REMEMBERING THE ROMAN PEOPLE

Remembering the Roman People

Essays on Late-Republican Politics and Literature

T. P. WISEMAN

OXFORD

UNIVERSITY PRESS

OXFORD
UNIVERSITY PRESS

Great Clarendon Street, Oxford OX2 6DP

Oxford University Press is a department of the University of Oxford.
It furthers the University's objective of excellence in research, scholarship,
and education by publishing worldwide in

Oxford New York

Auckland Cape Town Dar es Salaam Hong Kong Karachi
Kuala Lumpur Madrid Melbourne Mexico City Nairobi
New Delhi Shanghai Taipei Toronto

With offices in

Argentina Austria Brazil Chile Czech Republic France Greece
Guatemala Hungary Italy Japan Poland Portugal Singapore
South Korea Switzerland Thailand Turkey Ukraine Vietnam

Oxford is a registered trade mark of Oxford University Press
in the UK and in certain other countries

Published in the United States
by Oxford University Press Inc., New York

British Library Cataloguing in Publication Data

Data available

Library of Congress Cataloging in Publication Data

Data available

Typeset by SPI Publisher Services, Pondicherry, India
Printed in Great Britain
on acid-free paper by
MPG Biddles Ltd., King's Lynn, Norfolk

ISBN 978–0–19–923976–4

1 3 5 7 9 10 8 6 4 2

For Fergus Millar

Contents

List of Illustrations

Abbreviations

AIRF	*Acta Instituti Romani Finlandiae*
BCAR	*Bullettino della Commissione Archeologica Comunale di Roma*
BICS	*Bulletin of the Institute of Classical Studies*
CIL	*Corpus Inscriptionum Latinarum*
FGrH	*Die Fragmente der Griechischen Historiker*
ILLRP	*Inscriptiones Latinae Liberae Rei Publicae*
ILS	*Inscriptiones Latinae Selectae*
JRS	*Journal of Roman Studies*
NIS	*Nuova Italia Scientifica*
PLLS	*Papers of the Liverpool Latin Seminar*

Introduction

The modern word 'republic' is simply a transcription of the Latin phrase *res publica*. That is how it was spelt in the 'classical' Latin of our literary sources; but in the second century BC it was *res poplica*, and in the third probably *res populica*, the derivation from *populus* not yet obscured by changes in orthography.[1] The phrase meant 'the People's property', or 'the People's business'.[2]

In the Roman republic, only the People could make laws, only the People could elect magistrates and military commanders; even the Senate, composed as it was of ex-magistrates chosen by elected censors, was indirectly the creation of the People.[3] It is therefore paradoxical that modern historians of Rome regularly assume that the republic was always and necessarily an oligarchy.

How that assumption came to be the orthodox view is set out in Chapter 1 below.[4] It has not gone unchallenged; on the contrary, a series of studies by Fergus Millar forcefully insisted on the centrality of the People's role in the political life of the republic.[5] But entrenched attitudes are hard to shift, and Henrik Mouritsen reinstated

---

[1] *Res poplica*: CIL 1² 586.8 = *ILLRP* 512.8 (*c.*160 BC). *Populica* is not attested, but cf. *CIL* 1² 28 = *ILLRP* 35 (Populicius), *CIL* 1² 834 = *ILLRP* 357 (Poplicius) for early spellings of the name Publicius.

[2] Cicero *De republica*: 1.39: *est igitur, inquit Africanus, res publica res populi*... Repeated at 1.41, on the logical interdependence of *populus*, *ciuitas*, and *res publica*, and at 1.43, 1.48, 3.43–6. On the nature of Cicero's argument, see Schofield 1995.

[3] See Lintott 1999 for 'the constitution of the Roman republic'.

[4] First published in a collective volume of essays for the centenary of the British Academy (Wiseman 2002.285–310). I am grateful to the Academy for permission to reprint it here; I have added a few new references in square brackets.

[5] Millar 1984 (= 2002a.109–42), 1986 (= 2002a.143–61), 1989 (= 2002a.85–108), 1995 (= 2002a.162–82), 1998.

the orthodoxy with a new argument, that economic realities made it impossible for the *plebs* to take any significant part in politics.[6] Even Robert Morstein-Marx's excellent analysis of oratory before the People, which marks a significant step forward in our understanding of the realities of Roman politics, claims to demonstrate 'an élite hegemony over what was consequently a highly paternalistic public discourse that served, notwithstanding its agonistic aspects, to reinforce deference to the élite as a whole rather than to challenge it'.[7]

And that is how matters now stand: it can be assumed without argument that republican Rome was a 'profoundly hierarchical society' with an 'innately conservative governing class', and that 'the leading men of the most prominent political families, the nobility of office (*nobilitas*), dominated political life from their seats in the senate'.[8]

My own view is that Mouritsen's counter-attack was unconvincing, dependent on a forced interpretation of the eyewitness evidence of Cicero.[9] I think it is likely that the dominant aristocracy was a phenomenon of the second century BC, a corruption of the republican system rather than an inherent element of it.[10] There is always a danger in assuming that the situation taken for granted by our late-republican sources is all there ever was.

However, this book is not an attempt to define the nature of the Roman republic itself.[11] It is a sequence of particular studies with a

---

[6] Mouritsen 2001.36: 'Political activity in republican Rome was extremely time-consuming, and the urban *plebs* clearly had other more pressing concerns.' It is taken for granted that 'the *plebs* naturally remained outside the sphere of politics' (Mouritsen 2001.89).

[7] Morstein-Marx 2004.280–1.

[8] Quotations from Brennan 2004.32 and von Ungern-Sternberg 2004.89 (on the assumption that *The Cambridge Companion to the Roman Republic* should be a fair reflection of current mainstream opinion).

[9] See e.g. Mouritsen 2001.40–1 on Cicero *Ad Atticum* 1.16.11 (*illa contionalis hirudo aerarii, misera ac ieiuna plebecula*), *Ad Q. fratrem* 2.3.4 (*contionario illo populo*), and *De oratore* 1.118 (*haec turba et barbaria forensis*); he argues that Cicero was referring to 'those citizens, often of higher social standing, who regularly frequented the Forum and could be relied upon to turn up for a *contio* in support of the senate'.

[10] For a sketch on those lines, cf. Wiseman 2004.179–207.

[11] See Jehne 2006 for a good up-to-date account of the various suggested models. I agree with Mouritsen (2001.7) that ' "democracy" may not be very useful as an analytical tool', and that 'the simple question, "Was Rome a democracy or not?" by definition defies a straight answer'.

common underlying theme, the self-image of the Roman People. There is a good deal of detailed argument about comparatively obscure historical and literary questions, but I am not apologetic about that. In my opinion detailed argument is precisely what the subject needs. Zvi Yavetz's comment remains true after forty years:[12]

> An overall history of the Roman *plebs* would be highly desirable, but it is conceivable only after knowledge has been built up by a painful collection and comparison of individual facts.

Being able to answer the big questions in history depends on paying proper attention to the little ones.

But it is also important to have an overall framework into which the facts—or hypotheses—can be made to fit. Here too Yavetz's formulation may be helpful:[13]

> The Roman *plebs* was not some *Lumpenproletariat* but a class possessed of an ancient tradition, including the descendants of those who had once fought and overcome the patricians.

Our vision of the Roman republic is disproportionately influenced by the works of Cicero, a man whose attitudes were largely unsympathetic to that tradition. If we are to do it justice, we have to work hard to find other sources of information.

---

[12] Yavetz 1969.vii.
[13] Yavetz 1969.136; cf. Licinius Macer's appeal to the People to remember what their *maiores* had achieved (Sallust *Histories* 3.48.1, 6, 12, 15M).

1

Roman History and the Ideological Vacuum

I

For the twentieth century, the political history of Athens was essentially ideological, involving great issues of freedom and tyranny, while that of the Roman republic was merely a struggle for power, with no significant ideological content. 'Roman politicians', we are told, 'did not normally divide on matters of principle.'[1]

Why should that be? The Romans were perfectly familiar with the concepts and terminology of Greek political philosophy, and used them to describe their own politics. Cicero, writing in 56 BC, put it as clearly as anyone could wish: in the Roman republic, he said, there have always been two sorts of politician, by name and by nature respectively *populares* and *optimates*; the former speak and act for the *multitudo*, the latter for the elite.[2] The terms translate directly into Greek political language. The *populus* (whence *populares*) is the *demos*, and the *multi* (whence *multitudo*) are the *polloi*; the *optimi* (whence *optimates*) are the *aristoi*, and Cicero's 'elite', whom less friendly critics called 'the few' (*pauci*), are the *oligoi*.[3]

---

[1] Gruen 1974.50.

[2] Cicero *Pro Sestio* 96: *duo genera semper in hac ciuitate fuerunt eorum qui uersari in re publica atque in ea se excellentius gerere studuerunt; quibus ex generibus alteri se populares, alteri optimates et haberi et esse uoluerunt. qui ea quae faciebant quaeque dicebant multitudini iucunda uolebant esse, populares, qui autem ita se gerebant ut sua consilia optimo cuique probarent, optimates habebantur.*

[3] *Optimates* as *pauci*: Cicero *De republica* 1.51–2, 55. *Factio* and/or *potentia paucorum*: Caesar *Civil War* 1.22.5, Hirtius [Caesar] *Gallic War* 8.50.2; Sallust *Catiline* 20.9 (Catiline speech), 39.1, 58.11 (Catiline speech), *Jugurthine War* 3.4, 27.2, 31.19 (Memmius speech), *Histories* 1.12M, 3.48.27–8 (Macer speech); Livy 10.24.9 (P. Decius speech).

Not surprisingly, Greek authors who dealt with Roman politics used the concepts of democracy and oligarchy, the rule of the many or the rule of the best, without any sense that it was an inappropriate idiom.[4] So too the eighteenth- and nineteenth-century historians of Rome found it natural to refer to 'the popular side', 'the aristocratical faction', 'the democratic party', 'the oligarchs', and so on. Or it could be described in the language of Sallust and Tacitus, as a struggle between the Senate and the People.[5] The People's champion eventually won, but the result was the end of the republic and a return to monarchy.[6]

'Men generally look to this period of Roman history for arguments for or against monarchy, aristocracy, or democracy.'[7] So wrote Edward Freeman in 1859, summing up a long tradition: from Machiavelli to Mommsen, the history of the Roman republic was above all ideological. But twentieth-century scholarship turned its back on all that. Here is a representative assessment by a very distinguished historian:

How does one analyze the politics of the period? It can be argued that they were very much as they had always been. The great families continued to maintain control through interlocking marriages and adoptions, a whole network of relationships and *amicitiae* which formed the principal branches of the oligarchy. Behind the more publicized activities of military conquerors and demagogic tribunes lay the subtle manipulations of senatorial factions.

Erich Gruen explicitly rejects the 'older scholarship', which 'reduced Roman politics to a contest between the "senatorial party" and the "popular party". Such labels obscure rather than enlighten understanding.'[8]

Of course the word 'party' is anachronistic, if it is taken to mean the disciplined political organizations made necessary by modern

---

[4] Esp. (but not solely) Plutarch, whose sources for late-republican politics included Sulla's memoirs and the *History* of Asinius Pollio. See Pelling 1986 [= Pelling 2002.207–36].

[5] See e.g. Sallust *Catiline* 38.3, *Jugurthine War* 41.2–5, *Histories* 1.11M; Tacitus *Dialogus* 36.3, *Histories* 2.38.1, *Annals* 4.33.1–2. It is the basis of Appian's history of the civil wars: Appian *Civil Wars* 1.1.

[6] See e.g. Plutarch *Brutus* 47.7; Appian preface 6, *Civil Wars* 1.6; Cassius Dio 52.1.1, 53.11.4–5.

[7] Freeman 1880.314, repr. from *National Review* (Apr. 1859).

[8] Gruen 1974, 48, 50.

mass suffrage. But the 'older scholarship' didn't mean that; it meant what Livy meant when in a highly ideological context—the opposition to the tyrannical Decemvirs—he used *partes* with reference to *optimates* and *populares*. *Partes* is normal Latin for a political or ideological grouping;[9] granted that its modern derivative is now misleading, is that any reason to deny the history of the Roman republic its entire ideological dimension? How can this view be squared with what Cicero says?

Cicero's analysis was not at all dispassionate. On the contrary, it was the tendentious self-justification of a controversial politician at the crisis of his career—the best sort of evidence, and at the same time the most difficult to use. To understand it properly, I think we have to look again at a familiar story, one that had begun two generations before Cicero wrote.

II

Tiberius Gracchus' agrarian bill in 133 BC was a measure in favour of the poor against the rich and powerful (Plutarch and Appian are explicit about that), but it soon became a power struggle between the People's tribune and the Senate. Our sources claim that previously Senate and People had been in harmony;[10] what that means, and how long it had lasted, is a question to which we shall return, but certainly Gracchus put an end to it. Inconvenient tribunician proposals could be checked by getting one of the other tribunes to interpose a veto, and then waiting for the end of the would-be legislator's term of office. Gracchus countered that, first by getting the assembly to depose the vetoer on the grounds that he was acting against the People's will,[11] and secondly by standing for election to a second year's tribunate himself.

---

[9] Livy 3.39.9 (M. Horatius speech): *cuius illi partis essent, rogitare. populares?...* *optimates? Partes* in general: e.g. Cicero *Pro Roscio Amerino* 137, *Pro Quinctio* 69–70, *In Verrem* 2.1.35, *In Catilinam* 4.13, *Ad Atticum* 1.13.2; Sallust *Catiline* 4.2, *Jugurthine War* 40.2–3, 73.4; Velleius Paterculus 2.28.1, 2.62.6, 2.72.1; Suetonius *Diuus Iulius* 1.3. See Strasburger 1939.784–8.

[10] Sallust *Jugurthine War* 41 (until 146), Dionysius of Halicarnassus 2.11.2–3 (until 123), Plutarch *Tiberius Gracchus* 20.1.

[11] Plutarch *Tiberius Gracchus* 11.3, 15.2; Appian *Civil Wars* 1.12.51.

The effect on the Senate was dramatic. When the consul declined to take executive action, the *pontifex maximus* announced 'Then let those who want to save the republic follow me,' and led out a large group of senators and their supporters to beat Gracchus to death.[12] In their view, by going against the unwritten rules of the republic as they understood it, he was aiming at tyranny and therefore justly killed. 'Thus perish whoso else may do such deeds,' commented the great Scipio Aemilianus, quoting Homer.[13]

And perish they did, beginning with Gaius Gracchus in 121. Against him, as against others in later years, the Senate formalized its position with a decree that the consul 'should see to it that the republic be not harmed'.[14] Once again, it was a particular definition of the republic that prevailed: mobilizing the citizen body to pass laws in its own interest was interpreted as tyranny.

Tiberius Gracchus' *lex agraria* was for dividing public land among the citizens; Gaius Gracchus' *lex frumentaria* was for using public money to subsidize a guaranteed corn supply for the urban poor. On the one hand:[15]

quid tam iustum enim quam recipere plebem sua a patribus, ne populus gentium uictor orbisque possessor extorris aris ac focis ageret? quid tam aequum quam inopem populum uiuere ex aerario suo?

What could be so just as the commons getting back its own property from the senators, so that a world-conquering People should not live banished from its altars and hearths? What could be so fair as the treasury supporting a People that had no resources of its own?

On the other hand:[16]

multis in rebus multitudinis studium ac populi commodum ab utilitate rei publicae discrepabat.

---

[12] Valerius Maximus 3.2.17, Velleius Paterculus 2.3.1–2, Plutarch *Tiberius Gracchus* 19.3–6, Appian *Civil Wars* 1.16.68–70. [See below, pp. 178–87.]

[13] Plutarch *Tiberius Gracchus* 21.4 (Homer *Odyssey* 1.47); cf. Velleius Paterculus 2.4.4 (*iure caesum*).

[14] Cicero *In Catilinam* 1.4, *Philippics* 8.14; Plutarch *Gaius Gracchus* 14.3; Lintott 1999.89–93.

[15] Florus 2.1.2–3 (from Livy?). [Cf. Sallust *Jugurthine War* 31.8 (Memmius' speech).]

[16] Cicero *Pro Sestio* 103.

In various matters the desire of the many and the advantage of the People were not consistent with the good of the republic.

Here were two rival ideologies, two mutually incompatible understandings of what the republic was. That is surely what Cicero and Sallust mean when they say that the Gracchan crisis split the state into two *partes*; the Greek philosopher Posidonius put it that Gaius Gracchus wanted to abolish *aristokratia* and establish *demokratia*.[17] Those are different formulations of the same phenomenon—an ideological conflict between 'parties', identified as aristocratic (*optimates*) and democratic (*populares*), which would last until the republic itself collapsed.

In his history of the Jugurthine War, Sallust describes Opimius' destruction of Gaius Gracchus and his followers as the victory of the *nobilitas* over the *plebs*.[18] (He consistently uses *nobilitas* for the dominant oligarchy, varying it occasionally with *pauci* or *senatus*.) The reversal of that victory, he tells us, was one of his reasons for choosing the subject:[19]

quia tunc primum superbiae nobilitatis obuiam itum est; quae contentio diuina et humana cuncta permiscuit eoque uecordiae processit ut studiis ciuilibus bellum atque uastitas Italiae finem faceret.

because at that time the arrogance of the nobility was first challenged, a conflict which threw into confusion everything human and divine, and reached such a level of madness that through political conflict it ended in war and the devastation of Italy.

That was probably written at the time of the civil war of 41–40 BC, which resulted in the destruction of Perusia. So Sallust's book will show how the ideological conflict developed from the 'struggles of Senate and People', as Tacitus later phrased it,[20] into the sequence of

---

[17] Cicero *De republica* 1.31; Sallust *Jugurthine War* 41.5, 42.1; Diodorus Siculus 34/35.25.1 (Posidonius *FGrH* 87 F111b). On C. Gracchus, cf. Appian *Civil Wars* 1.22.93 (destroying the Senate's power), Plutarch *Gaius Gracchus* 5.3 (changing the constitution ἐκ τῆς ἀριστοκρατίας εἰς τὴν δημοκρατίαν).

[18] Sallust *Jugurthine War* 16.2, 42.1–4; cf. Plutarch *Gaius Gracchus* 11.2, 14.2 on Opimius and his allies as ὀλιγαρχικοί.

[19] Sallust *Jugurthine War* 5.1–2; cf. 31.2 (Memmius' speech) on the *superbia paucorum* [and see further pp. 35–8 below].

[20] Tacitus *Dialogus* 36.3 (*assidua senatus aduersus plebem certamina*), *Annals* 4.32.1 (*plebis et optimatium certamina*).

full-scale civil wars that still continued in his own time. Two of the protagonists of Sallust's story are the People's hero Marius (whose election as consul is the main 'challenge to the nobility') and the aristocratic Sulla, each introduced with a character-sketch that hints at future events.[21] His readers didn't need to be told what resulted from their rivalry.

The earliest contemporary evidence for the People's point of view comes from the mid-eighties BC, in the examples from a rhetorician's manual. Here, for instance, the fate of the People's champions is used to illustrate the figure *paronomasia*:[22]

Tiberium Graccum rem publicam administrantem prohibuit indigna nex diutius in eo commorari. Gaio Gracco similis occasio est oblata, quae uirum rei publicae amantissimum subito de sinu ciuitatis eripuit. Saturninum fide captum malorum perfidia per scelus uita priuauit. tuus, o Druse, sanguis domesticos parietes et uultum parentis aspersit. Sulpicio, cui paulo ante omnia concedebant, eum breui spatio non modo uiuere sed etiam sepeliri prohibuerunt.

Tiberius Gracchus was a statesman, but an unworthy killing prevented him from continuing in that role. To Gaius Gracchus came a similar fate, which snatched away a great patriot from the embrace of the citizen body. Saturninus, betrayed by trust, the treachery of wicked men deprived of life. Drusus, your blood spattered the walls of your house and the face of your mother. For Sulpicius, to whom at first they conceded everything, soon they allowed neither life nor burial.

It was a great tradition of Gracchan martyrs.[23] What did for Saturninus in 100 BC was again the Senate's decree and 'whoever wants to save the republic...';[24] for Drusus in 91 an assassin's knife was enough, while Sulpicius in 88 was hunted down at the orders of a consul who had just taken the city by military force. All of them had been duly elected as tribunes of the People, and passed their legislation by due process in the assembly. But Sulla regarded the tribunes' powers as tyrannical.[25]

---

[21] Sallust *Jugurthine War* 63.1–6, 95.4. The final sentence (114.4) is equally pregnant.

[22] *Rhetorica ad Herennium* 4.31 (cf. 4.68 on the martyrdom of Ti. Gracchus).

[23] Saturninus and the memory of Ti. Gracchus: Appian *Civil Wars* 1.32.141; cf. Cicero *Pro Rabirio perduellionis reo* 20, Valerius Maximus 9.7.1. Livius Drusus *per Gracchana uestigia*: Seneca *Consolatio ad Marciam* 16.4; cf. Florus 2.5.6. Sulpicius in the Gracchan tradition: Cicero *Pro Cornelio* [fr. 5 Crawford] in Asconius 80C.

[24] Cicero *Pro Rabirio perduellionis reo* 20, *De uiris illustribus* 73.10.

[25] Appian *Civil Wars* 1.59.267 (cf. 1.57.253, his reason for the march on Rome).

His own tyranny was described at the time (here too we now have contemporary evidence) as the victory of the *nobilitas*.[26] The lower orders had fought their betters, and lost; now everyone knew his place again.[27] The republic would be ruled by the Senate's authority, as it had been before the 'struggle of the orders', and the tribunes and popular assembly would have no power.[28] As for opposition, the proscriptions would see to that; the final total of dead was 4,700.[29] The counter-revolution was meant to be permanent.

But the result of the Senate's rule was a spectacularly corrupt oligarchy, resulting in a reform movement that demanded, and in 70 BC eventually obtained, the full restoration of the tribunes' powers. Cicero, prosecuting one of the worst culprits, had this to say to the senators on the jury:

tulit haec ciuitas quoad potuit, quoad necesse fuit, regiam istam uestram dominationem in iudiciis et in omni re publica tulit; sed quo die populo Romano tribuni plebi restituti sunt, omnia ista uobis, si forte nondum intellegitis, adempta atque erepta sunt.

As long as it could and as long as it had to, the republic put up with that monarchical domination of yours in the courts, and in the whole of public life. But in case you don't yet realize it, all that was snatched from you and taken away on the day the tribunes were restored to the Roman People.

Is it really true, as Erich Gruen assumes, that the Romans wouldn't understand the phrase 'senatorial party'?[30]

Cicero the *popularis* was an ambitious young senator with no inherited connections, making his way on talent alone and using it for the currently powerful cause. Seven years later, when he was

---

[26] Cicero *Pro Roscio Amerino* 138, 141–2, 149.

[27] Cicero *Pro Roscio Amerino* 136: *quis enim erat qui non uideret **humilitatem cum dignitate** de amplitudine contendere? quo in certamine perditi ciuis erat se ad eos iungere quibus incolumibus et domi dignitas et foris auctoritas retineretur. quae perfecta esse et **suum cuique honorem et gradum redditum** gaudeo, iudices, uehementerque laetor, eaque omnia deorum uoluntate, studio populi Romani, consilio et imperio et felicitate L. Sullae gesta esse intellego.*

[28] Appian *Civil Wars* 1.59.266–7; on *patrum auctoritas* (Livy 8.12.15, Cicero *De republica* 2.56), see Oakley 1998.525–7.

[29] Valerius Maximus 9.2.1; Florus 2.9.25 (from Livy?) gives 2,000 senators and *equites*.

[30] Cicero *In Verrem* 2.5.175; cf. *Pro Cluentio* 136 (*cum inuidia flagraret ordo senatorius*). Gruen 1974.50.

consul, the reformers had lost the moral high ground. There was serious hardship among the poor; the tribunes attacked the Senate, and vainly brought in proposals for land distribution and debt relief; but the self-styled 'standard-bearer of the oppressed' was Catiline, a patrician playboy with a record of murder and extortion.[31] Cicero could plausibly claim for himself the status of a *popularis*, complete with honorific references to the Gracchi, while now defending the Senate's authority.[32]

In October 63, alarmed by reports of an armed uprising in Etruria and a planned *coup d'état* in Rome, the Senate passed the same emergency decree that had authorized the killing of Gaius Gracchus in 121 and of Saturninus in 100.[33] Catiline left Rome to take command of the rebel army; five of his associates were arrested, and on 5 December Cicero had them executed without trial. Once again, Roman politics were ideologically polarized.

On the one hand, Cicero had acted like a tyrant. That was the view of the tribunes of 62, and of Caesar, now in his praetorship and a conspicuous *popularis*; Cicero knew that it was only by allying himself with Caesar that he could have 'peace with the multitude'.[34] It was also the view of Clodius, another patrician playboy, who now emerged as leader of the demand that Cicero should be put on trial before the People, or otherwise summarily dealt with.[35]

On the other hand, Cicero was the saviour of the republic, hailed as 'father of his country' by Catulus, the leading figure in the Senate

[31] Hardship: Sallust *Catiline* 33 (C. Manlius). Tribunes: Cicero *De lege agraria* [esp. 2.11–13], Cassius Dio 37.25.4; Cicero *Pro Rabirio perduellionis reo* 20 (*hos patres conscriptos qui nunc sunt in inuidiam uocatis*). Catiline: Cicero *Pro Murena* 50–1, cf. Sallust *Catiline* 20.2–21.2 (programme speech). For the politics of the sixties BC, see Wiseman 1994.

[32] Cicero *De lege agraria* 2.6–10, *Pro Rabirio perduellionis reo* 11–15: speeches delivered before the People early in 63 BC, but revised for publication in 60 (Cicero *Ad Atticum* 2.1.3).

[33] Cicero *In Catilinam* 1.4, *Philippics* 8.14–15; cf. *Pro Sulla* 21, *In Pisonem* 14, *Pro Milone* 8, *Philippics* 2.18 (Senate's responsibility).

[34] Plutarch *Cicero* 23.2 (δυναστεία), cf. Cicero *Pro Sulla* 21 (*regnum*); Cicero *In Catilinam* 4.9 on Caesar, *in re p. uiam quae popularis habetur secutus. Multitudo*: Cicero *Ad Atticum* 2.3.4 (60 BC), cf. Suetonius *Diuus Iulius* 16 on their rioting in support of Caesar in 62.

[35] Cicero *Ad Atticum* 1.16.10 (*rex*), 2.22.1, *Ad Q. fratrem* 1.2.16, *Pro Flacco* 96–7, *Pro Sestio* 40.

and (what comes to the same thing) the quintessential optimate.[36] Cicero's own accounts of his consulship emphasized *aristokratia*, and one of them no doubt lies behind Plutarch's account of the climactic moment (the translation is by John and William Langhorne, 1770):[37]

καὶ πρῶτον ἐκ Παλατίου παραλαβὼν τὸν Λέντλον ἦγε διὰ τῆς ἱερᾶς ὁδοῦ καὶ τῆς ἀγορᾶς μέσης, τῶν μὲν ἡγεμονικωτάτων ἀνδρῶν κύκλῳ περιεσπειράμενων καὶ δορυφορούντων, τοῦ δὲ δήμου φρίττοντος τὰ δρώμενα καὶ παριέντος σιωπῇ, μάλιστα δὲ τῶν νέων, ὥσπερ ἱεροῖς τισι πατρίοις ἀριστοκρατικῆς τινος ἐξουσίας τελεῖσθαι μετὰ φόβου καὶ θάμβους δοκούντων.

First he took Lentulus from the Palatine hill, and led him down the Via Sacra, and through the middle of the Forum. The principal persons in Rome attended the consul on all sides, like a guard; the People stood silent at the horror of the scene; and the youth looked on with fear and astonishment, as if they were initiated that day in some awful ceremonies of aristocratic power.

The idiom came naturally in the politics of the time. 'He spoke like an aristocrat' was Cicero's private (and bilingual) comment when Pompey, addressing the People after his return from the East, praised the Senate's authority to the disgust of the *populares*.[38]

At first, the People's view prevailed. The triumph of the *populares* came in 59–58 BC, Caesar's consulship followed by the tribunate of Clodius. There was a rush of reform legislation, including Gracchan land laws and a Gracchan corn law; Cicero was exiled by popular vote, his house torn down and a shrine of Liberty erected on the site;[39] the Senate was quite explicitly excluded from the political process.[40] But then the pendulum swung back. The consuls of 57 got Cicero recalled by the centuriate assembly, in which the votes of

---

[36] Cicero *In Pisonem* 6: *me Q. Catulus, princeps huius ordinis et auctor publici consili, frequentissimo senatu parentem patriae nominauit.* Catulus as *optimas*: Cicero *Ad Atticum* 1.20.3, *Pro Sestio* 101. *Res p. conseruata*: Cicero *Ad familiares* 5.2.7 (Jan. 62), *In Pisonem* 6, etc.

[37] Plutarch *Cicero* 22.1, probably from Cicero's Greek monograph περὶ ὑπατείας: Pelling 1985.313–6 [= Pelling 2002.46–9].

[38] Cicero *Ad Atticum* 1.14.2 (μαλ' ἀριστοκρατικῶς); 1.14.6 for the reaction.

[39] Cicero *Ad Atticum* 3.15.5 on his exile: *legem illam in qua popularia multa sunt. Libertas*: Cicero *De domo* 110–12, Plutarch *Cicero* 33.1, Cassius Dio 38.17.6.

[40] Cassius Dio 38.4.1, Appian *Civil Wars* 2.10 (Caesar in 59). Cicero *Pro Sestio* 28 (Gabinius in 58): *errare homines si etiam tum senatum aliquid in re publica posse arbitrarentur.*

the wealthy predominated.[41] The site of his house was restored to him, the shrine deconsecrated. There were protest demonstrations round the Senate-house ('protect the People's Liberty!'), and Cicero was even attacked by an armed mob in the street. But he had his own security guards, and the people were denied their vengeance.[42]

That is the context of Cicero's disquisition on *optimates* and *populares*, the passage with which this chapter begins. He stitched it into the text of a speech given in early March 56 BC, when he had successfully defended, on a political charge, one of the optimate tribunes of the previous year who had helped to bring about his return. At the time of writing, still in his post-recall euphoria, Cicero was attacking the legality of Caesar's land laws—the very citadel, as he put it, of the *popularis* cause.[43]

What matters is the premiss of his argument, not the content of it. We don't have to share his view that all patriotic citizens are by definition *optimates*, and that *populares* can only be criminal, bankrupt or insane. But we do, I think, have to accept the assumption on which it is based, that the republic was divided into two rival ideological camps—two *partes*, as he put it in a speech to the Senate—and that this rivalry had been fundamental in Roman politics since the time of the Gracchi.[44] That is, our most explicit evidence comes from within the conflict itself; it is in the highest degree tendentious, but it cannot simply be waved away as an anachronism.

The story can be briefly concluded. Cicero backed down, knowing that he was a marked man unless he made his peace with Caesar.[45] The *optimates* were determined that neither Caesar nor Clodius should hold legislative office again. When Clodius stood for the praetorship in 52, with a predictably radical programme, he was

---

[41] Appian *Civil Wars* 1.59.266 (οἱ ἐν περιουσίᾳ καὶ εὐβουλίᾳ)—'the Roman People' by Sulla's definition.

[42] Cicero *Ad Atticum* 4.1.6, 4.2.3, 4.3.3 (*clamor, lapides, fustes, gladii*).

[43] Cicero *Ad Q. fratrem* 2.6.1 (noisy Senate meeting, 5 Apr.), *Ad familiares* 1.9.8 (*in arcem illius causae inuadere*); cf. *Ad Atticum* 1.19.2 and 20.4 for the 'triumvirs' as *populares*.

[44] Cicero *Pro Sestio* 96 (*duo genera*), 97–9 (tendentious definitions), 103–5 (history of rival ideologies); *Post reditum in senatu* 33 (*duae partes*).

[45] Cicero *Ad Atticum* 4.5.1–3 (his 'palinode'); 8.11d.7 (cf. 8.3.5) on *popularis* threats against him.

murdered in a brawl on the Appian Way. His body was brought to Rome and given an impromptu funeral in the Forum; the Roman People burned down the Senate-house as his funeral pyre.[46] Caesar in 49 planned to return from Gaul to a second consulship, with *popularis* tribunes urging his cause. As against Gaius Gracchus in 121, Saturninus in 100, and the Catilinarians in 63, the Senate passed its decree 'that the consuls should see to it that the republic be not harmed'. Rather than wait for the fate of their predecessors, the tribunes fled to Caesar, who marched on Rome 'to free the People from the tyranny of the few'.[47]

Although the outbreak of civil war retrospectively overshadowed them, the events of 52 BC symbolized the struggle and its outcome. One of the *popularis* tribunes of that year, who must have been present at the burning of the Senate-house, was Sallust.[48] Ejected from the Senate by an optimate censor, restored and rewarded by the victorious Caesar, he then retired from politics to become a historian. By the time he had written his monographs on Catiline and on the post-Gracchan 'challenge to the nobility', he had seen Caesar become permanent dictator by vote of the popular assembly; he had seen outraged senators assassinate the man they saw as a tyrant; he had seen Cicero trying to guide a restored republic by resuming optimate politics; he had seen Caesar's son and two of his political heirs become joint dictators by vote of the popular assembly; and he had seen Cicero's head and hands nailed up on the *rostra*. When Sallust described Roman politics as a struggle between the People and the Senate (*plebs* and *patres*), he knew what he was talking about.[49]

But that wasn't how it seemed to the greatest Roman historian of the twentieth century. Sir Ronald Syme blamed Sallust for giving rise to a false doctrine, 'namely the belief that Rome had a regular two-party system, Optimates and Populares'. But that 'regular system', like

---

[46] Programme: Cicero *Pro Milone* 33, 87, 89; *Scholia Bobiensia* 173St. Pyre: Cicero *Pro Milone* 90, Asconius 33C, Cassius Dio 40.49.3.

[47] Caesar *Civil War* 1.5.3 (decree), 1.22.5 (*ut se et populum Romanum factione paucorum oppressum in libertatem uindicaret*).

[48] Asconius 37C, 49C.

[49] For the people granting power to Caesar and the Triumvirs (and to Augustus), see Lintott 1999.40: 'they were in theory permitted to abolish the Republic by legislation'. Sallust on *plebes/patres*: e.g. *Catiline* 33.3, 38.1; *Jugurthine War* 27.3, 30.1, 84.3; *Histories* 1.11M, 3.48.1M.

the 'organised Popular Party' referred to a sentence or two later, is a mere straw man (Sallust says no such thing), and when in the same passage Syme refers to *nobiles* who were 'advocates of the People's cause', he has tacitly conceded the very case he attacks.[50]

Syme's interests lay elsewhere, as a more famous passage shows:[51]

In all ages, whatever the form and name of government, be it monarchy, republic, or democracy, an oligarchy lurks behind the façade; and Roman history, Republican or Imperial, is the history of the governing class...

The political life of the Roman Republic was stamped and swayed, not by parties and programmes of a modern and parliamentary character, not by the ostensible opposition between Senate and People, *Optimates* and *Populares*, *nobiles* and *novi homines*, but by the strife for power, wealth and glory. The contestants were the *nobiles* themselves, as individuals or in groups, open in the elections and in the courts of law, or masked by secret intrigue.

One can't help feeling that that doesn't quite encompass the Gracchi, or even Cicero. For Syme, the strife was for power, wealth and glory; for Sallust, it was for '*liberty*, glory or domination'.[52] The difference is not insignificant.

III

After the Tarquins were expelled, the new republic enjoyed internal harmony for as long as there was a danger that they might return. Once that danger was past, wrote Sallust in the introduction to his *Histories*,[53]

seruili imperio patres plebem exercere, de uita atque tergo regio more consulere, agro pellere et ceteris expertis soli in imperio agere. quibus saeuitiis at maxume

---

[50] Syme 1964.17–18, citing Strasburger 1939 and, 'for the social basis of Roman political life', Gelzer 1912, Münzer 1920, and Taylor 1949.

[51] Syme 1939.7 and 11. Cf. 152: 'the realities of Roman politics were overlaid with a double coating of deceit, democratic and aristocratic'.

[52] Sallust *Histories* 1.7M: *nobis primae dissensiones uitio humani ingenii euenere, quod inquies atque indomitum semper **in certamine libertatis aut gloriae aut dominationis agit***.

[53] Sallust *Histories* 1.11M (Augustine *City of God* 2.18) (trans. Henry Bettenson, Penguin Classics), except that his final phrase is 'between the two *parties*'. Livy (2.21.5–6) tacitly follows Sallust's sequence of events.

faenore oppressa plebes, quom adsiduis bellis tributum et militiam simul
toleraret, armata montem sacrum atque Auentinum insedit tumque tribunos
plebis et alia iura sibi parauit. discordiarum et certaminis utrimque finis fuit
secundum bellum Punicum.

the patricians reduced the plebeians to the condition of slavery; they disposed of the lives and persons of the *plebs* in the manner of kings; they drove
men from their lands; and with the rest disenfranchised, they alone wielded
supreme power. Oppressed by such harsh treatment, and especially by the
load of debt, the plebeians, after enduring the simultaneous burden of
tribute and military service in continual wars, at length armed themselves
and took up a position on the Mons Sacer and the Aventine; thus they
gained for themselves the tribunes of the *plebs* and other rights. The Second
Punic War brought an end to the strife and rivalry between the two sides.

Those events—the armed plebeians forcing concessions from a tyrannical oligarchy—are constantly appealed to by the late-republican
populares portrayed by Sallust. In the next generation, the historians
of early Rome found it natural to portray the 'struggle of the orders'
in terms of *optimates* and *populares* (in Livy's Latin) or *demotikoi* and
aristokratikoi (in Dionysius' Greek).[54] The sense of continuity is
unmistakable: as Cicero said, there had *always* been those two sorts
of politician in the republic.[55]

It is possible that that was true. The republic may well have been in
constant tension between the respective interests of the many and the
few. Sallust's periodization is schematic (harmony requires fear of an
external enemy, so conflict continued until the Hannibalic War), but
he may still be essentially right; the 'period of concord' broken by
Tiberius Gracchus' legislative programme may well have been un-
typical and comparatively short-lived.[56] But no one can now be
certain, because of the absence of contemporary evidence.

What *is* clear, on the other hand, is that some of the second- and
first-century historians whom Livy and Dionysius used as sources
must have interpreted and elaborated the old stories in ways that

[54] Sallust *Catiline* 33.3 (C. Manlius), *Jugurthine War* 31.6 and 17 (C. Memmius),
Histories 1.55.23M (M. Lepidus), 3.48.1M (Macer). Livy : n. 8 above; Seager 1977.
Dionysius: e.g. 7.65.1, 7.66.2, 7.67.1 (on 'the first *stasis*', 7.66.1).

[55] Cicero *Pro Sestio* 96 (n. 1 above).

[56] On popular issues in the period between the 'struggle of the orders' and the
Gracchi, see Lintott 1987; on *libertas* throughout the republic, see Wiseman 2000 [=
2008.84–139].

would be exemplary for their own times.[57] As one instance out of many, take the case of Spurius Maelius, who in 439 BC supplied corn to the people and was suspected of aiming at tyranny. He was killed by Servilius Ahala at the order of the dictator Cincinnatus. There was no trial, just a summary execution like that of Tiberius Gracchus, with which it was often compared. In Dionysius, Maelius is an innocent man cut down 'like an animal' before the eyes of the horrified populace; in Livy, Ahala is congratulated for saving the republic.[58] Both ideologies were represented in the tradition—and they had an impact. Marcus Brutus was inspired by the example of Ahala, from whom he was descended on his mother's side, to 'save the republic' by killing Caesar.[59]

Here too, however, the presuppositions of twentieth-century scholarship have been an obstacle to understanding.

In the narratives of both Livy and Dionysius, the first act of the 'struggle of the orders' begins when a dreadful figure stumbles into the Roman Forum. Filthy, emaciated, his back a mass of recent scars, he tells his story to the People. He is a Roman citizen, a veteran of the republic's wars who fell into debt when his farm was destroyed by the Sabines; after all he owned had gone to pay the interest, he himself was seized by the creditor and subjected to a regime of hard labour, imprisonment, and frequent floggings.[60] Popular indignation and senatorial intransigence leads to the secession of the *plebs* the following year (494 BC), which in turn results in the establishment of the tribunate.

The main recurring economic themes of the 'struggle of the orders' were corn supply, land distribution, and debt. The first two were Gracchan issues, no doubt elaborated in contemporary terms by historians of the post-Gracchan period like the optimate Piso.[61] But debt—particularly debt as a result of war in Italy, debt as suffered by old soldiers—was an issue that became acute in 89 BC, and lasted

---

[57] For a convenient selection, see Gutberlet 1985.

[58] Dionysius of Halicarnassus 12.4.7–8, Livy 4.13.3–7. Gracchan parallel: Cicero *In Catilinam* 1.3, *Pro Milone* 72, *De republica* 2.49, *De amicitia* 36–7.

[59] Cicero *Ad Atticum* 2.24.3, 13.40.1, *Philippics* 2.26; Plutarch *Brutus* 1.3. Ahala on Brutus' coin-issue in 54 BC: Crawford 1974.455–6.

[60] Livy 2.23.1–9, Dionysius of Halicarnassus 6.26.1–2.

[61] Piso's politics: Cicero *Pro Fonteio* 39, *Tusculan Disputations* 3.48; *Scholia Bobiensia* 96St. Text, translation, and commentary in Forsythe 1994.

as an ongoing problem at least until the late sixties.[62] An influential historian who wrote in that period was Licinius Macer; he was tribune in 73 BC, and according to Sallust he took an outspoken part in the *popularis* campaign to get the powers of the tribunate restored after Sulla's legislation.[63]

We know one thing for certain about Macer as a historian: he conspicuously praised his ancestors, the Licinii of the fourth century BC.[64] Prominent among his heroes was surely Licinius Stolo, one of the two determined tribunes who pressed home the plebeian demands for debt relief, land reform, and the sharing of the consulship, supposedly for ten successive years. Macer may well be responsible for the version of events, not followed by Livy, which alleged a secession of the *plebs* on that occasion, and the election of Licinius Stolo as the first plebeian consul.[65] Similarly, it was surely Macer who named two Licinii among the founding college of tribunes in 493.[66]

Sallust, narrating Macer's tribunate in the third book of his *Histories*, gave him a splendid speech. It begins like this:[67]

si, Quirites, parum existumaretis quid inter ius a maioribus relictum uobis et hoc a Sulla paratum seruitium interesset, multis mihi disserundum fuit docendique quas ob iniurias et quotiens a patribus armata plebes secessisset utique uindices parauisset omnis iuris sui tribunos plebis; nunc hortari modo relicuom est et ire primum uia qua capessundam arbitror libertatem.

---

[62] Appian *Civil Wars* 1.54.232–9, Valerius Maximus 9.7.4, Livy *Epitome* 74 (89 BC); Festus 516L (88 BC); Velleius Paterculus 2.32.2 (86 BC); Cicero *De officiis* 2.84, *In Catilinam* 2.8, Cassius Dio 37.25.4 (63 BC). Veterans: Cicero *In Catilinam* 2.20, Sallust *Catiline* 16.4.

[63] Sallust *Histories* 3.48M. Text and commentary in Walt 1997. [In his review of Walt (Cornell 1999.229), Tim Cornell points out that 'the identification of the politician C. Licinius Macer with the historian Licinius Macer is not at all certain. The latter's *praenomen* is nowhere preserved . . . Even if he was named Gaius, nothing prevents us from postulating two different men of the same name—nothing, that is, apart from Occam's razor, an instrument of questionable value in ancient history.' But why should we *wish* to do so? See Ch. 3 below on Macer.]

[64] Livy 7.9.5 (on C. Licinius Calvus *cos.* 361): *quaesita ea propriae familiae laus leuiorem auctorem Licinium facit.*

[65] Livy 6.34–42 ('376–367 BC'); detailed discussion in Oakley 1997.645–61. Secession: Ampelius 25.4, Ovid *Fasti* 1.643–4 (cf. Livy 6.4.10 *prope secessionem*). Stolo first consul: auct. *De uir. ill.* 20.2.

[66] Dionysius of Halicarnassus 6.89.1 (contrast Asconius 77C); [see below, pp. 61–3]. 'Licinius Macer must be the one ultimately responsible' (Forsythe 1994.292).

[67] Sallust *Histories* 3.48.1–2M; Frier 1975.94–5.

'Romans: if you didn't understand what the difference is between the rights bequeathed to you by your ancestors and this slavery devised by Sulla, I would have to go on at length and explain how often, and because of what injustices, the plebeians in arms seceded from the patricians, and how they achieved tribunes of the *plebs* as defenders of all their rights. As it is, all I need to do is encourage and go before you on the road I believe we must take to win liberty.'

There is no point wondering whether the real Licinius Macer said this in 73 BC. It is Sallust writing nearly forty years later, and he and his readers knew Macer's *History*. When one historian gives a speech to another (as Tacitus did with Cremutius Cordus), it can hardly be innocent of intertextual allusion. Here, the hint is unmistakable: the imagined *Quirites*, like Sallust's readers, don't need telling about the heroic plebeians of the past, because it's all in Macer's history— including the secession of 367 BC that other historians didn't have.[68]

At the end of his speech, Sallust's Macer is scathing about the low expectations of his present-day audience:

abunde libertatem rati, scilicet quia tergis abstinetur at huc ire licet et illuc, munera ditium dominorum. atque haec eadem non sunt agrestibus, sed caeduntur inter potentium inimicitias donoque dantur in prouincias magistratibus.

'You think you have liberty in abundance just because your backs are spared and you're allowed to move around—gifts from your masters, the rich. And country people don't even have that: they are flogged when the men of power quarrel, and sent as gifts to magistrates in the provinces.'

Enslavement for debt was forbidden by the *lex Poetelia*, the flogging of Roman citizens by the *lex Porcia*—but enforcement of those laws depended on the protective power of the tribunes.[69] Their *ius auxilii*, the one power Sulla had left them, applied only in the city and for a mile outside the walls. Beyond that, there was no defence if magistrates allowed such abuses to happen. And they did.

Again, Sallust gives the evidence. Ten years after Macer's tribunate the peasants rose in revolt. Their leader was an old soldier, Gaius

---

[68] See n. 65 above. Implicit at 3.48.1 (*quotiens*) and at 3.48.15: *ne uos ad uirilia illa uocem, quo tribunos plebei, modo patricium magistratum, libera ab auctoribus patriciis suffragia maiores uostri parauere.* The *uirilia illa* were the secessions ('Be men today, Quirites, . . .'), and the *patricius magistratus* was the consulship, won in 367 BC.

[69] Sallust *Histories* 3.48.26–7M; Livy 8.28 (*lex Poetelia*), Sallust *Catiline* 51.21 (*lex Porcia*).

Manlius, to whom Sallust attributes this message to the Roman commander:[70]

deos hominesque testamur, imperator, nos arma neque contra patriam cepisse neque quo periculum aliis faceremus, sed uti corpora nostra ab iniuria tuta forent, qui miseri egentes, uiolentia atque crudelitate faeneratorum plerique patriae, sed omnes fama atque fortunis expertes sumus. neque quoiquam nostrum licuit more maiorum lege uti neque amisso patrimonio liberum corpus habere: tanta saeuitia faeneratorum atque praetoris fuit.

'We call gods and men to witness, Imperator, that we have taken up arms not against our country or to endanger others, but in order that our bodies may be safe from abuse. We are poor and wretched. Thanks to the violence and cruelty of the moneylenders, many of us have been deprived of our native land, all of us of our good name and possessions. Not one of us was allowed the traditional protection of the law, or to keep our bodies free when our inheritance was lost. Such has been the savagery of the moneylenders and the magistrate.'

For Sallust, the issues that sparked the 'struggle of the orders' were still unresolved after four centuries. In this passage of *Catiline*, in the preface to the *Histories* (pp. 16–17, above), and in the speech of Macer in book 3, the theme and phraseology are the same: freedom and slavery, cruelty and arrogance, the physical maltreatment of the poor by the rich and powerful. And if, as it surely must, the speech of Macer reflects Macer's history, then we may with some confidence infer the nature of that history—an ideologically committed narrative presenting the plebeians' achievement of freedom and the tribunate in the light of Sulla's attempt to reverse those gains.[71]

That in turn allows the hypothesis—by its nature unprovable, but plausibly explaining the phenomena—that passages in Livy or Dionysius that betray a particular sympathy for the oppressed plebeians and their tribune champions may be influenced by, or even recast versions of, Licinius Macer's tendentious narrative.[72] One likely

[70] Sallust *Catiline* 33.1 (cf. 33.3, *saepe ipsa plebs…armata a patribus secessit*). Manlius an ex-centurion: Cassius Dio 37.30.5.
[71] Macer's interest in the origin of the dictatorship was probably because of Sulla: Dionysius of Halicarnassus 5.74.4 and 77.4, with Gabba 1991.142.
[72] To deny this possibility a priori, as do Luce 1977.165–9 and Cornell 1995.4–5, seems to me to misplace the burden of proof.

example is the scene with which the whole long story begins, that scarred and haggard figure telling his story in the Forum in 495 BC.

It is important to remember that this hypothesis depends entirely on Sallust's treatment of Macer and his themes. Sallust's own historical persona was politically neutral, as befitted one who had retired from the conflict before he began to write.[73] But he had been a *popularis* tribune in his time, and he knew what could cause the Roman People to burn down the Senate-house. As for Macer, who never reached the serenity of retirement, his history was written during a life of active politics.[74] From the interaction of the two we can gain some idea of how *populares* saw Roman history, a necessary corrective to the Ciceronian attitudes which otherwise dominate our view of the late republic. Indeed, the very existence, and importance, of Macer's version of the political history of Rome may be the reason why in his *De republica* Cicero devoted a whole book to a liberal-optimate narrative of his own.[75]

I have dealt with Macer's ideological position at what may seem unnecessary length, since literary scholars, discussing Livy's sources, have largely taken it for granted that this 'vehement supporter of the Popular party... is undoubtedly responsible for much of the pro-plebeian element in the early books of the *Ab Urbe Condita*'.[76] That was Mommsen's view as well—but late twentieth-century historians have reacted against it, and even against the idea that *anything* useful can be said about the lost historians of the Roman republic. See for instance the firmly expressed opinion of Tim Cornell:[77]

---

[73] Sallust *Catiline* 4.1–2; cf. 38.3–4, *Jugurthine War* 40.3, 41.5, *Histories* 1.12M.

[74] [Or a period of forced inactivity: p. 80 below.] He committed suicide in 66 BC, two years after his praetorship (Cicero *Ad Atticum* 1.4.2, Valerius Maximus 9.12.7, Plutarch *Cicero* 9.1–2). The history was probably unfinished, since there are no surviving fragments after 299 BC (Livy 10.9.10).

[75] Cicero *De republica* 2.3 (Scipio): *nostram rem publicam uobis et nascentem et crescentem et adultam at iam firmam atque robustam ostendero.*

[76] Walsh 1961.122–3. See also (e.g.) Ogilvie 1965.7–12, Briscoe 1971.9–10, Oakley 1997.92.

[77] Cornell 1986.86. [The opinion is equally firm twenty years on (Cornell 2005.64): 'From an unprejudiced study of the fragmentary evidence it is clear that we know far less about the lost annalistic sources of Livy and Dionysius than is often claimed. The fact that we know so little about historians such as Valerius Antias and Licinius Macer makes it impossible to identify passages that might derive from them, and pointless to try.']

Even if it were possible to distinguish with certainty between those parts of Livy and Dionysius that derive from (e.g.) Licinius Macer and those that come from Valerius Antias, we should gain little, partly because of our general ignorance of those writers, but more particularly because their contributions are unlikely to have had a decisive effect on the character of the tradition.

For Macer at least, that seems to me a very difficult position to maintain.

There is now at last a thorough and scholarly edition of, and commentary on, the 'fragments' of Licinius Macer. Siri Walt begins her long and detailed introduction by pointing out how much, in fact, we know about the author.[78] That offers a valuable corrective to Cornell's allegation of general ignorance—and yet Walt ends up expressing a series of agnosticisms even more explicit than his.

First, we are not to suppose that the *popularis* politics of the late republic were in any sense ideological: there was no 'popular party', just individual politicians choosing the *popularis ratio* as a political strategy to achieve their own particular ends.[79] Second, we are not to suppose that the speech Sallust gave Macer has anything to do with what a tribune of 73 BC might really have said, or with the actual issues of the time: it is just free invention based on what Sallust thought appropriate to Macer's great ancestor Licinius Stolo in the fourth century BC.[80] Third, we are not to suppose that Macer in particular had any influence on the politically tendentious presentation of historical episodes in Livy and Dionysius: Mommsen's *Tendenzthese*, like the work of the nineteenth-century *Quellenforscher*

---

[78] Walt 1997.1: 'Im Gegensatz zu vielen anderen ... sind wir über die Biographie des C. Licinius Macer relativ gut unterrichtet.'

[79] Walt 1997.10–11, 21–8. 'Die Verknüpfung der popularen Methode mit der Volksversammlung und der Gegensatz *populares/optimates* könnte nun die Vorstellung erwecken, es habe sich bei den Popularen um eine demokratische Partei gehandelt. Dies ist aber von der modernen Popularenforschung widerlegt worden' (10). 'Die moderne Popularenforschung hat gezeigt, dass die *popularis ratio* nicht das beistehende System in Frage gestellt habe, sondern ein Mittel gewesen sei, um innerhalb des Systems Einfluss zu gewinnen' (25). The reference is to Gelzer 1912 and Strasburger 1939.

[80] Walt 1997.11–28, esp. 13 f. But if it was 'eine Konstruktion Sallusts, der sich inspirieren liess von Macers Darstellung der Ständekämpfe in dessen *annales*' (13, after Syme 1964.200 and 207), surely that invalidates the third point? The inconsistency reappears at Walt 1997.104 (third and fourth paragraphs).

that depended on it, is not valid.[81] And finally, we are not to suppose that 'political propaganda' had any place in late-republican life or literature: Macer was a politician operating within the conventions of an aristocratic system, and a historian whose creative reconstructions had no distinguishable ideological content.[82]

In the light of the evidence I have presented above, I think it is fair to describe all these propositions as deeply paradoxical. They are based, quite explicitly, on *neuer Forschung*,[83] a twentieth-century way of thinking about Roman politics with the ideology taken out. It is time to look at this phenomenon in its historical context.

IV

MENENIUS   Alack,
You are transported by calamity
Thither where more attends you, and you slander
The helms o' th' state, who care for you like fathers,
When you curse them as enemies.
FIRST CITIZEN Care for us? True indeed! They ne'er cared for us yet.
Suffer us to famish, and their store-houses crammed with grain;
make edicts for usury, to support usurers; repeal daily any
wholesome act established against the rich, and provide more
piercing statutes daily to chain up and restrain the poor. If the wars
eat us not up, they will; and there's all the love they bear us.

---

[81] Walt 1997.47–50, 102–5; cf. 72–5, grouping all the 'late annalists' together without distinction. 'Das Bild, das man von den Annalisten hat, steht schon vor der eigentlichen Quellenforschung fest und beruht auf *äusserlichen und sachfremden* Kriterien wie der demokratischen Einstellung Macers' (49, my italics).

[82] Walt 1997.104: 'Wir können nun in der Kritik noch einen Schritt weitergehen und uns fragen, ob politische Propaganda in diesem Sinne in Rom überhaupt denkbar ist . . . Auch die populare Methode war ein Mittel der Nobilitätspolitik, die die Herrschaft der Aristokratie nie ernsthaft in Frage stellte.' 105: 'Die Anachronismen der römischen Annalisten sind folglich nicht politisch bedingt. Bei der Vorstellung, Macer habe ein "populares Geschichtwerk" verfasst, handelt es sich um eine moderne Konstrukt, das sich nicht beweisen lässt.'

[83] Walt 1997.104: 'Dieses Schema [aristocratic v. democratic parties] ist aber von der neueren Forschung widerlegt worden.' See n. 79 above.

William Shakespeare, *Coriolanus*, Act 1, Scene 1 (produced probably in
1608, the year after the Levellers' riots in the English midlands)

> GRACCHUS Détruisez, renversez ces abus sacrilèges,
> Tous ces vols décorés du nom de privilèges.
> Jusqu'ici, peu jaloux de votre dignité,
> Vous avez adoré le nom de liberté:
> Elle n'existe point dans les remparts de Rome,
> Partout où l'homme enfin n'est point égal à l'homme.
> Mais la fin de vos maux est en votre pouvoir;
> Et punir ses tyrans c'est remplir un devoir.
> LE PEUPLE Jusqu'au fond de nos cœurs sa voix se fait entendre;
> C'est la voix de son frère.

Marie-Joseph de Chénier, *Caïus Gracchus*, Act 1, Scene 4 (produced in February 1792, six months before the establishment
of the French Republic)

> Ye good men of the Commons, with loving hearts and true,
> Who stand by the bold tribunes that still have stood by you,
> Come, make a circle round me, and mark my tale with care,
> A tale of what Rome once hath borne, of what Rome yet may bear.
>
> .   .   .   .
>
> 'Now, by your children's cradles, now, by your fathers' graves,
> Be men today, Quirites, or be for ever slaves!'

Thomas Babington Macaulay, *Lays of Ancient Rome*, 'Virginia'
(published in 1842, the year the petition for the People's Charter
was presented to Parliament)

Throughout the long history of radical politics, the struggles for the
liberty of the Roman People have been an example and an inspir-
ation.[84] Even in papal Rome itself, for five months in 1849 those
ideals prevailed over autocracy: 'La forma del Governo dello Stato
Romano sarà la Democrazia pura, e prenderà il glorioso nome di
Repubblica Romana.'[85]

One of the incidental effects of the revolutionary fervour in Europe
in 1848–9, and of the reaction that followed it, was the dismissal of the
young Theodor Mommsen from his post as Professor in Roman Law
at Leipzig. An active liberal, Mommsen took refuge for two years in

---

[84] See e.g. Peltonen 1995, Norbrook 1999, Richard 1994, Parker 1937. 'On ne peut
jamais quitter les Romains' (Montesquieu, *L'Esprit des lois*, 1748).

[85] *House of Commons Parliamentary Papers* 1851.lvii.156: item 3 of the decree
passed by the 'Roman Constituent Assembly' on the night of 8–9 Feb. 1849.

Zurich, where he wrote the classic Roman history of the nineteenth century.[86]

Mommsen believed that the establishment of the republic was the result not of popular enthusiasm for liberty, 'as the pitiful and deeply falsified accounts of it represent', but of two political parties uniting for a moment in the face of a common danger, like the Whigs and Tories in 1688.[87] (It is sobering to remember that Mommsen was almost as close in time to 1688 as we are to him.) However, 'every aristocratic government of itself calls forth a corresponding opposition party'. In Rome's case, the effect of the struggle of the orders, and the admission of the plebeians to government, was the creation of 'a new aristocratic and a new democratic party'.

The formation of these new parties began in the fifth century [i.e. 353–254 BC], but they assumed their definite shape only in the century which followed. The development of this change is, as it were, drowned amidst the noise of the great wars and victories, and the process of formation is in this case more concealed from our view than in any other in Roman history. Like a crust of ice gathering imperceptibly over the surface of a stream and imperceptibly confining it more and more, this new Roman aristocracy silently arose; and not less imperceptibly, like the concealed current slowly swelling beneath, there arose in opposition to it the new party of progress.

The breaking of the ice came with the Gracchi, and the 'democratico-monarchical revolution' that followed.[88]

Mommsen believed that the 'party names' of *optimates* and *populares* had become meaningless. 'Both parties contended alike for shadows'; the Roman revolution arose not out of 'paltry political conflict' but out of the economic and social conditions which the Roman government had allowed to develop; it was 'a great conflict between labour and capital'.[89] Nevertheless, Mommsen constantly uses the 'party names', in translation, as he describes the politics of the revolutionary period as the struggle of the democrats against the aristocracy.

Mommsen's *History* was hugely influential: it won him the Nobel Prize for Literature as late as 1902. The English translation, by

---

[86] Wiedemann 1996. The *Römische Geschichte* was published in 1854–6: I cite it below from the most widely available edition of the English translation.

[87] Mommsen 1910.1.257.

[88] Mommsen 1910.1.304, 305; 2.295, 339.

[89] Mommsen 1910.3.71, 72, 73.

W. P. Dickson, appeared in 1862–75, but in England Mommsen had a rival. Charles Merivale's *History of the Romans under the Empire* (1850–64) and *The Fall of the Roman Republic* (1853) were expanded into *A General History of Rome from the Foundation of the City* (1875). Its final manifestation was as the *History of Rome to the Reign of Trajan* (Everyman's Library, 1911), designed to form a continuous narrative with Gibbon's *Decline and Fall*. Throughout Merivale's work, Roman politics were disputed between the popular and senatorial parties.

From Mommsen and Merivale alike, the educated public of the late nineteenth and early twentieth centuries understood that the Roman republic was in near-constant tension between democracy and oligarchy, reform and reaction, the People and the Senate.[90] Nor was it an illusion: the evidence was there, in Cicero, Sallust, Livy, and Dionysius. What *was* an illusion was the old idea that the issues applied straightforwardly to the modern world. In the age of Marx, Nietzsche, and Freud, all such simple certainties were under attack.

Mass suffrage had made necessary, and mass literacy had made possible, a different sort of politics and a new concept of what a political party must be. As early as 1852, Marx himself noted the difference:[91]

Camille Desmoulins, Danton, Robespierre, Saint-Just, Napoleon, the heroes as well as the parties and the masses of the old French Revolution, performed the task of their time in Roman costume and with Roman phrases, the task of unchaining and setting up modern *bourgeois* society . . . The new social formation once established, the antediluvian colossi disappeared and with them resurrected Romanity—the Brutuses, Gracchi, Publicolas, the tribunes, the senators and Caesar himself. Bourgeois society in its sober reality . . . no longer comprehended that ghosts from the days of Rome had watched over its cradle.

However, Marx was wrong about Caesar. Now that the great powers aspired to empire, Caesar's name was appealed to more than ever. It usefully symbolized two glamorous topical themes, imperial conquest

---

[90] See e.g. Merivale 1911.215, on Gaius Gracchus: ' "Caius made the republic double-headed," was the shrewd remark of antiquity; but in fact the powers of the Roman state, the consuls and the tribunes, the Senate and the people, were always arrayed with co-ordinate powers one against the other, and Caius only introduced a fresh element of discord where there existed already others which could never long be held in equilibrium together.'

[91] Marx and Engels 1979.104, from 'Der 18te Brumaire des Louis Napoleon', *Die Revolution* 1 (1852).

and popular autocracy.[92] The Roman paradigm was now not the republic but the man who destroyed the republic.

It was against that background that the first 'modernist' interpretation of Roman republican politics, the 26-year-old Matthias Gelzer's *Die Nobilität der römischen Republik,* appeared in 1912. Ideological issues had no place in his analysis. For Gelzer, political life was the pursuit of power—that is, election to office—by the exploitation of personal and patronal relationships (*Nah- und Treuverhältnisse*). There were no parties, and factions were just ad hoc combinations to secure election. When standing for the consulship, the candidate 'should avoid taking up a position on any political question, whether in the senate or in the assembly, so that every man will expect him to intervene in his interest'.[93]

Gelzer took that piece of advice from Quintus Cicero's essay to his brother about electoral strategy, the *Commentariolum petitionis.* But Quintus was writing very specifically for the election campaign of a 'new man' who needed all the support he could get; it didn't necessarily apply in general. Besides, what he actually said is a bit different from Gelzer's paraphrase:[94]

atque etiam in hac petitione maxime uidendum est ut spes rei publicae bona de te sit et honesta opinio; nec tamen in petendo res publica capessenda est neque in senatu neque in contione. sed haec tibi sunt retinenda: ut senatus te existimet ex eo quod ita uixeris defensorem auctoritatis suae fore, equites R. et uiri boni ac locupletes ex uita acta te studiosum oti ac rerum tranquillarum, multitudo ex eo quod dumtaxat oratione in contionibus ac iudicio popularis fuisti te a suis commodis non alienum futurum.

Also, the main thing to be sure of in this campaign is that politically people should have high hopes and a good opinion of you. But while you're campaigning you mustn't take any political position, either in the Senate or in the assembly. This is what you must take care of: that the Senate should think from your way of life that you'll be a defender of its authority; that the Roman knights and the rich and respectable should think from your career that you'll be in favour of peace and quiet; and that the many should think

---

[92] On 'Caesarism', see now Baehr 1998, esp. 186–90 (Max Weber on modern parties).

[93] Gelzer 1912.45 = Gelzer 1962.64 = Gelzer 1969.56.

[94] Q. Cicero *Commentariolum petitionis* 53; cf. 5, *persuadendumque est iis nos semper cum optimatibus de re publica sensisse, minime popularis fuisse.*

that since you've been a *popularis*, at least in your speeches in the assembly and the courts, you won't be hostile to their interests.

No hint in Gelzer of the Senate and the *multitudo*—or of *popularis* speeches. This, I think, is the moment when the ideological vacuum was created.

In 1920 appeared Friedrich Münzer's *Römische Adelsparteien und Adelsfamilien*, a brilliantly original reading of the political history of the republic according to the patterns of names in the consular *fasti*. Münzer certainly didn't reject the ideological (the editor of the English translation tries to explain away his use of 'democracy' and 'democratic'), but since the aristocratic 'parties' of his title were essentially electoral alliances, the book could be seen as a history of Roman politics in Gelzerian terms.[95] So the two names are cited very frequently together, as joint founders of the modern view, in works of Roman history published in the mid-twentieth century.[96]

That view was established as orthodoxy by Hermann Strasburger's Pauly-Wissowa article on *optimates*, which appeared in 1939. Yes, Cicero says *duo genera semper in hac ciuitate fuerunt*, but it is anachronistic to infer two political groupings of government and opposition. The idea of 'parties' was borrowed from seventeenth-century England and used for Rome without any serious thought. Mommsen's whole approach was vitiated by this assumption, but Gelzer's pathbreaking work, completed and confirmed by Münzer, has corrected the misunderstanding. The whole history of the late republic needs rethinking, with the misleading evidence discounted; Greek authors used inappropriate Greek concepts (democracy, aristocracy), while Latin authors of the imperial period could not understand what was for them no longer a living reality.[97] As for the contemporary sources, Strasburger was too honest a scholar to

---

[95] Münzer 1920 = 1999, with R. T. Ridley at 1999.xxv–vi on 'democratic'. e.g. 1920.422–3 = 1999.358 on the Gracchan movement, 'this great antagonism between the democratic party and the nobility' and its effect on noble families: 'Torn between revolutionary and reactionary movements, the sons of these families could no longer follow a middle course as their ancestors had done; they perished in futile struggles with the superior strength of the right and left.' See also 1920.15–20 = 1999.20–24 on Licinius Macer, 'a vehement democrat and enemy of the aristocracy'.

[96] Most explicitly in Badian 1958.vii: 'Gelzer and Münzer, who revolutionized the approach to the study of this period.' Cf. among others Syme 1964.17 n. 3, Gruen 1968.2 n. 2, Scullard, 1970.381–2 nn. 4–5.

[97] Strasburger 1939.774–82 (esp. 779 on Gelzer and Münzer).

conceal the evidence that counted against his view, but he argued it away with the confidence of a true believer.[98] There was no democracy in Rome; the *populares* were individuals using the masses as a tool to achieve their own political ends; none of their proposals would have changed the self-evident leadership of the nobility.[99]

By the time Christian Meier's article on *populares* appeared in Pauly-Wissowa in 1965, all this was accepted doctrine. It was stated without argument, and with no sense of paradox, that the *popularis ratio* was a political method, as it were a career choice for achieving one's own ambitions.[100] One might have thought that the deaths of Tiberius and Gaius Gracchus, Saturninus, Livius Drusus, Sulpicius, and Clodius were prima facie evidence that being a radical tribune was not likely to bring you to the consulship; but perhaps these were just epiphenomena, not affecting the essential pattern.[101]

Meanwhile, in the English-speaking world the nature of Roman politics had been subjected to cold scrutiny in Ronald Syme's great book *The Roman Revolution*. Basing himself explicitly on Münzer's method, and clearly influenced by the rise of Stalin, Mussolini, and Hitler (the book was published the week after the invasion of Poland in September 1939), Syme kept his eye firmly fixed on *Machtpolitik*:[102]

The rule of Augustus brought manifold blessings to Rome, Italy and the provinces. Yet the new dispensation, or 'novus status', was the work of fraud and bloodshed, based upon the seizure of power and redistribution of property by a revolutionary leader...

One thing was clear. Monarchy was already there and would subsist, whatever principle was invoked in the struggle, whatever name the victor chose to give to his rule, because it was for monarchy that the rival Caesarian leaders contended.

When Syme used the word 'party', it was with all the overtones of Europe in the 1930s. Power for its own sake was his subject.

---

[98] Strasburger 1939.782–4 (*populares*), 784–8 (*partes*), 788–90 (*factio*).

[99] Strasburger 1939.790–7; cf. 782 ('*Popularis* wird ein Politiker genannt, der... einer bezeichnenden staatsrechtlichen Taktik bedient').

[100] Meier 1965.549–68 (esp. 553–4 on Gelzer and Strasburger). Already in Taylor 1949.13–15, though she thought Strasburger's attack on Mommsen had 'gone too far'.

[101] For an extreme version of that view, see Gruen 1974.4–5: 'Civil war need not be read as a token of the Republic's collapse.'

[102] Syme 1939.2, 258; cf. viii on 'the supreme example and guidance of Münzer'. On Syme and *The Roman Revolution*, see Raaflaub and Toher 1990.

Less overwhelming, but also influential in its way, was Lily Ross Taylor's *Party Politics in the Age of Caesar* (1949). Like Gelzer, she took Quintus Cicero's advice to his brother as a general rule, not just for the particular circumstances of a new man in 64 BC; her analogy for Roman politics was the American system of party conventions in a Presidential election year, when the Republican and Democrat hopefuls relied on their personalities for success and kept quiet about political issues.[103]

So Gelzer gave you the norm, aristocrats exploiting connections and patronage to get their consulships, and Syme gave you the crisis, as power was usurped by a 'chill and mature terrorist'.[104] Either way, you were not to suppose that there were causes that men would die for. And so you could end up as Siri Walt has done, unable to recognize a radical activist, the historian of the Roman People, because she has been taught to believe that such men did not exist.

V

Of course, there have been dissenting voices—Wirszubski on *libertas*, Brunt on social conflicts, de Ste Croix on the class struggle, most recently Millar on the urban crowd—but increasingly they have had to argue against a prevalent orthodoxy.[105] Much more characteristic of twentieth-century assumptions is the recent biography of Publius Clodius, which in a thirty-one-page introductory chapter on 'politics and popularity in the late Roman Republic' never once refers to the fact that the People's champions had been assassinated. 'The explosive careers of the Gracchi,' we are told, 'truncated and inconclusive, lent and lend themselves to varying interpretations.' As for Clodius, in pursuing his own career he showed 'how the *via popularis* could safely, even triumphantly, be trod'.[106] But it was no safer for him than it had been for his martyred predecessors.

---

[103] Taylor 1949.8; the system of 'primaries' has evolved somewhat since then. See nn. 93–4 above for Gelzer and Q. Cicero.

[104] Syme 1939.191, on Octavian in 43 BC.

[105] Wirszubski 1950; Brunt 1971; de Ste Croix 1981.332–72; Millar 1998.

[106] Tatum 1999.12, 238; 'it is perverse to question the aristocratic locus of political initiative and activity in Rome' (10).

Even after three generations, the sheer inertia of the Gelzer model seems to prevent the ideological content of republican politics, amply attested in contemporary authors, from being accepted as a given. Evidently historians still feel nervous about discussing *optimates* and *populares* as if the terms had a real meaning.

No doubt it would be unjust to attribute to modern scholarship what was said in 1866 about 'the credulous unphilosophical spirit, the ignorance of practical politics, the conservative tone of mind, and the literary *esprit de corps* too common among historians'. E. S. Beesly's complaint was not that his colleagues ignored ideology, but that they sympathized with the wrong side.[107] It is true, though, that twentieth-century academics have been less involved in real politics than, for instance, Mommsen was; and it may even be that university life predisposes one to think that cliques, patronage, and the pursuit of office are all that count. But I think there is a more general reason too.

Although it is unlikely that the Roman paradigm will ever lose its significance in Western culture, what it signifies varies from one age to the next. For the last four or five generations we have thought of Rome as the imperial power. Our Roman myths have been *Quo Vadis?* and *I, Claudius*; in the idiom of television, 'Rome' means a triumphal arch, or legionaries' boots on a paved road, with horns and drums and a portentous voice-over. If we need a radical reading, it has to be *Spartacus*.

But now the modern empires have gone (including the one that laid claim to Spartacus), and popular sovereignty is a real political issue. The Roman republic is becoming interesting again.[108] If we are to understand it, we need to hear all its voices. In 121 BC, with Opimius' Cretan archers closing in and his own followers deserting him, Gaius Gracchus fled for sanctuary to the temple of Diana on the Aventine. On his knees, arms outstretched, he prayed aloud to the goddess: 'For this ingratitude and treachery, may the Roman People be slaves for ever!'[109] Whether he really did so hardly matters: the story was told, for a Roman audience, and that fact itself shows us what the republic was like.

---

[107] Beesly 1866.421 = 1878. 40. For Beesly, see Wiseman 1998a.121–34.

[108] [See now Millar 2002b.]

[109] Plutarch *Gaius Gracchus* 16.5 (λέγεται). Cf. Sallust's Licinius Macer (*Histories* 3.48.13 and 26M) on the People's *ignauia*.

2

The Fall and Rise of Gaius Geta

What difference will it make to our understanding of republican political history if we 'put the ideology back', and take the concerns of the Roman People seriously? As a test case, let us consider a very obscure and puzzling episode of the late second century BC, mentioned fifty years later in a speech of Cicero's.

I

In his speech for Aulus Cluentius in 66 BC, Cicero needed to convince the jury that the censors' expression of disapproval (*animaduersio*) was not like condemnation in a court of law:[1]

neque in re nota consumam tempus; exempli causa ponam illud unum, C. Getam, cum a L. Metello et Cn. Domitio censoribus ex senatu eiectus esset, censorem esse ipsum postea factum, et cuius mores erant a censoribus reprehensi, hunc postea et populi Romani et eorum qui in ipsum animaduerterant moribus praefuisse.

I shan't waste time on a matter of common knowledge. I shall just give this one example, that Gaius Geta, although he had been expelled from the Senate by the censors Lucius Metellus and Gnaeus Domitius, was himself afterwards elected censor; a man whose moral character had been criticized by the censors was afterwards responsible for the moral character of the Roman People, and of the men who had criticized himself.

Who was Gaius Geta? The name must have been familiar at the time (Cicero didn't need to give the *nomen gentilicium*), but it is not mentioned in any surviving narrative source.

---

[1] Cicero *Pro Cluentio* 119, whence Valerius Maximus 2.9.9.

The necessary information is provided by the consular list from Antium, set up probably in the seventies BC, fragments of which happen to survive for the years in question:[2]

(*116 BC*)	C. LICINI. [Ge]THA	Q. F[abi.Maxim]
(*115 BC*)	M. AEMI[li.] SCAVRVS	M. C[aecil. Metel]
	[L.] CAECILI. Q.F. <Q.>N. METE	CN. D[omiti. Ahen. cens]
	LVSTRVM FECERVNT	
(*108 BC*)	[S]ER. SVLPICI. GALBA	M. AVRELI. SCAVR
	C. LICINI. GE[t]HA	Q. FABI. MAX. CENS
	[l]VS[tr]VM FECER[unt]	

The bare data imply a dramatic story, no doubt told at length in the lost books 112 and 113 of Livy's history. C. Licinius Geta was expelled from the Senate the year after his consulship, and one of the consuls in the year of his expulsion was M. Aemilius Scaurus, memorably described by Sallust as 'aristocratic and energetic, a political intriguer greedy for power, position and wealth'.[3] The censors of 115 BC expelled no fewer than thirty-two senators.[4] In 109 BC Scaurus was censor himself; he refused to resign when his colleague died, and had to be forced out of office by the tribunes of the *plebs*.[5] The new censors elected to carry out the *lustrum* were Geta himself and his consular colleague of eight years earlier.

For Valerius Maximus, the reversal of fortune was a moral lesson: disgrace sharpened Geta's energies, and he strove all the more earnestly to make the citizens think him worthy of the censorship.[6] Perhaps so, but one may also infer a political conflict of some intensity.

---

[2] *Fasti Antiates maiores* (Degrassi 1947.162–3); Cassiodorus and the late chronographers also give the name under 116 BC (Degrassi 1947.472–3). See also Sherk 1969.74 (n. 94 below), giving his affiliation *P.f.*

[3] Sallust *Jugurthine War* 15.4: *homo nobilis inpiger factiosus, auidus potentiae honoris diuitiarum.*

[4] Livy *Epitome* 112—evidently the culmination of the book, since the result of their *lustrum* was in book 113.

[5] Plutarch *Moralia* 276f (*Quaestiones Romanae* 50). Cf. *Fasti Antiates maiores* (Degrassi 1947.162–3): [cens.] ABDICAVE[runt] LVSTRVM NON FECER.

[6] Valerius Maximus 2.9.9: *ignominia uirtutem acuit...*

II

Our only narrative sources for the political history of the late second century BC are Sallust's *Jugurthine War* (discussed in this section) and the first part of Appian's *Civil Wars* book 1 (discussed in Section III). Sallust and Appian are very intelligent and well-informed authorities, enormously valuable on the events they choose to report, but unfortunately (for our purposes) they are very selective in their concentration on particular themes.

Sallust gives two reasons for his choice of subject in the *Jugurthine War*: first, the nature of the war itself, with its frequent reversals of fortune;[7] and second, the fact that it marked the first challenge to the arrogance of the Roman aristocracy, the beginning of a conflict that led to the civil wars of Sallust's own time.[8] At first, he comments only on the corruptibility of the aristocrats, the *auaritia* which made them susceptible to Jugurtha's bribes.[9] But when he comes to describe the outcome of the senatorial debate in 117 or 116 BC, when the Numidian king Adherbal vainly pleaded his case against Jugurtha's usurpation, he opens up a wider perspective.

The debate was won by 'the party that put profit or favour before the truth',[10] and an embassy of ten senators was sent to Numidia to divide the kingdom between the two claimants:[11]

quoius legationis princeps fuit L. Opimius, homo clarus et tum in senatu potens, quia consul C. Graccho et M. Fuluio Flacco interfectis acerrume uictoriam nobilitatis in plebem exercuerat.

---

[7] Sallust *Jugurthine War* 5.1: *primum quia magnum et atrox uariaque fortuna fuit.* Cf. Polybius 1.13.11 on περιπέτειαι, Cicero *Ad familiares* 5.12.4–5 on *temporum uarietates fortunaeque uicissitudines* in history.

[8] Sallust *Jugurthine War* 5.1–2: *dehinc quia tunc primum superbiae nobilitatis obuiam itum est.* His reference to *bellum atque uastitas Italiae* was probably written about the time of the Perusine War.

[9] Sallust *Jugurthine War* 8.1 (Romans at Numantia), 13.5 (*auaritia nobilitatis*), 16.4 (Scaurus, n. 3 above); the theme continues at 28.5 and 29.1 (Bestia), 37.2–3 (Albinus).

[10] Sallust *Jugurthine War* 16.1: *uicit tamen in senatu pars illa quae uero pretium aut gratiam anteferebat* (cf. *Oxford Latin Dictionary* s.v. *pars* §16a–b).

[11] Sallust *Jugurthine War* 16.2.

The leader of the delegation was Lucius Opimius, a distinguished man who was powerful in the Senate at that time because when he was consul, after the killing of Gaius Gracchus and M. Fulvius Flaccus, he had ruthlessly exploited the aristocracy's victory over the *plebs*.

Sallust did not need to tell his readers what had happened in 121 BC. The Senate had passed a decree 'that the consul L. Opimius should see to it that the *res publica* suffers no harm';[12] on the authority of that recommendation, Opimius had crushed Gracchus and his supporters by armed force and then executed more than three thousand prisoners, mostly innocent of any crime and without the benefit of a trial.[13]

That background of 'the aristocracy's victory over the *plebs*' is equally important in Sallust's next main episode. After Jugurtha had killed Adherbal and taken possession of the whole of Numidia, popular opposition to the clique of senators in Jugurtha's pay is presented as a full-scale attack by the tribune Gaius Memmius on the cruelty and arrogance of the aristocracy.[14] Sallust's Memmius reminds the citizens of what happened to the followers of the Gracchi— all those plebeians killed in prison, a process controlled not by law but by the arbitrary will of the aristocrats.[15] What was at stake was the liberty of the Roman People.[16]

Memmius failed to get his inquiry into Jugurtha's bribery of senators, and when C. Mamilius succeeded two years later righteous indignation had soured into political vindictiveness.[17] At this point, when the plebeians were displaying an arrogance like that of their aristocratic oppressors,[18] Sallust inserts a digression on party politics

---

[12] Cicero *In Catilinam* 1.4, cf. *De oratore* 2.132–4, *Philippics* 4.14; Livy *Epitome* 61, Plutarch *Gaius Gracchus* 14.3–4. See Lintott 1999.89–93 on 'the so-called Last Decree'.

[13] Orosius 5.12.10 (from Livy?): *ex quibus plurimi ne dicta quidem causa innocentes interfecti sunt*; Plutarch *Gaius Gracchus* 17.5, 18.1. See also Velleius Paterculus 2.7.3 (Opimius' *crudelitas* and *saeuitia*), Appian *Civil Wars* 1.26.119.

[14] Sallust *Jugurthine War* 27.2, 30.3 (*multa superba et crudelia facinora nobilitatis ostendere*), 31 (speech).

[15] Sallust *Jugurthine War* 31.7: '*item uostri ordinis multi mortales in carcere necati sunt: utriusque clades non lex uerum lubido eorum finem fecit.*' Cf. 31.26: '*nam inpune quae lubet facere, id est regem esse.*'

[16] *Libertas*: 30.3; 31.5, 16, 17, 22. *Seruitus* and *dominatio*: 31.11, 16, 20, 22–3. Unlawful killing of tribunes: 31.2, 13.

[17] Sallust *Jugurthine War* 40.3 (*magis odio nobilitatis . . . quam cura rei publicae*), 40.5 (*ex rumore et lubidine plebis*).

[18] Sallust *Jugurthine War* 40.5: *uti saepe nobilitatem, sic ea tempestate plebem ex secundis rebus insolentia cepit.* However, Sallust does not use the word *superbia*: that seems to be reserved for the *nobilitas* (5.1, 30.3, 31.2, 31.12, 64.1).

at Rome.[19] The dramatic date is 109 BC, the year Gaius Geta was elected to the censorship. Here, if anywhere, we may hope to find an explanation for his fall and rise.

Already in his previous monograph Sallust had identified the destruction of Carthage in 146 BC as the turning point of Roman history, after which virtue gave way to greed and arrogance and cruelty duly followed.[20] In repeating that analysis, Sallust now specifies the outcome—a political polarization between the aristocrats and the Roman People, pursuing their respective *dignitas* and *libertas* to the detriment of the republic.[21] The aristocrats exploited their dominant position to enrich themselves, driving the wives and children of citizens on military service from their farms in order to expand their own estates.[22] The crisis came—'like an earthquake', says Sallust—when two aristocrats with a conscience attacked the injustice in defence of the liberty of the *plebs*.[23]

It is important to register the moral tone of Sallust's indictment. The aristocracy is *guilty*; its activities are *crimes*, exemplified by the killing of Tiberius and Gaius Gracchus and M. Fulvius Flaccus.[24] Sallust prides himself on his non-partisan approach,[25] but he knows that here the balance of blame falls more on one side than the other:[26]

et sane Gracchis cupidine uictoriae haud satis moderatus animus fuit. sed bono uinci satius est quam malo more iniuriam uincere. igitur ea uictoria nobilitatis ex

---

[19] Sallust *Jugurthine War* 41.1: *mos partium et factionum ac deinde omnium malarum artium…*

[20] Sallust *Catiline* 10.5 (also in a digression, 5.9–13.5): *namque auaritia fidem probitatem ceterasque artis bonas subuortit; pro his superbiam crudelitatem, deos neglegere, omnia uenalia habere docuit.* Velleius Paterculus chose to divide his two-volume history of Rome at 146 BC.

[21] Sallust *Jugurthine War* 41.2 (*ante Carthaginem deletam… neque gloriae neque dominationis certamen inter ciuis erat*), 41.5 (*namque coepere nobilitas dignitatem, populus libertatem in lubidinem uortere*).

[22] Sallust *Jugurthine War* 41.8: *interea parentes aut parui liberi militum, uti quisque potentiori confinis erat, sedibus pellebantur.* Cf. Cassius Hemina fr. 17P = 21 Santini (Nonius 217L), Plutarch *Tiberius Gracchus* 8.1–4, Appian *Civil Wars* 1.7.29.

[23] Sallust *Jugurthine War* 41.10 (*quasi permixtio terrae*), 42.1 (*postquam Ti. et C. Gracchus… uindicare plebem in libertatem et paucorum scelera patefacere coepere.*).

[24] Sallust *Jugurthine War* 42.1. For *nobilitas noxia*, cf. 27.3 (the Senate's *delicti conscientia*), 40.1 (*conscii sibi*); for *scelera*, cf. 30.4 (*facinora*), 41.10 (*iniusta potentia*).

[25] Sallust *Catiline* 4.2 (*mihi a spe metu partibus rei publicae animus liber erat*), *Histories* 1.6M.

[26] Sallust *Jugurthine War* 42.2–4.

lubidine sua usa multos mortalis ferro aut fuga extinxit plusque in relicuom sibi timoris quam potentiae addidit. quae res plerumque magnas ciuitates pessum dedit, dum alteri alteros uincere quouis modo et uictos acerbius ulcisci uolunt.

It is true that in their eagerness for victory the attitude of the Gracchi was too unrestrained, but it is more proper for a good man to accept defeat than to use evil means to overcome a wrong. The aristocracy used its victory just as it chose, getting rid of many people by killing or banishing them; it thus added more to its future fear than its future power. This has been the usual cause of the ruin of great states, when each side wants to defeat the other by any means at all, and takes too ruthless a vengeance when it has done so.

The portentous conclusion reminds us of Sallust's premiss, that the political conflict caused by the arrogance of the aristocracy led directly to the civil wars and the devastation of Italy.

It was the censors who monitored moral behaviour, and stood for the values of the community against individual self-interest.[27] But when the censors of 115 BC demoted one of the previous year's consuls, who became censor himself seven years later, it seems clear that not even this bulwark of common standards was proof against the ruthless partisan politics of the late second century.[28]

III

Our other source for Gaius Geta's lifetime is book 1 of Appian's *Civil Wars*. Though less explicitly than Sallust, Appian too traces the origin of civil war to a moral cause, the greed of the rich.

He begins by explaining that the Romans kept much of the land they conquered in public ownership, and allowed any citizen to farm any part of it at a rent of one-tenth of the crop.[29] In fact, that is an oversimplification. The writings of the land surveyors (*agrimensores*) reveal how many different expedients were employed by the Romans

---

[27] See e.g. Cicero *De prouinciis consularibus* 21 (*commune officium censurae*), Valerius Maximus 2.9.pref. (*censuram pacis magistram custodemque*).

[28] For aristocratic *factiosi*, see Sallust *Jugurthine War* 8.1, 15.4, 27.2, 28.4, 29.2, 31.1, 31.4, 31.15. Cf. Cicero *De republica* 3.23: *cum autem certi propter diuitias aut genus aut aliquas opes rem publicam tenent, est factio sed uocantur illi optimates.*

[29] Appian *Civil Wars* 1.7.26–7; cf. Plutarch *Tiberius Gracchus* 8.1.

of the fourth and third centuries BC to allocate, define, and defend territories taken from defeated enemies.[30] However, Appian's source was no doubt accurate enough in describing the situation as it later developed.

His point is that the system was exploited by the rich. They bought out or forced out the poorer smallholders in order to create large estates that could be worked by slaves, who were not liable, as citizen farmers were, to call-up for military service.[31] At some point in the early second century BC, an attempt was made to curb this abuse:[32]

μόλις ποτὲ τῶν δημάρχων εἰσηγουμένων ἔκριναν μηδένα ἔχειν τῆσδε τῆς γῆς πλέθρα πεντακοσίων πλείονα μηδὲ προβατεύειν ἑκατὸν πλείω τὰ μείζονα καὶ πεντακοσίων τὰ ἐλάσσονα. καὶ ἐς ταῦτα δ᾽ αὐτοῖς ἀριθμὸν ἐλευθέρων ἔχειν ἐπέταξαν, οἳ τὰ γιγνόμενα φυλάξειν τε καὶ μηνύσειν ἔμελλον.

Eventually, and with difficulty, on the initiative of the tribunes, they decided that no one should hold more than five hundred *iugera* of that land or graze on it more than a hundred larger beasts [cattle] and five hundred smaller [sheep]. To this end they required landowners to employ a number of free men, whose task was to monitor what was going on and report it.

The aim of the legislation was to recover the land that was held over the legal limit and sell it to the poor in small lots.[33]

However, the tribunes' authority extended no further than the city walls (or perhaps 1 mile beyond),[34] and no doubt the monitors on whom the enforcement of the law depended could be bribed or terrorized as easily as the rich landlord's poor neighbours. At any

---

[30] See e.g. Frontinus *De agrorum qualitate* (Campbell 2000.2–3), Hyginus *De limitibus* (Campbell 2000.82–3) and Siculus Flaccus *De condicionibus agrorum* (Campbell 2000.104–5) on *ager arcifinius, ager occupatorius, ager quaestorius* etc. Helpful discussion in Campbell 2000.472–4 (473 on Appian).

[31] Appian *Civil Wars* 1.7.2–9; cf. Sallust *Jugurthine War* 41.8 (n. 22 above), Plutarch *Tiberius Gracchus* 8.2. For the same phenomenon in the 1st cent. BC, cf. Cicero *De lege agraria* 3.14, Horace *Odes* 2.18.23–8.

[32] Appian *Civil Wars* 1.8.33, cf. Plutarch *Tiberius Gracchus* 8.2. The tribunes' law pre-dates 167 BC (Aulus Gellius 6.3.37 = Cato *Pro Rhodiensibus* fr. 167 Malcovati); Brunt 1988.21 includes it among the laws omitted by Livy in books 21–40: 'Livy's narrative of internal events between 218 and 167 is very defective.'

[33] Appian *Civil Wars* 1.8.34: ἡγούμενοι τὴν λοιπὴν γῆν αὐτίκα τοῖς πένησι κατ᾽ ὀλίγον διαπεπράσεσθαι.

[34] Dionysius of Halicarnassus 8.87.6, Appian *Civil Wars* 2.31.123; cf. Livy 3.20.7, Cassius Dio 51.19.6. For the unpunished abuse of the rural poor, cf. Sallust *Histories* 3.34.27M (Macer's speech), *Catiline* 33 (Manlius' message).

rate, the abuse continued, until Tiberius Gracchus as tribune in 133 BC restated the earlier law in his own *lex agraria*, and set up a commission of senior senators to see to its implementation.[35]

For Appian, the murder of Tiberius Gracchus was an abomination,[36] the first step in an unstoppable progress to civil war. And it was the land question that brought about the second step too, as the landowners resisted the confiscation of their illegal holdings and the hopes of the plebeians were frustrated;[37] that was what made Gaius Gracchus stand for election as tribune, to vindicate his murdered brother with a new agrarian law.[38]

Of course Gaius' legislative programme went far beyond that, and no doubt the Senate had more reasons than one to encourage the consul to use armed force against him in 121 BC. (Like Sallust, Appian notes the cruelty of Opimius' treatment of Gracchus' supporters.[39]) But it is the land question on which the historian of the civil wars continues to concentrate:[40]

νόμος τε οὐ πολὺ ὕστερον ἐκυρώθη τὴν γῆν, ὑπὲρ ἧς διεφέροντο, ἐξεῖναι πιπράσκειν τοῖς ἔχουσι· ἀπείρητο γὰρ ἐκ Γράκχου τοῦ προτέρου καὶ τόδε. καὶ εὐθὺς οἱ πλούσιοι παρὰ τῶν πενήτων ἐωνοῦντο ἢ †ταῖσδε ταῖς† προφάσεσιν ἐβιάζοντο. καὶ περιῆν ἐς χεῖρον ἔτι τοῖς πένησι, μέχρι Σπούριος Θόριος δημαρχῶν εἰσηγήσατο νόμον, τὴν μὲν γῆν μηκέτι διανέμειν, ἀλλ᾽ εἶναι τῶν ἐχόντων, καὶ φόρους ὑπὲρ αὐτῆς τῷ δήμῳ κατατίθεσθαι καὶ τάδε τὰ χρήματα χωρεῖν ἐς διανομάς. ὅπερ ἦν μέν τις τοῖς πένησι παρηγορία διὰ τὰς διανομάς, ὄφελος δ᾽ οὐδὲν ἐς πολυπληθίαν. ἅπαξ δὲ τοῖς σοφίσμασι τοῖσδε τοῦ Γρακχείου νόμου παραλυθέντος, ἀρίστου καὶ ὠφελιμωτάτου, εἰ ἐδύνατο πραχθῆναι, γενομένου, καὶ τοὺς φόρους οὐ πολὺ ὕστερον διέλυσε δήμαρχος ἕτερος, καὶ ὁ δῆμος ἀθρόως ἁπάντων ἐξεπέπτωκει.

Not long afterwards, a law was passed making it legal for the recipients to sell the land which was the subject of dispute; for even this had been forbidden

[35] Appian *Civil Wars* 1.8–9.34–7; cf. Plutarch *Tiberius Gracchus* 8.2–4, 13.1, *ILLRP* 467–73 (Campbell 2000.452–3).
[36] Appian *Civil Wars* 1.2.5, 1.17.71 (τόδε μύσος). See pp. 178, 223 below.
[37] Appian *Civil Wars* 1.21.86, 88.
[38] The continuity is explicit in Livy *Epitome* 60, Florus 2.3.2, Orosius 5.12.4. Cf. Cicero *De officiis* 2.80: *quid? nostros Gracchos… nonne agrariae contentiones perdiderunt?*
[39] Appian *Civil Wars* 1.26.119: καὶ τοὺς συμφρονήσαντας ὁ Ὀπίμιος συλλαβὼν ἐς τὴν φυλακὴν ἐνέβαλέ τε καὶ ἀποπνιγῆναι προσέταξε.
[40] Appian *Civil Wars* 1.27.121–3. For the epigraphic *lex agraria* and its problematic relation to Appian's account see Lintott 1992.47–55, Crawford 1996.53–60.

by (the law of) the elder Gracchus. The rich immediately started buying it from the poor, or forcing them out on invented pretexts.[41] The situation of the poor became even worse, until a tribune, Spurius Thorius,[42] brought in a law to the effect that the land should no longer be divided up but belong to those in possession of it, that they should pay rent for it to the People, and that the income should be distributed. This was some consolation for the poor, because of the distributions, but it did not help to increase the population [i.e. of landholding citizens]. By these devices the Gracchan law—an excellent and most useful one, if it could have been put into practice—was undone once and for all. Not long afterwards another tribune abolished the rent, and the People lost absolutely everything.

That is what Sallust described as the victory of the aristocracy over the *plebs*.[43]

The following sentence of Appian's analysis is hard to translate and may be textually corrupt,[44] but it seems to say that by fifteen years after 'the legislation of Gracchus' both the land distributions and the agrarian laws had come to an end. If, as is usually supposed, he is referring to Gaius Gracchus, then the period he has just described is 123–108 BC. Once again, we have come to the date of Gaius Geta's censorship.

IV

Appian makes it clear that the People, and the Gracchi on their behalf, expected the community's property to be shared in common.[45] A similar egalitarian point is made by Appian's near-contemporary the land surveyor Siculus Flaccus: 'Gracchus', he says, 'understood that it is a harmful custom that anyone should possess a greater area of land than can be cultivated by the possessor himself.'[46]

---

[41] I translate A. Emperius' emendation πλασταῖς for ταῖσδε ταῖς, reported in Schneidewin 1855.

[42] The MS reading Βόριος or Βούριος cannot be right (no such name is attested), and Cicero twice refers to the agrarian law of a Sp. Thorius (*De oratore* 2.284, *Brutus* 136).

[43] Sallust *Jugurthine War* 16.2, 42.4 (see above, pp. 36, 38).

[44] Appian *Civil Wars* 1.27.124. See Gabba 1956.64–9, contra Crawford 1996.58.

[45] Appian *Civil Wars* 1.10.40 (the People's anger at being deprived of τὰ κοινά), 1.11.44 (Ti. Gracchus on the justice of τὰ κοινὰ κοινῇ διανέμεσθαι).

[46] Siculus Flaccus *De condicionibus agrorum* (Campbell 2000.102–3). The *praeno-men* of 'Gracchus' is lost in a textual lacuna; *pace* Campbell 2000.369, I think it sounds more like Tiberius.

That maxim dates back to Manius Curius in his second or third consulship, 275–274 BC.[47] It was the time of the retreat of Pyrrhus, and the definitive establishment of the Roman People as undisputed masters of Italy; C. Fabricius, another plebeian hero, was censor. That was evidently when Curius divided up the huge swathe of territory that he had conquered as consul for the first time in 290 BC, the Sabine and Picene lands which were later organized as the last of the thirty-five tribes, *Quirina* and *Velina*.[48] Like the territory of Veii 120 years earlier, the arable land was allotted to individuals in parcels of 7 *iugera* each,[49] about 1.7 hectares or 4.3 acres; as Curius announced, it is the sign of a bad citizen to want more than one man can cultivate himself.[50]

Curius emphasized his point by refusing the 50-*iugera* allotment granted him by the Senate and People. An alternative version of his announcement makes it the sign of a bad citizen to want more than everyone else receives.[51] In his world of equal citizens, the commander gets no more than his soldiers.

The loss of Livy book 14 is particularly unfortunate for our understanding of the ethos of that particular time.[52] We can get a glimpse of how it was exploited later, as in the tradition of Curius' humble farmhouse inspiring the young Marcus Cato,[53] but it is only through the uncertain medium of ancient etymology that we can try to guess how Curius presented his land distribution to the Roman People.

---

[47] For the implied date, see Valerius Maximus 4.3.5b, Columella 1.pref.14, *De uiris illustribus* 33.4–6.

[48] Livy *Epitome* 19 (241 BC); cf. Velleius Paterculus 1.14.7 on full citizenship granted to the Sabines in 268 BC.

[49] Valerius Maximus 4.3.5b, Columella 1.pref.14, Pliny *Nat. Hist.* 18.18; cf. Livy 5.30.8 (Veii).

[50] Pliny *Nat. Hist.* 18.18 (*perniciosus ciuis*, n. 70 below), Plutarch *Moralia* 194e, *Crassus* 2.8 (reading Μα<νιου Κου>ρίου with Ziegler), *De uiris illustribus* 33.6; the two last references give the allotments as 14 *iugera* each.

[51] Valerius Maximus 4.3.5b (*parum idoneus rei p. ciuis*), Frontinus *Stratagems* 4.3.12 (*malus ciuis*), Columella 1.3.10, *De uiris illustribus* 33.5–6.

[52] Livy *Epitome* 14 only has the story of Curius as *cos.* 275 selling the property of a man who failed to appear for the legionary call-up.

[53] Plutarch *Cato maior* 2.1–2. For the story of Curius' reception of the Samnite embassy, see also Cicero *De republica* 3.40, *De senectute* 55–6, Valerius Maximus 4.3.5a, Pliny *Nat. Hist.* 19.87, Athenaeus 10.419a, *De uiris illustribus* 33.7; cf. Aulus Gellius 1.14, Frontinus *Stratagems* 4.3.2, where the story is told of C. Fabricius.

Why was the *tribus Quirina* so called? According to Festus it was named after the Sabine town of Cures, but since Cures was enrolled in the *tribus Sergia* that cannot be the whole story.[54] The obvious analogy is with Quirinus, the god of the *Quirites* and the *curiae*;[55] his festival on 17 February (*Quirinalia*) was one of the 'large-letter' dates from the archaic calendar, but his temple on the Quirinal, symbolic of the cohesion of the citizen body, had been dedicated only three years before Curius' first consulship.[56] Another relevant deity is Juno Quiritis, or Cur(r)itis, for whom there were sacrificial 'tables' in each of the thirty *curiae*;[57] she was the principal goddess of Falerii, which was conquered by the Romans (after a revolt) in the very year the *tribus Quirina* was established.[58]

Both of these cults were supposedly initiated by Titus Tatius in his joint kingship with Romulus after the war for the Sabine women.[59] The citizens of the newly combined Roman-Sabine city were called *Quirites*, and the *curiae* into which they were divided were named after the Sabine women themselves.[60] A series of interlocking aetiologies derives

---

[54] Festus 304L (*Quirina tribus a Curensibus Sabinis appellationem uidetur traxisse*). Cf. Taylor 1960.63–4 for an involved attempt to save Festus' credit, rightly dismissed by Badian 1962b.203.

[55] Varro *De lingua Latina* 5.73 (*Quirinus a Quiritibus*), Ovid *Fasti* 2.479, Festus (Paulus) 43L. The *curio maximus* presided at the *Quirinalia*, when citizens were reminded to which *curia* they belonged (Ovid *Fasti* 2.527–32).

[56] Livy 10.46.7, Pliny *Nat. Hist.* 7.213 (293 BC). Cohesion: e.g. the 'patrician and plebeian' myrtle trees in front of the temple (Pliny *Nat. Hist.* 15.120) and the identification of Quirinus as the deified founder-hero (Cicero *De republica* 2.20, *De legibus* 1.3, Ovid *Fasti* 2.505–12, *De uiris illustribus* 2.14).

[57] Quiritis: *Fasti Antiates maiores* and *Fasti Paulini* on 7 October (Degrassi 1963.20–1, 153), *CIL* 11.3125. Curritis: *Fasti Arvalium* on 7 Oct. (Degrassi 1963.36–7), *CIL* 11.3100, 3126. Curitis: Festus (Paulus) 55L, Servius on *Aeneid* 1.8, 4.59, Servius *auctus* on *Aeneid* 1.17, Martianus Capella 2.149, scholiast on Persius 4.26. *Mensae*: Dionysius of Halicarnassus 2.50.3, Festus (Paulus) 56L.

[58] Faliscan goddess: *CIL* 11.3100, 3125–6, Tertullian *Apologeticus* 24.8; cf. *Liber coloniarum* (Campbell 2000.170–1) on the *colonia Iunonia quae appellatur Faliscos*. Conquest: Polybius 1.65.2, Livy *Epitome* 20, Valerius Maximus 6.5.1b; *Fasti triumphales* on 241 BC (Degrassi 1947.76–7).

[59] Quirinus: Varro *De lingua Latina* 5.74, Dionysius of Halicarnassus 2.50.3 (Enyalios); for Quirinus as Enyalios, see Dionysius of Halicarnassus 2.48.2, Plutarch *Romulus* 29.1, *Moralia* 285d (*Quaestiones Romanae* 87). Juno Quiritis/Cur(r)itis: Dionysius of Halicarnassus 2.50.3.

[60] *Quirites*: Varro *De lingua Latina* 6.68, Livy 1.13.5, Plutarch *Romulus* 19.7. *Curiae*: Dionysius of Halicarnassus 2.47.3, Plutarch *Romulus* 14.1, Festus (Paulus) 42L; disputed by Valerius Antias fr. 3P, and also by Varro (see p. 83 below).

all these *quir-* and *cur-* items from two sources: first, the Sabine town of Cures, supposedly Tatius' native city,[61] and second, the Sabine word *curis*, meaning a spear.[62]

It is possible that the whole story of Titus Tatius and the Sabines was a creation of the third century BC; that was Mommsen's view,[63] and it remains an attractive hypothesis, though by its nature unprovable. What matters for the present argument is the name of the *tribus Quirina*, in which all those *7-iugera* farmers were enrolled. Perhaps they thought of it as Curius' land, or as land won by the spear.[64] Or perhaps it was the citizens' land, the land of the *Quirites*.[65]

Romulus had divided the land into equal portions, representing the equality of his citizens; when new lands were captured, they were divided equally too.[66] It is likely that that ideal was still valued by the Roman People in the late second century BC.[67] And I think it can be shown that it was associated in particular with the family of C. Licinius Geta.

V

Appropriately, the evidence comes from the agricultural writers Columella and Varro.

[61] Derivations from *Cures*: Varro *De lingua Latina* 5.51, 6.68 (*collis Quirinalis, Quirites*); Livy 1.13.5 (*Quirites*); Ovid *Fasti* 2.480 (Quirinus); Plutarch *Romulus* 19.7, *Numa* 3.4 (*Quirites*); Festus (Paulus) 43L, 54L (Quirinus, *Quirites*); Festus 304L (*collis Quirinalis, tribus Quirina*); scholiast on Lucan 5.32 (*curia*), scholiast on Persius 4.25 (Juno Curitis); Lydus *De magistratibus* 1.5 (Quirinus).

[62] Derivations from *curis*: Varro fr. 387 Funaioli (Cures); Ovid *Fasti* 2.475–8 (Quirinus); Plutarch *Romulus* 29.1, *Moralia* 285c–d (Quirinus, Juno Curitis); Festus (Paulus) 43L, 55L (Quirinus, Juno Curitis); Servius on *Aeneid* 1.8, 1.292 (Juno Curitis, Quirinus); Macrobius *Saturnalia* 1.9.16 (Quirinus); Polemius Silvius on 17 Feb. (Quirinus); Isidore *Origines* 9.2.84 (Quirinus).

[63] Mommsen 1886 = 1906.22–35; cf. Wiseman 1995.127, 2004.143–7. Contra Cornell 1995.75–6, who takes the legend as evidence for a Sabine element in archaic Rome.

[64] Cf. Herodotus 8.74.2, 9.4.2 (δοριάλωτου χώρης), Diodorus Siculus 17.17.2 (Ἀσίαν...δορίκτητον).

[65] Mommsen (1887.172 n. 9) believed that 'the name of the last *tribus* was to mark the completion of the *populus Romanus quirites*'.

[66] Dionysius of Halicarnassus 2.7.4, 2.28.3; cf. Ch. 4 below on Romulus' 'constitution'.

[67] See above, nn. 45–6. Cf. Florus 2.1.3–4 on the legislation of the Gracchi: *quid tam aequum quam inopem populum uiuere ea aerario suo? quid ad ius libertatis aequandae magis efficax...?*

At the point in his first book where he argues that a small farm well cultivated will bring in more than a big one badly cultivated, Columella very properly mentions Manius Curius and his 7-*iugera* allotments. But Curius is not his first example:[68]

ideoque post reges exactos Liciniana illa septena iugera, quae plebis tribunus uiritim diuiserat, maiores quaestus antiquis rettulere quam nunc nobis praebent amplissima uetereta. tanta M'. quidem Curius Dentatus...

For that reason, those Licinian 7 *iugera* each after the expulsion of the kings, which the tribune of the *plebs* had divided up individually, brought in greater returns to the men of old than our extensive fallow lands provide for us now. That indeed was the amount which Manius Curius Dentatus...

Most of our sources about the expulsion of the Tarquins refer only to the royal property being handed over to the *plebs* to be looted without restraint; Dionysius, however, adds that the land was divided up 'among those who had no allotment'.[69] The detail of the 7-*iugera* lots and the juxtaposition with Manius Curius also appear in Pliny, with the same chronological marker 'after the expulsion of the kings'.[70] But only Columella refers to a tribune of the *plebs* called Licinius.[71]

This pseudo-historical scenario is clearly inconsistent with the view of both Cicero and Livy that the secession of the *plebs* and the foundation of the tribunate took place sixteen years after Tarquin's expulsion.[72] That may be why Licinius the tribune has not found a place in T. R. S. Broughton's *Magistrates of the Roman Republic*. But

---

[68] Columella 1.3.10, with a reference back to 1.pref.14 on Curius.

[69] Livy 2.5.2, Plutarch *Publicola* 8.1, Florus 1.9.3; Dionysius of Halicarnassus 5.13.2 (τοῖς μηδένα κλῆρον ἔχουσι), cf. 2.7.4 for Romulus allotting κλήρους ἴσους.

[70] Pliny *Nat. Hist.* 18.18: *Manii quidem Curii... nota dictio est perniciosum intellegi ciuem cui septem iugera non essent satis; haec autem mensura plebei post exactos reges adsignata est.*

[71] Recent scholarship is unhelpful here. See e.g. Cotta Ramosino 2004.170 n. 12, who assumes without argument that the reference is to a tribune of 493 BC, and Noè 2001.338–9, who attributes *errori grossolani* to Columella and seems to think (if I understand her correctly) that he was referring to the 2nd-cent. tribune mentioned by Varro (n. 73 below). The Pliny passage (n. 70), referred to by Noè only in a different context (2001.341), proves that Columella's *post reges exactos* is more than just a 'vague indication'.

[72] Cicero *Pro Cornelio* fr. 48 Puccioni = 47 Crawford (Asconius 76C: *anno XVI post reges exactos*); Livy 2.33.1–3 (Sp. Cassius and Post. Cominius are the sixteenth consular pair Livy records). According to Dionysius of Halicarnassus 6.74.3, the secession took place in the seventeenth year.

Columella's statement is clear enough. There was evidently a trad-ition that attributed a 7-*iugera* allotment, symbolic of a community of equals, to the founding moment of the republic, and described the legislator as already a tribune of the *plebs*. Not only that, but Colu-mella's phraseology ('those Licinian *iugera*') seems to imply that the name of the tribune was somehow significant.

An explanation may be found in the first book of Varro's *Res rusticae* (37 BC), at the point where the author, assembling the parti-cipants of his dialogue, welcomes the arrival of C. Licinius Stolo:[73]

> *cuius maiores de modo agri legem tulerunt (nam Stolonis illa lex quae uetat plus D iugera habere ciuem R.) . . . eiusdem gentis C. Licinius, tr. pl. cum esset, post reges exactos annis CCCLXV primus populum ad leges accipiendas in septem iugera forensia e comitio duxit.*

His ancestors passed the law on the limit of land (for the famous law prohibiting a Roman citizen from owning more than 500 *iugera* was a Stolo's) . . . From the same family C. Licinius, when he was tribune of the *plebs* 365 years after the expulsion of the kings, was the first to lead the People out of the Comitium into the 7 *iugera* of the Forum for receiving laws.

Both these allusions need careful attention.

Who was the Licinius Stolo who passed the 500-*iugera* law? It sounds like the law referred to by Appian and Plutarch,[74] and since Velleius Paterculus specifies that Gaius Gracchus' agrarian law was a re-enactment of the *lex Licinia*,[75] it is possible that Varro's Licinius Stolo was a tribune of the early second century BC.

Livy, however, attributes the law to the C. Licinius Stolo who with L. Sextius supposedly held the tribunate for ten consecutive years—including five years when no other magistrates were elected—before the 'Licinio-Sextian rogations' were voted into law in 367 BC.[76] Plutarch has a variant of the same story, in which Stolo is *magister*

---

[73] Varro *Res rusticae* 1.2.9. Stolo was later one of the senior *XVuiri* at the Secular games of 17 BC (*CIL* 6.32323.150, 167).

[74] See above, n. 32; the law referred to by Cato was the *plebiscitum Stolonis* (Tiro, quoted in Aulus Gellius 6.3.40).

[75] Velleius Paterculus 2.6.3: *uetabat quemquam ciuem plus quingentis iugeribus habere, quod aliquando lege Licinia cautum erat.* How long ago is *aliquando*?

[76] Livy 6.34–42 (6.35.5 for the agrarian proposal, cf. 10.13.14, 34.4.9). For the absurdities of Livy's narrative at this point, see Wiseman 1995.107–8 and Oakley 1997.646–9.

equitum to an unnamed dictator who allows the agrarian law to pass; the anonymous *De uiris illustribus* has yet another version, with Stolo as the first plebeian consul, evidently enacting the law in that capacity.[77] There was also a moralizing sequel to the story: Stolo was found guilty under his own law, and fined.[78]

Some scholars are prepared to believe in a fourth-century *lex Licinia* which 'was later modified and supplemented' by the law Appian and Plutarch refer to.[79] It seems to me just as likely that the fourth-century law was the fictional retrojection of a real second-century *lex Licinia* into the heroic context of the plebeian victory in the 'struggle of the orders'. One naturally thinks of Licinius Macer as a possible originator, since Livy mentions Macer's praising of his own family;[80] but though Macer may have introduced the idea into formal historiography, it seems obvious that a political conflict between *plebs* and aristocracy would provide the most plausible context for its first invention.

To return to the Varro passage: it is normally assumed without argument that Varro was referring to a fourth-century Licinius Stolo, as in Livy.[81] I suggested above that, on the contrary, he may have been referring to a second-century Licinius Stolo, author of the law Appian and Plutarch refer to; and I believe there is a good reason to prefer that alternative.

Commenting on Virgil's advice to 'praise big estates but cultivate a small one', Columella refers to Manius Curius' third-century land allocation;[82] after that (*mox*), even though 'our victories'—presumably in the Hannibalic War—had created wide areas of empty land, it was still illegal for a senator to own more than 50 [*sic*] *iugera*, 'and Gaius Licinius was condemned under his own law because in his excessive desire for property he had exceeded the landholding limit he had proposed by tribunician legislation in his own magistracy'.[83]

---

[77] Plutarch *Camillus* 39.5 (cf. Livy 6.39.3–4, Cassius Dio 7.29.5–6); *De uiris illustribus* 20.2–3.

[78] Livy 7.16.9, Dionysius of Halicarnassus 14.12, Valerius Maximus 8.6.3, Plutarch *Camillus* 39.5; cf. Columella 1.3.11, who, however, dates the trial of 'C. Licinius' after the conquests of M'. Curius in 290 BC.

[79] See e.g. Oakley 1997.654–9 (quotation from p. 658).

[80] Livy 7.9.5: *quaesita ea propriae familiae laus leuiorem auctorem Licinium facit.*

[81] See e.g. Oakley 1997.654–5, with 657–8 on Tiro (n. 74 above).

[82] Columella 1.3.10; Virgil *Georgics* 2.412–3.

[83] Columella 1.3.11: *suaque lege C. Licinius damnatus est, quod agri modum quem in magistratu rogatione tribunicia promulgauerat immodica possidendi libidine transcendisset…*

Quinquaginta (50) may be a slip or a textual error for *quingenta* (500)—but what matters is that Columella clearly believed that the author of the *lex Licinia de modo agrorum* passed his law in the second century BC. Naturally, Columella was very familiar with Varro's *Res rusticae*, even quoting it verbatim,[84] and his testimony makes it much more likely than not that Varro too had been referring to a second-century tribune.

The second allusion in the Varro passage is to another second-century Licinian tribune, 365 years after the expulsion of the kings (145 BC on Varro's chronology), who led the People out from the Comitium into 'the 7 *iugera* of the Forum'.[85] What does the phrase mean? The Forum piazza is roughly 6,000 square metres in area, the equivalent of about 2.4 *iugera*. Filippo Coarelli argues that *septem iugera* should be emended to *saepta iugera*, taking it as a reference to the 'sacred delimitation' of the Forum area.[86] But in that case, why use the word *iugera* at all? A term of measurement needs a numeral, or it is meaningless.

As we have seen, '7 *iugera*' was a phrase with symbolic connotations. When the elder Pliny refers to 'the law of Licinius Stolo' and Stolo's later condemnation (evidently accepting the Livian date),[87] he goes on to refer, like Columella, to the 7-*iugera* allotment after the expulsion of Tarquin.[88] Is that why Varro dated his second exemplary Licinius '365 years after the expulsion of the kings'?

That was a significant period of time, a 'year of years' or 'great year' such as that noted by Livy's Camillus after the sack of Rome, and later by the embattled pagans who hoped that AD 365 would see the end of Christianity.[89] Varro was interested in that sort of Pythagorean number-lore,[90] and though we have no idea what his source was for this item, it may well have been chronologically close to the event.

---

[84] See e.g. Columella 1.pref.15 and 17, quoting Varro *Res rusticae* 2.pref.3 and 1 respectively.

[85] See above, n. 73. Cf. Cicero *De amicitia* 96 on C. Licinius Crassus: *is primus instituit in forum uersus agere cum populo.*

[86] Coarelli 1985.130–1.

[87] Pliny *Nat. Hist.* 18.17—implied date before 250 BC?

[88] Pliny *Nat. Hist.* 18.18; see above, nn. 68 and 70.

[89] Livy 5.54.5, Augustine *City of God* 18.53; see Hubaux 1958.60–88.

[90] See e.g. Censorinus *De die natali* 9.1–11.2 (Varro *Logistorici* fr. 92 Chappuis). For Pythagoreanism in the late republic, see Griffin 1994.707–10.

Many years ago, Frank E. Brown suggested that Varro's mysterious reference to 'the 7 *iugera* of the Forum' might be a quotation from the tribune's own speech, 'with a description of the center of the Forum as common property of the people'.[91] Certainly the idea of the Roman People claiming back the Forum is appropriate to the time. In the first half of the second century the aristocracy had filled the piazza with honorific portrait statues; they were removed by the censors of 159 BC, who allowed only statues authorised by either the People or the Senate.[92]

Whether or not the tribune's speech was preserved, it is possible to detect the outlines of a *popularis* argument:

1. Tarquin was rich, arrogant, and tyrannical; the People rose against him; the land he occupied became the People's land; the tribune Licinius fixed fair shares for all, 7 *iugera* per man.

2. That was the beginning of Roman freedom, but now the great year has come full circle; the story begins again.

3. The aristocracy are rich, arrogant, and tyrannical; the People must rise against them; the land they occupy is the People's land; the tribune Licinius demands fair shares for all, 7 *iugera* per man.

And for a start (he may have said), let's at least make it clear that we own the Forum.

Plutarch attributes to C. Gracchus the new custom of addressing the People in the Forum rather than the Comitium.[93] That is no doubt a mistake; but it does at least suggest how ideologically significant Licinius' innovation was.

VI

To summarize so far: we have identified four separate Licinian tribunes, legendary or historical, who championed the right of the plebeians to farm the land owned by the People: first, the Licinius

---

[91] Cited by Taylor 1966.121 n. 28.
[92] Pliny *Nat. Hist.* 34.30 (Piso fr. 37P = 47 Forsythe); *De uiris illustribus* 44.3.
[93] Plutarch *Gaius Gracchus* 5.3.

(*praenomen* unknown) in the first year of the republic, who supposedly divided up the land at 7 *iugera* per citizen; second, C. Licinius Stolo in 367 BC, who supposedly established 500 *iugera* as the maximum legal holding; third, C. Licinius Stolo at some date between about 200 and 170 BC, who passed the real law about 500 *iugera* which the Gracchi tried to enforce; and fourth, C. Licinius Crassus in 145 BC, who let the People occupy the whole Forum and alluded in some way to the ancestral 7-*iugera* norm.

C. Licinius Geta was the presiding magistrate at the Senate meeting that resolved on the annexation of Phrygia, transferring the territory from the kingdom of Pontus to the newly created Roman province of Asia.[94] Now that that transaction has been convincingly dated to 122 BC,[95] we can place Geta's praetorship in the year of Gaius Gracchus' second tribunate, and attribute to him too Gracchus' concern to maximize the revenues of the Roman People.[96] It is consistent with what we know of his family, and there is other evidence too for the importance of the Licinii in the political tradition of the Roman *plebs*.

To start with, there is a comment by Cicero, addressing the Roman People as consul in January 63 BC. He is attacking Rullus' proposed agrarian law, and in particular the intention that Rullus himself should lead the commission responsible for administering it:[97]

> *qui licet? leges enim sunt ueteres neque eae consulares, si quid interesse hoc arbitramini, sed tribuniciae uobis maioribusque uestris uehementer gratae atque iucundae; Licinia est lex et altera Aebutia, quae non modo eum qui tulerit de aliqua curatione ac potestate sed etiam conlegas eius, cognatos, adfinis excipit, ne eis ea potestas curatioue mandetur.*

How is that lawful? For there are old laws—and laws not of consuls, if you think that makes any difference, but of tribunes, laws very pleasing and agreeable to you and to your ancestors. There is the Licinian law and the second Aebutian law, which excludes not only the man who has passed a law

---

[94] Sherk 1969.74 (no. 10 line 6); however, Sherk's restoration of the missing part of the line depends on the assumption that the SC is datable to 116 BC.

[95] Ramsey 1999.236–43, on the strength of new information about the accession date of Mithridates VI Eupator.

[96] Ramsey 1999.239–42, discussing C. Gracchus *Dissuasio legis Aufeiae* fr. 44 Malcovati (Aulus Gellius 11.10.3): *aput uos uerba facio ut uectigalia uestra augeatis, quo facilius uestra commoda et rem publicam administrare possitis.*

[97] Cicero *De lege agraria* 2.21.

about any responsibility or power, but also his colleagues and relatives, from having that power or responsibility granted to them.

The *lex Licinia* was evidently the more important of the two laws mentioned, since elsewhere Cicero cites it alone;[98] perhaps 'the second *lex Aebutia*' simply extended the list of prohibited persons. What matters for our purposes is that in establishing the principle the *lex Licinia* was regarded as a law in the *popularis* tradition, protecting the public interest by preventing private gain. Its date is unknown, but was probably in the second century BC.[99]

Late in that century a *lex Licinia sumptuaria* was passed, a law (well attested in the sources) which also seems to have escaped the notice of Broughton's *Magistrates*.[100] It postdates 143 BC,[101] and is attributed to a P. Licinius Crassus Dives, evidently a son of P. Crassus Dives Mucianus, who was consul in 131 BC.[102] He must have passed the law as tribune some time in the last two decades of the second century.

The law restated, with revisions, the terms of the consular *lex Fannia* of 161 BC. No more than 30 *asses* per day were to be spent on dining, except for certain specified holidays, when 100 *asses* might be spent, and weddings, for which the limit was 200 *asses*. The impact of this legislation may be judged from references to it in the fragments of the lost literature of the time. Lucilius put it bluntly:[103]

> *legem uitemus Licini.*
>
> Let's evade Licinius' law.

Laevius in his *Erotopaegnia* saw the law as saving animals from the butcher's knife:[104]

---

[98] Cicero *De domo* 51: *quod ne id quidem per legem Liciniam, ut ipse tibi curationem ferres, facere potuisti.*

[99] Weiss 1925.

[100] Aulus Gellius 2.24.7–10, Macrobius *Saturnalia* 3.17.7–10, Festus (Paulus) 47L.

[101] Macrobius *Saturnalia* 3.17.6–7: after the *lex Didia*, which was 18 years after the *lex Fannia* of 161 BC.

[102] Macrobius *Saturnalia* 3.17.7, cf. Plutarch *Gaius Gracchus* 15.4—*pace* Münzer 1927.288, who assumes that the reference is to P. Crassus, later *cos.* 97 BC, and the second *cognomen* an error by Macrobius or his source. For the Crassi Divites, cf. Cicero *Ad Atticum* 2.13.2, with Shackleton Bailey 1965.379.

[103] Fr. 1200 Marx = 599 Warmington = 1223 Krenkel (Aulus Gellius 2.24.10). For the Lucilian background, see Gruen 1992.304–6.

[104] Fr. 23 Courtney (Aulus Gellius 2.24.9).

> *lex Licinia introducitur,*
> *lux liquida haedo redditur.*

The Licinian law is introduced, the liquid light is restored to the kid.

It is likely that the law was also mentioned by Varro in his Menippean satire *Bimarcus*, datable to the seventies or sixties BC, though the text of the relevant fragment is very uncertain.[105]

Sumptuary legislation, like agrarian, was designed to preserve the egalitarian ethos of the citizen body by controlling ostentatious expenditure on private gratification. The Roman People did not like private luxury; they valued the traditional republican ideal of personal frugality and resources spent on public benefits.[106] Only a dangerous citizen would want more than a 7-*iugera* farm or a 30-*asses* dinner.[107]

That ideal is forcefully exploited in the speech Sallust gives to Marius, newly elected as consul for 107 BC. Marius reminds the People that his education has been in the hard school of practical soldiering:[108]

hostem ferire, praesides agitare, nihil metuere nisi turpem famam, hiemem et aestatem iuxta pati, humi requiescere, eodem tempore inopiam et laborem tolerare. his ego praeceptis milites hortabor, neque illos arte colam, me opulenter, neque gloriam meam, laborem illorum faciam. hoc est utile, hoc ciuile imperium. nam quom tute per mollitiam agas, exercitum supplicio cogere, id est dominum non imperatorem esse. haec atque alia talia maiores uostri faciundo seque remque publicam celebrauere.

Strike the enemy, stand guard, fear nothing except disgrace, endure cold and heat alike, sleep on the ground, put up with hard work and lack of food at the same time—these are the lessons I shall use to motivate the soldiers, and I shan't be mean with them and generous to myself, or give myself the glory and leave them all the work. My way of command is the proper one for citizens, for living in luxury yourself while you compel your army with

---

[105] Fr. 67 Buecheler/Astbury/Krenkel = 64 Cèbe (Nonius 309L). The MSS reading is: *nos ergo nihil egimus quod legem Lucanam luci claro latam non latam scutulans.* Cf. Krenkel 2002.111–2, who reads *nos ergo nihil egimus, quod legem Liciniam luci claro latam σκότῳ uitamus.* See Ch. 7 below on Varro's *Menippeans*.

[106] Cicero *Pro Murena* 76: *odit populus Romanus priuatam luxuriam, publicam magnificentiam diligit.* Custom of *maiores*: e.g. Cicero *Pro Flacco* 28, Sallust *Catiline* 7.6, 9.1–3.

[107] Cf. nn. 49–50 above.

[108] Sallust *Jugurthine War* 85.33–6.

punishments is to be not a commander but a slave-master. It was by acting in the way I propose that your ancestors gained fame both for themselves and for the republic.

One of the grounds on which Sallust's Marius attacks the arrogant and effete aristocracy is precisely their devotion to luxurious dining: '*I* don't have a chef who cost more than a farm manager.'[109]

Lucilius died in 102 BC, according to Jerome, so when Marius was elected the *lex Licinia sumptuaria* was probably a quite recent statute. No doubt there were plenty of wealthy Romans who tried to evade it; but Macrobius reports that the *optimates* were very keen that it should be acted on immediately.[110] It may be that Sallust's arrogant aristocrats were on the defensive, eager to demonstrate that they too stood for old-fashioned values.[111] It was the duty of the censors to protect the moral values of the citizen body, and there were censors in office in the year Marius was elected to the consulship. One of them was C. Licinius Geta.

VII

After the murder of Tiberius Gracchus in 133 BC, 'the Senate, wishing to conciliate the People in the present state of affairs, no longer opposed the division of the land, but proposed to the citizens that a commissioner be elected in place of Tiberius. They took a vote and elected Publius Crassus, a relative of Gracchus; for his daughter Licinia was married to Gaius Gracchus.'[112] This was P. Licinius Crassus Dives Mucianus, *pontifex maximus* and later consul in 131 BC.[113] So the author of the *lex Licinia sumptuaria* was probably Gaius Gracchus' brother-in-law.[114]

---

[109] Sallust *Jugurthine War* 85.39 (cf. 41 *in conuiuiis, dediti uentri*).

[110] Macrobius *Saturnalia* 3.17.7: *tantum stadium ab optimatibus impensum est…* Evasion: n. 103 above.

[111] Note that M. Scaurus passed a sumptuary law as consul in 115 BC (Pliny *Nat. Hist.* 8.223, Aulus Gellius 2.24.12, *De uiris illustribus* 72.5).

[112] Plutarch *Tiberius Gracchus* 21.1, cf. Campbell 2000.452–3 for the *tresuiri agris iudicandis adsignandis*; Münzer 1920.268–70 = 1999.246–7.

[113] Cicero *Academica priora* 2.13, Plutarch *Tiberius Gracchus* 9.1.

[114] Macrobius *Saturnalia* 3.17.7 (*Licinia lex lata est a P. Licinio Crasso Diuite*); see above, n. 102.

Licinia next appears in the historical record on the morning of her husband's death, begging him not to go to the Aventine, in a scene that owes much to that of Hector and Andromache in the sixth book of the *Iliad*.[115] As Gracchus walks away to meet his fate, Licinia falls fainting to the ground; her servants lift her up and carry her unconscious to the house of her brother Crassus.[116]

As Friedrich Münzer noted long ago, Plutarch's scene is influenced not only by Homer but also by tragedy.[117] Indeed, it may ultimately go back to a real tragic drama.[118] The suggestion is not, of course, that Plutarch knew such a play and transcribed his scene directly from it, but rather that his source was a historian whose own narrative of events was conditioned by what he had seen performed on stage at the *ludi scaenici*. A likely possibility is Valerius Antias, with whose work we know Plutarch was familiar.[119] On the one hand, Antias evidently dealt with the late republic at length, combining archival research with 'stereotyped set pieces and spurious precision',[120] and was therefore an obvious source for Plutarch to turn to for the second century BC; on the other hand, he was particularly interested in *ludi*, including *ludi scaenici*,[121] and even in the fragments of his work the influence of dramatic performance can be detected.[122]

If Licinia's tragedy was indeed a play, when was it first performed? Hardly in the immediate aftermath of C. Gracchus' death, when Opimius 'ruthlessly exploited the victory of the aristocracy'.[123] But

---

[115] Plutarch *Gaius Gracchus* 15.2–3, cf. Homer *Iliad* 6.390–502.

[116] Plutarch *Gaius Gracchus* 15.4.

[117] Münzer 1920.270 = 1999.247 on 'Plutarchs schöne, wenngleich von Homer und der Tragödie beeinfluuste Schilderung des letzten Abschieds beider Gatten.'

[118] A *fabula praetexta* on C. Gracchus is inferred by Meiser 1887.32–6, Wiseman 1998a.52–9, Beness and Hillard 2001.135–40. The idea is dismissed by Keaveney 2003 and Flower 2006.302 n. 41.

[119] Plutarch *Romulus* 14.6, *Numa* 22.4, *Moralia* 323c. Plutarch's life of Valerius Publicola is generally thought to be largely dependent on Antias: see e.g. Münzer 1891, esp. 70–1, and Wiseman 1998a.75–89.

[120] As cogently argued by Rich 2005 (quotation from p. 161).

[121] Censorinus *De die natali* 17.8, 10, 11 (Antias frr. 19P, 22P, 55P on *ludi saeculares*), Asconius 69C (Antias fr. 37P on *ludi Romani*), Livy 36.36.4 (Antias fr. 40P on *ludi Megalenses*), Livy 39.22.8–9 (Antias fr. 46P on *ludi uotiui*).

[122] Arnobius 5.1 (Antias fr. 6P) for the comedy of Numa, Picus, Faunus and Jupiter, a story told also by Plutarch (*Numa* 15.3–6); Egeria was the heroine of it (Ovid *Fasti* 3.262, Plutarch *Numa* 15.6), and Egeria as Numa's consort is described by Plutarch (*Numa* 8.6) as a δρᾶμα. See Wiseman 1998a.21–3.

[123] Sallust *Jugurthine War* 16.2, 42.4; see above, nn. 11–13.

Opimius' position started to become vulnerable in 116 BC, when as leader of the senatorial commission to Numidia he accepted Jugurtha's bribes.[124] One of the consuls of 116 BC was C. Licinius Geta. If Geta allowed some courageous aedile to put on 'the tragedy of Gaius Gracchus' at the *ludi plebeii*, it might explain why the censors of the following year not only demoted Geta from the Senate but also banished the acting profession from the city.[125] Hazardous though it is, that conjecture can take its place with the rest of the circumstantial evidence we have accumulated in order to make sense of what happened to Gaius Geta.

He belonged to a *gens* with a conspicuous tradition of legislation in the interests of the Roman *plebs*, and in particular the equal distribution of land to the poor. Licinian concern with the agrarian question had been kept up by P. Crassus (*cos.* 131 BC), father-in-law of C. Gracchus and member of the Gracchan land commission. However, P. Crassus was killed in Asia in 130 BC,[126] and his daughter was widowed by Opimius' brutal suppression of Gracchus and his supporters in 121 BC.

The first resistance to the triumphantly arrogant aristocracy came in 118 BC, with the contested foundation of the colony at Narbo Martius in the newly conquered province of Transalpine Gaul.[127] The People's will in that matter was carried out thanks to a precocious speech by a young man who would become one of Rome's great orators, the hero of Cicero's *De oratore*. He too was a Licinius, L. Licinius Crassus (consul in 95 BC, but dead before his time in 91).[128] It is possible that the election

---

[124] Sallust *Jugurthine War* 16.3–4, 20.1; Plutarch *Gaius Gracchus* 18.1.

[125] Cassiodorus *Chronica* 131–2 Mommsen (*MGH auct. ant.* 11): *his consulibus L. Metellus et Cn. Domitius censores artem ludicram ex urbe removerunt praeter Latinum tibicinem cum cantore et ludum talarium.* Geta: n. 1 above.

[126] Livy *Epitome* 59, Velleius Paterculus 2.4.1, Strabo 14.1.38 (646), Valerius Maximus 3.2.12, etc.

[127] L. Crassus frr. 15–17 Malcovati, esp. Cicero *Brutus* 160: *voluit adulescens in colonia Narbonensi causae popularis aliquid attingere.* Date: Velleius Paterculus 2.7.8, Eutropius 4.23; detailed discussion in Sumner 1973.94–7 and Crawford 1974.71–3, 298–9 (no. 282).

[128] See Rawson 1971.82–8 = 1991.25–33 for Crassus as a moderate optimate 'who sometimes talked like a *popularis*' (p. 85 = 29). The fragments of his speeches include an insistence that the Senate's only master is the Roman People (fr. 24 Malcovati = Cicero *De oratore* 1.225), and objections to the exercise of arbitrary power (*libido*) which are reminiscent of the speech of Sallust's Memmius (frr. 26, 41 Malcovati = Cicero *Orator* 219, *De oratore* 3.4, cf. n. 15 above). However, Crassus also attacked Memmius (frr. 20–1 Malcovati = Cicero *De oratore* 2.240, 267).

of C. Licinius Geta to the consulship of 116 BC was another indication of the changed political climate.

What Geta did in his consulship is not recorded, but it must have been conspicuous in one way or another for the censors to eject him from the Senate the following year. Since the consuls that year were M. Metellus, brother of one of the censors,[129] and M. Aemilius Scaurus, whom Sallust picked out as symptomatic of aristocratic intrigue,[130] it is hard to believe that the expulsion was not politically motivated. It was about this time, though we don't know exactly when, that the whole *raison d'être* of the Gracchan land legislation was undermined by a law allowing the allocated plots to be sold without restriction.[131]

The aristocrats' counter-attack did not last long. In 112 BC Jugurtha defied Rome by killing Adherbal and taking over his kingdom, and the Roman People knew that a clique of aristocrats had been bribed to let him get away with it.[132] Once again, as in 133 BC, the Senate had a guilty conscience and feared the People's reaction.[133] An army was sent, but its commander (L. Bestia, *cos.* 111 BC) was bribed in his turn, as was his chief adviser, M. Scaurus.[134] The tribune C. Memmius took the opportunity to exploit the People's indignation, and his wide-ranging attack on the aristocracy's cruelty and arrogance shifted the political balance; late in 110 BC a special inquiry was set up into Jugurtha's bribery.[135] Four ex-consuls were condemned and exiled, including Opimius.[136] Gaius Gracchus was avenged at last.

Scaurus avoided condemnation by getting himself elected as one of the three judges on the inquiry; he was also censor in 109 BC, until forced to resign by the tribunes.[137] It was in that tense political atmosphere that the People elected Gaius Geta to the censorship,

---

[129] For the disproportionate influence of the Metelli from 123 to 102 BC, see Velleius Paterculus 2.11.3, with Cicero *De finibus* 5.82, Pliny *Nat. Hist.* 7.59.

[130] See above, n. 3. Scaurus had been defeated in the election for 116 (Cicero *Pro Murena* 36).

[131] Appian *Civil Wars* 1.27.121 (n. 40 above).

[132] Sallust *Jugurthine War* 27.2: C. Memmius (as tribune designate) on *pauci factiosi*.

[133] Sallust *Jugurthine War* 27.3; cf. Plutarch *Tiberius Gracchus* 21.1.

[134] Sallust *Jugurthine War* 28.4–29.5.

[135] Sallust *Jugurthine War* 30–1 (Memmius), 40 (*quaestio Mamilia*).

[136] Cicero *Pro Sestio* 140, *Pro Plancio* 70, *Brutus* 128.

[137] Sallust *Jugurthine War* 40.4 (*quaesitor*); n. 5 above (censor).

and a year later they elected Marius as consul. These events were only a temporary setback for the aristocracy; murder and civil war would soon put them back in power.[138] But at least the plebeians were fighting back, and Gaius Geta's fall and rise can be seen as a part of that process.

In itself, the explanation of one minor episode in the long history of Roman politics may not be of much consequence. But I hope the detailed investigation may be more broadly useful in bringing together some of the scattered and neglected evidence for the political ideology of the Roman People.

[138] For Sulla's victory as the triumph of the *nobilitas*, see Cicero *Pro Roscio Amerino* 135–42. Murder: e.g. L. Saturninus, C. Glaucia, L. Equitius, P. Sulpicius, and the 4,700 proscription victims of 82–81 BC.

3

Licinius Macer, Juno Moneta, and Veiovis

I

Twenty-four years after Gaius Geta's censorship, one of the moneyers responsible for the issue of Rome's coinage in 84 BC was called C. Licinius L.f. Macer.[1] The filiation shows that he was not Geta's son, but he may have been a nephew. He was tribune of the *plebs* in 73 BC, an occasion featured in the third book of Sallust's *Histories*, where Macer was given a lengthy speech.[2]

It is normally assumed that this Roman politician was the historian Licinius Macer, used extensively by Livy and Dionysius of Halicarnassus as a source for the early republic. The identification was taken for granted in Chapter 1 above (first published in 2002), but since it is questioned by a very distinguished authority on Roman historiography,[3] some justification for the assumption must be offered.

'From an unprejudiced study of the fragmentary evidence,' writes Tim Cornell,[4] 'it is clear that we know far less about the lost annalistic sources of Livy and Dionysius than is often claimed.' However, that is only true of Licinius Macer if the politician and the historian are *not* identical. Where does the onus of proof lie? Given that the historian's younger contemporary Sallust, reporting the politician's

This chapter has been much improved by comments made on an earlier version by Stephen Oakley and Tim Cornell. I am also particularly grateful to Prof. Oakley for letting me see the draft of his material on Macer for the forthcoming edition of the *Fragmentary Roman Historians*.

[1] Crawford 1974.370 (no. 354).
[2] Sallust *Histories* 3.48M (= 3.34 McGushin).
[3] See above, pp. 19–23, esp. nn. 63 and 77.
[4] Cornell 2005.64.

campaign to restore the historic political powers of the tribunes, gave him a fine speech full of allusions to the heroic plebeians of the early republic,[5] I think it is more likely than not that the two were identical, and that Sallust was exploiting the fact. That is, it seems to me less prejudicial to assume their identity than to insist on the formal possibility that there were two men of the same name interested in the same things at the same time.

Until there is reason to believe otherwise, I think we may accept it as a working hypothesis that the historian was a determined *popularis*, at least in 73 BC when the restoration of the tribunes' historic powers was a fiercely contentious political issue. That is certainly consistent with the family tradition we identified in Chapter 2.

II

It was Sulla who effectively abolished the tribunes' powers. According to Appian, he did it as consul in 88 BC.[6] But then Sulla went off to the East, and the implementation of his reactionary agenda had to await his return in 82, when renewed civil war established him as dictator 'to make laws and revise the constitution'.[7] In the intervening period, especially the 'three years without war' from 86 to 84,[8] Sulla's opponents were in power, and able to hope—vainly, as it turned out—that it would never happen. It was in that period, as *triumvir monetalis* in 84 BC, that Licinius Macer began his career.[9]

Sallust's Macer, tribune in 73 BC, begins his speech to the Roman People by contrasting the rule of law handed down by their ancestors with 'this slavery created for you by Sulla'. He goes on to point out that nothing had changed with Sulla's death, and it was not until the tribunate of Sicinius in 76 that the restoration of the tribunes' powers could even be proposed.[10]

---

    [5] Sallust *Histories* 3.48.1, 12, 15, 17M.
    [6] Appian *Civil Wars* 1.59.265–7.
    [7] Appian *Civil Wars* 1.99.462.
    [8] *Triennium sine armis*: Cicero *Brutus* 308.
    [9] See n. 1 above, Section IV below.
    [10] Sallust *Histories*. 3.48.1, cf. 9 (Sulla's death), 8 (L. Sicinius), 10–11 (Sicinius' successors).

At this point it is worth considering the conflicting traditions about the original establishment of the tribunate after the first secession of the *plebs* to the Mons Sacer. Our earliest evidence comes from Cicero's defence of Cornelius in 65 BC: praising the bravery of the early plebeians in the face of patrician tyranny, he refers to their secession as the restoration [*sic*] of their own *leges sacratae*.[11] The language is very similar to that of Macer's speech in Sallust, and the use of *restituere* (which Asconius thought must be a copyist's error) was perhaps a reminder to the audience of the restitution of the tribunes' powers just five years earlier.[12]

According to Cicero, the plebeians elected two tribunes, whom he does not name. Asconius comments as follows:[13]

ceterum quidam non duo tr. pl., ut Cicero dicit, sed quinque tradunt creatos tum esse singulos ex singulis classibus. sunt tamen qui eundem illum duorum numerum quem Cicero ponant: inter quos Tuditanus et Pomponius Atticus, Livius quoque noster. idem hic et Tuditanus adiciunt tres praeterea ab illis duobus qui collegae <essent lege> creatos esse. nomina duorum qui primi creati sunt haec traduntur: L. Sicinius L.f. Velutus, L. Albinius C.f. Paterculus.

Some authorities, on the other hand, report that not two tribunes of the *plebs* (as Cicero says) but five were elected at that time, one from each of the *classes*. However, there are those who give the same number as Cicero does, namely two; they include Tuditanus, Pomponius Atticus, and our own Livy. This same authority [i.e. Livy?] and Tuditanus add that three others were elected by those two by law to be their colleagues. The names of the two who were first elected are reported as these: L. Sicinius L.f. Velutus and L. Albinius C.f. Paterculus.

It is not clear where Asconius got the two names he quotes; Tuditanus and Atticus, like Cicero, are cited only for the *number* of the original tribunes, not their identities.[14] Piso in the late second century BC also said there were two (he believed the number was increased to five only

---

[11] Cicero *Pro Cornelio* fr. 48 Crawford = 49 Puccioni (quoted in Asconius 76C): *leges sacratas ipsi sibi restituerent.*

[12] Cf. Cicero *In Verrem* 5.175, to an imagined senatorial jury in 70 BC: 'As long as it could and as long as it had to, the republic put up with that monarchical domination of yours [*regiam istam uestram dominationem*] in the courts and in the whole of public life. But in case you don't yet realize it, all that was snatched from you and taken away on the day the tribunes were restored to the Roman People.'

[13] Asconius 76–7C.

[14] *Pace* Broughton 1951.16 n. 1.

in 471 BC); it is not known whether he named the original two, but Livy's report of his item on 471 may suggest that he didn't.[15]

Livy's own account of the original tribunes is as follows:[16]

ita tribuni plebei creati duo, C. Licinius et L. Albinius; hi tres collegas sibi creauerunt. in his Sicinium fuisse, seditionis auctorem; de duobus qui fuerint minus conuenit. sunt qui duos tantum in sacro monte creatos tribunos esse dicant, ibique sacratam legem latam.

And so two tribunes of the *plebs* were elected, C. Licinius and L. Albinius; they then elected three colleagues, one of whom is said to have been Sicinius, the instigator of the revolution. There is less agreement about who the other two were. There are those who say only two tribunes were elected on the Mons Sacer, and that it was there that the *lex sacrata* was passed.

Previously, Livy had made only one brief mention of Sicinius the *auctor seditionis*, ignoring the version later exploited by Dionysius and Plutarch, which made C. Sicinius 'Belloutos' and L. Iunius Brutus the ringleaders of the secession.[17] Asconius' 'L. Sicinius Velutus and L. Albinius Paterculus' evidently came from yet another version.

I think it is reasonable to infer from all this that the earlier tradition, as represented by Tuditanus (perhaps) and Piso, assumed that the plebeians elected only two tribunes, and did not offer names for them. Since Claudius Quadrigarius evidently began his narrative only with the sack of Rome in 387 BC,[18] the possible authors of the various versions which named the original tribunes are Cn. Gellius,[19] Licinius Macer, Valerius Antias, Aelius Tubero, Cornelius Nepos, Atticus, and Varro;[20] one might add for completeness Procilius, Cornelius, and Lutatius, all cited by Varro on the origin of the

---

[15] Piso fr. 23P = 30 Forsythe (Livy 2.58.1–2): Livy says 'he also names the tribunes', implying perhaps that he hadn't before.

[16] Livy 2.33.2–3: *Albinius* is Sigonius' emendation for the MSS' *Albinus*.

[17] Livy 2.32.2, cf. 34.9. Contrast Dionysius of Halicarnassus 6.70.2, 72.1, 89.1, Plutarch *Coriolanus* 7.1. According to Dionysius (6.89.1), the original college of tribunes consisted of Brutus, Sicinius, C. Licinius, P. Licinius, and C. Visellius Ruga.

[18] See the quotations from his first book in Aulus Gellius 17.2.12, 14, 24, 26 (frr. 1, 4, 5, 7P).

[19] For Gellius on the early republic, see Dionysius of Halicarnassus 6.11.2, 7.1.4, Cicero *De diuinatione* 1.55 (frr. 19–21P).

[20] See Varro *De lingua Latina* 5.81, on the first tribunes and the 'secession to Crustumerium'; book 2 of his *De uita populi Romani* dealt with the early Republic, books 20 and 21 of the *Antiquitates humanae* with the workings of the republican constitution and the powers of the magistrates.

Lacus Curtius,[21] but it is hard to think of any other writers on the early republic whom Livy and Dionysius may have used.

Since Livy remarks that Licinius Macer went out of his way to praise his own ancestors,[22] it is an easy guess that the source of Livy's version of the first college of tribunes—C. Licinius as one of the original two, Sicinius, who started it all, as one of the subsequent three—was Macer himself.[23]

All the authors of these various versions had to either refute or ignore the argument of 'Clodius'—often, and reasonably, identified as Claudius Quadrigarius—that practically no authentic records survived from the period before the Gallic sack.[24] One of the few things we know for certain about Licinius Macer's history is that he claimed to have a list of magistrates for the fifth century BC, in 'linen books' which he had found in the temple of Juno Moneta.[25] As Alfred Klotz convincingly argued many years ago, that may have been Macer's answer to Quadrigarius.[26]

III

In Livy's (probably Licinian) account, one of the first two tribunes was L. Albinius. Ogilvie takes the very obscurity of the name as evidence for its authenticity,[27] but a historiographical explanation is surely more likely. Perhaps it was the name of another late-republican *popularis*.

---

[21] Varro *De lingua Latina* 5.148–50. Lutatius is presumably the author of *Communes historiae*: H. Peter attributes the fragments to Q. Catulus the elder (frr. 6–13P, and add *Origo gentis Romanae* 9.2, 11.3, 13.7, 18.1).

[22] Livy 7.9.5, *quaesita ea propriae familiae laus*.

[23] Understandably taken for granted by Ogilvie 1965.313: 'C. Licinius: rudely interpolated by his namesake and descendant.' Dionysius' version (n. 17 above), with two Licinii and a Sicinius, may imply elaboration by a historian later than, but sympathetic to, Macer's interpretation; Aelius Tubero (cf. Livy 4.23.2, 10.9.10) is an obvious possibility.

[24] Plutarch *Numa* 1.1 (Κλώδιός τις ἐν ἐλέγχῳ χρόνων), cf. *Camillus* 22.1; Livy 6.1.2 ('most public and private documents perished in the burning of the city'). For 'Clodius' as Quadrigarius, see most recently Forsythe 2005.63.

[25] Livy 4.7.11–12 (444 BC), 4.13.7 (439 BC), 4.20.8 (436 BC), 4.23.1–3 (434 BC); Oakley 1997.7–8.

[26] Klotz 1937.219, rightly followed by Frier 1975.94–6, and 1979/1999.153–9.

[27] Ogilvie 1965.313: 'The Albinii were an Etruscan family (Schulze 118 f) who continued in the honourable obscurity of minor senatorial rank (cf. Cicero, pro

The best known L. Albinius in Roman history is the pious plebeian who rescued the Vestal Virgins as they fled from the approaching Gauls;[28] according to his *elogium* in Agrippa's Pantheon, when the Gauls had gone he brought the Vestals back again from Caere to Rome.[29] That story was part of a version of the 'Camillus legend' in which patrician arrogance and incompetence led to disaster, redeemed only by the exemplary behaviour of plebeians. I have suggested elsewhere that in its essentials it may date back to the plebeians' demand for power-sharing in the 370s,[30] but that does not exclude much later elaboration, for example by giving names to anonymous characters.[31]

The rival version had patrician heroes—not only M. Furius Camillus himself, but the courageous M. Manlius, who was woken by Juno's geese and repulsed the Gauls' night attack on the Capitol,[32] and the pious Fabius Dorsuo, who walked through the Gauls' lines and back in order to carry out a necessary sacrifice.[33] The origin of that version is also the origin of the cult of Juno Moneta, 'the Warner'. Her temple was vowed in 345 BC, the consulship of M. Fabius Dorsuo, by the dictator L. Furius Camillus, whose *magister equitum* was Cn. Manlius Capitolinus.[34] Juno was the Warner not only because of the geese story, but also because she had supposedly warned the Romans to

Sestio 6) for long years of the Republic. It is unlikely that they would have had the opportunity or the motive to invent so famous an ancestor if he had not existed.' As it turns out, the Cicero reference is irrelevant: P. Sestius' father-in-law was probably called Albanius (Shackleton Bailey 1991.5).

[28] Livy 5.40.7–10, Valerius Maximus 1.1.10, Plutarch *Camillus* 21.1–2, Florus 1.13.12.

[29] *CIL* 6.1272: [*urbe recup*]*erata sacra et uirigines* [*Romam reu*]*exit*. Pantheon: Cozza 1983.116–17.

[30] Wiseman 2004.126–8.

[31] Two other exemplary plebeians remained nameless: the soldier who captured the Veientane *haruspex* (Livy 5.15.5–6) and the young man who asked Juno if she wanted to go to Rome (Livy 5.22.4–5).

[32] Livy 5.47.4–7, Diodorus Siculus 14.116.6–7, Dionysius of Halicarnassus 13.7.3–8.2, Plutarch *Camillus* 27.2–5, Florus 1.7.15, *De uiris illustribus* 24.4.

[33] Livy 5.46.1–3, Valerius Maximus 1.1.11, Florus 1.7.16, Appian *Gallic Wars* fr. 6, Cassius Dio 7.25.5–6.

[34] Livy 7.28.1–4; *Fasti triumphales* on 338 BC (Degrassi 1947.68–9) for L. Furius' *cognomen*. Cf. Wiseman 2004.129–30.

defend the Capitol in the first place.[35] That, however, was one revision the patricians were not able to establish: the old story of the disembodied voice at the grove of Vesta, heard and reported by a plebeian who was then mocked by the patrician magistrates,[36] could not be dislodged.

Two centuries later, when *plebs* and *patres* were again locked in fierce political conflict,[37] the old stories took on new exemplary life. After the destruction of Gaius Gracchus and his supporters in 121 BC, the consul L. Opimius built a grand and provocative temple of Concordia on the lower slope of the Capitol overlooking the Forum; it was claimed, perhaps now for the first time, that Camillus had done the same in 367 BC.[38] The site was immediately below the temple of Juno Moneta on the Capitoline *arx*, as Ovid makes clear:[39]

> *candida, te niueo posuit lux proxima templo,*
> *qua fert sublimes alta Moneta gradus:*
> *nunc bene prospicies Latiam, Concordia, turbam…*

Fair goddess, the next day [16 January] placed you in your snow-white temple, where lofty Moneta lifts her steps on high. Well will you look out now, Concord, on the Latin throng…

Of course it is good if Concord watches over the citizens. But when Opimius, as a new Camillus, set up the temple after 121 BC, the Roman People recognized it for what it was—a monument to discord and the abuse of power.[40] Did the Juno Moneta temple similarly advertise the power of the nobility?

---

[35] Scholiast on Lucan 1.380: *Moneta dicta est, quod monuisset ut Capitolium tuerentur.* Other aetiologies in Cicero *De diuinatione* 1.101, 2.69 and Suda *s.v.* 'Moneta' (μ1220).

[36] Cicero *De diuinatione* 1.101, Livy 5.32.6–7, Plutarch *Camillus* 14, Zonaras 7.23.3.

[37] Senate v. People: Sallust *Jugurthine War* 41.2–5, Appian *Civil Wars* 1.1.1. Sallust usually defines the two sides as *populus* or *plebes* on the one hand, *nobilitas* or *pauci* on the other: *Jugurthine War* 16.2, 27.2, 30.3, 31 (Memmius' speech), 41.5–7, 42.1, etc.

[38] Opimius' temple: Varro *De lingua Latina* 5.156 ('above the Graecostasis'), Festus 470L ('between the Capitol and the Forum'), Cassius Dio 58.11.4 (close to the *carcer*); Ferroni 1993 with fig. 188. 'Camillus': Plutarch *Camillus* 42.4, Ovid *Fasti* 1.641–4. See Levick 1978, esp. 218–20.

[39] Ovid *Fasti* 1.637–9, referring to the temple as rebuilt by Tiberius in AD 10.

[40] Plutarch *Gaius Gracchus* 17.6, Augustine *City of God* 3.25; cf. Sallust *Jugurthine War* 16.2 (p. 36 above).

In an ambitious and wide-ranging recent argument, Andrew Meadows and Jonathan Williams seek to associate Moneta as a symbol of 'monumentality'—coined money, weights and measures, historical memory[41]—with 'the unprecedented turn taken by [Roman] coin design in the late second century BC'.[42] Down to about 137 BC, the Roman coinage carried predictable symbols of the community that issued it; after that date, practically every issue was different, with most of the designs evidently relevant to the family histories of the moneyers responsible.

That is certainly an important phenomenon, and perhaps not irrelevant to the aristocratic arrogance (*superbia nobilitatis*) which Sallust thought was characteristic of the period.[43] But the claim that 'Moneta guaranteed the standard of the coinage, and therefore she also ensured the authenticity of the scenes that appeared on her coinage',[44] is something of a non sequitur. Besides, if it is so fundamental that the goddess of the mint was also the guardian of historical memory, why did the series of 'monumental' family-history issues begin only in about 137 BC?

What Meadows and Williams leave out of their analysis is the idea of political conflict. It would be wrong, they say,[45] to take the new issues

as an indication of the incipient 'privatization' of the coinage in the period of the late Republic, still less as a part of the collapse of common Republican institutions in anticipation of the fall of the Republic itself. Rather, this change is suggestive of the ways in which the story of the *populi Romani gesta* ('the deeds of the Roman people') was mostly understood by members of the great political families from the partial viewpoint of their own traditions, the public memory and recognition of which they tried their best to foster

---

[41] *Moneta* as the mint: Livy 6.20.13, Suda *s.v.* 'Moneta' (μ1220); Coarelli 1996a. Measures: Hyginus Gromaticus on the *pes monetalis*, Campbell 2000.90.2–9. Moneta as Mnemosyne: Livius Andronicus *Odusia* fr. 23M (Priscian in *Grammatici Latini* 2.198K), cf. Homer *Odyssey* 8.480–1; Hyginus *Fabulae* pref. 27.

[42] Meadows and Williams 2001, quotation from p. 37.

[43] Sallust *Jugurthine War* 5.1, 31.2, 31.12, 64.1, 85.1, etc. See above, pp. 35–8.

[44] Meadows and Williams 2001.48. Cf. 37: 'Just as Moneta guaranteed the surveyor's *pes* and the moneyer's silver, so she kept indisputable records of Rome's past, and cast-iron evidence for the pedigrees of Rome's oldest families.'

[45] Meadows and Williams 2001.43–4.

and cultivate from generation to generation. There was no inherent tension or conflict between a proper sense of Roman civic patriotism and public proclamation of the family's outstanding record of achievement in the service of the Roman state.

That may have been how the *nobiles* saw it, but in the late second century BC those who spoke for the Roman People had a quite different view of the *nobilitas*. Sallust makes that abundantly clear, both in his own analysis and in the speeches he gives to C. Memmius in 111 BC and to C. Marius in 108.[46] As an ex-*popularis* tribune himself,[47] the historian knew what he was talking about.

Sallust perceived a direct continuity between the arrogant aristocracy of the late second century BC and the civil wars of his own time.[48] There is no reason to doubt his judgement: the best possible contemporary evidence proves that in 80 BC it was taken for granted that Sulla's victory was the victory of the *nobilitas*.[49] Not surprisingly, therefore, Sallust's Licinius Macer begins his speech to the People on the restoration of the tribunes' powers with a reference to the power of the *nobiles*:[50]

neque me praeterit quantas opes nobilitatis solus, inpotens, inani specie magistratus pellere dominatione incipiam.

I'm well aware how great are the resources of the *nobilitas* which I am setting out to dislodge from domination, single-handed, powerless, in the empty shadow of a magistracy.

And he makes exactly the same point as Sallust's Memmius and Sallust's Marius about the way the aristocrats have taken over the republic.[51]

Both sides in the conflict appealed to the distant past. Sulla's constitutional reforms were a conscious reversal of the concessions won by

---

[46] Sallust *Jugurthine War* 31.9–10 (Memmius), 41.7 (author's analysis), 85.19–22 (Marius), etc.

[47] Asconius 37, 49C—in 52 BC, the year the Roman People burned down the Senate-house.

[48] Sallust *Jugurthine War* 5.1–2; cf. *Catiline* 12.2, 20.9 on post-Sullan *superbia*.

[49] Cicero *Pro Roscio Amerino* 16, 135, 138, 142.

[50] Sallust *Histories* 3.48.3M; *dominatio* also at sections 6, 10, 11, 23, 28.

[51] Sallust *Histories* 3.48.5–6, 18M; cf. n. 46 above.

the plebeians in the 'struggle of the orders';[52] Sallust's Macer, on the
other hand, calls on the People to recover the *libertas* their ancestors
had won by armed secession.[53] So it seems unlikely that when Macer
the historian cited documents found in the temple of Moneta he was
somehow endorsing the Roman aristocracy's claim to power.[54]

IV

A whole new chapter has now been added to the history of the
Juno Moneta temple by Pier Luigi Tucci's investigations on the
arx of the Capitol (see Fig. 1).[55] The original fourth-century temple
is now firmly sited in the 'Aracoeli Garden' north-east of the Palazzo
Senatorio. It faced south-east, looking over the Forum, and was
evidently constructed on the site of an earlier building, from which
the remains of *cappellaccio* walls survive; the literary sources say it was
the house either of Titus Tatius or of M. Manlius Capitolinus.[56]

   However, the existence of two huge concrete foundations on the
site indicate that by the imperial period the temple had been
destroyed or demolished and replaced by something quite different.[57]
There is no reason in principle why a historic temple could not have
been replaced on a different site; that must have happened, for
instance, with the temple of Jupiter Stator after the fire of AD 64.[58]
But when did it happen with Moneta? And where was she moved to?

   [52] Appian *Civil Wars* 1.59.266, the reimposition of *patrum auctoritas*.
   [53] Sallust *Histories* 3.48.1, 12, 15M; cf. 1.11M for Sallust's own comment on the
secessions.
   [54] See above, n. 25. Meadows and Williams 2001.48: 'Macer's recovery of the Linen
Rolls in her temple is the literary equivalent of a moneyer's imposition of a scene
from his family's traditions onto a coin: both imply a strong and persuasive claim to
reliability and genuineness.'
   [55] Tucci 2005.
   [56] Tucci 2005.11–21. House of T. Tatius: Solinus 1.21, Plutarch *Romulus* 20.4.
House of Manlius Capitolinus: Livy 6.20.13, 7.28.4–6, Ovid *Fasti* 6.183–5; cf. Cicero
De domo 101 (at the *duo luci*).
   [57] Tucci 2005.20–1.
   [58] Tacitus *Annals* 15.41.1 for its destruction; it was close to the Forum (Appian
Civil Wars 2.11.40), at the foot of the Palatine (ps.Cicero *Pridie quam in exilium iret*
24), on or near the Nova Via (Livy 1.41.4), by the Porta Mugonia (Dionysius of

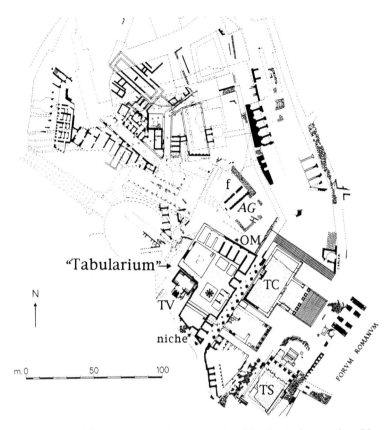

Fig. 1. Plan of the *arx*, the northern summit of the Capitol; reproduced by permission of Pier Luigi Tucci. 'Tabularium' refers to the Roman complex below the Palazzo Senatorio, evidently constructed by Q. Catulus *cos.* 78 BC; the asterisk marks Tucci's proposed site for the rebuilt temple of Juno Moneta. *AG*: Aracoeli garden (concrete foundations marked 'f'). OM: suggested site of the republican mint (*officina monetae*). TV: temple of Veiovis. TC: temple of Concordia. TS: temple of Saturn.

Tucci's brilliant solution is based on the lost inscription which identified the so-called 'Tabularium':[59]

Halicarnassus 2.50.3). The post-Neronian temple was in *Regio IV*, near the temple of Venus and Rome and the Basilica of Maxentius (*Notitia urbis Romae*).

[59] *CIL* 6.1314 = *ILS* 35 = *ILLRP* 367.

Q. LVTATIVS Q.F. Q.[n.] CATVLVS COS.
SVBSTRVCTIONEM ET TABVLARIVM
DE S.S. FACIVNDVM COERAVIT [ei]DEMQVE
PRO[bauit]

Q. Lutatius Q.f. Catulus, consul, saw to the building of the substruction and archive on the instruction of the Senate, and he also approved (the work).

What Catulus built in 78 BC was the great arcaded facade that gave the Roman Forum a unified monumental backdrop at its north-east end, masking the dip between the two summits of the Capitol, and extending the area of the northern summit (the *arx*) with an artificial platform 70 metres wide and 50 metres deep.[60] The nearest parallels, in both form and date, are the platforms that supported the temples of Hercules Victor at Tibur and Jupiter Anxur at Tarracina.[61]

The inscription identifies it as a 'substruction'—but a substruction for what? Something was to be built on the platform, and it was probably a temple, for what else would deserve so grandiose a support? Whatever it was, it had an archive (*tabularium*), like the Hercules temple at Tibur.[62] Tucci's answer to the question is compelling: Catulus' substruction was designed to carry the new temple of Juno Moneta, 80 metres or so south of the old site and looking out over the Forum even more dramatically.[63] The new suite of seven rooms behind the *uia tecta* of the arcade is convincingly identified as the late-republican offices of the mint (*moneta*).[64]

No doubt the plan had the approval of Sulla, before his sudden death that same year;[65] the temple vowed by the patrician dictator (Camillus) was now warning the citizens more visibly than ever.

As soon as Sulla was dead, the tribunes demanded the restoration of their powers, but without success.[66] Then came news of a rebellion in Etruria against the Sullan colonists there, and the consuls M. Lepidus and Q. Catulus were sent to put it down. The two men were bitter

---

[60] Tucci 2005.7–9; Delbrueck 1907.23–46.
[61] Coarelli 1987.85–112 with figs. 26–7 (Tibur), 113–40 with figs. 33–6 (Tarracina).
[62] Aulus Gellius 19.5.4 (*bibliotheca*).
[63] Tucci 2005.21–31.
[64] Tucci 2005.10; Coarelli 1996a.
[65] Tucci 2005.24: 'the rebuilding of both mint and Temple of Juno Moneta may well have been ordered by Sulla himself.' However, Sulla was a private citizen in 79–78 BC.
[66] Granius Licinianus 33–4 Flemisch.

enemies, and the Senate required them to take an oath that they would not resort to war on each other.[67] As soon as his year of office expired, considering himself now free of his oath, Lepidus put himself at the head of the rebel forces and marched on Rome, promising to restore the powers of the tribunes and rescind Sulla's acts.[68]

Of all the civil wars of the late republic, that of 77 BC is the least well documented. Our sources tell us nothing of the political arguments in Rome, though Lepidus evidently had enough support for the Senate to have granted him proconsular *imperium*.[69] Early in the year, before new consuls could be elected, the Senate did what it had done against C. Gracchus in 121 BC and Saturninus in 100 BC: it gave the magistrates and those with *imperium*—in this case Catulus as proconsul—the authority to act as they saw fit to protect the republic.[70] The proposal was made by a senior ex-consul, who observed that all the *nobilitas* were behind it.[71]

Armed with such powers, defending the city at the Milvian Bridge and the Janiculum, how did the 'leaders and standard-bearers of the Sullan domination' deal with those who disagreed with them?[72] Our sources are silent, except for a brief phrase in Licinius Macer's speech to the Roman People in Sallust:[73]

Sulla mortuo, qui scelestum imposuerat seruitium, finem mali credebatis: ortus est longe saeuior Catulus.

With the death of Sulla, who had imposed on you a wicked slavery, you thought your troubles were over; but then came Catulus, far more savage.

That probably refers to summary executions, as had happened on the two previous occasions.[74]

---

[67] Appian *Civil Wars* 1.107.502 (cf. 1.105.491 for their enmity), Granius Licinianus 34 Flemisch.

[68] Sallust. *Histories* 1.77.14M (Philippus' speech) on *tribunicia potestas*. Sulla's *acta* in general: Livy *Epitome* 90, Granius Licinianus 33 Flemisch, Florus 2.11.2, *De uiris illustribus* 77.3.

[69] Sallust *Histories* 1.77.5–7M.

[70] Sallust *Histories* 1.77.22M; cf. Cicero *In Catilinam* 1.4, *Philippics* 8.14 (121 BC), *Pro Rabirio perduellionis reo* 20 (100 BC).

[71] Sallust *Histories* 1.77.21 (Philippus' speech): *adest . . . nobilitas omnis*.

[72] Florus 2.11.6 (*Sullanae dominationis duces atque signiferi*), cf. Orosius 5.22.6 (Catulus as *Sullanus dux*). Lepidus was defeated in a battle 'not far beyond the Campus Martius' (Appian *Civil Wars* 1.107.504).

[73] Sallust *Histories* 3.48.9M.

[74] Sallust *Jugurthine War* 31.7 (121 BC), Appian *Civil Wars* 1.33.146 (100 BC).

While these grim events were taking place, Catulus' 'substruction and archive' were being completed on the Capitol slope, and the new temple of Juno Moneta (if Tucci is right) was being constructed on the platform above. It is hard to imagine the historian Licinius Macer consulting the linen books in Catulus' new *tabularium*.[75]

V

Fortunately, there is no need to imagine it. Macer may well have done his research in the old Juno Moneta temple, which he must have known well as a moneyer in 84 BC. As it happens, the new archaeological evidence may help us with an old problem about his coin-types.

The obverse of Macer's *denarius* issue shows the head and shoulders of a young god, seen from behind with a thunderbolt in his right hand (see Fig. 2). He is confidently identified in all the standard catalogues, by Grueber and Sydenham as Veiovis, by Crawford as Apollo.[76]

At first sight, the latter seems the better choice: the design had been used once before, by L. Caesius in 112 or 111 BC, accompanied by the

Fig. 2. *Denarius* of C. Licinius L.f. Macer. Obverse: young god holding thunderbolt.

[75] See above, p. 70.
[76] Grueber 1910.320, no. 2467; Sydenham 1952.116, no. 732; Crawford 1974.370, no. 354.1. For Apollo, and a speculative political interpretation, see Luce 1968.

legend *AP* in monogram, and the same monogram was used by one of Macer's immediate predecessors, M'. Fonteius C.f. in 85 BC, next to the laureate head of a young god with thunderbolt below.[77] It ought to mean *AP*(*ollo*), the identification made necessary by the unfamiliar attribute. Not only that, but Ovid states explicitly that Veiovis did *not* carry thunderbolts.[78]

However, it is more complicated than that. *Vediouis pater* is first attested on the altar set up to him in the second century BC at Bovillae by the members of the Julian *gens* (*genteiles Iuliei*).[79] A temple had been built for him on the Tiber island in 194 BC,[80] and another on the Capitol in 192 BC.[81] But there is a strange phenomenon here. Only the calendars attribute to Veiovis the Tiber island cult on 1 January; the literary sources all say it was Jupiter's. Even the Capitol cult on 7 March, for which Vitruvius, Ovid, and Aulus Gellius name Veiovis, is attributed by Livy to Jupiter. Aulus Gellius believed that while *Iouis* and *Diouis* were derived from *iuuare* 'to help', *Vediouis* was the harmful equivalent, with the prefix *ue-* used in a negative sense; that theory appears also in the 'Vatican Mythographer', who makes Veiovis 'the bad Jupiter'.[82]

It is also possible, though the evidence is very uncertain, that Veiovis could be thought of as a wielder of thunderbolts. Describing Julian's campaign against the Alamanni in AD 358, Ammianus Marcellinus narrates a sudden failure of nerve on the part of the cavalry commander Severus. In the Fulda manuscript (*V*), the text runs as follows:[83]

mortem fortasse metuens aduentantem ut in tagetinicis libris legitur uegonicis fulmine mox tangendos adeo heuetari ut nectores nitruum nec maiores possint audire fragores

---

[77] Crawford 1974.312, no. 298.1; 369–70, no. 353.1.

[78] Ovid *Fasti* 3.438: *fulmina nulla tenet*.

[79] *CIL* 1².1439 = *ILS* 2988 = *ILLRP* 270. See Weinstock 1971, plate 2.1–2.

[80] Livy 34.53.7, Vitruvius 3.2.3 (shared with Faunus), Ovid *Fasti* 1.291–3 (shared with Aesculapius); *Fasti Antiates maiores* and *Fasti Praenestini* for 1 January, Degrassi 1963.2, 110–11 (shared with Aesculapius).

[81] Livy 35.41.8; Vitruvius 4.8.4, Ovid *Fasti* 3.430, Aulus Gellius 5.12.2; *Fasti Antiates maiores* and *Fasti Praenestini* for 7 Mar., Degrassi 1963.6, 120–1.

[82] Aulus Gellius 5.12.8–10; *Mythographus Vaticanus* 3.6.1 (*Veiovis id est malus Iouis*).

[83] Ammianus Marcellinus 17.10.2. I omit a phrase accidentally repeated from the previous line and deleted by the scribe.

That is, correcting all the corruptions but one:

mortem fortasse metuens aduentantem, ut in Tagetis libris legitur †uegonicis† fulmine mox tangendos adeo hebetari ut nec tonitrum nec maiores possint audire fragores.

perhaps fearing his approaching death, as we read in the books of Tages that those about to be struck by a thunderbolt are so dulled that they can hear neither thunder nor any louder noises.

The Fulda manuscript dates from the ninth century, but it was evidently copied from a manuscript at Hersfeld (*M*), which must be the archetype of all the surviving manuscripts. Although only six leaves of *M* now survive, it was complete when Sigismundus Gelenius used it for his edition of 1533. However, as L. D. Reynolds remarks, 'Gelenius... failed to distinguish in his edition between those readings which he had taken from or based on *M* and his own arbitrary and audacious conjectures'.[84] So we cannot know how authoritative his reading of our sentence is:

...ut in Tagetis Tusci libris legitur, Veiouis fulmine mox tangendos...

...as we read in the books of Etruscan Tages, that those about to be struck by the thunderbolt of Veiovis...

Modern editions emend *uegonicis* to *et Vegoicis*, and make Ammianus say 'as we read in the books of Tages and Vegoia', which certainly makes good sense.[85] But Gelenius' reading also deserves respect, since we know that Etruscan lore was interested in the nine different gods who send thunderbolts;[86] and it may even come from the archetype.

So far, then, we have a Veiovis who was interchangeable with Jupiter, could be thought of as a harmful Jupiter, and may even have wielded thunderbolts like Jupiter. But there is also good evidence that he was thought of as a god of the underworld, invoked in the *deuotio*.[87] And yet another area of conjecture is revealed by Aulus Gellius, who adds this comment on the god's harmful nature:[88]

---

[84] Reynolds 1983.6–8, quotation from p. 8.
[85] For Vegoia, see Campbell 2000.254–9, and Servius on *Aeneid* 6.72.
[86] Pliny *Nat. Hist.* 2.138: *Tuscorum litterae nouem deos emittere fulmina existimant...*
[87] Macrobius *Saturnalia* 3.9.10 (*deuotio* of Carthage, 146 BC): *Dis pater Veiouis Manes, siue uos quo alio nomine fas est nominare...*
[88] Aulus Gellius 5.12.11–12, referring back to 5.12.2.

simulacrum igitur dei Vediouis, quod est in aede de qua dixi, sagittas tenet,
quae sunt uidelicet partae ad nocendum. quapropter eum deum plerumque
Apollinem esse dixerunt; immolaturque ritu humano capra eiusque animalis
figmentum iuxta simulacrum stat.

Therefore the statue of the god Vediovis which is in the temple I referred to
[between the *arx* and the *Capitolium*] holds arrows, which are obviously
intended to cause harm. For that reason they have often said that the god is
Apollo; and a she-goat is sacrificed by the *ritus humanus*, and an image of
that animal stands next to the statue.

The *ritus humanus* was evidently appropriate to the cult of the
dead;[89] the significance of the she-goat itself is quite obscure. But
Gellius' main point is clear: Veiovis was regularly identified as Apollo
precisely because he carried dangerous weapons.

It is an obvious possibility that a thunderbolt in the god's hand
was interpreted as three arrows, and therefore appropriate to the
archer god.[90] What is certain is that the cult statue, discovered in
1939, represented a god with Apollo's youthful physique.[91]

The prefix *ue-*, taken as a negative by Aulus Gellius, was given a
different meaning by other interpreters. They said it meant 'small',
and so the youthful god was 'young Jupiter'.[92] Ovid used that interpretation, but he knew it was only a guess:[93]

> *uis ea si uerbi est, cur non ego Veiouis aedem*
> *aedem non magni suspicer esse Iouis?*

If that is the force of the word, why should I not suspect that the temple of
Veiovis is the temple of not-big Jupiter?

In a classic dialogue fifty years before, Cicero had questioned the
whole technique of inferring the nature of the gods from the etymology of their names, and Veiovis had been one of his examples of its
inadequacy.[94]

---

[89] Festus (Paulus) 91L: *humanum sacrificium dicebant, quod mortui causa fiebat.*
[90] See e.g. Cook 1914.711–12, Latte 1960.82.
[91] Weinstock 1971, plate 2.3. Unfortunately the head and arms are missing.
[92] Festus (Paulus) 519L: *ue enim syllabam rei paruae praeponebant, unde Veiouem*
paruum Iouem.
[93] Ovid *Fasti* 3.447–8.
[94] Cicero *De natura deorum* 3.62 (Cotta on *enodatio nominum*).

Ovid explains the she-goat as the one that suckled the infant Jupiter,[95] and he insists that the god holds no thunderbolts because the young Jupiter was unarmed until the rebellion of the Giants.[96] That is clearly inconsistent with Aulus Gellius' report of a god holding arrows; but in any case, amid all these conflicting interpretations of the god it would be quite arbitrary to pick out Ovid's 'no thunderbolts' as being somehow uniquely authentic.[97]

The most economical explanation of the coin-types of L. Caesius and C. Licinius Macer is that those moneyers accepted the identification of Veiovis as Apollo, and of his weapon as a thunderbolt. Moreover, the related type of the head of a young god with thunderbolt below, also with the monogram *AP(ollo)*, must refer to the same deity.[98] That type was used in 86 BC by the moneyers whose names are abbreviated as GAR. OGVL. VER, and in 85 BC by M'. Fonteius C.f.,[99] whose reverse design shows a winged child on a goat, two *pilei* (symbols of *libertas*), and a *thyrsus* (symbol of Liber Pater). The inference must be that Veiovis-Apollo had a particular significance during the brief ascendancy of Sulla's opponents, and therefore that Licinius Macer's choice of type was consistent with his political attitude a decade later.

Veiovis' Capitoline temple was 'between the two groves' (*inter duos lucos*), or 'between the *Capitolium* and the *arx*',[100] exactly the same two descriptions as are offered by our sources for the site of Romulus' asylum.[101] According to Dionysius, who gives both descriptions, Romulus built a temple there, 'but to which of the gods or *daimones* I cannot say for certain'.[102] Ovid is much more confident:[103]

> *una nota est Marti Nonis, sacrata quod illis*
> *templa putant lucos Veiovis ante duos.*

[95] Ovid *Fasti* 3.443–4, cf. 5.111–28.
[96] Ovid *Fasti* 3.438–42, cf. 5.35–46.
[97] *Pace* Luce 1968.26: 'whoever the young god with the thunderbolt is, he is not Veiovis'.
[98] See n. 77 above.
[99] Crawford 1974.364–6 and 369–70, nos. 350A and 353.
[100] Vitruvius 4.8.4, Ovid *Fasti* 3.430, *Fasti Praenestini* for 7 Mar. (Degrassi 1963.120–1); Aulus Gellius 5.12.2.
[101] Livy 1.8.5, Dionysius of Halicarnassus 2.15.4, Velleius Paterculus 1.8.5; Strabo 5.3.2 (230).
[102] Dionysius of Halicarnassus 2.15.4.
[103] Ovid *Fasti* 3.429–34.

> *Romulus ut saxo lucum circumdedit alto,*
> *'quilibet huc' dixit 'confuge: tutus eris.'*
> *o quam de tenui Romanus origine creuit,*
> *turba uetus quam non inuidiosa fuit!*

There is one mark [in the calendar] for the Nones of March, because they think that on the Nones the temple of Veiovis was consecrated before the two groves. When Romulus surrounded the grove with a high stone wall, he said 'Whoever you are, take refuge here: you'll be safe.' Oh, from how poor an origin have the Romans risen, how unenviable the ancient populace was!

The god of the asylum was Veiovis, and the rival interpretations of the god make Dionysius' uncertainty very understandable.

Romulus' refuge was a symbol of equality: all comers were welcome, whatever their background.[104] Of course that idea was ideologically contentious, and pejorative descriptions of the 'infamous asylum' and the rabble it attracted are not hard to find.[105] They correspond to the late-republican *optimates'* view of the Roman People. Sulla was no doubt unusual in telling the citizens openly that they were like lice in a tunic, but if Cicero the *nouus homo* could refer to them in private letters as 'dregs' (*faex*), we may be sure that Catulus and his fellow-*nobiles* were no less contemptuous.[106]

So it is not likely to be accidental that Catulus' 'substruction' monopolized practically the whole area 'between the two groves', leaving only the barest room for the temple of Veiovis itself, which was dwarfed beneath the great walls of the platform. The only space left for the 'grove of the asylum' was in the niche opening on to the street just south of the temple, 3 to 4 metres deep and less than 5 metres wide.[107] Catulus' building dominated what had once been the Romulean topography, and if Tucci's hypothesis is right, it left

---

[104] Livy 1.8.5–6, Dionysius of Halicarnassus 2.15.4, Florus 1.1.9, Plutarch *Romulus* 9.3. In one tradition this was the origin of the *plebs*: the newcomers were contrasted with 'those who know their fathers', the original patricians (Dionysius of Halicarnassus 2.8.3–4, Plutarch *Romulus* 13.2, cf. Livy 10.8.10).

[105] Strabo 5.3.2, 230 (σύγκλυδας), Juvenal 8.273–5 (*infame*), Justin 38.7.1 (*conluuies conuenarum*), Minucius Felix *Octauius* 25.2, etc; cf. Dionysius of Halicarnassus 1.4.2, 1.89.1, 2.8.3, 7.70.1.

[106] Appian *Civil Wars* 1.101.472 (Sulla); Cicero *Ad Atticum* 1.16.11, 2.1.8, *Ad Quintum fratrem* 2.5.3. Good collection of material in Hellegouarc'h 1963.532–4.

[107] Delbrueck 1907.37–40 and Tafel III; Tacitus *Histories* 3.71.3 for the *lucus asyli*.

Veiovis cowering behind and far below the new temple of Juno
Moneta, the goddess whose function it was to warn the citizens.

Did Veiovis lose his thunderbolt in this aristocratic reconstruction? That can only be a guess, but it would at least explain Ovid's
comment about the statue. Young Jupiter, unarmed, was ideologically harmless in an age when the *pater patriae* had put an end to all
the strife and violence.[108] It had been very different eighty years
earlier for C. Licinius Macer, historian and activist—about whom
we do know something after all, and can infer a good deal more.

VI

The political events of 78–73 BC are extremely ill-attested, but a story
can be pieced together from the few bits of information that survive.
Archaeological evidence usually provides only a relative chronology,
but in the case of Tucci's investigations on the Capitoline *arx* the
record of Catulus' inscription allows a reading of the data in historical time. The iconography of coin-types is often a puzzle to which
the key is lost, but the literary evidence on Veiovis, contradictory
though it is, does offer a plausible explanation of Licinius Macer's
denarius issue. Putting all these inferences together, I think we are
entitled to draw two tentative conclusions about Macer's lost history.

The first is a general point: given the continuing relevance in
contemporary politics of the issues of the early republic, particularly
the rights and powers of the plebeian tribunes, it is more likely than
not that Macer's history was politically contentious.[109] The second is
more specific: given the ferocity of the political conflict, the balance
of probability is against Macer having used the archive in the new
building constructed by his enemy Catulus. Since he drew attention
to his use of documents from the temple of Juno Moneta,[110] we may

---

[108] Suetonius *Diuus Augustus* 58.2 on the achievement of consensus; cf. *SC de Cn.
Pisone patre* 46–7 ('all the evils of civil war having long been buried by the *numen* of
diuus Augustus').

[109] For a brief sketch on those lines see Wiseman 2004.199–200.

[110] See n. 25 above; frr. 16–19 Walt = 13–15 and 27P.

infer that he did so before the temple was rebuilt on a new site as a symbol of aristocratic dominance. That in turn would imply that he was writing his history in the eighties BC.

However, that date is impossible if Siri Walt is right about Macer's account of the first *ouatio* (P. Postumius in 503 BC).[111] Against all the other sources, who say that the *ouans* wore a crown of myrtle, Dionysius, citing Macer, says he wore laurel.[112] In 71 BC M. Crassus insisted on wearing a laurel wreath for his *ouatio* after the war against Spartacus, and Walt suggests that his friend Macer provided him with a supposedly historical precedent.[113]

It is an attractive idea, but there is a strong argument against the implied date of composition. Macer died suddenly in 65 BC, having just been found guilty of extortion;[114] his provincial command must have followed a praetorship in 69 or 68 BC. He was also a hard-working orator in the courts.[115] It is very hard to suppose that so substantial a history was written in the mere interstices of a busy political career.[116] Senators who wrote history normally did so after their political ambitions were realised, or abandoned,[117] but untimely death left Macer no chance of that.

Untypically, therefore, he may have written his history earlier in life; the *impudentia* which Cicero attributes to it might be thought of as a young man's characteristic.[118] As for Crassus' *ouatio*, we might suppose that Macer had already attributed a laurel wreath to the first *ouans* for reasons of his own—he evidently liked being in a minority of one[119]—and Crassus was able to appeal to an existing historical precedent. Similarly, we might suppose that Sicinius the tribune of 76

---

[111] Walt 1997.237.

[112] Dionysius of Halicarnassus 5.47.2–3 (Macer fr. 9P = 13W).

[113] Cicero *In Pisonem* 58, Pliny *Nat. Hist.* 15.125, Aulus Gellius 5.6.23. Crassus defended Macer at his trial (Plutarch *Cicero* 9.1–2).

[114] Valerius Maximus 9.12.7 (*uir praetorius*), Plutarch *Cicero* 9.1–2; cf. Cicero *Ad Atticum* 1.4.2.

[115] Cicero *Brutus* 238 ('the most diligent of *patroni*').

[116] Cf. Cicero *De legibus* 1.8–9 and Pliny *Letters* 5.8.7–8 on the time and effort needed for writing history; Macer's was at least 16 books long (fr. 22P = 11W).

[117] See e.g. Piso (who wrote as *censorius*), Sallust, Pollio, Tacitus.

[118] Cicero *De legibus* 1.7, where the *orationes* are evidently speeches in the history.

[119] See e.g. frr. 2–5, 8, 10, 13, 16–18P = frr. 4–7, 16, 20–2, 28W; also fr. 3W (not in Peter), on the death of Remus.

BC saw himself as repeating the exploit of his ancestor, who instigated the first secession in the version we have identified as Macer's.[120]

If that reasoning is sound, we need to ask how the younger Macer found time to write his history, and why he was motivated to do so. Perhaps we should put the question differently: what did Macer do during Sulla's dictatorship? My guess is that he kept out of sight and devoted himself to creating the narrative that would prove Sulla wrong.

---

[120] See above, nn. 10 and 16. Sallust's Macer says that no one had dared raise the subject of the restoration of the tribunes' powers before Sicinius (Sallust *Histories* 3.48.8M); untrue in fact (cf. Granius Licinianus 34 Flemisch and Sallust *Histories* 1.77.14M on 78–77 BC), that flourish may betray the influence of Macer's history of the first secession (cf. Livy 2.33.2 on Sicinius the *seditionis auctor*).

4

Romulus' Rome of Equals

The story of Romulus' asylum, whenever it was first created, implies a community where equality was valued more than hierarchy. So too does the belief that Romulus distributed the territory of his new city in equal lots, and did the same with new land acquired by conquest.[1] However, that part of the foundation legend appears only in Dionysius of Halicarnassus, and not in the narrative proper but in a long descriptive section on the institutions of Romulus' city. Where did Dionysius get it from?

I

The second book of the *Roman Antiquities* begins with the creation of Romulus' city. Once the walls and buildings were constructed, it was time to decide about a constitutional system, κόσμος πολιτείας.[2] On the advice of his grandfather Numitor, Romulus called an assembly of the Albans and local Latins who made up his people; there were a little over three thousand of them left after the murderous battle in which Remus and Faustulus had been killed.[3] He urged them to think

---

[1] Asylum: above, p. 77 n. 104. Equal lands: Dionysius of Halicarnassus 2.7.4, 2.28.3. All otherwise unspecified references below are to Dionysius' *Roman Antiquities*.

[2] 2.3.1 (2.1–2 are a recapitulation of the story so far): ἀπῄτει δ' ὁ καιρὸς καὶ περὶ κόσμου πολιτείας ᾧ χρήσονται σκοπεῖν.

[3] 2.3.1; cf. 1.85.1–2, 1.86.1, 1.87.1, 2.4.1, 2.30.2 for the authority of Numitor; 1.85.4, 1.87.3 for the mixture of Albans and Latins; 1.87.3 (ὀλίγῳ πλείους ὄντας τρισχιλίων), 2.2.4 (3,000 foot, 300 horse), 2.16.2 (3,000 foot, less than 300 horse) for the surviving numbers.

about the form of their constitution, τὸ τῆς πολιτείας σχῆμα, and offered them a choice of the three standard models, monarchy, oligarchy, and democracy. They conferred among themselves, decided in favour of monarchy, their own ancestral constitution, and offered Romulus the kingship.[4] Romulus accepted, secured confirmation of the gods' will by augury (lightning from the left), and called another assembly to establish the custom of augury as a condition of election, a rule observed by the Romans ever after.[5] Dionysius adds a disapproving comment about the contempt for divine authority in his own day, the first of several such observations distributed unobtrusively throughout his work.[6]

Now that his readers are prepared for it, Dionysius introduces his narrative of the reign of the first king:[7]

ὁ δὲ Ῥωμύλος ἀποδειχθεὶς τοῦτον τὸν τρόπον ὑπό τε ἀνθρώπων καὶ θεῶν βασιλεὺς τά τε πολέμια δεινὸς καὶ φιλοκίνδυνος ὁμολογεῖται γενέσθαι καὶ πολιτέαν ἐξηγήσασθαι τὴν κρατίστην φρονιμώτατος. διέξειμι δ' αὐτοῦ τὰς πράξεις τάς τε πολιτικὰς καὶ τὰς κατὰ πολέμους, ὧν καὶ λόγον ἄν τις ἐν ἱστορίας ἀφηγήσει ποιήσαιτο.

It is agreed that Romulus—who in this manner was proclaimed king by both men and gods—was both skilled and daring in war and very wise in setting forth the most excellent constitution. I shall relate such of his deeds, both political and in warfare, as may be appropriate for narration in a history.

The *diuisio* thus announced between political and military achievements is clearly reflected in the narrative: sections 7–29 are marked out explicitly as Romulus' constitutional system,[8] while 30–55 deal with his wars.[9]

---

[4] 2.3–4, esp. 3.5–6 on τὸ τῆς πολιτείας σχῆμα, 4.1 on τὴν ὑπὸ τῶν πατέρων δοκιμασθεῖσαν (sc. πολιτείαν).

[5] 2.5–6.1 (digression on the origin of augury at 5.2–5).

[6] 2.6.2–4 (e.g. the defeat of Crassus at Carrhae). Cf. 2.11.3 (destruction of ἁρμονία), 2.14.3 (loss of the Senate's authority), 2.19.2 (corrupted morals), 2.74.5 (greed for others' property), 4.24.4–8 (abuse of manumissions), 5.60.2 (tyrannical arrogance of leaders), 10.17.6 (frugality abandoned). Dionysius is consistently respectful of τὸ δαιμόνιον: 1.77.3, 2.56.6, 2.68.1–2, 8.56.1 (hostility towards sceptics).

[7] 2.7.1.

[8] 2.7.2 (ἐρῶ δὲ πρῶτον ὑπὲρ τοῦ κόσμου τῆς πολιτείας)—2.29.2 (τοιοῦτος μὲν δή τις ὁ κόσμος ἦν τῆς κατασκευασθείσης ὑπὸ Ῥωμύλου πολιτείας); cf. n. 2 above.

[9] 2.30.1 (αἱ δὲ ἄλλαι πράξεις αἵ τε κατὰ τοὺς πολέμους ὑπὸ τοῦ ἀνδρὸς γενόμεναι καὶ αἱ κατὰ πόλιν, ὧν ἄν τις καὶ λόγον ποιήσαιτο ἐν ἱστορίας γραφῇ τοιαυταί τινες παραδίδονται)—2.56.1 (οὗτοι συνέστησαν οἱ πόλεμοι Ῥωμύλῳ λόγου καὶ μνήμης ἄξιοι).

By separating the categories in this artificial way, Dionysius invites his readers to suppose that Romulus created all the institutions of his city, in a single legislative programme, before planning the *casus belli* of the first and greatest of his wars, the abduction of the Sabine women. That assumption seems to be confirmed by Dionysius' choice between rival traditions on two separate points. First, the date of the abduction:[10]

ταῦτα δὲ γενέσθαι τινὲς μὲν γράφουσι κατὰ τὸν πρῶτον ἐνιαυτὸν τῆς Ῥωμύλου ἀρχῆς, Γναῖος δὲ Γέλλιος κατὰ τὸν τέταρτον· ὃ καὶ μᾶλλον εἰκός. νέον γὰρ οἰκιζομένης πόλεως ἡγεμόνα πρὶν ἢ καταστήσασθαι τὴν πολιτείαν ἔργῳ τηλικούτῳ ἐπιχειρεῖν οὐκ ἔχει λόγον.

Some authors write that this took place in the first year of Romulus' reign, but Cn. Gellius says it was in the fourth. That is more likely, for it makes no sense that the leader of a newly founded city should undertake an enterprise of this kind before establishing its constitution.

Second, the honours given to the women after their success in making peace between the Romans and Sabines:[11]

τινὲς μὲν γὰρ αὐτῶν γράφουσι τά τε ἄλλα πολλὰ καὶ μεγάλα δωρήσασθαι ταῖς γυναιξὶ τοὺς ἡγεμόνας καί δὴ καὶ τὰς φράτρας τριάκοντα οὔσας, ὥσπερ ἔφην, ἐπωνύμους τῶν γυναικῶν ποιῆσαι· τοσαύτας γὰρ εἶναι γυναῖκας τὰς ἐπιπρεσβευσαμένας. Οὐάρρων δὲ Τερέντιος τοῦτ' αὐτοῖς τὸ μέρος οὐχ ὁμολογεῖ παλαίτερον ἔτι λέγων ταῖς κουρίαις τεθῆναι τὰ ὀνόματα ὑπὸ τοῦ Ῥωμύλου κατὰ τὴν πρώτην τοῦ πλήθους διαίρεσιν, τὰ μὲν ἀπ' ἀνδρῶν ληφθέντα ἡγεμόνων, τὰ δ' ἀπὸ πάγων.

Some authors write that among the many other distinctions conferred on the women, the two leaders also named the *curiae* after them (there were thirty *curiae*, as I stated earlier), since the same number of women had formed the embassy. But Terentius Varro disagrees with them on this point, saying that the names had been previously given to the *curiae* by Romulus at the time of the original division of the people, some of them taken from the leading men, others from the *pagi*.

But there was a price to pay for this arrangement of material. Inevitably, Dionysius has to put the whole (very political) story of

---

[10] 2.31.1 (Gellius fr. 11P), contra Fabius Pictor *FGrH* 809 F5 (Plutarch *Romulus* 14.1).

[11] 2.47.3–4 (Varro *Antiquitates humanae* fr. 4.6 Mirsch), contra Livy 1.13.6, Festus (Paulus) 42L; cf. Plutarch *Romulus* 14.6, 20.3. The reference back is to 2.7.2.

Titus Tatius, his joint kingship and his murder by the men of Lavinium, into the 'wars' section. He acknowledges the breakdown of his *diuisio* by slipping the extra phrase 'and in the city' into his introduction to the second section of narrative.[12] So why did he make things difficult for himself in this way?

II

The obvious answer is that he took his constitutional material from a source that was not primarily interested in chronology—a descriptive text, not a narrative one. The once-popular view that Dionysius had simply incorporated a first-century BC *Tendenzschrift*, aimed at influencing Sulla or Caesar or Octavian,[13] was decisively refuted by Balsdon long ago.[14] But Balsdon went too far in the other direction.

In his discussion of the 'capsule' (as he calls sections 7–29), Balsdon rightly emphasizes the author's own input, as Dionysius constantly draws attention to Greek parallels that support his overall thesis that the Romans were themselves of Greek descent.[15] But it does not follow that Dionysius created the whole thing from 'what he read in a number of different sources about Romulus'.[16] 'The capsule is a coherent unit. That is clear.'[17] But it is not wholly coherent with Dionysius' own narrative. In form and structure, at least, it must be someone else's work.

That form and structure may be analysed as follows:

[12] Tatius: 2.46.2, 2.47.1–2, 2.50.1–53.1. Extra phrase: 2.30.1 (n. 9 above): καὶ αἱ κατὰ πόλιν.

[13] Pohlenz 1924; von Premerstein 1937.8–12; Gabba 1960 = 2000.69–108.

[14] Balsdon 1971.

[15] See e.g. 2.7.3, 8.2–3 (ὡς ἄν τις εἰκασείε), 12.3–4, 13.4 (τοῦτό μοι δοκεῖ), 14.2, 17.1–4, 20.1–21.1, 22.1–2 (ὡς ἐγὼ πείθομαι), 23.3 (δοκεῖ μοι), 24.2–6, 26.2–3. Cf. also 2.29 and 2.23.5–6 for Dionysius' own observations of Roman customs.

[16] Balsdon 1971.27.

[17] Balsdon 1971.24. Cf. Gabba 1960.180 = 2000.73: 'che si tratti, quindi, di una serie di capitoli a sè stanti e derivanti da una fonte particolare non sembra vi possa essere dubbio.'

A. A system for peace and war (7.2–14.4).[18]

    i. Division of People and land into three *tribus* and thirty *curiae*, led respectively by *tribuni* and *curiones* (7.2–4).

    ii. Separation of *patres* and *plebeii* (8.1–4).

    iii. *Patres* to be priests, magistrates, and judges; plebeians to be farmers and wealth-creators (9.1).

    iv. Patronage: mutual responsibilities of patrons and clients (9.2–11.3).

    v. Senators: one chosen by king, three by each *tribus*, three by each *curia*, total one hundred (12.1–4).

    vi. Bodyguard of young men (*celeres*), ten chosen by each *curia*, total three hundred (13.1–4).

    vii. Honours and powers of king (14.1), Senate (14.2), and People (14.3).

    viii. Same system in war: *tribuni* command *tribus*, *centuriones* command centuries, *decuriones* command groups of ten (14.4).[19]

B. Measures to increase manpower (15–17).[20]

    i. All sons and first-born daughters to be brought up; infanticide prohibited except for monstrous births (15.1).

    ii. Immigration encouraged: *asylum* established (15.2–4).

    iii. Conquered populations to be colonized, not slaughtered or enslaved (16.1–3).

C. Measures to achieve the favour of the gods (18.2–23.6).[21]

    i. Establishment of temples, altars, cults, festivals (18.2–3).

    ii. Appointment of priests for public sacrifices, two from each *curia*, to serve for life (21.1–3).

    iii. Wives and children of priests to be involved in rites as appropriate (22.1).

    iv. One *haruspex* from each *tribus* to be present at sacrifices (22.3).

---

[18] Marked as such at 7.2 (αὐταρκέστατον ἐν εἰρήνῃ τε καὶ κατὰ πολέμους) and 15.1 (κεκοσμημένην πρὸς εἰρήνην τε ἀποχρώντως καὶ πρὸς τὰ πολέμια ἐπιτηδείως). Cf. also 14.4 (οὐ μόνον τὰ πολιτικὰ πράγματα … ἀλλὰ καὶ τὰ πολεμικὰ).

[19] With 7.3, this implies one *tribunus* from each *tribus*, in command of 1,000 men. *Centuriae* have not been mentioned before; at 7.4 *decuriae* were subdivisions of *curiae*.

[20] Marked as such by the use of πολυάνθρωπος at 15.1 and 16.3.

[21] Announced at 18.1 (τήν παρὰ τῶν θεῶν εὔνοιαν) and 18.2 (εὐσεβῆ … πόλιν).

    v. All priests to be elected by *curiae*, election confirmed by augury (22.3).[22]

    vi. Particular cults established for *curiae*; frugal sacrifices (23.1–4).

D. Measures to encourage temperance and justice (24–9).[23]

    i. Romulus' laws, both written and unwritten (24.1).

    ii. Establishment of marriage by *confarreatio*, spouses' possessions and sacred rites held in common (25.1–7).

    iii. Establishment of *patria potestas*: son in father's total control, may be sold into slavery up to three times (26.4–27.4).

    iv. Degrading activities deputed to slaves and foreigners; citizens to engage in agriculture and warfare (28.1–2).

    v. Citizens to stay on their farms except for market-days (28.3).

    vi. Booty to be divided equally among citizens (28.3).

    vii. Justice to be swift and formidable (29.1).

E. Measures to encourage bravery in war (no details given).[24]

At only two points in his exposition of this material does Dionysius name a source. The first occasion is on item A(vi), Valerius Antias' alternative explanation of the *celeres* (named not from their speed but from their leader).[25] That is no help for identifying the main source, but the second case, on item C(ii), may be more useful. Emphasizing Romulus' immediate appointment of no fewer than sixty priests, something unmatched in any other city-foundation, Dionysius names his authority: 'I am saying what Terentius Varro, the most experienced man of his time, has written in his *Antiquities*.'[26] As we noted above, it was Varro who insisted that the *curiae* had already been

---

[22] 22.3 (ὑπὸ τῶν ἐξηγουμένων τὰ θεῖα διὰ μαντικῆς), cf. 5.1 (διαμαντεύσασθαι), 5.2 (τῶν οἰωνοῖς μαντευομένων) on confirmation by augury.

[23] Announced in advance at 18.1 (τὴν σωφροσύνην τε καὶ δικαιοσύνην) and 18.2 (σώφρονα καὶ τὰ δίκαια ἀσκοῦσαν...πόλιν); cf. also 24.2 (δικαίους καὶ σώφρονας), 28.1 (τὸ σωφρόνως ζῆν...καὶ τὰ δίκαια πρὸ τῶν κερδαλέων αἱρεῖσθαι).

[24] Announced in advance at 18.1 (τὴν ἐν τοῖς πολέμοις γενναιότητα) and 18.2 (τὰ πολέμια ἀγαθὴν...πόλιν). However, Dionysius reports only a selection of Romulus' measures (24.1, 29.2).

[25] 2.13.2 (Valerius Antias fr. 2P); cf. 2.8.3 for a similar dispute (no sources named) about why the *patres* were so called.

[26] 2.21.2: λέγω δὲ ἃ Τερέντιος Οὐάρρων ἐν ἀρχαιολογίαις γέγραφεν, ἀνὴρ τῶν κατὰ τὴν αὐτὴν ἡλικίαν ἀκμασάντων πολυπειρότατος. Cf. Cardauns 1976.62, 182; from the *Antiquitates diuinae* or *humanae*? No doubt the latter (priests elected by the *curiae*), but since Mirsch did not include it among the *Ant. hum.* fragments, it would have been helpful if Cardauns had at least given it a number.

named before the abduction of the women, implying the same order of narration as in Dionysius.[27]

Friedrich Cornelius drew the obvious conclusion in a footnote in 1940: Dionysius took the whole 'capsule' from Varro's *Antiquities*.[28] Given the interest generated by Dionysius' account of the 'constitution of Romulus', it seems extraordinary that no one since then has taken Cornelius' point seriously. Chris Smith perhaps comes closest, in his important new book on the *gens*:[29]

> The question which one would so much like to be able to answer is where Dionysius' account comes from. Varro was clearly a key source.

Can we not be more definite, and assert that in *Antiquitates Romanae* 2.7–29 Dionysius was reproducing, with comments of his own, what he found in Varro's *Antiquitates rerum humanarum et diuinarum*? It would be an obvious source for him to consult,[30] and since he actually names it in his text, hesitation seems unnecessary.

Accepting the idea as a working hypothesis, let us see if the details of Dionysius' exposition cast any light on the question.

III

To begin with item A(i): Varro certainly referred to 'the original division of the people', as Dionysius himself later informs us,[31] and

---

[27] 2.47.4 (p. 83 above).

[28] Cornelius 1940.27 n. 59: 'Wie man in den Kapitel II, 7–29 eine politische Tendenzschrift aus der Zeit Caesars hat erblicken können (Pohlenz, Hermes, 59 (1924), S. 157 ff.) ist mir unbegreiflich. Dionysios sagt ausdrücklich (II 21,2), λέγω δὲ ἃ Τερέντιος Οὐάρρων ἐν ἀρχαιολογίαις γέγραφεν. (Er zitiert für eine Abweichung II 13,2 Antias). Was Hinweis auf die Zeit Caesars in diesem Abschnitt ist, z.B. der Auszug des Crassus gegen die Parther, II 6,4, paßt sehr gut in die Schrift des Varro.' Cornelius' inference is referred to without comment by Gabba 1960.199 = 2000.87 n. 67, and Balsdon 1971.27 n. 55.

[29] Smith 2006b.197; cf. 350 on 2.21–3 ('This entire passage clearly owes much to Varro').

[30] Cf. Quintilian 1.6.12: *Varro in eo libro quo initia Romanae urbis enarrat*—no doubt referring to *Antiquitates humanae* book 4, or conceivably *De uita populi Romani* book 1.

[31] Varro *Antiquitates humanae* fr. 4.6 Mirsch (n. 11 above).

at least three of the four references to it in *De lingua Latina* are immediately compatible with Dionysius' account:[32]

(a) *ager Romanus primum diuisus in partis tris, a quo tribus appellata Titiensium Ramnium Lucerum. nominatae, ut ait Ennius, Titienses ab Tatio, Ramnenses ab Romulo, Luceres, ut Iunius, ab Lucumone; sed omnia haec uocabula Tusca, ut Volnius, qui tragoedias Tuscas scripsit, dicebat.*

Roman territory was originally divided into three parts, from which (each of the) Titienses, Ramnes, and Luceres is called a *tribus*. According to Ennius, the Titienses were named after Tatius and the Ramnenses after Romulus, and according to Iunius, the Luceres were named after Lucumo; but all these words are Etruscan, as Volnius, who wrote tragedies in Etruscan, used to say.

(b) *tribuni militum, quod terni tribus tribubus Ramnium Lucerum Titium olim ad exercitum mittebantur.*

Tribuni militum (are so called) because in the past three of them were sent to the army by each of the three *tribus* Ramnes, Luceres, and Titii.

(c) *milites, quod trium milium primo legio fiebat ac singulos tribus Titiensium Ramnium Lucerum milia militum mittebant.*

Milites (are so called) because originally the legion was made up of three thousand, and each of the *tribus* Titienses, Ramnes, and Luceres sent a thousand *milites*.

Varro's reference to Volnius' opinion in the first passage may be an allusion to an argument developed at length elsewhere (most likely in the *Antiquities*) against the conventional explanation of the three names;[33] just as the original *curiae* could not have been named after the Sabine women, so an original *tribus* could hardly have been named after Tatius. It may be significant that Dionysius does not name the three *tribus* in item A(i).

The *legio* of the third passage, consisting of a thousand men from each *tribus*, is consistent with Dionysius' observation at item B(iii), and elsewhere in his narrative, that Romulus had three thousand foot soldiers at the time of the foundation.[34]

---

[32] Varro *De lingua Latina* 5.55, 5.81, 5.89.

[33] Ennius *Annales* 1.lix Sk, Cicero *De republica* 2.14, Livy 1.13.8, Plutarch *Romulus* 20.1, ps.Asconius 227St, *De uiris illustribus* 2.11, Servius on *Aeneid* 5.560.

[34] See n. 3 above; also Plutarch *Romulus* 13.1, where the derivation of *legio* translates that of Varro (*De lingua Latina* 5.87, 6.66).

How many cavalry did he have? Dionysius says three hundred (presumably the *celeres* of item A(vi)), which may or may not be consistent with the fourth passage in *De lingua Latina*:[35]

(d) *Turma terima (E in U abiit), quod ter deni equites ex tribus tribubus Titiensium Ramnium Lucerum fiebant. itaque primi singularum decuriarum decuriones dicti, qui ab eo in singulis turmis sunt etiam nunc terni.*

Turma is *terima* (the E has become a U), because three times ten cavalrymen were made up from the *tribus* Titienses, Ramnes, and Luceres. And so the leaders of each *decuria* were called *decuriones*, who as a result of that are three to each *turma* even nowadays.

It seems clear from Livy that Ramnes, Titienses, and Luceres could be thought of as equestrian *centuriae*,[36] and a *centuria* cannot be divided into three *turmae* of thirty men. If Romulus' three hundred cavalry are Varronian, as his three thousand infantry certainly are, then Varro, unlike Livy, must have structured them not as $3 \times (10 \times 10)$ but as $10 \times (3 \times 10)$, ten *turmae* each consisting of a *decuria* from each *tribus*.

When explaining, at item A(viii), that Romulus' division of the citizen body functioned equally as the structure of the army, Dionysius puts it like this:[37]

ὁπότε γὰρ αὐτῷ φανείη στρατιὰν ἐξάγειν, οὔτε χιλιάρχους τότε ἔδει ἀποδείκνυσθαι κατὰ φυλὰς οὔτε ἑκατοντάρχους κατὰ λόχους οὔτε ἱππέων ἡγεμόνας οὔτε ἐξαριθμεῖσθαί τε καὶ λοχίζεσθαι.

For whenever the king decided to lead out his army, there was no need for tribunes to be chosen at that moment tribe by tribe, or centurions century by century, or leaders of cavalry, nor for them to be numbered and put in centuries.

If he had thought that the cavalry were organized as three *centuriae*, there would have been no need for Dionysius to make separate mention of their 'leaders' (ἱππέων ἡγεμόνες). They must be the commanders of the ten *turmae*, who in the second century BC were chosen from among the three *decuriones* in each unit.[38] So it looks as if here too Dionysius reproduces the Varronian scheme.

---

[35] Varro *De lingua Latina* 5.91; the same derivation is given by Festus 484L (Curiatius fr. 3 Funaioli). Varro's definition of a *turma* as thirty-six *equites* (Servius *auctus* on *Aeneid* 11.503) may refer to a later configuration; cf. Polybius 6.25.3–11 on the development of the Roman cavalry.

[36] Livy 1.13.8, 1.36.2; also *De uiris illustribus* 2.11.

[37] 2.14.4.

[38] Polybius 6.25.1–2, calling them ἰλάρχαι, from ἴλη = *turma*; cf. Vegetius 2.14.2 for *decurio* as commander of a *turma* of 32 men in the fourth century AD.

IV

At the end of his lengthy discussion of the Roman system of *patronatus* (item A(iv)), Dionysius points to the success of the institution in securing civic concord at Rome for 630 years. So *concordia* broke down in 122/1 BC, as Dionysius goes on to explain:[39]

ἐξ οὗ δὲ Γάιος Γράκχος ἐπὶ τῆς δημαρχικῆς ἐξουσίας γενόμενος διέφθειρε τὴν τοῦ πολιτεύματος ἁρμονίαν, οὐκέτι πέπαυνται σφάττοντες ἀλλήλους καὶ φυγάδας ἐλαύνοντες ἐκ τῆς πόλεως καὶ οὐδενὸς τῶν ἀνηκέστων ἀπεχόμενοι παρὰ τὸ νικᾶν.

Ever since C. Gracchus, in the exercise of his tribunician power, destroyed the harmony of the constitution, they have never yet ceased from killing each other and driving each other out of the city, not refraining from any irreparable act in the pursuit of victory.

It is a surprising date.

In Dionysius' time, as now, the origin of civil conflict at Rome was normally defined as the murder of Tiberius Gracchus in 133 BC, that violently symbolic moment when a group of senators led by the *pontifex maximus* attacked an assembly of the Roman People and beat the presiding tribune to death. In the opinion of Cicero, Sallust, Velleius, and the well-informed but unidentified sources of Appian, Florus, and Cassius Dio, that was the turning point.[40] Why should Dionysius take a different line? It can hardly have been his own idea, and by great good fortune we happen to know who he got it from.

In Nonius Marcellinus' dictionary, the use of *biceps*, 'two-headed', applied to an abstract noun is illustrated by a quotation from the fourth book of Varro's *De uita populi Romani*:[41]

in spem adducebat non plus soluturos quam uellent; iniquus equestri ordini iudicia tradidit ac bicipitem ciuitatem fecit, discordiarum ciuilium fontem.

He encouraged them to hope that they would pay no more than they wanted; he unjustly handed over the courts to the equestrian order and made the citizen body two-headed, the origin of the civil conflicts.

---

[39] 2.11.2–3, cf. 1.75.3 for the foundation in 752/1 BC.

[40] Cicero *De republica* 1.31, Sallust *Histories* 1.17M, Velleius Paterculus 2.3.3, Appian *Civil Wars* 1.2.4–8, Florus 3.12.7–8, 3.14.1, Cassius Dio fr. 83.1.

[41] Nonius 728L (Varro *De uita p. R.* fr. 114 Riposati = 425 Salvadore).

The subject must be Gaius Gracchus; the object of the first clause must be the Roman citizens who benefited from his *lex frumentaria*, to supply grain at a subsidized price.[42] But the origin of the *discordiae ciuiles* was in Varro's view the law passed in Gracchus' second tribunate (122 BC) which required the *iudices* in the criminal courts to be not senators but *equites*.[43] That gave political power to men who had not been elected to office, whose qualification was not public responsibility but only wealth.

Varro was in his twenties when the notorious condemnation of P. Rutilius destroyed any moral authority the *Gracchani iudices* may have had.[44] That scandal led directly to the *lex iudiciaria* of Livius Drusus,[45] and it is striking that Florus, in explaining Drusus' policy, quotes Varro's comment about Gaius Gracchus:[46]

iudiciaria lege Gracchi diuiserant populum Romanum et bicipitem ex una fecerant ciuitatem.

The Gracchi had divided the Roman people by their judiciary law and made the previously unified citizen body two-headed.

Had Florus read the *De uita populi Romani*? It is possible, given his emphasis on the corrupting influence of King Attalus' legacy, which Varro certainly mentioned in that work.[47] However, we should remember Varro's habit of repetition and self-citation.[48] It is not inconceivable that the '*biceps ciuitas*' diagnosis had already featured in the *Antiquities*.

There were no rival sources of authority in Romulus' constitution. Dionysius makes it clear that the *patres* were to be judges as well as magistrates and priests; the king himself would judge the most

---

[42] See Rickman 1980.158–61.

[43] Diodorus Siculus 34/35.25.1 (τὸ χεῖρον τῆς πολιτείας τοῦ κρείττονος κύριον ἐποίησε), Pliny *Nat. Hist.* 33.34 (*discordi popularitate in contumeliam senatus*), etc. Second tribunate: Appian *Civil Wars* 1.22.91–2.

[44] Cicero *Brutus* 115 (*quo iudicio conuulsam penitus scimus esse rem publicam*), *In Pisonem* 95; Livy *Epitome* 70, Velleius Paterculus 2.13.2, Cassius Dio fr. 97.1–2.

[45] Cicero *Pro Rabirio Postumo* 16; Velleius Paterculus 2.13.2, Florus 3.17.1–4.

[46] Florus 3.17.3. The evasive plural *Gracchi*—no doubt meant to conceal the inconsistency with Florus' view of Ti. Gracchus (n. 40 above)—appears also at Pliny *Nat. Hist.* 33.34: *iudicum autem appellatione separare eum ordinem primi omnium instituere Gracchi discordi popularitate in contumeliam senatus.*

[47] Florus 3.12.7–8; Varro *De uita p. R.* fr. 112 Riposati = 415 Salvadore.

[48] See e.g. *De lingua Latina* 5.56; 6.13, 18, 52; 7.36; 9.26.

serious cases, but others were left to the Senate's responsibility, and the senators had been elected by the *tribus* and *curiae*.[49] That distribution of rights and duties secured the *concordia* which Gaius Gracchus destroyed; no doubt Dionysius' source thought that the equestrian jurors were motivated not by temperance and justice but by the pursuit of gain, which Romulus deplored.[50] It seems inevitable that the source was Varro.

V

So far we have been concerned with items in Romulus' constitution which may have come from the *Antiquitates rerum humanarum*. But since the lawgiver insisted also on piety towards the gods (item C(i)), the *Antiquitates rerum diuinarum* are relevant too.[51]

In the introduction to that work, Varro drew his famous distinction between the gods of the poets, the gods of the philosophers, and the gods of the city.[52] Of these three types of theology, the first is the *genus mythicon*, which is characterized by 'slanders against the gods' and 'unworthy stories' invented by poets and playwrights.[53] That vocabulary, faithfully transmitted by Augustine, is recognizable also in Dionysius:[54]

τοὺς δὲ παραδεδομένους περὶ αὐτῶν μύθους, ἐν οἷς βλασφημίαι τινές ἔνεισι κατ' αὐτῶν ἢ κακηγορίαι, πονηροὺς καὶ ἀνωφελεῖς καὶ ἀσχήμονας ὑπολαβὼν εἶναι καὶ οὐχ ὅτι θεῶν ἀλλ' οὐδ' ἀνθρώπων ἀγαθῶν ἀξίους, ἅπαντας ἐξέβαλε καὶ παρεσκεύασε τοὺς ἀνθρώπους τὰ κράτιστα περὶ θεῶν λέγειν τε καὶ φρονεῖν μηδὲν αὐτοῖς προσάπτοντας ἀνάξιον ἐπιτήδευμα τῆς μακαρίας φύσεως.

---

[49] 2.9.1 (judges), 12.2 (elected), 14.2 (Senate's judgement), 14.3 (people's right to ἀρχαιρεσιάζειν).

[50] 2.12.2 (ὁμόνοια), 28.1 (τὰ κερδαλέα αἱρεῖσθαι). Cf. Diodorus Siculus 37.5 and Livy *Epitome* 70, on the Asia *publicani* in the nineties BC.

[51] Compare 2.18.3 (ἱερὰ μὲν οὖν...κατεστήσατο) with Varro *Antiquitates diuinae* fr. 5 Cardauns (*quae a ciuitatibus instituta sunt*).

[52] Varro *Antiquitates diuinae* frr. 6–11 Cardauns.

[53] Fr. 7 Cardauns: *in eo sunt multa contra dignitatem et naturam immortalium ficta.* For *crimina deorum*, see Augustine *City of God* 4.26, 4.27, 6.6 (cf. 6.7 *dedecora*); for *indigna*, ibid. 6.1, 6.6, 6.7, 6.8, Tertullian *Ad nationes* 2.1.13, Arnobius *Aduersus nationes* 4.35. See Wiseman 1998a.18–20.

[54] 2.18.3, item C(i).

But he rejected all the traditional myths about the gods which contain blasphemies and slanders against them, regarding such stories as wicked, useless, and unseemly, unworthy not only of the gods but of good men as well, and he accustomed people to speak and think the best about the gods, attributing to them no conduct unworthy of their blessed nature.

Varro's examples of such stories included 'gods born from the head, from the thigh, from drops of blood, gods stealing, gods committing adultery, gods in servitude to mortals'.[55] Dionysius refers to 'wars, wounds, bindings, and servitudes of the gods among men';[56] he may well have been using Varro's list. Dionysius also specifies the castration of Caelus (Ouranos), Saturn devouring his children, and Jupiter overthrowing Saturn's rule and imprisoning him in Tartarus, all of them stories for which allegorical explanations were presented by Varro in the *Antiquities*.[57]

It is also worth noticing that Dionysius, like Varro, makes the point that the general public are prone to accept the deplorable myths, whereas only the educated few understand the theology of the philosophers.[58] And in the next paragraph, item C(ii) on the election of priests, Dionysius cites 'Terentius Varro in his *Antiquities*'.[59]

VI

In his section on temperance and justice, at item D(ii), Dionysius demonstrates the long-lasting effect of Romulus' legislation on marriage:[60]

ὁμολογεῖται γὰρ ἐντὸς ἐτῶν εἴκοσι καὶ πεντακοσίων μηδεὶς ἐν Ῥώμῃ λυθῆναι γάμος· κατὰ δὲ τὴν ἑβδόμην ἐπὶ ταῖς τριάκοντα καὶ ἑκατὸν ὀλυμπιάσιν

---

[55] Varro *Antiquitates diuinae* fr. 7 Cardauns (Augustine *City of God* 6.5)—respectively the births of Minerva, Bacchus and Pegasus, Mercury's theft of Apollo's cattle, Jupiter's many liaisons, and Apollo in servitude to Admetus.

[56] 2.19.1—respectively the gods at war in *Iliad* 21, the woundings of Aphrodite and Ares in *Iliad* 5, the binding of Zeus at *Iliad* 1.399–406, and Apollo and Admetus again.

[57] Varro *Antiquitates diuinae* frr. 241, 242, 245, 247 Cardauns.

[58] 2.20.2; Varro *Antiquitates diuinae* frr. 19, 21 Cardauns.

[59] 2.21.2, n. 26 above.

[60] 2.25.7. The *a.u.c.* date is 232/1 BC on Dionysius' reckoning (cf. n. 39 above); the Olympiad is 232–229 BC.

ὑπατευόντων Μάρκου Πομπωνίου καὶ Γαίου Παπιρίου πρῶτος ἀπολῦσαι
λέγεται τὴν ἑαυτοῦ γυναῖκα Σπόριος Καρουίλιος ἀνὴρ οὐκ ἀφανής,
ἀναγκαζόμενος ὑπὸ τῶν τιμητῶν ὀμόσαι τέκνων ἕνεκα γυναικὶ συνοικεῖν
(ἦν δ᾽ αὐτῷ στείρα ἡ γυνή).

For it is agreed that no marriage was dissolved at Rome for 520 years; but in
the 137th Olympiad, when M. Pomponius and C. Papirius were consuls,
Sp. Carvilius, a man of some distinction, is said to have been the first to divorce
his wife, since he was required by the censors to take an oath that he was living
with a wife for the sake of producing children (for his wife was barren).

M. Pomponius Matho and C. Papirius Maso were consuls in 231 BC,
a year when there were indeed censors in office.[61] The distinguished
man must be Sp. Carvilius Maximus, consul in 234 and 228 BC, who
bore the *agnomen* 'Ruga'.[62] However, other sources give other dates
for Sp. Carvilius and the first divorce at Rome.

Valerius Maximus puts the event in the 150th year *ab urbe condita*,
Plutarch in the 230th—respectively 604 and 524 BC.[63] Those dates,
obviously impossible for Sp. Carvilius,[64] have been argued away by
modern scholars, Valerius' as a textual corruption, Plutarch's as a
misunderstanding of his source.[65] Perhaps so; but since the Twelve
Tables evidently legislated for divorce, and Valerius Maximus himself
reports a divorce in 307 BC,[66] it may be that one branch of the

---

[61] *Fasti Capitolini consulares* (Degrassi 1947.44–5). However, *uit*(*io*) *facti abd-*
(*icauerunt*), and new censors were elected the following year to carry out the *lustrum*.

[62] Aulus Gellius 4.3.2 (*uir nobilis*); he was probably son of Sp. Carvilius Maximus,
consul in 293 and 272 BC. For the family, see Feig Vishnia 1996.

[63] Valerius Maximus 2.1.4; Plutarch *Theseus-Romulus comparison* 6.3, *Lycurgus-
Numa comparison* 3.7.

[64] The elder Carvilius (n. 62 above) was an exemplary *nouus homo* (Velleius Paterculus 2.128.1); see Syme 1956.262–4 = 1979.310–13. *Pace* Feig Vishnia 1996.435–6,
the quaestor Sp. Carvilius who supposedly accused Camillus in 391 BC looks like
an anachronistic invention (Pliny *Nat. Hist.* 34.13, with Ogilvie 1965.698–9 on Livy
5.32.8–9).

[65] In the Loeb text of Valerius, Shackleton Bailey prints Aldus' emendation
uicesimum et quingentesimum (making him agree with Dionysius) in place of the
MSS reading *centesimum et quinquagesimum*. For Plutarch, see Flacelière 1948.102–3,
who argues that he was confused by the date ('in the reign of Tarquin the Proud')
given for the first recorded quarrel between a wife and her mother-in-law, which is
also recorded at *Lycurgus-Numa comparison* 3.7.

[66] Crawford 1996.632–3 (Cicero *Philippics* 2.69, Gaius in *Digest* 48.5.44); Valerius
Maximus 2.9.2 on L. Annius or Antonius, ejected from the Senate by the censors of
307 BC for divorcing his wife *nullo amicorum consilio adhibito*.

tradition took the (not unreasonable) view that a date in the 230s was impossibly late for the first-ever divorce at Rome.[67]

More interesting for our purposes are two passages in Aulus Gellius. The first is taken from Ser. Sulpicius' book *On Dowries*, and it places Sp. Carvilius' divorce 'in the 523rd year after the foundation of the city, in the consulship of M. Atilius and P. Valerius'.[68] M. Atilius Regulus and P. Valerius Flaccus were consuls in 227 BC, but *ab urbe condita* 523 is 231 BC on the Varronian chronology. Servius Sulpicius evidently used a different system. The second passage is one of the items in Gellius' long list of synchronisms and dates of cultural history, put together, as he says, from various 'chronicles';[69] the sources he happens to name are Cassius Hemina, Cornelius Nepos (three times), Varro (three times), and Porcius Licinus.[70] Here Gellius offers no consular date, but puts Sp. Carvilius' divorce in *ab urbe condita* 519.[71]

These confusing data can best be understood by setting out (see Table 1) the relevant part of the consular *fasti* against the dates 'from the foundation of the city' offered (*a*) by Dionysius and (*b*) by Servius Sulpicius in Gellius' first passage (in bold). For comparison, I add (*c*) the equivalent *ab urbe condita* dates in the Varronian system. Asterisks mark years when censors were in office.

If Gellius in the second passage was using one of these systems,[72] his date of *ab urbe condita* 519 would represent (*a*) 232 BC, (*b*) 231 BC, or (*c*) 235 BC. Only the second of these was a 'censorial' year.[73]

It seems likely, therefore, that Gellius in his second passage dated the divorce to the same year as Dionysius, using the same *ab urbe*

---

[67] For the actual innovation that may have been involved, see Watson 1965.

[68] Aulus Gellius 4.3.2: *anno urbis conditae quingentesimo uicesimo tertio M. Atilio P. Valerio consulibus.* On Ser. Sulpicius, see Harries 2006.84–5.

[69] Aulus Gellius 17.21.1, *excerpebamus ex libris qui chronici appellantur… excerptiones nostras uariis diuersisque in locis factas.*

[70] Aulus Gellius 17.21.3 (Cassius Hemina fr. 8P, Nepos *Chronica* fr. 2P), 8 (Nepos *Chronica* fr. 4P), 24 (Varro *Annales* fr. 2P, Nepos *Chronica* fr. 5P), 43 (Varro *De poetis* 1), 45 (Varro *De poetis* 1, Porcius Licinus fr. 1 Courtenay).

[71] Aulus Gellius 17.21.44, *anno deinde post Romam conditam quingentesimo undeuicesimo.*

[72] I ignore the possibility that he was using the same system as the Augustan *fasti* (*a.u.c.* numbers one lower than Varro's), because that would put the divorce in Sp. Carvilius' own consulship (234 BC); it is hardly conceivable that none of our sources would have mentioned that he was consul at the time.

[73] See n. 61 above.

Table 1

BC date	consuls	ab urbe condita date		
		(a) D.	(b) S.	(c) V.
235	T. Manlius, C. Atilius II	516	515	519
*234	L. Postumius, Sp. Carvilius	517	516	520
233	Q. Fabius, M'. Postumius	518	517	521
232	M. Aemilius, M. Publicius	519	518	522
*231	**M. Pomponius, C. Papirius**	**520**	519	523
*230	M. Aemilius, M. Iunius	521	520	524
229	L. Postumius II, Cn. Fulvius	522	521	525
228	Sp. Carvilius II, Q. Fabius II	523	522	526
227	**P. Valerius, M. Atilius**	524	**523**	527

condita chronology as Ser. Sulpicius. In Gellius' first passage, Servius himself dated it five years later; but his *ab urbe condita* date coincides with the Varronian date for the year Dionysius gives. I suggest that Ser. Sulpicius and Varro agreed that the divorce took place in *ab urbe condita* 523,[74] but disagreed over which consular year that date represented; and that in Gellius' second passage (for which the source is not stated) Varro's consular date is accepted and Servius' *ab urbe condita* date adjusted to fit. In that case we can safely infer that Dionysius was following Varro's version, and has given us Varro's consular date; but the *ab urbe condita* date he gives is the result of his own independent research into Roman chronology.[75]

VII

In Romulus' constitution, those who did the fighting were also those who did the farming:[76]

εἰ μὲν εἰρήνην ἄγοιεν ἐπὶ τοῖς κατ' ἀγρὸν ἔργοις ἐθίζων ἅπαντας μένειν, πλὴν εἴ ποτε δεηθεῖεν ἀγορᾶς, τότε δ' εἰς ἄστυ συνιόντας ἀγοράζειν, ἐνάτην ὁρίζων ἡμέραν ταῖς ἀγοραῖς.

[74] For scholarly correspondence between Ser. Sulpicius and Varro, see Aulus Gellius 2.10.1–4 (Varro *Epistolicae quaestiones* fr. 228 Funaioli).

[75] See 1.74.2–75.3 (summarizing a separate monograph).

[76] 2.28.3, item D(v). On the *nundinae*, see Frayn 1993.3–5, 17–23.

In time of peace he accustomed them all to remain at their tasks in the country, except for occasions when they needed a market, and then to come together in the city and do their buying and selling; he had set aside every ninth day for the markets.

The purpose of that was to habituate the Romans to virtuous pursuits, and prevent them from being corrupted by the 'sedentary and banausic' life of the city-dweller.[77]

That ancestral custom is praised by Varro in the preface to his second book of *Res rusticae*:[78]

uiri magni nostri maiores non sine causa praeponebant rusticos Romanos urbanis. ut ruri enim qui in uilla uiuunt ignauiores quam qui in agro uersantur in aliquot opera faciendo, sic qui in oppido sederent quam qui rura colerent desidiosiores putabant. itaque annum ita diuiserunt ut nonis modo diebus urbanas res usurparent, reliquis septem ut rura colerent.

It was not without reason that those great men, our ancestors, valued rural Romans over urban ones. For as in the country those who live in villas are lazier in doing any job than those who work in the fields, so they thought that those who were sedentary in town were more indolent than those who cultivated the land. And so they divided up the year in such a way that they carried out their business in town only every ninth day, so that they could cultivate the land for the remaining seven.

I think it is likely that this passage presupposes an earlier Varronian treatment of the subject, no doubt in the *Antiquities*, and that that treatment was Dionysius' source.

Of course, that is not demonstrable. But I hope that the cumulative effect of all these parallels may make it unnecessary to resist, and attractive to accept, the opinion expressed by Friedrich Cornelius, so briefly and so long ago, on the source of Dionysius' account of Romulus' constitution.[79] The benefit of that is not inconsiderable, if it means that we can recover, at least in broad outline, a substantial chapter of Varro's lost masterpiece.

---

[77] 2.28.1, on ἐπιδιφρίους καὶ βαναύσους καὶ προσαγωγοὺς ἐπιθυμιῶν αἰσχρῶν τέχνας, which were to be carried out by slaves and foreigners.

[78] Varro *Res rusticae* 2.pref.1 (whence Columella 1.pref.17). Cf. also Festus 176L: *nundinas feriatum diem esse uoluerunt antiqui, ut rustici conuenirent mercandi uendendique causa.*

[79] See n. 28 above.

What makes it interesting for the argument of this book is the fact that Varro's family was enrolled in the *tribus Quirina*;[80] his ancestral home was in the Sabine *ager Reatinus*.[81] It is important to remember that Reate was not a city but a prefecture, the market and administrative centre for the rich lands that were divided up among the citizen body after the conquests of Manius Curius in the third century BC.[82] It seems clear that Varro's praise of the farmer-citizens of Rome was a reflection of his own family tradition.[83] No doubt his great-great-great-great-grandfather received one of those equal 7-*iugera* plots when the conquered territory was first shared out. It would be natural for such people to believe that Romulus—who was also Quirinus—had established the principle of equality at the very origin of Rome.

[80] Varro *Res rusticae* 3.2.1 (Q. Axius a *tribulis* of the author); *Inscriptiones Graecae* 7.413.12 = Sherk 1969.134 (Κόιντος Ἄξιος Μαάρκου υἱὸς Κυρίνᾳ).

[81] Symmachus *Letters* 1.2 (Varro as *Reatinus*); cf. Varro *Res rusticae* 2.pref.6 and 2.8.3 on Varro's horses and asses *in Reatino*, 3.2.3, 5, 9 and 12 on *uillae Reatinae*.

[82] See above, pp. 42–4. Cicero *De natura deorum* 2.6 (whence Valerius Maximus 1.8.1) for the *praefectura Reatina*. Festus 262L: *praefecturae eae appellabantur in Italia in quibus et ius dicebatur et nundinae agebantur.*

[83] Cf. Varro *Logistorici* fr. 25 Chappuis (Nonius 155L) on his own upbringing: *mihi puero modica una fuit tunica et toga, sine fasceis calciamenta, ecus sine ephippio, balneum non cotidianum, alueus rarus.*

5

Macaulay on Cicero

Where would we be without Cicero? The survival of so many of his letters, speeches, and dialogues means that we are incomparably better informed about Roman politics in his lifetime than in any other period. It is no accident that the first two chapters of this book began with explanations of passages from Cicero's works. But there is a price to pay for this enormous benefit. We know Cicero so well that we may find ourselves taking his attitudes for granted, as if there were no other way of looking at his world; and even when we try to use other information to achieve some kind of perspective, the sheer volume of the Ciceronian corpus gives the illusion that his view must be the prevailing one.

To understand Cicero, not only as an individual to whose private thoughts we have unparalleled access, but also as a politician whose actions and opinions were both influential and deeply controversial, requires a quite exceptional degree of historical insight. One man who had that quality was Thomas Babington Macaulay.

I

Even as a schoolboy, Macaulay liked Cicero particularly,[1] and by the time he was at Cambridge he regarded him as a moral and political paradigm: 'My opinions, good or bad,' he wrote to his father at 18,

---

[1] Aged 14 in a letter to his mother, 23 Aug. 1815 (Pinney 1974.66): 'But I am like my favourite Cicero about my own productions. It is all one to me what others think of them.'

'were learnt...from Cicero, from Tacitus, and from Milton.'[2] His phenomenal appetite for reading, and his equally phenomenal memory, gave him a mastery of the works of Cicero that can rarely have been matched since antiquity.[3]

At 34, already well known from his precocious parliamentary career, he wrote to his sister from Calcutta:[4]

I still retain...my thirst for knowledge; my passion for holding converse with the greatest minds of all ages and nations; my power of forgetting what surrounds me, and of living with the past, the future, the distant, and the unreal. Books are becoming everything to me.

During his three years in India he read all of Cicero twice, and under the influence of *De finibus*, the *Academica*, and the *Tusculan Disputations*, even imagined giving up politics altogether.[5] But that was just a momentary mood, and the letters and the speeches enabled him to 'hold converse' with Cicero as a politician and as a man:[6]

Am busily engaged with Cicero, whose character, moral and intellectual, interests me prodigiously. I think that I see the whole man through and through.

Apart from the brilliant Preface to the *Lays of Ancient Rome* (1842), Macaulay published nothing on the classical world. As his nephew and biographer puts it, 'a Life of Pericles, or a Life of Cicero, are among the unwritten biographies which were buried with him under the pavement of Poet's Corner in the transept of the Abbey'.[7] However, his *obiter dicta* make up for the loss.

Macaulay not only read voraciously;[8] he also commented at length on what he was reading, either in the margins of his books or in his

---

[2] A letter of Sept. 1819, explaining his indignation at the 'Peterloo massacre' (Pinney 1974.133).

[3] Trevelyan 1932.1.48–50 (memory); 1.410, 2.443–50 (reading and rereading of classical authors in Calcutta).

[4] Ibid. 1.358. Cf. Pinney 1976.129, from a letter to T. F. Ellis, 8 Feb. 1835: 'What a blessing it is to love books as I love them;—to be able to converse with the dead, and to live amidst the unreal.'

[5] Trevelyan 1932.2.422; Pinney 1976.158–9 (letter to Ellis, 30 Dec. 1835). Cf. Trevelyan 1932.2.314 n. 1: rereading *De finibus*, Macaulay commented 'I always liked it the best of his philosophical works; and I am still of the same mind'.

[6] Letter to Ellis, 25 Aug. 1835 (Pinney 1976.153).

[7] Trevelyan 1932.2.423.

[8] Cataloguers of the books he owned have noted 'the characteristic thumb- and finger-prints of mixed blood and lather that appear on books read by TBM when shaving' (typescript addition to Hunt 1968 by Alistair Elliot, Librarian of the University of Newcastle upon Tyne, 21 Nov. 1969).

letters and journals. The marginalia to Cicero were evidently inscribed in the thirteen-volume Bipontine edition reported in the manuscript catalogue of his library.[9] Where those volumes are now is a mystery; they do not appear in the catalogue of books from Macaulay's library that were sold by auction on 4–6 March 1863, nor are they among the Macaulay items at Wallington Hall, Northumberland.[10] We must be content with the selection of Macaulay's marginalia that was transcribed and commented on by his nephew in 1907, where Cicero is one of the authors most prominently featured.[11] With the letters and the journals we are in a much better position, since both collections have now been published in modern annotated editions.[12]

A combination of these resources enables us to put together Macaulay's 'far from unsympathetic analysis' of Cicero's 'mobile, and singularly interesting, character'.[13]

II

Since his own first oratorical triumph had been at the age of 30,[14] it is not surprising that Macaulay liked Cicero's early speeches. Here he is on *Pro Roscio Amerino*:[15]

I cannot help thinking that he strengthened the language after Sulla's resignation. But, after making full allowance for re-touching, it is impossible

---

[9] 'Division II, shelfs 2,3,4'; the MS is at Wallington Hall, but there is a photocopy in the Wren Library, Trinity College Cambridge.

[10] The former is accessible in the Wren Library, Trinity College Cambridge; for the latter, see Hunt 1968.

[11] Trevelyan 1907.38–55 = 1932.2.422–33.

[12] Letters ed. Thomas Pinney, 6 vols., 1974–81; journals ed. William Thomas, 5 vols., 2008. I am very grateful to Mr Thomas for allowing me to consult his edition before publication.

[13] Trevelyan 1907.43 = 1932.2.426.

[14] 1 Mar. 1831, the Reform Bill debate.

[15] Trevelyan 1907.43–4 = 1932.2.426. Cf. Thomas 2008.2.233 (journal, 12 Apr. 1850) on the *Pro Quinctio, Pro Roscio Amerino,* and *Pro Roscio comoedo*: 'they are inferior in magnificence, no doubt, but superior, I think, in force and sharpness to the more celebrated orations of his manhood'.

to deny that he performed a bold service to humanity and to his country. *Si sic omnia!*

And on the first speech against Verres:[16]

There is great force about this speech. Cicero had not attained that perfect mastery of the whole art of rhetoric which he possessed at a later period. But on the other hand there is a freedom, a boldness, a zeal for popular rights, a scorn of the vicious and insolent gang whom he afterwards called the *boni*, which makes these early speeches more pleasing than the later. Flattery,—and after his exile, cowardice,—destroyed all that was generous and elevated in his mind.

The third part of the *actio secunda* against Verres he describes as 'a very powerful speech indeed':[17]

It makes my blood boil, less against Verres than against the detestable system of government which Cicero was so desirous to uphold, though he himself was not an accomplice in the crimes which were inseparable from it.

'I believe', he wrote,[18] 'that when Cicero was adopted into the class of nobles, his tastes and opinions underwent a change, like those of many other politicians.' And that change came with the consulship.

Macaulay's full statement of his diagnosis comes in a comment on the fourth speech against Catiline. 'Fine declamation, but it is no answer to Caesar's admirable speech.' As he goes on to explain,[19]

this was the turning point of Cicero's life. He was a new man, and a popular man. Till his Consulship he had always leaned against the Optimates. He had defended Sulla's victims. He had brought Verres to justice in spite of strong aristocratical protection. He had always spoken handsomely of the Gracchi and other heroes of the democratic party. He appears, when he became consul, to have been very much liked by the multitude, and much distrusted by the nobles. But the peculiar circumstances in which he was now placed rendered it his duty to take the side of the aristocracy on some important questions. He supported them on the Agrarian Law. He also took vigorous measures against Catiline. They began to coax and flatter him. He went further. He was hurried by adulation, vanity, and vindictive feeling into

---

[16] Trevelyan 1907.44 = 1932.2.426.
[17] Ibid. 44 = 426–7.
[18] Ibid. 41 n. 1 = 425 n. 1 (context not stated).
[19] Ibid. 45–6 = 427.

a highly unconstitutional act in favour of the nobles. He followed, with more excuse indeed, the odious example set by Scipio Nasica and by Opimius. From that time he was an instrument in the hands of the grandees, whom he hated and despised: and who fully returned his hatred, and despised, not his talents indeed, but his character.

That 'odious example' of the killing of the Gracchi was Macaulay's constant point of reference.[20]

Trevelyan's transcripts of the marginalia rarely reveal which exact phrase in Cicero Macaulay was commenting on, but sometimes we can get close. Trevelyan writes:

> At a serious crisis in Roman history [Cicero] told Atticus that the leaders of the aristocratic party cared nothing about the ruin of the Republic as long as their fishponds were safe, and believed themselves to have attained celestial honours if they had great mullets which came up to be fed by hand.

That is a conflation of two passages from 60 BC:[21]

ceteros iam nosti: qui ita sunt stulti ut amissa re publica piscinas suas fore saluas sperare uideantur.

nostri autem principes digito se caelum putent attingere si mulli barbati in piscinis sint qui ad manum accedant.

Against one or other of those sentences in his text Macaulay wrote: 'These are your *boni*!'

The passage in *Pro Sestio* where 'Cicero asked what sort of men were these *Optimates*, who so well deserved their honourable title,' is easily identifiable as the opening of the famous digression on the two rival traditions of Roman politics. *Quis ergo iste optimus quisque?*, asks Cicero, and Macaulay replied:[22]

---

[20] Ibid. 41 = 424–5, on *De officiis*: 'he protested vehemently whenever the author thought fit to draw his examples of the just man made perfect from Scipio Nasica and Lucius Opimius,—the pair of worthies who murdered the brothers Gracchi'. Cf. also Trevelyan 1932.2.425 n. 1: 'Publius Nasica, . . . who, (said Macaulay), by so doing, gave the first example to Marius, Cinna, Caesar, and Antony of settling civil disputes by arms.' However, that is not in Trevelyan 1907, and not cited verbatim; we can be sure Macaulay would have mentioned Sulla.

[21] Ibid. 46 = 427–8; Cicero *Ad Atticum* 1.18.6 (20 Jan.), 2.1.7 (c. 3 June).

[22] Ibid. 49 = 429; Cicero *Pro Sestio* 97. For the character of L. Domitius Ahenobarbus (*cos.* 54 BC), see Suetonius *Nero* 2.2–3.

The murderers of the Gracchi, the hirelings of Jugurtha, the butchers of Sulla, the plunderers of the provinces, the buyers and sellers of magistracies,—such men as Opimius and Scaurus, Domitius Ahenobarbus and Caius Verres.

'Cicero's opinion of the nobles', Trevelyan writes, 'went steadily down as his experience of them became more intimate. The time came when he confided to Atticus that they were altogether insupportable. "I cannot endure," he said, "to be the object of their sneering talk. They certainly do not merit the name of *boni*."' Despite the quotation marks, that seems to be a paraphrase of two passages in a letter of 6 March 49 BC:[23]

audio enim bonis uiris, qui et nunc et saepe antea magno praesidio rei publicae fuerunt, hanc cunctationem nostram non probari multaque mihi et seuere in conuiuiis, tempestiuis quidem, disputari.

me quidem alius nemo mouet, non sermo bonorum, qui nulli sunt ...

It was surely that last phrase that made Macaulay write in the margin 'You have found it out at last!'

The correspondence with Atticus was what Macaulay enjoyed most in Cicero's works, but as Trevelyan explains, the text in it that he most admired was not by Cicero himself:[24]

[It] was Caesar's answer to Cicero's message of gratitude for the humanity which the conqueror had displayed towards those political adversaries who had fallen into his power at the surrender of Corfinium. It contained, (so Macaulay used to say,) the finest sentence ever written. ... *Nor am I disturbed when I hear it said that those, whom I have sent off alive and free, will again bear arms against me; for there is nothing which I so much covet as that I should be like myself and they like themselves.*

In his copy of *De bello ciuili* Macaulay noted that Caesar 'was on the right side, as far as in such a miserable government there could be a right side'. Pompey, he thought, would have been incapable of Caesar's humanity in victory: 'whether he inclined to it or not, [he] must have established a reign of terror to gratify the execrable aristocracy whose tool he had stooped to be'.[25]

---

[23] Ibid. 46 = 428; Cicero *Ad Atticum* 9.1.3 and 4.
[24] Ibid. 42 and n. 1 = 425 and n. 2; Cicero *Ad Atticum* 9.16.2 (p. 194 below).
[25] Trevelyan 1932.2.445; see p. 200 below for the plans of the *boni* in 48 BC.

Not surprisingly, Macaulay did not approve of Cicero's attitude after the Ides of March. 'His whole conduct was as bad as possible. His love of peace, the best part of his public character, was overcome by personal animosity and wounded vanity.' At the end of the *Philippics* he gave a severe verdict:

As a man, I think of Cicero much as I always did, except that I am more disgusted with his conduct after Caesar's death. I really think that he met with little more than his deserts from the Triumvirs. It is quite certain, as Livy says, that he suffered nothing more than he would have inflicted. There is an impatience of peaceful counsels, a shrinking from all plans of conciliation, a thirst for blood, in all the Philippics, which, (whatever he may say,) can be attributed only to personal hatred, and is particularly odious in a timid man.

'A hard saying', comments Macaulay's biographer.[26] How justified it was, we shall see in Chapter 9.

III

Macaulay's considered view deserves respect. He knew the texts at least as well as any scholar, and he applied to them the practical experience of a politician who knew about oratory—and the aristocratic establishment—at first hand. Gladstone recalled that whenever Macaulay rose to speak in the House of Commons, 'it was a summons like a trumpet call to fill the benches'.[27] And a distinguished modern historian observes that the great virtue of Macaulay's *History of England* 'is his unerring grasp of political reality':[28]

Uninterested in abstract ideas, insensitive in his approach to persons, Macaulay had nevertheless an unfailing appreciation of political situations.

---

[26] Trevelyan 1907.52–3 = 1932.2.431–2; see below, pp. 203 (hatred), 128 (Livy). For a more favourable view, cf. ibid. 52 = 431 on *Philippics* 3: 'The close of this speech is very fine. His later and earlier speeches have a freedom and an air of sincerity about them which, in the interval between his Consulship and Caesar's death, I do not find. During that interval he was mixed up with the aristocratical party, and yet afraid of the Triumvirate. When all the great party-leaders were dead, he found himself at the head of the state, and spoke with a boldness and energy which he had not shown since his youthful days.'

[27] Quoted in Trevor-Roper 1979.18.

[28] Trevor-Roper 1979.39.

Himself a politician, who had lived through the excitement of the parliamentary struggle for Reform and had enjoyed personal experience of government both in England and in India, he understood the pressures of politics, the need and the moment of action.

That applied equally to the politics of Rome.

Readers must judge for themselves whether Macaulay's approach to Cicero was insensitive. I conclude with his reaction to two late items in the correspondence.[29] First, a letter to Antony on 26 April 44 BC:

quod mecum per litteras agis unam ob causam mallem coram egisses; non enim solum ex oratione, sed etiam ex uultu et oculis et fronte, ut aiunt, meum erga te amorem perspicere potuisses. nam cum te semper amaui, primum tuo studio, post etiam beneficio prouocatus, tum his temporibus res publica te mihi ita commendauit ut cariorem habeam neminem.

I only wish that you had addressed me face to face, instead of by writing; for you might then have perceived not by my words alone, but by my countenance, my eyes, and my forehead, the affection that I bear to you. For,—as I always loved you for the attentions you have shown me, and the services you have done me,—so, in these later days, your public conduct has been such that I hold no one dearer than you.

Second, a letter in February 43 BC to Gaius Trebonius, who had detained Antony outside the Senate at the time of the assassination:

quam uellem ad illas pulcherrimas epulas me Idibus Martiis inuitasses! reliquiarum nihil haberemus... quod uero a te, uiro optimo, seductus est tuoque beneficio adhuc uiuit haec pestis, interdum, quod mihi uix fas est, tibi subirascor.

Would to heaven you had invited me to that noble feast which you made on the Ides of March! No remnants, most assuredly, would have been left behind.... I have a grudge even against so good a man as yourself when I reflect that it was through *your* intervention that this pest of humanity is still among the living.

'Infamous!', wrote Macaulay.

---

[29] Cicero *Ad Atticum* 14.13b.1, *Ad familiares* 10.28.1; trans. as in Trevelyan 1907.53–4 = 1932.2.432–3.

6

Cicero and Varro

Cicero's correspondence is a matchless historical resource for understanding the political world of the late republic from the inside. But it can be deceptive. Cicero was not as open and frank with all his correspondents as he was with Atticus and Quintus, and in any case we only have one side of the story;[1] without the replies, how can we know what his addressees' attitudes were? A particularly revealing example is Marcus Varro, with whom Cicero was in regular contact by letter in the spring and early summer of 46 BC.

I

As prominent *Pompeiani*, both Cicero and Varro had been in uneasy exile from Rome for well over a year after the battle of Pharsalus. Pardoned eventually by Caesar, they returned cautiously to their villas, Cicero in October 47, Varro probably in January 46.[2] By April Cicero was back in the city, and wondering whether to accept Varro's invitation to Cumae:[3]

etsi uide, quaeso, satisne rectum sit nos hoc tanto incendio ciuitatis in istis locis esse; dabimus sermonem iis qui nesciunt nobis, quocumque in loco simus, eundem cultum, eundem uictum esse. <sed> quid refert? tamen in sermonem incidemus.

---

[1] The one significant exception is the correspondence between Caelius Rufus in Rome and Cicero in Cilicia (*Ad familiares* 2.8–15 and 8.1–14).
[2] Cicero *Ad familiares* 14.20 (Cicero to Tusculum), 9.1 (Varro to either Tusculum or Cumae).
[3] Cicero *Ad familiares* 9.3.1 (trans. D. R. Shackleton Bailey, Penguin Classics).

But pray ask yourself whether it is quite proper for us to be down there at such a time of national convulsion. We shall be giving a chance for gossip to those who don't know that, wherever we are, our style and way of life remain the same. And yet, what does it matter? They will gossip about us anyway.

The *incendium ciuitatis* to which Cicero refers was the war in Africa, where Caesar, consul for the third time, was facing the combined forces of Juba's Mauretanians (and elephants) and the *optimates* under Metellus Scipio and Cato.

In fact, the war was already over when Cicero wrote his letter. A few days later came the news of Caesar's overwhelming victory, with fifty thousand dead on the field of Thapsus.[4] Cicero wrote again:[5]

tibi autem idem consilium do quod mihimet ipsi, ut uitemus oculos hominum, si linguas minus facile possimus; qui enim uictoria se efferunt quasi uictos nos intuentur, qui autem uictos nostros moleste ferunt nos dolent uiuere.

To you I have the same advice to offer as to myself. Let us avoid men's eyes, even if we cannot easily escape their tongues. The jubilant victors regard us as among the defeated, whereas those who are sorry for the defeat of our friends feel aggrieved that we are still among the living.

Until it was clear what the victor had in mind,[6] it was better to keep one's head down:[7]

sed haec tu melius, modo nobis stet illud, una uiuere in studiis nostris, a quibus antea delectationem modo petebamus, nunc uero etiam salutem; non deesse si quis adhibere uolet, non modo ut architectos uerum etiam ut fabros, ad aedificandam rem publicam, et potius libenter accurrere; si nemo utetur opera, tamen et scribere et legere πολιτείας, et, si minus in curia atque in foro, at in litteris et libris, ut doctissimi ueteres fecerunt, nauare rem publicam et de moribus ac legibus quaerere.

But you will judge better than I. Only let us be firm on one point—to live together in our literary studies. We used to go to them only for pleasure, now we go for salvation. If anyone cares to call us in as architects or even as workers to help build a commonwealth, we shall not say no, rather we shall hasten cheerfully to the task. If our services are not required, we must still

---

[4] *De bello Africano* 86.1, Plutarch *Caesar* 53.2 (an incredible figure).

[5] Cicero *Ad familiares* 9.2.2 (trans. Shackleton Bailey).

[6] Ibid. 9.2.4: *magni autem intererit qui fuerit uictoris animus.*

[7] Ibid. 9.2.5 (trans. Shackleton Bailey). For *studia nostra*, see also 9.3.2 (*artes nostrae*), 9.6.5, 9.8.1 (*coniunctio studiorum*), 9.8.2.

read and write 'Republics'. Like the learned men of old, we must serve the state in our libraries, if we cannot in Senate-House and Forum, and pursue our researches into custom and law.

The constant use of the first-person plural indicates the nature of the relationship.[8] Here, surely, are two men who saw eye to eye on everything important, in life, literature, and politics.

A year or so later, in the summer of 45 BC, Cicero recast the four books of his newly written *Academica* in order to dedicate the work to Varro. He set the new scene at Cumae, where they both had villas:[9]

in Cumano nuper cum mecum Atticus noster esset, nuntiatum est nobis a M. Varrone uenisse eum Roma pridie uesperi et nisi de uia fessus esset continuo ad nos uenturum fuisse. quod cum audissemus, nullam moram interponendam putauimus quin uideremus hominem nobiscum et studiis eisdem et uetustate amicitiae coniunctum.

When my friend Atticus was with me recently at my place at Cumae, a message came from Marcus Varro that he had arrived from Rome the previous evening and that if he wasn't too tired from the journey he would come straight on to us. When we heard that, we thought we should go and see him without delay; for he is attached to us both by our common studies and by the length of our friendship.

But that was for public consumption; the letters to Atticus reveal a more complicated story.

First from Arpinum in June and July, then from Tusculum in July and August, Cicero bombarded his friend with letters about the recasting of the dialogue. How do you know Varro would like to be in it? Why hasn't he said anything? Is he jealous of someone? Are you sure it's a good idea?[10] Cicero can see problems, but doesn't want to put them on paper.[11] Atticus is nervous about taking responsibility,[12] and for good reason: Varro is like Homer's Achilles, 'a man to be feared, who would blame even the blameless'.[13]

---

[8] Besides the passages quoted, see also *Ad familiares* 9.5.2, 9.6.3 and 5, 9.8.2. Cf. Griffin 1994.701 on Varro as 'an older contemporary of Cicero, whom he resembled in social background and political sympathies'.

[9] Cicero *Academica* 1.1. (Book 2 is from the first edition, set in 60 BC and dedicated to Lucullus.)

[10] Cicero *Ad Atticum* 13.12.3, 13.1, 14.1, 16.1–2, 24.1, 25.3.

[11] Ibid. 13.19.5, 22.1 and 3.

[12] Ibid. 13.23.2, 24.1, 25.3, 35.2, 44.2.

[13] Ibid. 13.25.3, quoting Homer *Iliad* 11.654 (Patroclus to Nestor): *sed est, ut scis,* δεινὸς ἀνήρ· τάχα κεν καὶ ἀναίτιον αἰτιόῳτο.

The relationship had always been an uneasy one, as an earlier part of the Atticus correspondence demonstrates. In the summer of 59 BC Cicero had been looking for allies against the threat of Clodius' impending tribunate.[14] 'I'm satisfied with Varro,' he told Atticus; 'much can be done through him, and it will be stronger if you urge him on.'[15] Cicero himself was evidently not close enough:[16]

nuper me scis scripsisse ad te de Varronis erga me officio, te ad me rescripsisse eam rem summae tibi uoluptati esse. sed ego mallem ad ipsum scripsisses mihi illum satis facere, non quo faceret sed ut faceret. mirabiliter enim moratus est, sicut nosti, ἑλικτὰ καὶ οὐδέν ... *sed nos tenemus praeceptum illud,* 'τὰς τῶν κρατούντων ...'

The other day, you remember, I wrote to you about Varro's good offices towards me, and you wrote back that you were delighted to hear of it. But I would rather you had written to *him* that I was well content with him, not that this really *was* so but that it might become so. He is a strange person, as you know, 'crooked and not at all ...' But I am holding to the old maxim 'To put up with the rulers ...'

This time the analogy is not Homeric but Euripidean, and what it implies is very revealing.

The first quotation is from Andromache's outburst against the Spartans, after Menelaus has tricked her into leaving her place of safety at the altar:[17]

> ὦ πᾶσιν ἀνθρώποισιν ἔχθιστοι βροτῶν
> Σπάρτης ἔνοικοι, δόλια βουλευτήρια,
> ψευδῶν ἄνακτες, μηχανορράφοι κακῶν,
> ἑλικτὰ κοὐδὲν ὑγιές, ἀλλὰ πᾶν πέριξ
> φρονοῦντες, ἀδίκως εὐτυχεῖτ' ἀν' Ἑλλάδα.

O you whom all men hate most in the world, dwellers in Sparta, deceitful counsellors, masters of lies, crafty schemers of evil, whose thoughts are crooked and not at all wholesome but wholly devious, unjustly do you flourish in Greece!

---

[14] Cicero *Ad Atticum* 2.18.3, 19.1, 19.4–5, 20.2, 22.1–5, 23.3, 24.5.
[15] Ibid. 2.20.1, 21.6, 22.4.
[16] Ibid. 2.25.1 (trans. Shackleton Bailey, slightly adjusted); cf. also 3.8.3, 3.15.1 and 3, 3.18.1 (from exile).
[17] Euripides *Andromache* 445–9.

Andromache is a slave, and the whole play up to this point has insisted on her slave status.[18] Menelaus, on the other hand, is an autocrat, and pompously announces himself as such.[19] That, no doubt, is why the lines were in Cicero's mind: throughout the spring and summer of Caesar's consulship, his letters constantly refer to the political situation in terms of slavery and tyranny.[20]

The second quotation is from the *Phoenissae*. Polyneices, tricked by Eteocles of his share of power, explains to his mother Jocasta why exile is the greatest of evils:[21]

> Π. ἓν μὲν μέγιστον, οὐκ ἔχει παρρησίαν.
> Ἰ. δούλου τόδ᾽ εἶπας, μὴ λέγειν ἅ τις φρονεῖ.
> Π. τὰς τῶν κρατούντων ἀμαθίας φέρειν χρεών.
> Ἰ. καὶ τοῦτο λυπρόν, συνασοφεῖν τοῖς μὴ σοφοῖς.
> Π. ἀλλ᾽ ἐς τὸ κέρδος παρὰ φύσιν δουλευτέον.

P. The one worst thing is that there's no freedom of speech.
J. That's a slave's fate, not to say what one thinks.
P. You have to put up with the rulers' ignorance.
J. That too is wretched, to share the unwisdom of the unwise.
P. You have to gain by being a slave against your nature.

It is remarkable that Cicero should impute ignorance (*amathia*) to Varro, of all people. But it was the first half of the line that mattered, on the ignorance of *rulers*.

In 59 BC, the rulers were the consul Caesar and his allies.[22] Ever since the bitter conflict over the *lex agraria* early in the year, Caesar had ignored the Senate and taken political business directly to the People; his colleague Bibulus had been forced to retreat to his house.[23] The senatorial opposition saw that as a denial of their freedom of speech—in effect, enslavement.[24] The analogy with Andromache and Polyneices

---

[18] Andromache herself at lines 12–13, 25, 30, 64, 99, 110, 114, 187 and 401; the Chorus at 127 and 137; Hermione at 155; Menelaus at 366 and 433–5.

[19] Lines 366–7: γύναι, τάδ᾽ ἐστὶ σμικρὰ καὶ μοναρχίας | οὐκ ἄξι᾽, ὡς φῄς, τῆς ἐμῆς οὐδ᾽ Ἑλλάδος.

[20] Cicero *Ad Atticum* 2.8.1 (*reges*), 9.1 (*his dynastis*), 12.1 (*regnum*), 13.2 (*regnum*), 14.1 (ἐντυραννεῖσθαι), 17.1 (τυραννίδα), 18.1 and 2 (see n. 24 below), 21.1 (*dominatio*), 24.3 (Ahala or Brutus needed); *Ad Q. fratrem* 1.2.16 (*reges*).

[21] Euripides *Phoenissae* 391–5.

[22] Cicero *Ad Atticum* 2.18.1 (*qui tenent omnia*); see n. 20 above.

[23] Dio Cassius 38.4.1, 6.5–6; Appian *Civil Wars* 2.10.35–11.40.

[24] Cicero *Ad Atticum* 2.18.2 (*spes ut nulla sit aliquando non modo priuatos uerum etiam magistratus liberos esse*); ibid. 2.18.1 (*neque iam quo minus seruiamus recusamus*); Dio Cassius 38.6.4 (τῇ γὰρ τοῦ πλήθους σπουδῇ δεδουλωμένοι πάντες ἡσύχαζον).

applied particularly to Cicero, once Caesar had allowed Clodius to become a plebeian; like them, he was now unprotected against his mortal enemy.[25] Cicero later claimed that Caesar constantly cited the self-justification of the tyrant Eteocles:[26]

εἴπερ γὰρ ἀδικεῖν χρή, τυραννίδος πέρι
κάλλιστον ἀδικεῖν, τἄλλα δ' εὐσεβεῖν χρέων.

If one has to do wrong, the finest thing is to do wrong for absolute power; in everything else one should be virtuous.

That is the context in which he and Atticus thought of Varro. Far from being two of a kind, Cicero and Varro were on opposite sides of an ideological divide.

II

Varro was born in 116 BC (the consulship of Gaius Geta, as it happens).[27] According to St Augustine, he was born and brought up in Rome,[28] but Varro evidently thought of himself as a Sabine of Reate, with a suitably old-fashioned rural upbringing.[29] There is no necessary contradiction; since Reate was only 49 miles up the Via Salaria from Rome, one day's journey in summer, two in winter,[30] he may well have spent most of his boyhood in the country, coming to Rome only for the games and other special occasions.[31]

---

[25] Cicero *De prouinciis consularibus* 42 (*traduxit ad plebem inimicum meum*), *Pro Flacco* 4–5, 96–7 (Cicero's danger); n. 14 above. Cf. Euripides *Andromache* 435–63, *Phoenissae* 261–8, 358–64.

[26] Euripides *Phoenissae* 524–5; Cicero *De officiis* 3.82 (*in ore semper... habebat*), Suetonius *Diuus Iulius* 30.5. He also attributed to Caesar Eteocles' motivation τὴν θεῶν μεγίστην ὥστ' ἔχειν τυραννίδα (*Phoenissae* 506, Cicero *Ad Atticum* 7.11.1, Jan. 49 BC).

[27] Jerome *Chronicle* on Olympiad 166.1: *M. Terentius Varro philosophus et poeta nascitur.*

[28] Augustine *City of God* 4.1 (the supposed reason for Varro's assumption that *ludi scaenici* counted as *res diuinae*).

[29] See above, p. 98.

[30] Varro *Res rusticae* 3.2.14–15.

[31] Games: Cicero *In Verrem* 1.54 (also elections and census), *Ad familiares* 7.1.1, Ovid *Fasti* 3.779–84; cf. p. 97 above for market days.

Certainly he grew up tough (see Fig. 3). 'A good soldier and a good commander' is how he was described in his old age, by a man well qualified to make the judgement.[32] We don't know anything about his soldiering as a young man, but at least his service as a commanding officer can be tenuously documented from his own works. He used to speak of the time he went to Liburnia, the north-east Adriatic coast;[33] it may have been as quaestor to L. Cinna in 85 BC, or else as legate to C. Cosconius in 78–77.[34] In the war against Sertorius (77–72 BC) he was in Spain so long that his friends thought the local rabbits had followed him home.[35] In the pirates campaign of 67 BC he was in command of the naval forces between Sicily and Delos, taking the opportunity to visit the sites in Epirus where Aeneas had been;[36] he was decorated by Pompey with the *corona rostrata*, given for being the first man to board an enemy ship.[37] He reported Pompey's exploration of the Caspian in 66–65 BC, though whether he himself was a legate in the war against Mithridates is not known.[38]

In the interstices of all this military work, Varro also took his share of civilian responsibility. We know he was *triumuir capitalis*, tribune of the *plebs*, praetor and proconsul,[39] but the dates can only be conjectured. He may have been tribune during the 'three years of peace' from 86 to 84 BC, when he was in his early thirties;[40] the praetorship and subsequent

---

[32] Appian *Civil Wars* 4.47.202 (ἐστρατευμένος τε καλῶς καὶ ἐστρατηγηκώς). For Pollio as Appian's chief source, see Gabba 1956, esp. 229–49. Appian's description of Varro as ἐχθρὸς μοναρχίας is very like Pollio's self-description at *Ad familiares* 10.31.2–3; for Pollio, *princeps orator et ciuis*, honouring Varro in his new library, see Pliny *Nat. Hist.* 7.115.

[33] Varro *Res rusticae* 2.10.8 (Cossinius speaking, dramatic date 67 BC): *ut te audii dicere, inquit, cum in Liburniam uenisses...*

[34] Respectively Appian *Civil Wars* 1.77.354 (Badian 1962a.60 = 1964.230); Eutropius 6.4, Orosius 5.23.23 (Cichorius 1922.191–2).

[35] Varro *Res rusticae* 3.12.7 (Ap. Claudius speaking, dramatic date 50 BC): *in Hispania annis ita fuistis multis ut inde te cuniculos persecutos credam.*

[36] Varro *Res rusticae* 2.pref.6 (*cum piratico bello inter Delum et Siciliam Graeciae classibus praeessem*); Varro *Antiquitates humanae* fr. 2.12 Mirsch = Servius on *Aeneid* 3.349 (*Varro Epiri se fuisse dicit et omnia loca isdem dici nominibus quae poeta commemorat se uidisse*); cf. Pliny *Nat. Hist.* 3.101 for his plan to bridge the straits of Otranto.

[37] Pliny *Nat. Hist.* 7.115, 16.7; cf. Festus 156–7L.

[38] Varro ap. Pliny *Nat. Hist.* 6.51–2; Cichorius 1922.194–5 argues against autopsy.

[39] *Tr. cap.* and *tr. pl.*: Varro *Antiquitates humanae* fr. 21.1 Mirsch = Aulus Gellius 13.12.6. *Procos.* (and therefore praetor): inferred from Varro *De lingua Latina* 7.109 (*Septumio qui mihi fuit quaestor*).

[40] Cicero *Brutus* 308 (*triennium fere fuit urbs sine armis*). This date is ruled out by Cichorius (1922.202) on the quite unjustified assumption that Varro 'sein Leben lang auf

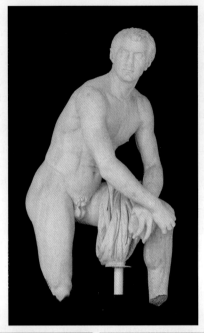

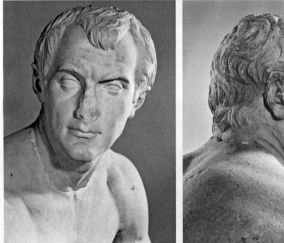

Fig. 3. Heroic portrait statue in the National Archaeological Museum, Naples. It stood in a niche in the *scaenae frons* of the first-century BC theatre at Cassino (Casinum), with an inscription describing the honorand as *patron (us) praef (ecturae)*; identified as Varro by Coarelli 1996b.418–33.

proconsulship must have been held between the Sertorian campaign and the war against the pirates, in either 70 and 69 or 69 and 68 BC. It is also likely that Varro was elected to one of the priestly colleges, perhaps the *quindecimuiri sacris faciundis*.[41]

Already as a young man he was a constitutional expert, very conscious of the limits of a magistrate's authority.[42] His view of the proper rights of a citizen comes out very clearly in a precious verbatim quotation from the *Antiquities*:[43]

qui potestatem neque uocationis populi uiritim habent neque prensionis, eos magistratus a priuato in ius uocari est potestas. M. Laeuinus aedilis curulis a priuato in praetorem in ius est eductus; nunc stipati seruis publicis non modo prendi non possunt sed etiam ultro submouent populum.

It is legally possible for a private citizen even to summon to law those magistrates who do not have the power of summoning the People as individuals or of arrest. Marcus Laevinus, a curule aedile, was brought to law before the praetor by a private citizen. Nowadays they are escorted by public servants; not only can they not be arrested, but they even go so far as to move the People away.

That sense of the People's status fits in well with the Varronian account of Romulus' city of equals that we identified in Chapter 4. It may also be reflected in Varro's use of such un-Ciceronian locutions as 'the Senate of the Roman People', 'the public augurs', 'the public gods of the Roman People',[44] appropriate to a traditionally egalitarian way of thinking about the republic.

---

seiten der Nobilität gestanden hat', and therefore would not have held office 'unter der Herrschaft der Gegenpartei, der Marianer'; Cichorius' own proposal (70 BC), as he admits, does not leave time for a praetorship and proconsulship before the pirate war of 67 BC.

[41] Cichorius 1922.197–9, an ingenious inference from Varro *De uita sua* fr. 1 Peter = Charisius *Ars grammatica* 1.89 Keil (1.113 Barwick): since Varro referred in his autobiography to Isis and Serapis, he may have been officially involved in the banning of the Egyptian cults in 59–58 BC (Varro *Antiquitates diuinae* fr. 46a–b Cardauns = Tertullian *Ad nationes* 1.10.17, *Apologeticus* 6.8; cf. Varro *De gente populi Romani* fr. 14 Fraccaro = Augustine *City of God* 18.5).

[42] Varro *Antiquitates humanae* fr. 21.1 Mirsch = Aulus Gellius 13.12.6: as *triumuir capitalis* he successfully challenged a tribune's right to summon him.

[43] Varro *Antiquitates humanae* fr. 21.3 Mirsch = Aulus Gellius 13.13.4.

[44] Respectively Varro fr. 58 Funaioli = Aulus Gellius 17.21.48 (*ab Atheniensibus ad senatum populi Romani negotii publici gratia legati sunt*); Varro *De lingua Latina* 5.33 (*ut nostri augures publici disserunt*); Varro *Antiquitates diuinae* fr. 228 Cardauns = Augustine *City of God* 7.17 (*de diis, inquit, populi Romani publicis . . . in hoc libro scribam*); cf. also Varro *Res rusticae* 1.1.3 on the Sibyl's books consulted *publice*. To be

At the time Varro came back from his long service in Spain, that way of thinking was under threat. The aristocrats whom Sulla had left in power proved themselves shockingly corrupt. The traditional checks to such exploitation of authority—the censorship, the power of the tribunes—had been removed by Sulla, but now the Roman People demanded their restoration, and in 71 BC they elected Pompey consul to carry it out.[45] Pompey asked his friend Varro to brief him on the proper procedure for summoning and consulting the Senate.[46] The little book Varro wrote for him is likely to have made clear the Senate's dependence on the authority of the Roman People.

The People were very anxious about the rivalry between Pompey and his colleague-elect, M. Crassus. It was only seven years since a quarrel between two consuls had resulted in civil war and brutal reprisals.[47] At a public meeting they called on the two to be reconciled, and only when the handshake was witnessed and acclaimed were they freed from their fear of new bloodshed.[48]

Eleven years later the situation was similar. Pompey had returned victorious from the great war the People had entrusted to him. The senatorial establishment was now confident again, and among its political victories was the defeat of a land-distribution bill proposed by one of the tribunes. That would have provided land for the citizens who had spent the last six years fighting for Rome in far-off lands; but the Senate would not allow it to pass.[49] Once again it was necessary for rivals to make common cause, but this time the People's consul would be Caesar:[50]

fair to Cicero, he does once refer to himself as *augur publicus*, in a letter full of private 'auguries' (*Ad familiares* 6.6.7, to A. Caecina in 46 BC); and see *In Verrem* 1.156–7, 3.93, 4.25, and 4.42 for his use of *senator populi Romani* in 69 BC.

[45] Cicero *Diuinatio in Caecilium* 7–10, *In Verrem* 1.43–5; Plutarch *Pompey* 21.4–5, 22.3. For the Senate's *dominatio . . . in omni re publica* see Cicero *In Verrem* 2.5.175 (p. 11 above).

[46] Aulus Gellius 14.7.1: *uti commentarium faceret* εἰσαγωγικόν (*sic enim Varro ipse appellat*).

[47] Fear of new *stasis*: Appian *Civil Wars* 1.121.561–2, Plutarch *Pompey* 21.3. Lepidus and Catulus in 78 BC: pp. 70–1 above.

[48] Appian *Civil Wars* 1.121.563–5. Appian ends his first book at this point, 'in about the sixtieth year of the civil wars, from the murder of Tiberius Gracchus'.

[49] Cicero *Ad Atticum* 1.18.6, 19.4 (cf. 2.9.2 on the *inuidiosa senatus potentia*); Dio Cassius 37.49–50.

[50] Appian *Civil Wars* 2.9.33 (cf. 4.47.202 for Varro as φιλόσοφός τε καὶ ἱστορίας συγγραφεύς). Caesar as *popularis*: Cicero *In Catilinam* 4.9, *Ad Atticum* 2.3.3–4, 19.2, 20.4, 21.1.

ἀγανακτῶν οὖν ὁ Πομπήιος προσεταιρίζεται Καίσαρα, συμπράξειν ἐς τὴν
ὑπατείαν ἐπομόσας· ὁ δ' εὐθὺς αὐτῷ Κράσσον διήλασσε. καὶ τρεῖς οἵδε τὸ
μέγιστον ἐπὶ πᾶσι κράτος ἔχοντες τὰς χρείας ἀλλήλοις συνηράνιζον.
καί τις αὐτῶν τήνδε τὴν συμφροσύνην συγγραφεὺς Οὐάρρων ἐνὶ βιβλίῳ περιλαβὼν
ἐπέγραψε Τρικάρανον.

Pompey was indignant and took Caesar into alliance, promising to work
with him for the consulship. Caesar immediately reconciled Pompey with
Crassus, and these three men, who had the greatest power in all things, put
their requirements together. A writer called Varro, encompassing their
consensus in one little volume, gave it the title *Tricaranus* [*Three-Heads*].

The nature of Varro's *Tricaranus* is a controversial question (to which
we shall return in the next chapter), but we have no reason to suppose
that its tone was critical;[51] on the contrary, the consensus of the three
allies was something to be glad of, like that of Pompey and Crassus in
71 BC.[52] Their opponents were the men whose luxurious villas Varro
later denounced as harmful to the republic.[53] The Roman People
wanted legislation for the distribution of land, and Caesar provided
it.[54] It was the way he overcame the Senate's obstructiveness that gave
rise to the optimate rhetoric about slavery and tyranny that we find in
Cicero's letters; Varro, on the other hand, helped to put the legislation
into practice as one of the *uigintiuiri agris dividendis*.[55]

We know what Cicero thought about the Roman People. The word
he uses in his private letters is *faex*, 'dregs'.[56] In his political dialogues,

[51] As is usually assumed: see e.g. Astbury 1967.407, Coffey 1976.150 ('a political
attack on the First Triumvirate'); Zucchelli 1976.615 ('l'attacco di Varrone'); Krenkel
2002.xiv ('Der Dreier-Bund des Caesar mit Pompeius und Crassus war Zielscheibe
des konservativen, traditionalistischen Republikaners Varro'), cf. n. 40 above. Better
judgement is shown by Fantham 2003.111: 'a political comment on the so-called first
triumvirate, but hardly a hostile one'.

[52] Mazzarino 1966.396: 'certamente, egli salutò con gioia la *concordia* (*symphrosýne*,
App. II 33) di Pompeo Cesare Crasso...'; cf. Plutarch *Crassus* 12.2 on the φιλοφροσύνη
of 71 BC.

[53] Varro *Res rusticae* 1.13.7 (*pessimo publico*); cf. 1.2.10 (*regie*), 3.2.16, 3.10, 6.6
(*luxuria*).

[54] Dio Cassius 38.1.1, 2.3, 4.1, 5.3, 6.4, 7.4; cf. Cicero *Ad Atticum* 2.3.4, 21.1 on the
wishes of the *multitudo*.

[55] Varro *Res rusticae* 1.2.10, Pliny *Nat. Hist.* 7.176.

[56] Cicero *Ad Atticum* 1.16.11 (*apud sordem urbis et faecem*, July 61), 2.1.8 (*in
Romuli faece*, June 60), *Ad Q. fratrem* 2.5.3 (*apud perditissimam illam atque infimam
faecem populi*, Mar. 56). Mistranslated as 'shit' by Morstein-Marx 2004.128
(cf. Dench 2005.16); in fact, Cicero disapproved of that particular term of abuse
(*De oratore* 3.164).

the idea of a Rome of equals is conspicuous by its absence: Romulus is praised not for setting up the all-comers' Asylum, but for creating an advisory Senate of *optimates*.[57] Equality is itself unequal, because it ignores differences of status.[58] Servius Tullius is commended as the most politically intelligent of the kings, because he kept the fundamental rule of politics, that the greatest number should not have the greatest power.[59] The verdict of 'Laelius the wise', a privileged contributor to the *De republica* dialogue (and a figure in whom Cicero liked to see himself), was that a state which was wholly in the control of the multitude did not deserve to be called a *res publica* at all.[60]

For Cicero the *populus* is 'unbridled', 'untamed',[61] needing the control of the Senate, or the *optimates*, or a single wise statesman, holding the reins.[62] That single wise statesman, the ideal citizen of Cicero's ideal republic,[63] is described in a different metaphor as the helmsman (*gubernator*), steering the ship of state.[64] How much the idea mattered to him may be seen from a letter to Atticus in the anxious days of February 49 BC, as Caesar was pursuing Pompey to Brundisium:[65]

[57] Cicero *De republica* 2.14–15, 23 (see pp. 76–7 above for the Asylum).

[58] Ibid. 1.43 (*ipsa aequabilitas est iniqua cum habet nullos gradus dignitatis*), 1.53 (*cum enim par habetur honos summis et infimis . . . ipsa aequitas iniquissima est*). Cf. *De legibus* 3.24 on the creation of the tribunate as a concession by the Senate: *inuentum est temperamentum quo tenuiores cum principibus aequari se putarent.*

[59] Cicero *De republica* 2.39: *curauitque quod semper in re publica tenendum est, ne plurimum ualeant plurimi.* Cf. 2.37 (Laelius) on Servius Tullius (*is qui mihi uidetur ex omnibus in re publica uidisse plurimum*); *De legibus* 3.44 on the *comitia centuriata*, set up by Servius (*descriptus enim populus censu ordinibus aetatibus plus adhibet consilii quam fuse in tribus conuocatus*).

[60] *De republica* 3.45: *ac nullam quidem citius negauerim esse rem publicam quam istam quae tota plane sit in multitudinis potestate.* For Laelius, cf. 1.8, 31.3 (privileged status); *Brutus* 213, *De amicitia* 1.1, *De officiis* 2.40, 3.16 (*sapientia*); *Ad familiares* 5.7.3 (Cicero as Laelius).

[61] *De republica* 1.53, 65 (*effrenatus*); 1.9, 49, 68 (*indomitus*).

[62] Reins (*habenae*): *De oratore* 1.226 (Senate), *De republica* 1.9 (*sapiens*). *Auctoritas*: *De republica* 2.55–6 (*principes*), *De legibus* 3.27–8 (Senate), 37–8 (*optimates*).

[63] Cicero *Ad Q. fratrem* 3.5.1: *de optimo statu ciuitatis et de optimo ciue.* For the *optimus status ciuitatis*, cf. *De republica* 1.33–4, 70–1; 2.33, 40–1; *De legibus* 1.15, 3.4.

[64] Cicero *De republica* 2.51 (*rector et gubernator rei publicae*), 5.5–6 (*rector*). *Gubernare rem publicam* (or *ciuitatem*): 1.45, 52; 2.15, 47; *De legibus* 3.28. *Regere rem publicam* (or *ciuitatem*): 1.11, 42, 47, 53; 2.15, 23; *De legibus* 3.14.

[65] Cicero *Ad Atticum* 8.11.1–2 = *De republica* 5.8 (trans. Shackleton Bailey, slightly adjusted). For *moderator rei publicae*, cf. *De republica* 1.45; also *De legibus* 2.15 (gods as *moderatores*).

consumo igitur omne tempus considerans quanta uis sit illius uiri quem nostris
<libris> satis diligenter, ut tibi quidem uidemur, expressimus. tenesne igitur
moderatorem illum rei publicae quo referre uelimus omnia? nam sic quinto,
opinor, in libro loquitur Scipio:

> *ut enim gubernatori cursus secundus, medico salus, imperatori uictoria,*
> *sic huic moderatori rei publicae beata ciuium uita proposita est, ut opibus*
> *firma, copiis locuples, gloria ampla, uirtute honesta sit; huius enim operis*
> *maximi inter homines atque optimi illum esse perfectorem uolo.*

hoc Gnaeus noster cum antea numquam tum in hac causa minime cogitauit.

I therefore spend all my time reflecting on the essential greatness of the
figure I have portrayed conscientiously enough, in your opinion at least, in
my volumes. Do you remember the standard which I want my ideal statesman to apply to all his actions? This is what Scipio says in Book V, I think:

> Just as a fair voyage is the object of the helmsman, health of the
> physician, victory of the general, so our statesman's object is the
> happiness of his countrymen—to promote power for their security,
> wealth for their abundance, fame for their dignity, virtue for their good
> name. This is the work I would have him accomplish, the greatest and
> noblest in human society.

To this our Gnaeus has never given a thought, least of all in the present
context.

Power, wealth, fame, virtue ... The People had to be kept in check in
order to achieve the values of the *optimates*. It is hard to resist the
impression that the ideal statesman was Cicero's self-flattering vision
of himself.[66]

The *De republica* was a great success,[67] as it deserved to be. What did
Varro make of it? From what little we know of his political views, we may
guess that the 'helmsman of the state' was not much to his taste. A few
years later, in the great work on the Latin language that he dedicated
to Cicero, he used the *gubernator* metaphor in a significantly different
way. Who has the right to correct linguistic usage? Only the People:[68]

populus enim in sua potestate, singuli in illius; itaque ut suam quisque
consuetudinem, si mala est, corrigere debet, sic populus suam. ego populi
consuetudinis non sum ut dominus, at ille meae est. ut rationi optemperare

---

[66] See e.g. Cicero *De diuinatione* 2.3 (*cum gubernacula rei publicae tenebamus*); *De
legibus* 3.37 (*eamque optimam rem publicam esse dico quam hic* [i.e. Cicero] *consul
constituerat, quae sit in potestate optimorum*). See now Lintott 2008.239–41.

[67] Cicero *Ad familiares* 8.7.4 (Caelius, May 51 BC): *tui politici libri omnibus uigent*.

[68] Varro *De lingua Latina* 9.6.

debet gubernator, gubernatori unus quisque in naui, sic populus rationi, nos singuli populo.

The People has power over itself, individuals are in the power of the People. So just as each person should correct his own usage if it is bad, so the People should correct its own. I am not in the position of a master of the People's usage, but it is of mine. As the helmsman ought to obey reason, and each member of the crew ought to obey the helmsman, so the People ought to obey reason, and we ought to obey the People.

III

Twice since the death of Sulla, in 71 and in 60 BC, the People's champions had pooled their resources against their common enemy. That did not happen in 50 BC. On the contrary, in December of that year the *optimates* requested Pompey to take command of all military forces in Italy and defend the republic against Caesar.[69] Pompey agreed—and the reason for that may be found in the violent events of two years before.

On 18 January 52 BC, a prominent senator was murdered in cold blood on the Via Appia.[70] The dead man was Publius Clodius, who as tribune in 58 had had Cicero sent into exile by popular vote for putting Roman citizens to death without trial. The man who ordered his killing was Titus Milo, who as tribune the following year had made it possible for Cicero to be recalled. At this time there was no effective government in Rome; constant political infighting had prevented the election of consuls and praetors, and only the tribunes were in office.[71]

Two of the tribunes encouraged the indignant populace to take Clodius' body from his house to the Forum, where it was displayed on the Rostra as they inveighed against Milo in a formal *contio*.[72] The People took deliberate action:[73]

---

[69] Appian *Civil Wars* 2.31.121, Plutarch *Pompey* 29.1, Dio Cassius 40.64.4.
[70] Asconius 31–2C, Dio Cassius 40.48.2; see below, pp. 188–91.
[71] Asconius 30–1C, Dio Cassius 40.46.3, 48.1. Cf. Asconius 34C: *factum erat s.c. ut interrex et tribuni plebis et Cn. Pompeius, qui pro cos. ad urbem erat, uiderent ne quid detrimenti res publica caperet.*
[72] Asconius 32–3C, Dio Cassius 40.48.3–49.2.
[73] Dio Cassius 40.49.2–3, cf. Asconius 33C.

τὸ γὰρ σῶμα τοῦ Κλωδίου ἀράμενοι ἔς τε τὸ βουλευτήριον ἐσήνεγκαν καὶ
εὐθέτησαν, καὶ μετὰ τοῦτο πυρὰν ἐκ τῶν βάθρων συννήσαντες ἔκαυσαν καὶ
ἐκεῖνο καὶ τὸ συνέδριον. οὕτω τε οὐχ ὁρμῇ τινι, οἷα που τοὺς ὄχλους ἐξαπιναία
καταλαμβάνει, ἀλλὰ ἐκ προαιρέσεως αὐτὸ ἔπραξαν ὥστε καὶ τὴν ἐνάτην τὸ
περίδειπνον ἐν αὐτῇ τῇ ἀγορᾷ, τυφομένου ἔτι τοῦ βουλτηρίου, ποιῆσαι.

They lifted up the body of Clodius and carried it into the Senate-house. They
laid it out [as for a funeral], and after that, heaping up a pyre from the
benches, they burned the body and the Senate building together. And they
did this not from some sudden impulse, such as often takes hold of crowds,
but so deliberately that even at the ninth hour they were holding the funeral
feast in the Forum, with the Senate-house still smouldering.

It was a demonstration of sovereignty.

Of the People's three champions against the aristocracy, Crassus
was dead and Caesar far away in Gaul. So they demanded that Pompey
be elected either dictator or consul.[74] For the *optimates*, the least bad
option was that he should be consul, but alone; Bibulus proposed it at
a Senate meeting (he didn't want Caesar recalled to be Pompey's
colleague), Cato added his support ('any government is better than
none'), and the election duly took place.[75] Milo was immediately put
on trial and condemned, with an armed guard in the Forum to protect
him and his defence counsel from the anger of the populace.[76]

Pompey's emergency legislation was regarded as the restoration of
political morality, a necessary healing process for the sick republic.[77]
His reputation as a statesman had never been higher.[78]

When his consulship was over, Pompey still had his proconsular
imperium from the *lex Trebonia* in 55 BC. He had been granted it by
the Roman People, and would resign it, as he observed pointedly in a
letter to the Senate, when those who gave it wished to take it back.[79]

---

[74] Asconius 33C, Dio Cassius 40.50.3.

[75] Dio Cassius 40.50.4; Plutarch *Cato minor* 47.3; Asconius 35–6C (*ab interrege…
creatus est*), omitting the necessary formality of the vote.

[76] Asconius 40–2C.

[77] Tacitus *Annals* 3.28.1: *tertium consul corrigendis moribus delectus*. Cf. Cicero *Ad
Atticum* 8.3.3 (*defensor rei publicae*), *Pro Milone* 68 (*omnes rei publicae partes aegras…
sanare*), Appian *Civil Wars* 2.28.107 (ἐς θεραπείαν τῆς πόλεως), Plutarch *Pompey* 55.3
(ἰατρός).

[78] Cicero *Ad Atticum* 7.1.4 (*in illo diuino tertio consulatu*), Velleius Paterculus
2.48.2 (*primus omnium ciuis*), Seneca *Ad Marciam de consolatione* 20.4 (*indubitatus
populi Romani princeps*); cf. Plutarch *Pompey* 57.1–2.

[79] Appian *Civil Wars* 2.28: ἑκὼν ἀποθήσομαι τοῖς ἀπολαβεῖν θέλουσιν.

Evidently Pompey shared the view of his friend Varro (now his legate in Spain, with two legions) about the sovereignty of the Roman People.[80] There is no reason to doubt his sincerity; after all, he had benefited from that sovereignty throughout his career. His position was quite consistent with Cicero's conviction that both Pompey and Caesar aimed at *dominatio*:[81] as the *optimates* saw it, holding power by popular vote without the benefit of the Senate's authority was exactly what *dominatio* meant.[82]

Also as the *optimates* saw it, the killing of Clodius had been a noble act; Milo should have been rewarded, not condemned.[83] So when that deputation came to Pompey in December 50 BC, it was not because there had been a meeting of minds. The hardliners needed Pompey, and the danger that Caesar would enter Italy with his army gave them their chance. Would Pompey defend the republic by force of arms? Pompey gave the honourable answer: 'Only if there is no better way.'[84] That was enough. The hardliners were not interested in negotiation; they would make sure that no better way was possible.[85]

It was a crisis that faced every Roman senator with acutely difficult choices. The respective reactions of Cicero and Varro are both attested in our sources, but in very different ways.

For Cicero, we have the best conceivable evidence—over eighty letters to Atticus from mid-December 50 to mid-May 49, in which he agonizes over the conflicting demands of honour, friendship, and the safety of his family.[86] Macaulay's judgement is worth recalling:[87]

---

[80] See n. 68 above: *populus enim in sua potestate, singuli in illius*. Varro in Spain: Caesar *De bello ciuili* 1.38.1–2; for the date, Cicero *Ad familiares* 9.13.1 (*ante bellum*).

[81] Cicero *Ad Atticum* 8.11.2 (*dominatio quaesita ab utroque est...uterque regnare uult*), 10.4.4 (*utrique semper patriae salus et dignitas posterior sua dominatione et domesticis commodis fuit*), 10.7.1 (*regnandi contentio est*).

[82] Cicero *Ad Atticum* 2.21.1 (n. 20 above); the *lex Trebonia* had attracted no less senatorial hostility than Caesar's legislation in 59 (Dio Cassius 39.33.2–36.1). Cf. also *Ad Atticum* 8.3.6 on Cinna's *dominatio* in 87–84 BC.

[83] Cicero *Pro Milone* 72–91; Asconius 41C (Brutus and others), 53–4C (Cato); see below, pp. 189–90.

[84] Appian *Civil Wars* 2.31.107 (εἰ μή τι κρεῖσσον).

[85] Plutarch *Pompey* 59.2–4, *Caesar* 31.1–2, Appian *Civil Wars* 2.32.127–9.

[86] Cicero *Ad Atticum* 7.4–10.18, esp. 7.9.4 (*equidem dies noctesque torqueor*, 27 Dec.), 7.21.3 (*mira me ἀπορία torquet*, 8 Feb.), 9.12.1 and 4 (*torqueor infelix... nunc doleo, nunc torqueor*, 20 Mar.). The clearest statements of his motivation are 9.10 and 9.13 (18 and 23 Mar.), 10.4.1–5 (14 Apr.), 10.8 (2 May); see also 8.11d (to Pompey, 27 Feb.), 9.11a (to Caesar, 19 or 20 Mar.). See now Lintott 2008.275–300 for an excellent running commentary on the whole sequence.

[87] Journal, 28 and 31 Aug. 1856 (Thomas 2008.4.323.324).

I have been reading of late those most interesting letters of Cicero which were written just after Caesar had taken up arms. What materials for history! What a picture of a mind which well deserves to be studied! . . . No novel ever interested me half so much, and often as I have read them, every sentence seems new.

Cicero wanted a negotiated solution; anything was preferable to civil war.[88] He had no confidence in Pompey's strategy, and no trust in his motives.[89] But he had an emotional commitment to him which outweighed everything else,[90] and when Pompey left Italy Cicero knew he would have to follow him, even without hope.[91]

In Varro's case our evidence comes from Caesar. The context is the aftermath of Pompey's flight from Brundisium:[92]

M. Varro in ulteriore Hispania initio cognitis eis rebus quae sunt in Italia gestae diffidens Pompeianis rebus amicissime de Caesare loquebatur: praeoccupatum sese legatione ab Cn. Pompeio teneri obstrictum fide; necessitudinem quidem sibi nihilo minorem cum Caesare intercedere, neque se ignorare quod esset officium legati qui fiduciariam operam obtineret, quae uires suae, quae uoluntas erga Caesarem totius prouinciae. haec omnibus ferebat sermonibus neque se in ullam partem mouebat.

Marcus Varro in Further Spain, having heard the news from Italy and doubting the success of Pompey's cause, initially spoke of Caesar in the friendliest terms. He himself, he said, was constrained by the prior obligation of his duty as Gnaeus Pompeius' legate, but the relationship that existed between him and Caesar was no less close; he knew what was required of a legate holding a charge of trust, but he also knew what his own resources were and how popular Caesar was throughout the province. This was what he said to everyone, and he made no move either way.

So begins Caesar's brief, dry narrative of how Varro then changed his tune and rashly decided to resist; one of his legions mutinied, and he had to surrender the other.[93] The story could have been told differently:

---

[88] *Ad Atticum* 7.6.2 (*sentiam enim omnia facienda ne armis decertetur*, 18 Dec.), 7.14.3 (*uel iniusta* [sc. *pax*] *utilior est quam iustissimum bellum cum ciuibus*, 25 Jan.), 9.6.7 (11 Mar.).

[89] See n. 81 above; *Ad Atticum* 8.11.2, 9.7.3, 9.10.2 and 6, 9.11.3, 10.7.1 for Pompey as a potential Sulla.

[90] *Ad Atticum* 9.5.3, quoting *Iliad* 18.96–9 (Achilles and Patroclus); cf. also 7.3.5, 7.20.2, 7.26.3, 8.7.2, 9.1.4, 9.6.4, 9.13.3.

[91] Ibid. 10.2.2 (5 or 6 May): *sine spe conamur ulla.*

[92] Caesar *De bello ciuili* 2.17.1–3.

[93] Caesar *De bello ciuili* 2.17.4–21.3.

how Varro, knowing himself outmatched, still did his duty to his friend as best he could.

Varro, like Cicero, made his way to Pompey's headquarters at Dyrrachium.[94] For the moment, that was where legitimate authority lay. The consuls were there, with at least four of the praetors and a majority of the Senate.[95] Cato was there too, having yielded Sicily to Caesar's legate Pollio. 'Do you bring the order of the Senate, or of the People?', he had demanded, and Pollio could only answer, 'I was sent by the man who controls Italy.'[96]

But the moral advantage soon slipped away. The leading *optimates* were more interested in the spoils of war than in constitutional correctness,[97] and once Caesar was legally elected as consul for the following year,[98] there was no argument from legitimacy left to use. Caesar claimed to have made war in defence of the freedom of the Roman People,[99] and now the People had given him constitutional authority.

Varro had dedicated his *Divine Antiquities* to Caesar as *pontifex maximus*;[100] now he was stuck with men like Domitius Ahenobarbus, Metellus Scipio, and Lentulus Spinther, who were quarrelling about who should have that honour once Pompey had got Caesar out of the way for them.[101] He must have found the experience even more difficult than Cicero did.[102]

---

[94] Cicero *De diuinatione* 1.68, 2.114; Plutarch *Caesar* 36.

[95] Velleius Paterculus 2.49.4 (*consulesque et maior pars senatus*). Praetors: Cicero *Ad Atticum* 8.12a.4, 9.8.1, Caesar *De bello ciuili* 1.24.3, 3.5.3 (C. Coponius, L. Torquatus, P. Rutilius Lupus); Velleius Paterculus 2.53.1 (M. Favonius).

[96] Appian *Civil Wars* 2.40.162; cf. 2.50.207 (Pompey on Caesar usurping the power of the *populus*).

[97] Cicero *Ad Atticum* 9.11.4 (Scipio, Faustus Sulla, Libo), 11.6.6 (Lentulus); Caesar *De bello ciuili* 1.4.2–3 (Lentulus and Scipio), Velleius Paterculus 2.49.3 (Lentulus). See below, p. 200.

[98] Caesar *De bello ciuili* 3.1.1 (*is enim erat annus quo per leges ei consulem fieri liceret*); Dio Cassius 41.43.1 (ἐκ τῶν νόμων).

[99] Caesar *De bello ciuili* 1.22.5, 3.91.2.

[100] Lactantius *Institutiones diuinae* 1.6.7, Augustine *City of God* 7.35.

[101] Caesar *De bello ciuili* 3.82.3–83.1, Plutarch *Pompey* 67.5, *Caesar* 42.2, Appian *Civil Wars* 2.69.285. For the *optimates'* attitude to Pompey see Plutarch *Pompey* 67.2–3, Cicero 38.1, Appian *Civil Wars* 2.67.278.

[102] Cicero *Ad familiares* 9.6.3 (to Varro, June 46 BC): *crudeliter enim otiosis minabantur, eratque iis et tua inuisa uoluntas et mea oratio.* For examples of Cicero's *oratio* at the time, cf. Plutarch *Cicero* 38.2–6.

The end of this unhappy episode illustrates the difference between the two men. When the shattering news of Pompey's defeat and flight came through to those left behind at Dyrrachium, the question for Cato was how to fight on. Plentiful military resources were still available, including a substantial fleet; but who was to command them? Here was Varro, full of military experience, including the command of a fleet in these very waters in 67 BC; true, he was in his late sixties, but he had led a legionary army only the year before. But Cato offered the command to Cicero.[103]

That was partly because Cicero was a *consularis*, and still (for what it was worth) in possession of proconsular *imperium*.[104] But it was probably more important that he was the obvious choice as the figurehead of the *optimates*—so much so that when he refused the command it is said that Pompey's son drew his sword and would have killed him as a traitor if Cato had not intervened.[105] Varro, in military terms incomparably better qualified, evidently wouldn't do.

IV

All of this long story may help to explain the paradox with which this chapter began, of Cicero's relationship with Varro in 46–45 BC. On the one hand, the semi-public letters *to* Varro, which we may be sure were meant to be read to others as well,[106] present two learned elder statesmen with everything in common; on the other, the private letters to Atticus *about* Varro reveal two touchy characters quite uncertain of each other's motives.[107] The main reason was no doubt literary rivalry—Varro's huge output had made him a celebrity[108]—but a less than complete political sympathy may have been part of it too.

---

[103] Plutarch *Cato minor* 55.3, *Cicero* 39.1–2.
[104] Cicero *Ad Atticum* 11.7.1 (his lictors, Dec. 48 BC).
[105] Plutarch *Cicero* 39.2, cf. *Cato minor* 55.3. Cicero was still the obvious figure-head on the Ides of March (Cicero *Philippics* 2.28–30, Dio Cassius 44.20.4).
[106] Cf. Cicero *Ad Atticum* 15.17.2 (reading a letter *in acroasi*), 1.16.8 (unusually, an *epistula quam nolo aliis legi*).
[107] See above, respectively nn. 2–8 and 10–13.
[108] Cicero *Ad Atticum* 13.19.3 (Varro was ἔνδοξος).

There is no sign of any such friction in the revised *Academica*.
Cicero begins by putting into Varro's mouth a self-deprecating
account of his contribution to philosophy as education:[109]

> *quae autem nemo adhuc docuerat nec erat unde studiosi scire possent, ea*
> *quantum potui (nihil enim magnopere meorum miror) feci ut essent nota*
> *nostris; a Graecis enim peti non poterant ac post L. Aelii nostri occasum ne a*
> *Latinis quidem. et tamen in illis ueteribus nostris, quae Menippum imitati non*
> *interpretati quadam hilaritate conspersimus, multa admixta ex intima philo-*
> *sophia, multa dicta dialectice, quae quo facilius minus docti intellegerent,*
> *iucunditate quadam ad legendum inuitati; in laudationibus, in his ipsis*
> *antiquitatum prooemiis philosophiae <more> scribere uoluimus, si modo*
> *consecuti sumus.*

'There are some things that no-one had taught before, and people interested
in the subject had no way of knowing them. You couldn't get them from
Greek authors, and after the passing of our friend Lucius Aelius, not from
Latin ones either. Those are the things I have made known to the Romans—
so far as I could, for I'm no great admirer of my own works. Still, I did
sprinkle some humour over that old stuff of mine from Menippus (imitated,
not translated), in which many ingredients from the heart of philosophy
were stirred in, and many things said in a dialectical way, so that less
educated people would be invited to read them by a kind of enjoyment
and find them easier to understand. In my eulogies, and in the introductions
to the actual *Antiquities*, I wanted—though I don't know whether I've
succeeded—to write in the proper manner of philosophy.'

Varro is made to refer to the most conspicuous parts of his enormously varied *oeuvre*. The 'old stuff' was the 150 books of Menippean
satires, which we shall look at in the next chapter. The 'eulogies' were
evidently the seventy-six books of *Logistorici*, essays on topics of
general interest which were based on the lives and characters of
particular Roman citizens.[110] The *Antiquities* were his masterpiece,

---

[109] Cicero *Academica* 1.8. I use the Teubner text (Otto Plasberg, 1922); the Loeb
text is much less satisfactory, and at one important point mistranslated.
[110] See e.g. *Atticus: On Gifts; Catus: On Bringing Up Children; Curio: On Worship-
ping the Gods; Fundanius Gallus: On Remarkable Phenomena; Marius: On Fortune;
Messalla: On Physical Health; Orestes: On Madness; Pius: On Peace; Scaurus: On the
Origins of Drama; Sisenna: On History; Tubero: On the Origins of the Human Race;*
fragments in Chappuis 1868. ('Orestes' was probably the son not of Agamemnon but
of L. Aurelius Orestes, consul in 103 BC.) For the number of volumes of both
Menippeae and *Logistorici*, see Jerome's (partial) list of Varro's works (Funaioli
1907.182).

twenty-five books on *res humanae* and sixteen on *res diuinae*, published probably in the fifties BC.[111]

Cicero knew that Varro's next major work, the twenty-five books *De lingua Latina*, would be dedicated to him.[112] He paid back the compliment with a deservedly famous tribute:[113]

tum ego, sunt, inquam, ista Varro. nam nos in nostra urbe peregrinantis errantisque tamquam hospites tui libri quasi domum deduxerunt, ut possemus aliquando qui et ubi essemus agnoscere. tu aetatem patriae, tu descriptiones temporum, tu sacrorum iura tu sacerdotum, tu domesticam tu bellicam disciplinam, tu sedum regionum locorum tu omnium diuinarum humanarumque rerum nomina genera officia causas aperuisti.

'Yes indeed, Varro,' I said. 'When we were strangers abroad and lost in our own city, your books led us back home, so to speak, so that at last we were able to recognise who and where we were. You revealed the age of our native land, its divisions of time, the rules of sacrifices and priesthoods; discipline at home and at war; the location of regions and places; and the names, types, functions and causes of all matters human and divine.'

Cicero here puts his finger on the quality that was characteristic of all Varro's writings—the aim to be of service to his fellow-citizens.[114] He himself claimed the same motive for the philosophical dialogues he wrote in 45–44 BC;[115] but there was a difference. Cicero never forgot his political agenda. Under Caesar's dictatorship he couldn't make speeches in the Senate or the Forum, so he used his books instead.[116] And once Caesar was safely dead, the optimate rhetoric came out in full force.[117] There is no such factious polemic in what survives of Varro's work.

---

[111] Contents listed in Augustine *City of God* 6.3; fragments in Mirsch 1882 and Cardauns 1976.

[112] Cicero *Academica* 1.2–3, *Ad Atticum* 13.12.3.

[113] Cicero *Academica* 1.9 (trans. Wallace-Hadrill 2005.66).

[114] Varro *Antiquitates diuinae* fr. 3 Cardauns = Augustine *City of God* 4.22 (*praestare se ciuibus suis*); cf. Varro *Res rusticae* 1.1.3, Pliny *Nat. Hist.* 35.11.

[115] Cicero *De diuinatione* 2.1–7, *De finibus* 1.10.

[116] Cicero *De diuinatione* 2.7 (*in libris enim sententiam dicebamus, contionabar*), *De officiis* 2.3.

[117] Cicero *De diuinatione* 2.23 (Caesar killed *a nobilissimis ciuibus*), 2.110 (Caesar as *rex*); *De officiis* 1.112, 2.23, 3.19 (Caesar as *tyrannus*); 3.83–4 (Caesar as *rex*); 1.26, 2.27–8, 2.84 (Caesar's abuse of power). See Dyck 1996.29–36 on *De officiis* as 'Cicero's political legacy' (30).

Both men had thought profoundly about the history of Rome (witness the *Antiquities* and the *De republica*), and in the fateful and dramatic months after the Ides of March each of them turned to historical writing.[118] Varro's work took the form of a biography of the Roman People.[119] Cicero's was entitled *My Policies*.[120]

In fact, Cicero's policies led straight to the Triumvirate and the proscriptions. His great, brave, doomed attempt to be the 'helmsman of the republic' against Antony (a legally elected consul) was the last fling of optimate politics in action, as divisive now as when Scipio Nasica led the senators to beat Tiberius Gracchus to death. According to Cicero in 44 BC, the killing of Gracchus had been a wise policy of benefit to the republic,[121] as he believed that of Caesar had been as well. For all the horror of Antony's revenge, the severed head and hands on the *rostra*, we should not forget Livy's measured judgement on Cicero's death:[122]

quae uere aestimanti minus indigna uideri potuit, quod a uictore inimico <nihil> crudelius passus erat quam quod eiusdem fortunae conpos ipse fecisset.

On an honest estimate it might have seemed less undeserved, in that he had suffered at the hands of his victorious enemy no more cruelly than he himself would have acted if he had had the same good fortune.

As we saw in the last chapter, Macaulay thought that was a just assessment.[123]

Varro too was proscribed. His property was confiscated and his library plundered.[124] But he survived, because his friends were determined

---

[118] Cicero *Ad Atticum* 14.17.6 (*librum illum meum* ἀνέκδοτον, 3 May 44 BC), 16.11.1–3 (*nostrum opus*, 5 Nov.), 16.13a(b).2 (*ardeo studio historiae*, 11 Nov.). Varro *De gente populi Romani* fr. 20 Fraccaro = Arnobius *Aduersus nationes* 5.8 (*ad usque Hirti consulatum et Pansae*—i.e. 43 BC, though they were already designated by Caesar).

[119] Four books *De gente populi Romani* (fragments in Fraccaro 1907), and four books *De uita populi Romani* (fragments in Riposati 1939 and Salvadore 2004). For '*de gente*' as a structural part of biography, cf. Suetonius *Diuus Augustus* 1.1, *Tiberius* 1.1, *Nero* 1.1, *Galba* 2–3.1, *Otho* 1.1, *Vitellius* 1.1.

[120] Asconius 83C (*in expositione consiliorum suorum*); Dio Cassius 39.10.2 (περὶ τῶν ἑαυτοῦ βουλευμάτων); Charisius *Ars grammatica* 1.146 Keil = 1.186 Barwick (*ratio consiliorum suorum*).

[121] Cicero *De officiis* 1.76, cf. 1.109, 2.43. See p. 181 below.

[122] Quoted in Seneca *Suasoriae* 6.22.

[123] See above, p. 105. So too Lintott 1968.65: 'a fair judgement on his partisan ruthlessness at the end'.

[124] Varro *Hebdomades* fr. 1 Chappuis = Aulus Gellius 3.10.17.

that he should.[125] He was 73 years old, not just a historian and philosopher but more importantly a citizen, a soldier, and a man who spoke his mind.[126] 'They will only be entitled to criticize me', he said, 'when their own policies aim at civil concord.'[127] That was what mattered to Varro.

[125] Appian *Civil Wars* 4.47.203 (φιλοτιμουμένων δε αὐτὸν ὑποδέξασθαι τῶν γνωρίμων); cf. Cicero *Philippics* 2.104 (*nullius salus curae pluribus fuit*).

[126] See above, nn. 32 and 13.

[127] Varro *De uita populi Romani* fr. 124 Riposati = Nonius 438L: *si modo ciuili concordia exsequi rationem parent, rumores famam differant licebit nosque carpant*. For *concordia ciuilis*, cf. Livy 9.19.17.

7

Marcopolis

That tough-minded, outspoken old man lived to see the end of civil war and the restoration of the authority of the Roman People.[1] He died in 27 BC,[2] leaving a unique reputation with posterity as the most learned of all the Romans.[3] But he had another reputation too, equally well deserved: Varro the poet, Varro the 'Menippean' satirist.[4] As a fellow-scholar centuries later explained, 'he was called "the Menippean" not after his master, who lived long before, but because of the similarity of their talent; for Menippus too had polished up his satires with poetry of every kind'.[5] Nearly six hundred fragments of

---

[1] Rich and Williams 1999, *aureus* of 28 BC (*imp. Caesar diui f. cos VI leges et iura p. R. restituit*); *Fasti Praenestini* on 13 Jan. = Degrassi 1963.113, with Millar 2000.6–7 (oak-leaf crown decreed to Augustus [*quod leges et iura* (?)] *p. R. rest*[*it*]*u*[*it*]); Sutherland 1984.79, *cistophorus* of 28 BC (*imp. Caesar diui f. cos. VI libertatis p. R. uindex*); *CIL* 6.701–2 = *ILS* 91 (*Aegypto in potestatem populi Romani redacta*); Augustus *Res gestae* 27 (*Aegyptum imperio populi* [*Ro*]*mani adieci*); Ovid *Fasti* 1.589 (*redditaque est omnis populo prouincia nostro*). See in general Millar 2002a. 314–20.

[2] Jerome *Chronica* on Olympiad 188.1: *M. Terentius Varro philosophus prope nonegenarius moritur.*

[3] See e.g. Dionysius of Halicarnassus 2.21.2 (ἀνὴρ τῶν κατὰ τὴν αὐτὴν ἡλικίαν ἀκμασάντων πολυπειρότατος); Quintilian 10.1.95 (*uir Romanorum eruditissimus*), cf. 12.11.24; Plutarch *Romulus* 12.3 (ἄνδρα Ῥωμαίων ἐν ἱστορίᾳ βιβλιακώτατον); Aulus Gellius 4.16.1 (Varro and Nigidius *uiros Romani generis doctissimos*); Augustine *City of God* 6.6 (*homo omnium acutissimus et doctissimus*), cf. 6.2.

[4] Poet: Cicero *Academica* 1.9 (*uarium et elegans omni fere numero poema fecisti*); Jerome *Chronica* on Olympiad 166.1 (*philosophus et poeta*). *Saturae Menippeae*: Aulus Gellius 2.18.7, 13.31.1 (also called *saturae Cynicae*, but evidently not by Varro himself); ibid. 1.17.4, 3.18.5, 13.11.1, 13.23.4; Macrobius *Saturnalia* 1.7.12, 2.8.2, 3.12.6, 5.20.13.

[5] ps.Probus on *Eclogues* 6.31 (p. 336 Hagen): *Menippeus non a magistro, cuius aetas longe praecesserat, nominatus, sed a societate ingenii, quod is quoque omnigeno carmine satiras suas expoliuerat.*

the *Menippean Satires* survive.[6] But before we can use them as historical evidence, some fundamental questions have to be asked.

I

First, what exactly *was* Roman satire? The evidence offers two quite different answers, which modern scholarship has failed to reconcile. On the one hand, Livy and Valerius Maximus, evidently using Varro himself, define *satura* as an early form of drama.[7] On the other hand, the surviving satires of Horace, Persius, and Juvenal are non-dramatic poems in hexameters.

The Livy passage is part of his excursus on the origins of Roman drama from the supposed introduction of *ludi scaenici* in 364 BC, to placate the gods at a time of plague. First, Etruscan performers were brought in, who danced to the music of the pipe; then the young Romans began to imitate them, adding jests in improvised verses; that in turn became a regular feature, now performed by professional actors (*histriones*).[8] Livy goes on:

> *qui non, sicut ante, Fescennino uersu similem incompositum temere ac rudem alternis iaciebant sed impletas modis saturas descripto iam ad tibicinem cantu motuque congruenti peragebant. Liuius post aliquot annis, qui ab saturis ausus est primus argumento fabulam serere, . . .*

They did not throw out rough improvised exchanges like Fescennine verse, as had been done previously, but began to perform *saturae* filled with musical measures in what was now a written song with pipe accompaniment and appropriate movement. After some years, Livius [Andronicus], who from *saturae* was the first to venture on composing a play with a plot, [allegedly introduced separate singers and actors].

Valerius Maximus' version of events is that 'then the performer's art developed slowly to the measures of *saturae*'.[9]

    [6] Text: Astbury 1985. Text, trans., and commentary: Cèbe 1972–99, Krenkel 2002.
    [7] Livy 7.2.7–8, Valerius Maximus 2.4.4. Excellent detailed discussion in Oakley 1998.40–58, 776–8.
    [8] Livy 7.2.1–6.
    [9] Valerius Maximus 2.4.4: *deinde ludicra ars ad saturarum modos perrepsit.*

A *satura* was not a play with a plot, but it was certainly a performance, and may well have involved the impersonation of characters by the *histriones*.[10] After Livius, the first authors known to have written *saturae* were the playwrights Ennius and Pacuvius,[11] and the original 'measures' (*modi*) of *satura* were no doubt the iambo-trochaic metres which by Livius' time had already been adapted for use in Latin drama.[12] Some of Ennius' *satura* fragments are in those metres, but some also in hexameters, the rhythm which he himself had made possible for use in Latin.[13] Of course the chief hexameter genre was epic; but Ennius also used it for parody didactic (*Hedyphagetica*), and could easily have emulated his neighbour Rhinthon of Tarentum in using it for the stage.[14]

The unknown source of John Lydus identifies Rhinthon's hexameter comedies as the origin of Roman satire:[15]

Ῥίνθωνα καὶ Σκίραν καὶ Βλαῖσον καὶ τοὺς ἄλλους τῶν Πυθαγόρων ἴσμεν οὐ μικρῶν διδαγμάτων ἐπὶ τῆς μεγάλης Ἑλλάδος γενέσθαι καθηγητάς, καὶ διαφερόντως τὸν Ῥίνθονα, ὃς ἑξαμέτροις ἔγραψε πρῶτος κωμῳδίαν. ἐξ οὗ πρῶτος λαβὼν τὰς ἀφορμὰς Λουκίλιος ὁ Ῥωμαῖος ἡρωικοῖς ἔπεσιν ἐκωμῴδησεν. μεθ' ὃν καὶ τοὺς μετ' αὐτόν, οὓς καλοῦσι Ῥωμαῖοι σατυρικούς, οἱ νεώτεροι τὸν Κρατίνου καὶ Εὐπόλιδος χαρακτῆρα ζηλώσαντες τοῖς μὲν Ῥίνθωνος μέτροις, τοῖς δὲ τῶν μνημονευθέντων διασυρμοῖς χρησάμενοι, τὴν σατυρικὴν ἐκράτυναν κωμῳδίαν. Ὁράτιος μὲν οὐκ ἔξω τῆς τέχνης χωρῶν, Πέρσιος δὲ τὸν ποιητὴν Σώφρονα μιμήσασθαι θέλων τὸ Λυκόφρονος παρῆλθεν ἀμαυρόν. Τοῦρνος δὲ καὶ Ἰουβενάλιος καὶ Πετρώνιος, αὐτόθεν ταῖς λοιδορίαις ἐπεξελθόντες, τὸν σατυρικὸν νόμον παρέτρωσαν.

We know that Rhinthon, Sciras, Blaesus, and the others of the sort like Pythagoras had been teachers of no insignificant precepts in 'Great Greece', and especially Rhinthon, who was the first to write comedy in hexameters. Lucilius the Roman took his start from him and became the first to write comedies in heroic verse. After him and those who came after him, whom the

---

[10] *Pace* Jocelyn 1967.13 n. 5, who asserts that 'talk of "dramatic" *satura* is confused and misleading'. That seems a somewhat arbitrary reading of Livy.

[11] Diomedes *Ars grammatica* 1.485 Keil, Porphyrion on Horace *Satires* 1.10.46.

[12] Brilliantly elucidated by Gratwick 1982a.84–93.

[13] For Ennius' *saturae* see Gratwick 1982b.156–60.

[14] Lydus' evidence (next note) is dismissed by Kaibel 1899.184, for no good reason.

[15] John Lydus *De magistratibus* 1.41 (trans. A. C. Bandy); cf. 1.pref. on his sources (Capito, Fonteius, Varro, 'all the Romans'). On Lydus' erudition see Maas 1992.54–6.

Romans call *saturici*, the later poets, because they had emulated the style of Cratinus and Eupolis and had used Rhinthon's metres and the caustic railleries of those mentioned above, strengthened the satiric comedy. Horace did not deviate from the art, but Persius in his desire to imitate the poet Sophron surpassed Lycophron's obscurity. Turnus, Juvenal, and Petronius, however, because they had capriciously made abusive attacks, marred the satiric norm.

We can have no idea how accurately Lydus has reproduced his source, nor how well informed the source was. But it is worth remembering that Horace too took for granted the derivation of Lucilian satire from Greek comedy.[16]

At this point we have to consider the currently prevailing view of the nature of early Roman literature, and Ennius in particular. In his excellent book on republican epic, Sander Goldberg assumed that it was from the beginning 'a genre for private circulation rather than public performance'.[17] Expanding the notion in a wider-ranging treatment of 'the construction of literature', he now posits a small, elite 'intepretive community' quite separate from the audience at the *ludi scaenici*:[18]

A Roman author not only knew who his readers were but could, at least for a time, choose them...

The plays of Plautus were not products of the same world—not written in the same way or for the same audience or with the same end in view—as the *Annales*...

Significant differences of conception and reception distinguish the texts created for stage performance in the rough-and-tumble world of the *ludi scaenici* from the book culture developing among Roman *nobiles* by the end of the Second Punic War.

It seems to me that this idea is both improbable a priori and inconsistent with what our sources say.

---

[16] Horace *Satires* 1.4.1–7: *Eupolis atque Cratinus Aristophanesque poetae...hinc omnis pendet Lucilius, hosce secutus | mutatis tantum pedibus numerisque.* See also Diomedes *Ars grammatica* 1.485 Keil on Roman satire as *archaeae comoediae charactere compositum* (very close to Lydus' formulation); Euanthius *De comoedia* 4.1 (Kaibel 1899.66) on Latin genres that exploited Old Comedy, including *fabulae Rhinthonicae*; and Donatus *De comoedia* 6.1 (Kaibel 1899.68) on *Rhinthonica* as a Latin comic genre.

[17] Goldberg 1995.43; cf. 132 for drama as 'on the margins of Roman society', and epic 'bring[ing] poetry into the mainstream of Roman culture'.

[18] Goldberg 2006.40, 44; cf. also 153–4, arguing that epic was written for the elite.

In the Hellenistic world of which Livius, Naevius, and Ennius were a part, hexameter poetry was something you heard at a festival.[19] Such poems might be short panegyrics, but there were also much longer works on the myth-history of particular places, the nearest parallel for the Roman epics of Naevius and Ennius.[20] Callimachus describes a long epic as something for the *people*; Strabo notes that poetry—and Homer above all—can fill whole theatres.[21] Epic poetry may have been demanding, but as Alan Cameron observes, 'at major festivals there will always have been several hundred and perhaps a few thousand who understood enough to enjoy themselves'.[22] How many were there at the *ludi Romani*?

Ennius was quite explicit: he expected his *Annales* to be famous 'widely among the peoples',[23] and that must have included the Roman People above all. When Naevius died, there was one copy of the *Bellum Punicum*, not yet divided into books;[24] presumably it was the poet's master-copy, not a book to be read in private but a performance script. Two centuries later, epics like Statius' *Thebaid* were still performed in the theatre, for a popular audience.[25] Indeed, we even have an eyewitness account of a performance of Ennius' *Annales* in the theatre at Puteoli in the reign of Marcus Aurelius.[26]

---

[19] Evidence and discussion in Hardie 1983.15–36 and 206; Cameron 1995.47–53. For the Latin pioneers as Hellenistic poets, see Feeney 2005.236–40.

[20] Cameron 1995.263–302 on Hellenistic epic, esp. 297–301. Cameron's judgement on the epics of Naevius and Ennius, that 'there is no precedent for either enterprise in Hellenistic epic' (288), seems to me much too sweeping; Ennius' epic could be called *Romais* (Diomedes *Ars grammatica* 1.484 Keil, with Skutsch 1985.46)—a close parallel to (e.g.) the eleven books of Menelaus of Aegae's *Thebais* (Cameron 1995.296).

[21] Callimachus *Epigrams* 30 = *Anthologia Palatina* 12.43.1–4 (ἐχθαίρω τὸ ποίημα τὸ κυκλικόν . . . σικχαίνω πάντα τὰ δημόσια); Strabo 1.2.8, C20 (δημωφελεστέρα καὶ θέατρα πληροῦν δυναμένη).

[22] Cameron 1995.58.

[23] *Annales* fr. 12–13 Skutsch (*latos <per> populos res atque poemata nostra . . . cluebunt*), rightly emphasized by Feeney 2005.236.

[24] Suetonius *De grammaticis* 2.2: *ut C. Octauius Lampadio Naeui Punicum bellum, quod uno uolumine et continenti scriptura expositura diuisit in septem libros.*

[25] Juvenal 7.82–6 (esp. 85 on the *uulgus*); cf. Statius *Siluae* 5.3.161–3 on the *Achilleid* in the theatre (*cunei*, 162). The same can be inferred for Virgil: Tacitus *Dialogus* 13.2 (*in theatro*); Donatus *Vita Vergilii* 11 (his celebrity), 29 (delivery and *hypocrisis*), 34 (performance with master-copy).

[26] Aulus Gellius 18.5.1–5.

I think we may assume that *all* Ennius' works—dramatic, epic, satiric—were equally designed for performance to a large audience. There is no need to assume that 'outside drama there was no tradition of festival performance' at Rome;[27] any kind of performance was possible at the *ludi scaenici*,[28] where all tastes had to be catered for, and something had to be happening on stage all day, for several days. That satire in particular was written for performance,[29] before a popular audience, may be seen from what Horace says about Lucilius:[30]

> *atqui*
> *primores populi arripuit populumque tributim*
> *scilicet uni aequus Virtuti atque eius amicis.*
> *quin ubi se a uulgo et scaena in secreta remorant*
> *uirtus Scipiadae et mitis sapientia Laeli,*
> *nugari cum illo et discincti ludere, donec*
> *decoqueretur holus.*

And yet he arraigned the People's leaders and the People tribe by tribe, well-disposed to Virtue alone, of course, and her friends. In fact when the brave scion of Scipio and gentle, wise Laelius had withdrawn from the crowd and the stage to a private place, they used to fool around with him and play in casual clothes while waiting until the vegetables cooked.

Scipio and Laelius were by the stage among the crowd as Lucilius, or the actor performing his work, satirized the audience; they were not reading him in a book. For Horace himself it was different, but only by his own choice:[31]

> *haec ego ludo*
> *quae neque in aede sonent certantia iudice Tarpa,*
> *nec redeant iterum atque iterum spectanda theatris.*

I play about with these trifles, which aren't designed either to resound in competition in the temple with Tarpa adjudicating, or to return to be seen again and again in the theatres.

---

[27] Cameron 1995.44, a dangerous argument from silence.

[28] For example, boxers, rope-dancers, and imitators of animal noises (Terence *Hecyra* prologues, Phaedrus 5.5).

[29] Rather than Goldberg 2006.19 ('a distinctly aristocratic genre') and 170 (the 'aristocrat' Lucilius 'circulat[ing] his poems among his friends'), I prefer to follow Gratwick 1982b.164: '[Lucilius] speaks to you and me, not to an audience of connoisseurs in a declamation hall.'

[30] Horace *Satires* 2.1.68–74 (trans. F. Muecke, slightly adapted).

[31] Horace *Satires* 1.10.37–9 (trans. P. M. Brown).

Now that he had Maecenas as a patron, he didn't need to do what would otherwise be essential.

II

Before Horace, then, Roman satire was evidently a theatrical genre. But what was *Menippean* satire in particular?

The answer that has been given in the last fifty years, ever since Northrop Frye's *Anatomy of Criticism* borrowed the phrase to account for works like *Gulliver's Travels* (fiction but not quite a novel),[32] is one we can leave to students of modern literature. As its latest chronicler observes, 'a genre that includes Johnson's *Dictionary* (1755) and *Portnoy's Complaint* (1969), *Utopia* (1516) and *The Waste Land* (1922) is less baggy than bulbous'; it has become 'the genre that ate the world'.[33] Menippus would have been amused.

He was a third-century BC 'Cynic' philosopher from Gadara in Syria, allegedly an ex-slave, who wrote in the 'serious-humorous' mode (*spoudogeloion*).[34] Cynics traditionally made a performance out of their own life, like Diogenes in his barrel, and we have one wonderful description which probably refers to Menippus himself:[35]

οὗτος, καθά φησιν Ἱππόβοτος, εἰς τοσοῦτον τερατείας ἤλασεν ὥστε Ἐρινύος ἀναλαβὼν σχῆμα περιῄει, λέγων ἐπίσκοπος ἀφῖχθαι ἐξ ᾅδου τῶν ἁμαρτονομένων, ὅπως πάλιν κατιὼν ταῦτα ἀπαγγέλλοι τοῖς ἐκεῖ δαίμοσιν. ἦν δὲ αὐτῷ ἡ ἐσθὴς αὕτη· χιτὼν φαιὸς ποδήρης, περὶ αὐτῷ ζώνη φοινική, πῖλος Ἀρκαδικὸς ἐπὶ τῆς κεφαλῆς ἔχων ἐνυφασμένα τὰ δώδεκα στοιχεῖα, ἐμβάται τραγικοί, πώγων ὑπερμεγέθης, ῥάβδος ἐν τῇ χειρὶ μειλίνη.

According to Hippobotus he had attained such a degree of audacity in wonder-working that he went about in the guise of a Fury, saying that he had come from Hades to take cognisance of sins committed, and was going to return and report them to the powers down below. This was his attire: a grey tunic reaching to his feet, about it a crimson girdle; an Arcadian hat on

---

[32] Frye 1957.308–12.

[33] Weinbrot 2005.1–2, cf. 12–16 on the contribution of Mikhail Bakhtin.

[34] Diogenes Laertius 6.8.99–101; Strabo 16.2.29, 759 (Μένιππος ὁ σπουδογέλοιος).

[35] Diogenes Laertius 6.9.102 (trans. R. D. Hicks, Loeb Classical Library), with von Fritz 1932.794: attributed to Menedemus, but the same passage in the *Suda* (s.v. *Phaios*, φ 180 Adler) refers to Menippus.

his head with the twelve signs of the Zodiac inwrought in it; buskins of tragedy; and he wore a very long beard and carried an ashen staff in his hand.

If the actor performing one of Varro's Menippean satires came on stage like that, it must have made quite an impact.

The theatrical context is explicit in several of the fragments. In *Glory (On Envy)*, the audience is addressed directly:[36]

> *uosque in theatro, qui uoluptatem auribus*
> *huc aucupatum concucurristis domo,*
> *adeste et a me quae feram cognoscite,*
> *domum ut feratis ex theatro litteras.*

And you in the theatre, who have rushed together here from your homes to hunt for pleasure for your ears, come and learn from me what I have for you, so you can take literature home from the theatre.

So too in *Donkey Hears the Lyre*, the performance evidently ended with the play-actor's traditional exit line: 'Farewell, and send me away with applause.'[37] Other characters are referred to: 'the most despised old man the Latin stage has ever seen' (*Double Marcus*);[38] an astrologer 'here in his tragic boots, explaining the ways and the sound of the star-bearing heaven with hollow bronze' (*Ulysses and a Half*).[39]

The satires were also books to be read. Cicero's Varro makes that clear in the *Academica*, and the fragments confirm it.[40] But with most ancient literature performance was the primary medium, as Kenneth Quinn rightly insists: 'You acquired a copy with the intention of having it performed for you by a professional reader, or as a record of a performance which you had heard... It was not in itself a substitute for performance.'[41] A fragment of *Right Measure* neatly juxtaposes the two media:[42]

---

[36] Fr. 218 = Nonius 510L. All references to the *Menippeans* are according to the numeration in Astbury 1985 and Krenkel 2002.

[37] See e.g. fr. 355 = Nonius 593L: *ualete et me palmulis producite*.

[38] Fr. 51 = Nonius 143L: *scena quem senem Latina uidit derisissimum*.

[39] Fr. 465 = Nonius 465L: *uias stelligeras aetheris explicans aere cauo sonitum hic in cothurnis*.

[40] Cicero *Academica* 1.8 (p. 126 above): *ad legendum inuitati*. Written *libelli*: frr. 59–60 = Nonius 612L, 719L (from *Double Marcus*); *Sailing Around (On Philosophy)* consisted of two *libri* (Nonius 190L, 252L, 282L).

[41] Quinn 1982.90.

[42] Fr. 304 = Nonius 259L, text as in Krenkel's edition. 'Petrullus' is not a known name, but cf. Suetonius *Vespasian* 1.2: T. Flavius Petro of Reate, a veteran centurion who fought for Pompey at Pharsalus.

> *sed, o Petrulle, ne meum taxis librum*
> *si tete pigeat hic modus scenatilis.*

But my dear Petro, you shouldn't touch my book if this stage style irritates
you.

The vast majority of the fragments are short quotations cited by
Nonius Marcellus (early fourth century AD) in his encyclopaedic
dictionary to explain particular words and usages. That does at
least mean that the fragments are a more or less random sample,
and therefore that the surviving titles—93 out of the original 150—
should give us an authentic flavour. The list is as follows:[43]

Aborigines (*On Human Nature*)	[1–5]
Agathon	[6–14]
Ajax the Straw Man	[18]
The Arms Verdict	[42–3]
Baiae	[44]
A Battle of Words	[242]
Beware of the Dog	[75]
The Big Barrel or The Little One	[92]
The Boar-Hunters	[293–303]
The City of Men (*On Astrology*)	[36–41]
Come On Then!	[15–17]
Daddy's Little Boy (*On Begetting Children*)	[552–5]
The Defeated (*On the Will to Win*)	[87–90]
The Dish Found Its Lid (*On Married Couples*)	[166–8]
Dog Historian	[231]
Dog Knighted	[220–1]
Dog Orator	[232]
Dogs' Handbook	[230]
Donkey Hears the Lyre	[348–69]
Double Marcus	[45–70]
Eight Pence (*On Money*)	[342–6]

---

[43] I have included two titles (*Mystic Guides* and *Tanaquil*) which Astbury relegates
to the 'doubtful' category (1985.99), as well as *Three Heads*, which both Cèbe and
Krenkel think was a 'political pamphlet'. In each case it seems to me that the type of
title suggests Menippean satire rather than any other Varronian mode.

It is likely that all the satires had second titles in Greek (περὶ δόξης, περὶ φιλοσοφίας,
etc), but only one of the three collections used by Nonius happened to preserve them
(Astbury 1985.xxii–xxiii).

Epitaph-Collectors (On Tombs)	[109–10]
Fighting Goats (On Pleasure)	[71–3]
Fighting Shadows (On Nonsense)	[506–10]
The Five-Day Festival	[440–8]
The Folded Tablet[44] *(On Provincial Government)*	[175–80]
For Postumius, Perfume Stinks	[420]
A Friend from Boyhood (On Constancy)	[511–15]
Ganymede	[74]
Gladiators Fighting Blind	[25–35]
Glory (On Envy)	[218–19]
Good Grief! (On Eulogies)	[370–83]
Gotcha! (On Luck)	[169–72]
Hercules, Help!	[213–16]
The Horse-Jumper (On Writing)	[85–6]
A Hundred Oxen (On Sacrifices)	[94–100]
A Husband's Duty	[83]
It's A Long Run From Your Family	[244–5]
The Kindly Ones	[117–65]
Know Yourself	[199–210]
Like a Dog	[82]
Lunched and Ready	[421–2]
The Magic Wand	[565–74]
Marcopolis (On Political Power)	[288–92]
Marcus' Boy	[269–87]
Maybe Tomorrow, Nothing Today	[77–8]
Menippus' Tomb	[516–39]
Mister Morning	[247–68]
The Mysteries	[326–32]
Mystic Guides	[II]
Oedipus-Thyestes	[347]
Old Men, Second Childhood	[91]
One Mule Scratches Another (On Separation)	[322–5]
Pappus or The Native[45]	[384]

[44] Astbury 1985.31 (apparatus criticus) for the possible readings: *Flextabula(e)* and *Flaxtabula(e)* seem the most likely. Pliny (*Nat. Hist.* pref. 24) cites it as a wittily modest title.

[45] Nonius 19L: *Pappo aut indige*—i.e. *indice* or *indige<na>*? Astbury prefers the former, Cèbe and Krenkel the latter.

---

[46] Astbury 1985.4 (apparatus criticus) for the possible readings: he prefers ἀλλ᾽ οὐ μένει σε, Cèbe and Krenkel ἄμμον μετρεῖς.

(*On Cuisine*)	[403–4]
(*On Departure*)	[405–10]
(*On Schools of Philosophy*)	[400–2]
(*On Thunder*)	[411–13]

The seven canine titles—*Beware of the Dog, Dog Historian, Dog Knighted, Dog Orator, Dogs' Handbook, Like a Dog,* and *Water Dog*— allude to the 'Cynic' style of philosophy, which Menippus practised. The Cynics specialized in ethical criticism; as Diogenes explained, 'I bite the wicked'.[47] Lucilius had already taken on that persona,[48] and though there is no sign of it in the few surviving Ennian fragments, it is possible that Roman *satura* exploited it from the start.[49] Despite Lucilius' decisive move to hexameters only, which was followed by Horace, Persius, and Juvenal, there was a recognizable satiric tradition from Ennius through Lucilius to Varro.[50]

That is worth bearing in mind when we read Quintilian's well-known account of Roman satire. '*Satura*', he says, 'is wholly our own,' and he goes on to refer to Lucilius, Horace, and Persius.[51] That he had in mind only hexameter satire is clear from his next sentence:[52]

alterum illud etiam prius saturae genus, sed non sola carminum uarietate mixtum, condidit Terentius Varro, uir Romanorum eruditissimus.

The other well-known type of satire, earlier but of mixed form with a variety not only of verse metres, was composed by Terentius Varro, the most learned of the Romans.

He must mean 'earlier than Lucilius' hexameters', the origin of his first type of satire. Since it was only the first type that was 'wholly our own', Quintilian's boast is not inconsistent with a Greek model (the

---

[47] Diogenes Laertius 6.2.60 (τοὺς δὲ πονηροὺς δάκνων); cf. 6.9.103–5 on the general characteristics of the Cynic way of life.

[48] Lucilius frr. 3–4 and 1000–1 Warmington; 'he consciously adopts the role of the cynic dog' (Gratwick 1982b.164).

[49] Gratwick (1982b.159) seems to me too dogmatic in denying even the possibility in Ennius.

[50] Porphyrion on Horace *Epistles* 1.3: *hic Florus* [Horace's addressee] *scriba fuit saturarum scriptor, cuius sunt electae ex Ennio Lucilio Varrone saturae.*

[51] Quintilian 10.1.93–4. His reference to satirists of his own day (*sunt clari hodieque et qui olim nominabuntur*) no doubt includes Turnus, whose two surviving fragments are in hexameters (Courtney 1993.362–3).

[52] Quintilian 10.1.95; my trans. is influenced by Winterbottom 1970.191.

Cynic tradition as expressed by Menippus) for the multi-metre satires of Ennius, early Lucilius, and Varro.

'A variety not only of verse metres' ought to imply that prose could be used too, as we know it was in Varro's *Menippeans*.[53] Far-reaching conclusions have been drawn from that. One of the best books on Roman satire refers to 'the alternative convention...in which prose discourse or narrative was interspersed with a variety of verse forms to enhance a moment of the story or to illustrate the argument'.[54] In the recent *Cambridge Companion to Roman Satire* the few contributors who even mention Varro refer uneasily to his 'literary experiments', 'essays', and 'fictional pieces'.[55] Something important has been lost sight of. Varro the satirist was not a prose writer who sometimes used verse, but a poet who sometimes used prose. Those who enjoyed his satires enjoyed them as poetry.[56]

At least twenty-five different metres are represented in the fragments. By far the most frequent is the iambic *senarius*, the regular metre of dramatic speech without musical accompaniment,[57] but the actor might also have to sing or chant in various other rhythms, including the frenetic Galliambi of the Great Mother's eunuchs, as well as engaging the audience in rhetorical or conversational prose. The *satura* was indeed a 'mixed dish',[58] not only a showpiece for a versatile performer but also a wonderfully entertaining medium for an author who wanted to reach the Roman People.

---

[53] See Astbury 1985.137 for the 208 certainly metrical fragments, 138–42 for the large number of others to which scholars have attempted to assign metrical form. On my count there are 362 fragments which Astbury prints as prose, 293 of which have at some point been read (however implausibly) as verse.

[54] Coffey 1976.149, introducing Menippean satire as the genre of Seneca's *Apocolocyntosis* and Petronius' *Satyrica* (neither of which is ever so described in the ancient sources).

[55] Relihan 2005.109, Mayer 2005.153, Henderson 2005.316; there are only ten very fleeting references to Varro (and no discussion) in the volume's 318 pages. So too in the latest 'companion to the Roman republic', the treatment of satire goes straight from Lucilius to Horace (Batstone 2006.552).

[56] See e.g. Aulus Gellius 6.16.1–3 (*lepide admodum et scite factis uersibus*); cf. Diomedes *Ars grammatica* 1.400 Keil (*in poetico libro*), and n. 4 above.

[57] Statistics at Astbury 1985.137: 68 *senarii* out of 208. The next most frequent are dactylic hexameters (18) and trochaic *septenarii* (17).

[58] Diomedes *Ars grammatica* 1.485 Keil: *a lance quae referta uariis multisque primitiis in sacro apud priscos dis inferebatur.*

III

According to Horace, Lucilius confided everything to his books:[59]

> *quo fit ut omnis*
> *uotiua pateat ueluti descripta tabella*
> *uita senis.*

That's how it happens that the old man's whole life is on view, as if drawn on a votive tablet.

Satura was always an autobiographical mode—or at least, that is what it purported to be.[60] So the third of our questions must be how far the first-person speaker of the *Menippean Satires* represents Varro himself.[61]

Certainly he is *called* Varro.[62] More to the point, he is called Marcus. Three of the titles feature him by that name (*Marcopolis*, *Marcus' Boy*, and *Double Marcus*), and it is repeatedly used by sceptical interlocutors as a way of illustrating his character. In *Double Marcus*, on *tropoi*:[63]

> *ebrius es, Marce: Odyssian enim Homeri ruminari incipis, cum περὶ τρόπων scripturum te Seio receperis.*

Marcus, you're drunk! You promised Seius you'd write him a book *On Ways of Life*, and now you're starting to chew over Homer's *Odyssey*!

In *The Folded Tablet (On Provincial Government)*:[64]

> *quare, o Marce, pransum ac paratum esse te hoc minume oportet.*

And so, my dear Marcus, it's not at all appropriate for you to be 'lunched and ready' in this matter.

In *Sixty Years Old*, on the degeneracy of modern Rome:[65]

---

[59] Horace *Satires* 2.1.32–4.

[60] For the *personae* presented by satirists, see Anderson 1982.3–10 (a classic polemic), 28–30 (Lucilius and Horace).

[61] All this section owes much to Cichorius 1922.207–26, 'Chronologisches und Autobiographisches aus den Menippeischen Satiren'.

[62] Fr. 562 = Nonius 191L: *ego nihil, Varro, uideo...*

[63] Fr. 60 = Nonius 612L; Marcus had evidently alluded to the ἄνδρα πολύτροπον (Homer *Odyssey* 1.1, 10.330).

[64] Fr. 175 = Nonius 735L.

[65] Fr. 505 = Nonius 770L.

erras, Marce, accusare nos: ruminaris antiquitates.

Marcus, you're wrong to accuse us. You're just chewing over how things used to be.

Another fragment from that satire reveals that Marcus breeds horses and asses in the Reate district, just like the real Marcus Varro.[66] And just like the real Marcus Varro, he likes to combine scholarship and country life.[67]

In *Donkey Hears the Lyre*, on music, someone appeals to eyewitness evidence:[68]

non uidisti simulacrum leonis ad Idam, eo loco ubi quondam subito eum cum uidissent quadrupedem Galli tympanis adeo fecerunt mansuem ut tractarent manibus?

Haven't you seen the statue of the lion at Mt. Ida? It's where the Galli once suddenly saw the beast, and made him so tame with their drums that they could stroke him with their hands.

If the speaker was Marcus, it may be relevant that the real Marcus Varro had been in Phrygia himself, thinking about musical instruments; as he mentioned in book 3 of his *Disciplinae*, he had seen pipes with four apertures in the temple of Marsyas.[69]

Marcus had evidently spent long years soldiering: he had hardly been given his adult toga when he changed it for military uniform.[70] He was an *eques*, and when his service was over he returned his horse to the censor.[71] That ceremony is reported in *Ulysses and a Half*, where the speaker compares himself to the wandering hero: 'I'm afraid that when I come home from Ilium, squatting on my haunches, no one will recognize me except the dog.'[72] The title implies an absence of thirty years (Ulysses was away for twenty)— and if the real Marcus Varro was given his adult toga at the age of 16,

---

[66] Fr. 502 = Nonius 97L; cf. *Res rusticae* 2.8.6, Pliny *Nat. Hist.* 8.167.

[67] Fr. 457 = Nonius 241L: *dum in agro studiosus ruror...*

[68] Fr. 364 = Nonius 775L.

[69] Varro fr. 44 Funaioli = ps.Acro on Horace *Ars poetica* 202 (*se ipsum ait in Marsyae templo uidisse*); the temple was presumably at Kelainai (Herodotus 7.26.3, Xenophon *Anabasis* 1.2.8).

[70] Fr. 223 = Nonius 863L: *toga tracta est et abolla data est; ad turbam abii fera militiai munera belli ut praestarem.*

[71] Fr. 478 = Nonius 122L: *in castris permansi; inde caballum reduxi ad censorem.*

[72] Fr. 471 = Nonius 423L.

thirty years would bring him to the censorship of 70 BC, when we happen to know that the parade of the *equites* was particularly spectacular.[73]

Marcus has views (still in *Ulysses and a Half*) about the quality of modern *equites*:[74]

itaque tum ecum mordacem calcitronem horridum miles acer non uitabat…
nunc emunt trossuli nardo nitidi uulgo Attico talento ecum.

So in those days a keen soldier didn't avoid a bad-tempered horse that would bite and kick…
Nowadays the cavaliers gleam with cosmetics, and normally buy their horse for an Attic talent.

That is a good example of Marcus' habitual style, always looking back to when things were better. In *Sixty Years Old* he pretends to have fallen asleep at the age of 10 and woken up fifty years later.[75] He doesn't like what he finds:[76]

> *ergo tum Romae parce pureque pudentis*
> *uixere. en patriam! nunc sumus in rutuba.*

So at Rome in those days they lived frugal, clean, modest lives. Look at our country now! We're in a mess.

There are many other examples of the contrast of then and now,[77] just as there are in the non-satirical works of the real Marcus Varro. We noted in the last chapter his sharp comment on the old and new behaviour of magistrates, and he is similarly censorious elsewhere, about gold and ivory statues of gods (as opposed to terracotta), or about villas with Greek names for all the rooms (as opposed to working farms).[78] The satirical persona is not very different from the author himself.

---

[73] Plutarch *Pompey* 72.4–6. See p. 113 above on Varro as 'soldier and commander'; of course his own absence had not been continuous (Cichorius 1922.218–19).

[74] Frr. 479–80 = Nonius 64L, 69L; cf. Pliny *Nat. Hist.* 33.35 for *equites* as *trossuli*.

[75] Frr. 485, 490–1 = Nonius 233L, 151L, 570L. Cf. n. 65 above.

[76] Fr. 488 = Nonius 245L; *en* for *in* is Lachmann's emendation.

[77] See e.g. frr. 181, 342, 495 (moral decline); 435 (the Forum a pigsty nowadays); 537 (not a trace of Numa's institutions).

[78] Varro *Antiquitates humanae* fr. 21.3 Mirsch = Aulus Gellius 13.13.4 (p. 115 above); *De uita populi Romani* fr. 15 Riposati = Nonius 239L; *Res rusticae* 2.pref.1–3.

Ancient readers evidently assumed they were identical; Ausonius, for instance, an intelligent and learned man, cites Varro's *Hebdomades* as the work of 'Marcus', with no further specification.[79] Of course that applied only to readers of the satires in book form. When they were first seen on the stage, it must have been obvious that 'Marcus' was an actor playing Varro, not Varro himself. Nevertheless, Varro was speaking through him.

IV

The datable fragments refer to the civil war in Africa in 81 BC (when Varro was 25), the slave revolt of Spartacus in 73–71, the censorship of 70–69, the sack of Delos by the pirates in 69, and the alliance of Caesar, Pompey, and Crassus in 60 (when Varro was 56).[80] If there were indeed 150 Menippean satires, as Jerome's list states, that gives an average of about seven per year, but Varro's military obligations make it unlikely that his output was steady or regular. Satires could of course be written abroad and sent to Rome (one thinks of Ovid's poems from exile), but the intensely urban subject matter counts against that idea. So if we were to suppose that the satires were written between 85 and 60 BC, and that (as a pure guess) Varro was in Rome for only five or six of those twenty-five years, then the average rate of composition would be between twenty-five and thirty per year.

Whether the output was slow and regular or intermittent and intense, the cumulative impact must have been very impressive. The nearest analogy might be a popular columnist in a mass-circulation newspaper, for in the Roman world the stage was the only mass medium available. Not everyone approved, as we see in *Donkey Hears the Lyre*:[81]

iurgare incipit dicens: quae scis atque in uulgum uulgas artemque expromis inertem.

---

[79] Ausonius *Mosella* 306–7: *decimo celebrata uolumine Marci | hebdomas.*

[80] Frr. 225, 193, 478, 529b (Astbury 1985.97), 556; *pace* Krenkel 2002.1107–8 (and many previous scholars), I see no reason to rule out the last of these (n. 43 above).

[81] Fr. 359 = Nonius 268L.

He started to get nasty. 'The things you know', he said, 'and publicize to the masses, and that "art without art" you're putting out...'

Varro was not like Horace, a freedman's son in need of a powerful protector. He was himself a prominent citizen, and what he knew included things his fellow-senators might well not want to have publicized.[82]

His constant theme is 'How best to live?'. In *The Kindly Ones*—the forty-nine fragments of which offer our best chance of reconstructing the whole plot of a satire—Marcus reports on a search for sanity in a crazy world, as he samples all the philosophical sects and religious cults that offer it. From a high watchtower he sees the People driven to madness by three Furies, the *Eumenides* of the euphemistic title, who probably represent the Stoics' trio of pathological desires—the pursuit of wealth, the pursuit of pleasure, the pursuit of fame.[83] In Latin, those are *auaritia*, *luxuria*, and *ambitio*, the three main reasons, in Sallust's analysis, for the corruption of the Roman republic.[84]

When Varro's satires were appearing in the seventies BC, that corruption was particularly in evidence. It took the form of bribery at the elections, followed by extortion in the provinces, followed by bribery in the courts.[85] The Roman People wanted traditional morality enforced in the traditional way by the censorship,[86] but no censors had held office since 86 BC; Sulla as dictator had ordered the republic in his own way, and the aristocracy he had left in power could do without any curb on their own behaviour.

In *Teaching Old Men*, Marcus reflects on the value of the censorship, and remembers the strict standards of Manius Curius.[87] Another

---

[82] Cf. Cicero *In Verrem* 1.27: *an me taciturum tantis de rebus eximistauistis?*

[83] Fr. 117, cf. 126 on *auaritia*. See Norden 1892.337–40 = 1966.73–6; for φιλοπλουτία, φιληδονία, and φιλοδοξία, see *Stoicorum ueterum fragmenta* 3.394–5 = Stobaeus *Ecl.* 2.90.7W, 2.91.10W, Cleanthes *Hymn to Zeus* 26–9, Plutarch *Moralia* 1049e, 1050d; cf. Cicero *De republica* 1.60. The third of the Furies is called *Infamia* (fr. 123); one pursues fame in order to escape her.

[84] Sallust *Catiline* 10.3–12.2, *Histories* 1.11–13M, 16M; see pp. 35–7 above.

[85] Cicero *In Verrem* 1 *passim*, esp. 34–7 and 44–7 on the indignation of the Roman People; *Pro Cluentio* 79, 130 on the *infamia* of the courts.

[86] Cicero *Diuinatio in Caecilium* 8: *iudicum culpa atque dedecore etiam censorium nomen, quod asperius antea populo uideri solebat, id nunc poscitur, id iam populare et plausibile factum est.*

[87] Frr. 195 (Curius), 196 (*hoc est magnum censorem esse...*).

paragon from the third century BC was Atilius Serranus, summoned to the consulship from sowing his fields.[88] Varro chose his name for a satire on elections:[89]

> *hunc uocasset e liquida uita in curiae uestrae faecem.*

[?The republic] would have called this man from his blameless life into your dregs of a Senate-house.

Marcus uses of the Senate the word Cicero used of the Roman People—but Cicero was the spokesman of the rich.[90]

In *Double Marcus*, the speaker casts a cold eye on a contemporary namesake of Manius Curius. It was typical of the men of those days that Curius refused to accept a land allotment any bigger than his soldiers got:[91]

aui et ataui nostri, cum alium et cepe eorum uerba olerent, tamen optume animati erant.

Our grandfathers and great-grandfathers had an excellent attitude, even though their words did smell of garlic and onion.

But different standards prevail nowadays, and the modern Manius has a grand new house to build:[92]

non te pudet, Mani, cum domi tuae uides conmilitonum tuorum cohortis seruis tuis ministrare caementa?

Aren't you ashamed, Manius, when at your house you see cohorts of your fellow-soldiers supplying your slaves with rubble for concrete?

It is paid for, of course, with plunder taken from Rome's provincial allies.[93]

In *Good Grief!*, Marcus reports the plight of the provincial who tries to invoke Roman justice:[94]

---

[88] Cicero *Pro Roscio Amerino* 50, *Pro Sestio* 72; Virgil *Aeneid* 6.844, Valerius Maximus 4.4.5, Pliny *Nat. Hist.* 18.20. He was probably C. Atilius *cos.* 245 (Wiseman 1998a.102).

[89] Fr. 452 = Nonius 526L; cf. fr. 450 = Nonius 397L (*et petere imperium populi et contendere honores*).

[90] See p. 117 above; Cicero *Ad Atticum* 1.19.4 (*is enim est noster exercitus, hominum, ut tute scis, locupletium*).

[91] Fr. 63 = Nonius 296L; see p. 42 above.

[92] Fr. 66 = Nonius 131L, 289L.

[93] Fr. 64 = Nonius 374L: *sociis es <hostis>, hostibus socius; bellum ita geris ut bella omnia domum auferas.*

[94] Fr. 378 = Nonius 38L.

*praetor uester eripuit mihi pecuniam. de ea questum ad annum ueniam ad
nouum magistratum, cum hic rapo umbram quoque spei deuorasset.*

'Your praetor stole my money. In a year's time I'll come and complain before
the new magistrate, although this robber would have swallowed up even the
shadow of a hope.'

These are the courts of the age of Verres. They feature also in *Sixty
Years Old*:[95]

quod leges iubent non faciunt. δὸς καὶ λάβε feruit omnino.
auidus iudex reum ducebat esse κοινὸν Ἑρμῆν.

They don't do what the laws command. It's a whole ferment of 'give and
take'.

The greedy juror regarded the defendant as a public gift from the gods.

And in *A Friend from Boyhood*, Marcus quotes the wrongdoers
themselves:[96]

hodie, si possumus quod debemus populo in foro medio luci claro decoquere.

'If today, in the middle of the Forum in broad daylight, we can melt away
what we owe to the People, . . . '

The indicative mood shows that they are sure they can get away
with it.

Only a few unhelpful fragments remain of the satire Varro called
Marcopolis. But it was subtitled *On Political Power* (περὶ ἀρχῆς), and
we know what he thought about that. In the fourth book of his
biography of the Roman People, written in the tense, unstable period
after the Ides of March, Varro gave his verdict on the corruption of
the republic:[97]

*tanta porro inuasit cupiditas honorum plerisque ut uel caelum ruere, dum-
modo magistratum adipiscantur, exoptent.*

Besides, most of them have been infected by so great a lust for honours that
they'd even long for the sky to fall, provided they get their magistracy.

Soon after that, the avengers of Caesar proscribed him—for 'hostility
to monarchy', Appian thought.[98] But Theodor Mommsen, that

[95] Frr. 498–9 = Nonius 808L, 436L.
[96] Fr. 512 = Nonius 310L.
[97] Varro *De uita populi Romani* fr. 121 Riposati = Nonius 802L.
[98] Appian *Civil Wars* 4.47.203.

hero-worshipper of Caesar, found space in his history for a generous and affectionate, if slightly patronizing, tribute to Varro; and he
was surely right to see the *Menippean Satires* as the last breath of the
old 'age of citizens' as it disappeared.[99]

Varro himself may have signed off in the satire called *Testament*.
True to Menippus to the last, the terms of Marcus' will include this
item:[100]

*e mea φιλοφθονίᾳ natis quos Menippea haeresis nutricata est tutores do qui rem
Romanam Latiumque augescere uultis.*

To the children born by my lady Enviousness, whom the Menippean school
has suckled, I give as guardians 'you who wish to augment the prosperity of
Rome and Latium'.

Ironically, he pretends that his criticism is merely envious; but his
quotation (perhaps from Ennius?) alludes to the ritual prayer of
those real guardians of Roman morality, the censors.[101]

After the successful census of 70–69 BC, Varro may have felt that
the task of telling the citizens how to live could be bequeathed to the
elected magistrates whose proper responsibility it was. But over forty
years were to pass before the next census, and the next purification of
the Roman People at the *lustrum*. In 28 BC Varro was 88 years old,
and legality had just been restored to the republic.[102] Let us hope he
was well enough to go to Rome and make his declaration as a citizen
before Marcus Agrippa and the young Caesar.

---

[99] Mommsen 1910.4.558–67, esp. 565 ('der letzte Hauch des scheidenden gutes
Geistes der alten Bürgerzeit').

[100] Fr. 542 = Nonius 767L; cf. Diogenes Laertius 6.8.101 for Menippus' διαθῆκαι.

[101] Valerius Maximus 4.1.10: *quo di immortales ut populi Romani res meliores
amplioresque facerent* (allegedly revised by Scipio Aemilianus). See p. 38 above.

[102] See n. 1 above.

8

The Political Stage

I

For the purposes of this book's argument, few episodes in the political history of the late republic are as revealing as Cicero's return to Rome from exile. This is how he reported it to Atticus:[1]

cum uenissem ad portam Capenam, gradus templorum ab infimo plebe completi erant. a quo plausu maximo cum esset mihi gratulatio significata, similis et frequentia <et> plausus me usque ad Capitolium celebrauit in foroque et in ipso Capitolio miranda multitudo fuit.

When I reached the Porta Capena I found the steps of the temples thronged by the common people, who welcomed me with vociferous applause. Like numbers and applause followed me to the Capitol. In the Forum and on the Capitol itself the crowd was spectacular.

The people Cicero refers to as *infima plebs* were the ordinary citizens of Rome.

The following day (5 September) he gave a speech of thanks to the Senate; he had one prepared for the Roman People too, but probably didn't deliver it.[2] Two days after that—for the day immediately following was a *dies ater*[3]—he plunged straight back into serious politics:[4]

---

[1] Cicero *Ad Atticum* 4.1.5 (trans. D. R. Shackleton Bailey).

[2] Cicero *Post reditum ad senatum*, *Ad Atticum* 4.1.5; see Lintott 2008.8–9 on the speech *Post reditum ad Quirites*.

[3] Varro *De lingua Latina* 6.29 (*dies postridie Kalendas Nonas Idus appellantur atri, quod per eos dies nihil noui inciperent*); Livy 6.1.12, Verrius Flaccus fr. 3 Funaioli = Aulus Gellius 5.17.1.

[4] Cicero *Ad Atticum* 4.1.6 (trans. Shackleton Bailey, slightly adjusted).

cum esset annonae summa caritas et homines ad theatrum primo, deinde ad senatum concurrissent, impulsu Clodi mea opera frumenti inopiam esse clamarunt, cum per eos dies senatus de annona haberetur et ad eius procurationem sermone non solum plebis uerum etiam bonorum Pompeius uocaretur idque ipse cuperet multitudoque a me ut id decernerem postularet, feci et accurate sententiam dixi.

The price of grain had risen very high, and people had been flocking first to the theatre and then to the Senate, clamouring at Clodius' instigation that the shortage was my doing. The Senate was meeting during those days to consider the grain situation, and there was a general demand, not only from the populace but from the honest men too, that Pompey should be asked to take charge of supplies. He himself was eager for the commission, and the crowd called on me by name to propose it. I did so in a full-dress speech.

Here the Roman People are the *multitudo*. They know what they want, and through the open doors of the Senate-house they make sure their wishes are known.[5] Such demonstrations could be quite intimidating for senators with unpopular views,[6] and on this occasion only three senators of consular rank had ventured to be present; the others said that it was not safe for them to give their opinion.[7]

   On Cicero's proposal, the Senate resolved that Pompey should be asked to take charge of the grain supply, and requested the consuls to bring forward legislation to that effect for the People to vote on:[8]

quo senatus consulto recitato continuo, <cum multitudo> more hoc insulso et nouo plausum meo nomine recitando dedisset, habui contionem. <eam> omnes magistratus praesentes praeter unum praetorem et duos tribunos pl. dederunt.

The Senate's resolution was immediately read out, and the People applauded in the tasteless modern fashion when my name was mentioned. I then gave a public speech; the invitation came from all the magistrates who were present, except for one praetor and two tribunes.

---

   [5] Open doors: implied by Cicero *Philippics* 2.112 and 5.18 (exceptionally closed); *In Catilinam* 4.3 (*in conspectu*), Livy 22.59.16 (*intueri potestis*), Pliny *Letters* 8.14.5 (*consilii publici spectatores*).
   [6] See e.g. Cicero *Ad Q. fratrem* 2.1.3 (*metu interiecto*), with Millar 1998.159 on the casualness of the reference; such scenes were evidently not uncommon. Cf. also Tacitus *Annals* 3.14.4, 5.4.2.
   [7] Cicero *Ad Atticum* 4.1.6. The three were M. Messalla (*cos.* 61), L. Afranius (*cos.* 60), and Cicero himself.
   [8] Cicero *Ad Atticum* 4.1.6 (Shackleton Bailey's text); cf. 1.13.3 for the procedure.

Only magistrates in office had the right to address the People in a *contio*; anyone else had to be invited.[9]

Cicero does not usually go into so much detail about the People's role in the political issues of the day. There are two reasons why he does so here: first, because on this occasion, unusually, his agenda coincided with that of the People; and second, because his purpose in giving Atticus such a detailed account was to report his success in recovering not only his authority in the Senate and the goodwill of the *optimates*, but also his 'brilliance in the Forum' (*splendor forensis*)[10]— and that meant brilliance in the eyes of the Roman People. Contemptuous though he often was of 'the Forum crowd',[11] Cicero was still glad of its good opinion when he could get it.

For twenty-three years, Cicero's brilliance in the Forum had been manifested in court cases, normally for the defence but once— memorably, against Verres—as a prosecutor. The forensic orator's audience consisted of, first, the jurymen on their benches (*subsellia*);[12] second, the praetor or his deputy (*iudex quaestionis*), seated with his advisers on the *tribunal*;[13] and finally, the crowd standing round (*corona*), enjoying the performance with appreciative shouts and gestures.[14] Spectators could also get a view of the proceedings from the balconies above the shops, or by using vantage points designed for viewing gladiatorial shows or theatrical games.[15]

To draw a crowd like that was one thing; it was quite another to speak from the *rostra* to the People as a whole. Cicero was 39, holding the second most senior magistracy in the *cursus honorum*, before he did that for the first time:[16]

---

[9] Morstein-Marx 2004.40–1.

[10] Cicero *Ad Atticum* 4.1.3: *splendorem nostrum illum forensem et in senatum auctoritatem et apud uiros bonos gratiam.*

[11] Cicero *De oratore* 1.118 (*haec turba et barbaria forensis*), cf. Livy 9.46.14 (*forensis turba* attributed to 304 BC); *Ad Atticum* 1.16.11 (*illa contionalis hirudo aerari, misera ac ieiuna plebecula*), *De domo* 89 (*multitudo ex seruis, ex conductis, ex facinerosis, ex egentibus congregata*). Contrast the more neutral description at *Pro Caelio* 22: *iam quae sit multitudo in foro, quae genera, quae studia, quae uarietas hominum uidetis.*

[12] Cicero *Pro Caelio* 67, *Brutus* 289–90.

[13] Cicero *De oratore* 1.168, *Brutus* 290 (n. 54 below).

[14] Catullus 53, Cicero *Brutus* 192, 289–90.

[15] Valerius Maximus 9.12.7 (view from *maenianum*); Cicero *Pro Cluentio* 93 (*gradus Aurelii* 'like a theatre'); see below, pp. 161–2.

[16] Cicero *Pro lege Manilia* 1–2.

quamquam mihi semper frequens conspectus uester multo iucundissimus, hic
autem locus ad agendum amplissimus, ad dicendum ornatissimus est uisus,
Quirites, tamen hoc aditu laudis, qui semper optimo cuique maxime patuit,
non mea me uoluntas adhuc, sed uitae meae rationes ab ineunte aetate susceptae
prohibuerunt . . . ita neque hic locus uacuus umquam fuit ab iis qui uestram
causam defenderent, et meus labor in priuatorum periculis caste integreque
uersatus ex uestro iudicio fructum est amplissimum consecutus.

Although your crowded assembly has always seemed to me the most pleasing of
sights, and this place in particular the grandest for political action and the most
distinguished for speech-making, nevertheless, citizens, this way to reputation,
open as it is to every man of merit, has so far been closed to me—not by my
wish, but by the plan of life I have adopted since my youth . . . This place was
never short of people to defend your interests, and my hard work defending
private citizens, honestly and scrupulously carried out, has now received by your
verdict the most honourable of rewards.

'This place', *hic locus*, was the *rostra*, 'the orator's greatest stage';[17] his
audience was the Roman People, summoned by criers through the
streets and now thronging the Forum and its temples like the auditorium of a giant theatre.[18]

Cicero's phrase *frequens conspectus uester* is hard to translate, but easy
to understand if one sees it through the eyes of the man on the *rostra*.
What he sees is a huge crowd (*frequentia*), and as the prefix of the verbal
noun implies, they all have their eyes fixed on him. Wherever Cicero
uses *hic locus* in this sense, he uses *conspectus* or *conspicere* as well.[19]

'Did you imagine', he had taunted Verres, 'that you'd never come
back into their sight, never come into the Forum of the Roman
People?'[20] It was taken for granted that the Forum belonged to the

---

[17] Cicero *De oratore* 2.338 (*quia maxima quasi oratoris scaena uideatur contionis*
esse); cf. *De diuinatione* 97 (*in scaena, id est in contione*).
[18] Cicero *Pro lege Manilia* 44: *uniuersus populus Romanus referto foro completisque*
omnibus templis ex quibus hic locus conspici potest. Criers: Livy 4.32.1 (*praeconibus per*
uicos dimissis), Festus (Paulus) 34L (*contio . . . per praeconem conuocatur*).
[19] Cicero *Pro lege Manilia* 44 (previous note); *De lege agraria* 2.6 (*aditum huius loci*
conspectumque uestrum), 2.56 on Sulla's sale of the goods of the proscribed (*ex hoc loco*
uendidit, nec quorum oculos offendebat, eorum ipsorum conspectum fugere ausus est).
[20] Cicero *In Verrem* 2.5.144: *numquam te in horum conspectum rediturum, num-*
quam in forum populi Romani uenturum . . . duxisti? For the same train of thought cf.
Rhetorica ad Herennium 4.9 (*tu in forum prodire, tu lucem conspicere, tu in horum*
conspectum uenire audes?), Cicero *De oratore* 2.226 (*tu lucem aspicere audes? tu hos*
intueri? tu in foro, tu in ciuium esse conspectu?). Other *in conspectu* references:
Rhetorica ad Herennium 4.38; Cicero *In Verrem* 2.1.122, 2.4.26, *De lege agraria* 1.7,
de oratore 3.4, *Philippics* 2.63.

citizens of Rome, and whatever happened there happened 'with the Roman People looking on'.[21] That politics was a spectacle, with the citizens as the audience, is made explicit by Quintus Cicero's treatise of advice for his brother's consular candidature in 64 BC:[22]

postremo tota petitio cura ut pompae plena sit, ut inlustris, ut splendida, ut popularis sit, ut habeat summam speciem et dignitatem . . .

Last of all, see that your whole campaign is full of show; that it is glorious and colourful, and pleasing to the People, that it has a fine appearance and dignity.

It had to be *splendida*; this self-presentation was the *splendor forensis* of which Cicero wrote to Atticus, spectacularly regained on his return from exile in September 57 BC.[23]

II

The two occasions when a Roman politician was most literally a performer before an audience were the triumph and the games.

Polybius explained the triumph to his Greek readers as 'a spectacle in which generals bring right before the eyes of the Roman People a vivid impression of their achievements'.[24] Cicero in the *Verrines* explains why commanders bring their prisoners (and their booty) back to Rome, 'so that the Roman People may *see* the fruits of victory in a splendid spectacle'.[25] In AD 71, Vespasian and Titus began their triumphal procession by driving through the theatres of Pompey, Balbus and Marcellus, 'to give the crowds a better view'.[26]

---

[21] *Inspectante populi Romani*: Cicero *In Verrem* 2.1.13, *In toga candida* fr. 5 Crawford (Asconius 87C), *Post reditum ad Quirites* 14, *In Vatinium* 34, *Philippics* 2.21, 3.12; Q. Cicero *Commentariolum petitionis* 10.

[22] *Commentariolum petitionis* 52 (trans. D. W. Taylor and J. Murrell). Cf. M. Caelius in Cicero *Ad familiares* 8.4.1, 8.14.1 and 4 (*spectaculum*), 8.11.3 (*scaena rei totius*).

[23] See above, n. 10.

[24] Polybius 6.15.8: δι' ὧν ὑπὸ τὴν ὄψιν ἄγεται τοῖς πολίταις ὑπὸ τῶν στρατηγῶν ἡ τῶν κατειργασμένων πραγμάτων ἐνάργεια (trans. Beard 2007.31, bringing out the sense of ἐνάργεια as *sub oculos subiectio*, Quintilian 9.2.40).

[25] Cicero *In Verrem* 2.5.77: *ut his per triumphum ductis pulcherrimum spectaculum fructumque uictoriae populus Romanus percipere possit.*

[26] Josephus *Bellum Iudaicum* 7.131: ἔπεμπον τὸν θρίαμβον διὰ τῶν θεάτρων διεξελαύνοντες, ὅπως εἴη τοῖς πλήθεσιν ἡ θέα ῥάων.

Those venues were not available to the republican *triumphator*, but even in the less magnificent pre-Augustan city the same principle of maximum publicity applied. Here is Plutarch's description of Aemilius Paullus' triumph in 167 BC:[27]

πεμφθῆναι δ' αὐτὸν οὕτω λέγουσιν. ὁ μὲν δῆμος ἔν τε τοῖς ἱππικοῖς θεάτροις, ἃ κίρκους καλοῦσι, περί τε τὴν ἀγορὰν ἰκρία πηξάμενοι, καὶ τἆλλα τῆς πόλεως μέρη καταλαβόντες, ὡς ἕκαστα παρεῖχε τῆς πομπῆς ἔποψιν.

They say it was conducted as follows. The People set up wooden stands, both in the horse-racing theatres which they call *circi* and also round the Forum, and they occupied all the other places in the city which provided a view of the procession.

Before Caesar built the Circus Maximus as a monumental chariot-racing arena, the only permanent seating there was provided by the *fori publici*, wooden 'public decks' about 12 feet high, supposedly dating back to the Tarquins.[28] How extensive they were is unknown, but in Cicero's time people watched the races from shops or booths (*tabernae*),[29] and the need for extra stands at Paullus' triumph implies that the permanent provision was limited.[30]

Plutarch's reference to the other vantage points in the city may remind us of the temple steps crowded with people at the Porta Capena when Cicero returned;[31] or of Tacitus' description of Nero's return to Rome after the execution of his mother, with the Roman People watching from tiers of seats set up along his route 'in the way triumphs are viewed'.[32] As for the stands set up 'around the Forum', they were probably the ones that were used for gladiatorial shows.[33]

The study of the 'prehistory' of the Roman amphitheatre has been put on a new footing by the work of Katherine Welch.[34] Her careful

---

[27] Plutarch *Aemilius Paullus* 32.2, cf. 34.7 on Aemilius as περίβλεπτος.
[28] Livy 1.35.8–9, 1.56.2, Dionysius of Halicarnassus 3.68.1; cf. Livy 29.37.2, 45.1.7, Festus (Paulus) 74L (*fori significant et circensia spectacula*).
[29] Cicero *Pro Murena* 73, cf. *Pro Milone* 65; Wiseman 1980.12–13 = 1987.182–3.
[30] For Caesar's great arena, see Dionysius of Halicarnassus 3.68.2–4, Pliny *Nat. Hist.* 36.102, Suetonius *Diuus Iulius* 39.2.
[31] See above, n. 1.
[32] Tacitus *Annals* 14.13.2: *extructos qua incederet spectaculorum gradus, quo modo triumphi uisuntur*.
[33] Plutarch *Gaius Gracchus* 12.3 (θεωρητήρια κύκλῳ κατασκευάσαντες); Cicero *Pro Sestio* 124 (*ex omnibus spectaculis usque a Capitolio*).
[34] See Welch 1991, 1994, 2007.

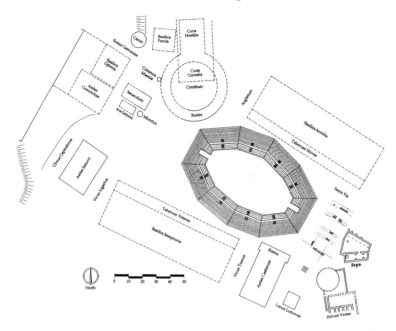

Fig. 4. Hypothetical plan of temporary seating for gladiatorial games in the republican Forum (Welch 2007.52, drawn by P. Stinson).

analysis of the Forum piazza as a gladiatorial arena, by which she aims to explain the oval shape of later purpose-built ampitheatres, has resulted in a brilliant and far-reaching hypothesis about how the spectators were accommodated.[35] Welch's book is superbly illustrated with reconstruction drawings (two of which I reproduce here as Figs. 4 and 5); but the very plausibility of the reconstructions makes it important to emphasise the problems they involve. First, this enclosed layout seems inconsistent with Cicero's reference to seats for spectators as far as the Capitol, and with the space on the Caesarian *rostra* which was reserved for the family of Servius Sulpicius Rufus to view the games and the gladiators.[36] Second, we are told

---

[35] Welch 2007.30–71, esp. 49–57.

[36] Cicero *Pro Sestio* 124 (n. 33 above), not addressed in the discussion of the passage at Welch 2007.38; *Philippics* 9.16 (*locum ludis gladiatoribusque*). See Welch 2007.282 n. 73, conceding that 'on certain grand occasions... the seating around the oval arena could have spread even up the slopes of the Capitol'; but it is hard to see how that is consistent with her reconstruction.

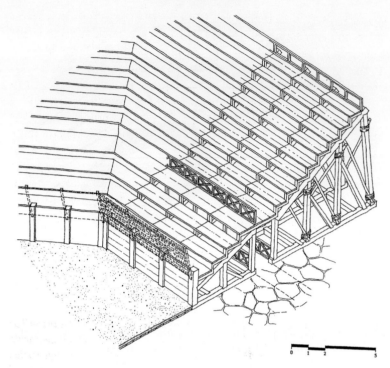

Fig. 5. Hypothetical construction details of temporary seating in the republican Forum (Welch 2007.63, drawn by P. Stinson).

that Gaius Gracchus, who objected to the wooden stands blocking the view of ordinary citizens, had them taken down overnight; that would not have been possible with such elaborate structures.[37]

It seems to me that the hypothesis depends too much on inference from the Caesarian underground passages below the paving of the piazza in front of the Basilica Iulia. Katherine Welch is surely right to see that complex as providing access from below not for gladiators but for caged beasts, and to associate it with the 'hunting theatre' constructed in the Forum for Caesar's triumph in 46 BC.[38] But that was a unique occasion, as our sources make clear,[39] and the underground

---

[37] Plutarch *Gaius Gracchus* 12.4; cf. Welch 2007.57, estimating that a workforce of 'perhaps 500–1000 men' would have needed 'from several days to one week' to take the structure down.

[38] Welch 2007.38–42; Dio Cassius 43.22.3–23.3.

[39] Pliny *Nat. Hist.* 15.78 (altar removed), 19.23 (awnings over the whole Forum); Suetonius *Diuus Iulius* 39.1 (senators as gladiators).

passages must have been specially excavated as part of the huge construction programme (funded, of course, by the conquest of Gaul) that saw the building of the Julian and Aemilian basilicas.[40] For wild beasts in the Forum, a substantial enclosed arena must have been necessary; but there is no need to read that necessity back into the days when railings were enough to separate the gladiators from the spectators.[41]

We know surprisingly little about the detailed topography of the republican Forum. The 'old shops' were on the south-west side of the piazza, and the 'new shops' on the north-east, but it is not known where exactly they were or how far they extended.[42] It was believed that the shops and porticos in the Forum dated back to the time of Tarquinius Priscus,[43] and that in 318 BC the censor Gaius Maenius built out balconies (*maeniana*) 'projecting beyond the columns', in order to give more room for spectators above.[44]

By the time Vitruvius was writing in the twenties BC, that layout was what defined the forum in a Roman town. A Roman architect could not build a Greek-style *agora*, with double colonnades and close-set columns:[45]

Italiae uero urbibus non eadem est ratione faciendum, ideo quod a maioribus consuetudo tradita est gladiatoria munera in foro dari. igitur circum spectacula spatiosiora intercolumnia distribuantur circaque in porticibus argentariae tabernae maenianaque superioribus coaxationibus conlocentur, quae et ad usum et ad uectigalia publica recta erunt disposita.

In the cities of Italy we must work to a different plan, because of the custom handed down from our ancestors of holding gladiatorial shows in the Forum. For that reason wider intercolumniations should be arranged round the shows, and bankers' shops should be provided in the porticos

[40] Cicero *Ad Atticum* 4.16.8, Plutarch *Caesar* 29.2–3; Wiseman 1998a.106–10.
[41] Cicero *Pro Sestio* 124 (*tantus ex cancellis fori plausus*); cf. Varro *Res rusticae* 3.5.4 (*ad speciem cancellorum scaenicorum et theatri*), Ovid *Amores* 3.2.63–4 (*cancelli* in the Circus Maximus).
[42] *Tabernae ueteres*: Plautus *Curculio* 480, Livy 44.16.10, Pliny *Nat. Hist.* 35.113 (quoting Varro). *Tabernae nouae*: Cicero *De oratore* 2.266, *Academica* 2.70, Varro *De lingua Latina* 6.59, Livy 3.48.5, 26.27.2.
[43] Livy 1.35.10, Dionysius of Halicarnassus 3.67.4.
[44] Festus 120L: *qui primus in foro ultra columnas tigna proiecit quo ampliarentur superiora spectacula.*
[45] Vitruvius 5.1.1–2. For the *tabernae argentariae*, see Varro *De lingua Latina* 6.91, *De uita populi Romani* fr. 72 Riposati (Nonius 853L), Plautus *Epidicus* 199, Pliny *Nat. Hist.* 21.8; detailed discussion in Papi 1999.

round about, with balconies on joists above, which will be appropriately placed for usefulness and public revenue.

As the phraseology implies (*distribuantur, disposita*), the republican Forum had not been completely surrounded by such porticos. There was still plenty of space to be exploited, for instance in the seventies BC with the *gradus Aurelii*, evidently a permanent stand of seats for spectators.[46]

From such vantage points the Roman People watched triumphal processions and gladiatorial games, and sometimes also the regular judicial business of the Forum.[47] It was an arena for various types of spectacle, and in each of them Roman politicians were on show. The magistrate in charge of the games, whether here or in the Circus Maximus, sat enthroned with as much pomp as the commander riding in his triumphal chariot.[48] His *tribunal* was like a stage—or perhaps it actually was one.

When Appius Claudius was praetor in 57 BC, he honoured with his presence the gladiatorial show given by Quintus Metellus Scipio in memory of his father. Cicero's tendentious account of the event contains a very revealing detail:[49]

is cum cotidie gladiatores spectaret, numquam est conspectus cum ueniret. emergebat subito, cum sub tabulas subrepserat, ut 'mater, te appello' dicturus uideretur. itaque illa uia latebrosior, qua spectatum ille ueniebat, Appia iam uocabatur. qui tamen quoquo tempore conspectus erat, non modo gladiatores sed equi ipsi gladiatorum repentinis sibilis extimescebant.

Although he was present every day at the gladiatorial games, he was never seen when he came. He used to creep up underneath the flooring and appear all of a sudden, as though he were going to cry out 'Mother, to thee I cry!' And so that

---

[46] Cicero *Pro Cluentio* 93 (*gradus illi Aurelii tum noui quasi pro theatro illi iudicio aedificati uidebantur*), cf. *Pro Flacco* 66. Not to be confused with the *tribunal Aurelium* (Cicero *De domo* 54, *Post reditum ad Quirites* 13, *Pro Sestio* 34, *In Pisonem* 11); both structures may have been part of a wider Forum project by either C. Cotta (*pr.* 78?, *cos.* 75) or M. Cotta (*pr.* 77?, *cos.* 74): see Festus 416L, with Lindsay's reading *postquam id* [i.e. the Forum] *Cotta strauit*.

[47] See above, n. 15.

[48] Propertius 3.18.17–18 on Marcellus: *i nunc, tolle animos et tecum finge trium-phos | stantiaque in plausum tota theatra iuuent*. Cf. also Juvenal 11.193–5 (*similisque triumpho*) on the praetor in the Circus at the *ludi Megalenses*.

[49] Cicero *Pro Sestio* 126: trans. R. Gardner (Loeb Classical Library), very slightly adjusted.

somewhat skulking path by which Appius came to see the games began to be called the Appian Way. Yet whenever he was seen, not only the gladiators but the very horses of the gladiators took fright at the sudden hissings.

The first of Cicero's two jokes alludes to a famous scene in Pacuvius' tragedy *Iliona*, where the ghost of the murdered boy Polydorus appears and pleads for burial.[50] We happen to know how the scene was staged in Cicero's time: the ghost 'came up out of the ground', which must mean through a trapdoor from under the stage, the device known to the Greeks as 'Charon's ladder'.[51]

Modern scholars, anachronistically imagining an amphitheatre-like structure, assume that Appius' sudden appearance was into the 'auditorium' or 'seating area'.[52] But a praetor in office had lictors, a *tribunal*, a curule chair; he would not be sitting shoulder to shoulder with the rest of the citizens. We are not well informed about *tribunalia*: on the one hand, they were evidently moveable;[53] on the other, they were substantial enough to accommodate the magistrate's *consilium* of advisers.[54] Were they dismantled on days when there was no public business in the Forum? Or were they used for other purposes? The latter seems most likely, if Appius' *tribunal* had a trapdoor entrance like a theatre stage.

Livy's account of the contracts let by the censors of 174 BC contains a puzzling item which may be relevant. Along with the road-paving and bridge-building, there was also the provision of 'a stage for the aediles and praetors'.[55] Where it was, and what it was for, is not known. Since the urban praetor was responsible for the *ludi Apollinares*, and the plebeian and curule aediles for the other annual *ludi*,

---

[50] *Scholia Bobiensia* 138 Stangl; cf. Cicero *Tusculan Disputations* 1.106, *Academica* 2.88, Horace *Satires* 2.3.60–2. For the plot, see Hyginus *Fabulae* 109.

[51] Cicero *Tusculan Disputations* 1.106 (*exoritur e terra*); cf. [Seneca] *Octauia* 593 for Agrippina's ghost (*tellure rupta Tartaro gressum extuli*). χαρώνιοι κλίμακες: Pollux 4.132.

[52] See e.g. Gardner 1958.206 n. *c*, Beacham 1991.251 n. 4, Welch 2007.279 n. 39. My own earlier suggestion that Appius used the underground passages (Wiseman 1990.246) is rightly dismissed by Welch (2007.279 n. 43).

[53] Cicero *In Vatinium* 21 (*continuatis tribunalibus*, an improvised causeway), Caesar *De bello ciuili* 3.20.1 (*tribunal suum iuxta ... praetoris urbani sellam collocauit*). There may have been permanent *tribunalia* too: see n. 46 above (*tribunal Aurelium*).

[54] Cicero *De oratore* 1.168 (*nobis in tribunali Q. Pompei praetoris urbani familiaris nostri sedentibus*), *Brutus* 290 (*compleatur tribunal*).

[55] Livy 41.27.5: *et scaenam aedilibus praetoribusque praebendam*.

most scholars assume that it was a stage for theatrical perform-ances.[56] However, as we shall see in the next section, the theatre games (*ludi scaenici*) were held in front of the respective temples of the deities honoured at each festival; there was no one place appro-priate to them all. For the circus games (*ludi circenses*), on the other hand, there was just the one venue—and in fact Livy's list of the censors' contracts in 174 goes on to list various items specific to the Circus Maximus.[57]

Perhaps the 'stage for the aediles and praetors' was a *tribunal* for the magistrates presiding at the *ludi circenses*. That cannot be certain; but the very fact that Livy uses the word *scaena* is sufficient con-firmation of what Cicero implies in his malicious description of Appius at the gladiatorial games: Roman magistrates were like actors, on show before an audience. The stage and the *tribunal* might be the same structure, used differently on different days.

III

When Cicero returned to the city from exile, so many well-wishers came to Rome to greet him that Clodius' supporters were able to claim that that was the reason for the grain shortage. When the crisis was debated in the Senate, they ran 'first to the theatre and then to the Senate', shouting that Cicero was to blame.[58] What theatre, where?

Fifty years ago, John Arthur Hanson established beyond question that the *ludi scaenici* of the Roman republic were performed in front of the temples of the respective divinities honoured in each of the

---

[56] 'Evidently as a permanent structure for all the *ludi* for which those magistrates were responsible' (Gruen 1992.206); 'presumably a single facility to be available for the various *ludi scaenici* in their charge' (Goldberg 1998.2); similarly Welch 2007.59. The passage is normally considered along with Livy 40.51.3 on the *theatrum et proscaenium ad Apollinis* provided by the censors of 179 BC; but the different terminology probably implies a different sort of structure.

[57] Livy 41.27.6, with Humphrey 1986.70–1; the corrupt text refers to the *carceres*, the *metae*, the 'eggs' for counting the laps, and *caueae ferreae* which were probably for wild-beast shows.

[58] Cicero *Ad Atticum* 4.1.6 (p. 154 above): *cum...homines ad theatrum primo, deinde ad senatum concurrissent.*

annual games.[59] Cicero is explicit in his description of the *ludi Megalenses*, 'which our ancestors wished to be held on the Palatine, in front of the temple in the very sight of the Great Mother';[60] and Livy's account of the 'theatre and proscenium' put up at the Apollo temple by the censors of 179 BC shows that the same applied to the *ludi Apollinares*.[61]

It is clear that the primary audience space was provided by the steps of the temples themselves, as is implied by Pompey's dedication in 52 BC of a 'temple of Victoria with steps that serve as a theatre'.[62] Indeed, we know from the archaeological evidence that there was no room in front of the Magna Mater temple for any other form of auditorium.[63] What the censors of 179 provided at the Apollo temple was probably an extension of the temple steps in the shape of a *theatrum*.

On the other hand, there is ample evidence for free-standing temporary stages and auditoria (*caueae*), which were constructed for each set of games and then taken down again.[64] Lucius Roscius' reservation of the first fourteen rows for the *equites* implies that they could be substantial structures, and ambitious magistrates competed with each other in lavishly decorating them.[65] The *theatrum* to which Clodius' supporters ran on 7 September 57 BC was evidently an example.

---

[59] Hanson 1959.9–26, the introductory chapter in an archaeological study of Roman 'theatre-temples'.

[60] Cicero *De haruspicum responso* 24 (trans. Hanson 1959.13): *quos in Palatio nostri maiores ante templum in ipso Matris magnae conspectu Megalesibus fieri celebrarique uoluerunt*. Cf. also Augustine *City of God* 2.4 (*coram deum matre*).

[61] Livy 40.51.3 (n. 56 above); Hanson 1959.18–24. There is no reason to suppose (with Gruen 1992.206 and Goldberg 1998.2, 10) that the contract was never carried out.

[62] Tiro in Aulus Gellius 10.1.7: *cum Pompeius . . . aedem Victoriae dedicaturus foret, cuius gradus uicem theatri essent*. See also Tertullian *De spectaculis* 10.5: *non theatrum sed Veneris templum nuncupauit, cui subiecimus, inquit, gradus spectaculorum*. The temple was presumably of Venus Victrix.

[63] See Goldberg 1998, a brilliant analysis of what the extant remains imply.

[64] Tacitus *Annals* 14.20.2: *nam antea* [before 55 BC] *subitariis gradibus et scaena in tempus structa ludos edi solitos*. Servius on *Georgics* 3.24 (citing Varro and Suetonius): *apud maiores theatri gradus tantum fuerunt, nam scaena de lignis ad tempus fiebat*. Cf. also Dio Cassius 37.58.4 on the Tiber flood of 60 BC: καί τι καὶ θέατρον πρὸς πανήγυρίν τινα ἐκ θύρων ᾠκοδομημένον ἀνετράπη. *Cauea*: Lucretius 4.75–80 (a view from the back), Cicero *De legibus* 2.38.

[65] *Lex Roscia* (67 BC): Asconius 78–9C, Plutarch *Cicero* 13.2–4. Decoration: Cicero *Pro Murena* 38 (*ludorum huius elegantiam et scaenae magnificentiam*), Valerius Maximus 2.4.6.

The *ludi Romani* were on at that time, and since those games were in honour of Jupiter Optimus Maximus, one would expect the performances to be in the *area Capitolina*, with the steps of the huge Capitoline temple accommodating the spectators. But how far are we to imagine the agitators running? The easiest inference from Cicero's account is that they were shouting their slogans in different parts of the Forum. A reference in Livy suggests that the Comitium, a theatre-like structure, could be used for the *ludi Romani*,[66] but since it was immediately outside the Senate-house, that cannot be the *theatrum* Cicero refers to on this occasion.

There were two aediles—plebeian or curule—in charge of each of the *ludi*. They could preside either together or separately,[67] and when they chose to act independently they must have done so at two separate 'theatres'. That is exactly what our sources tell us, despite modern scholars' reluctance to believe them,[68] in the only two episodes that provide any detail at all about the circumstances of the *ludi scaenici*.

The more explicit of the two is a narrative dated to either 53 or 52 BC, when Marcus Favonius was aedile. He deputed the stage games to his mentor Cato, while he himself went and sat with the spectators and joined in the applause.

ἐν δὲ τῷ ἑτέρῳ θεάτρῳ †Δουρίων† ὁ Φαωνίου συνάρχων ἐχορήγει πολυτελῶς· ἀλλ' ἐκεῖνον ἀπολείποντες οἱ ἄνθρωποι μετέβαινον ἐνταῦθα, καὶ συνέπαιζον προθύμως ὑποκρινομένῳ τῷ Φαωνίῳ τὸν ἰδιώτην καὶ τῷ Κάτωνι τὸν ἀγωνοθέτην.

In the other theatre Favonius' colleague Lurco[?] was presiding in lavish style. But people left him to go to the other place, and enthusiastically joined in the fun of Favonius playing the private citizen and Cato playing the president of the games.

---

[66] Livy 27.36.8: *comitium tectum esse memoriae proditum est et ludos Romanos semel instauratos ab aedilibus*. See below, n. 86.

[67] Suetonius *Diuus Iulius* 10.1, on Caesar in 65 BC: *ludosque et cum collega et separatim edidit*.

[68] 'It is ... very improbable that the two aediles should have organized the theatrical performances simultaneously but separately in two different theatres' (Linderski 1972.189–90 = 1995.239–40 on Plutarch *Cato minor* 46.4, followed by Ryan 1998.520). 'What is meant by the two *caveae* or the two *scaenae* is an utter mystery' (Lenaghan 1969.124 on Cicero *De haruspicum responso* 25, followed by Goldberg 1998.8–9).

We are not told which *ludi* they were, nor do we know whether Favonius was a plebeian or a curule aedile. But he and his colleague were certainly presiding at two separate theatres simultaneously.[69]

The other episode took place three or four years earlier. Our evidence for it is another piece of Ciceronian malice—his interpretation, in a speech to the Senate, of Clodius' presidency of the *ludi Megalenses* as curule aedile in 56 BC.[70] Clodius' entourage is described as 'a countless force of slaves, whipped up and brought together from every street in Rome', who 'at a given signal were suddenly let loose from every arch and doorway and rushed out on to the stage'.[71] The aedile 'had handed over the Senate and People of Rome, penned up as they were in the packed audience, hampered by the crowd and the narrow quarters, to a mob of jeering slaves'.[72]

What exactly was happening? Cicero chooses not to be explicit, launching instead into an indignant purple passage about the pollution of the Great Mother's games. When he returns to specifics, he does so in somewhat different terms:[73]

> *quo si qui liber aut spectandi aut etiam religionis causa accesserat, manus adferebantur, quo matrona nulla adiit propter uim consessumque seruorum . . . hos ludos serui fecerunt, serui spectauerunt, tota denique hoc aedile seruorum Megalesia fuerunt.*

Free men who came to watch, or even for religious reasons, could expect to be manhandled. No married woman attended because of the violence of the slaves and their presence in the audience . . . These games were celebrated by slaves, watched by slaves; in short, with *him* as aedile, the whole Megalesia belonged to slaves.

Here we have a new outrage, 'slaves' in the audience as well as on the stage, but it soon becomes clear that that was happening somewhere else:[74]

---

[69] Plutarch *Cato minor* 46.2–4. For the date (53 or 52 BC) see Linderski 1972 = 1995.231–50; for the identity of Favonius' colleague (M. Aufidius Lurco) see Ryan 1998 (though his explanation of the two theatres at 1998.520–1 is unnecessary).

[70] Cicero *De haruspicum responso* 22–6; commentary in Wiseman 1974.159–69.

[71] *De haruspicum responso* 22: *uis enim innumerabilis incitata ex omnibus uicis conlecta seruorum . . . repente e fornicibus ostiisque omnibus in scaenam signo dato inmissa inrupit.*

[72] Ibid. (trans. Shackleton Bailey, slightly adapted).

[73] Ibid. 24 (trans. Shackleton Bailey, slightly adapted).

[74] Ibid. 25 (trans. Shackleton Bailey).

quid magis inquinatum, deformatum, peruersum, conturbatum dici potest quam omne seruitium, permissu magistratus liberatum, in alteram scaenam inmissum, alteri praepositum, ut alter consessus potestati seruorum obiceretur, alter seruorum totus esset?

Could there be any worse defilement, disfigurement, perversion, confusion than this—the entire slave population freed by a magistrate's permission, let loose on to one stage and put in control of the other, so that one body of spectators was at the slaves' mercy, the other entirely made up of them?

Clodius had 'sent slaves into one auditorium and ejected free men from the other'.[75] No doubt he presided in person at one theatre, and at the other left his deputies in charge.[76] There is no mention of his colleague.

We can be fairly sure where each of these supposed outrages took place. Cicero's reference to the helpless audience being mocked by the 'slaves' suggests the cramped conditions in front of the temple itself.[77] The other theatre, with Clodius himself presiding, was probably at the foot of the Palatine slope directly below the temple.[78] This was the site, puzzlingly described by Velleius as 'from the Lupercal towards the Palatine', where the censors of 154 BC started to build a permanent theatre, only to have it destroyed by order of the Senate a few years later.[79] According to Appian the project was renewed in 107 BC, perhaps in connection with the rebuilding of the Magna Mater temple after the fire of 111; again, the theatre was demolished before completion.[80] The Lupercal site was linked to the temple precinct by the Scalae Caci,[81] and was no doubt thought of as under the goddess' influence, if not literally within her sight.

[75] *De haruspicum responso* 26 (trans. Shackleton Bailey): *tu in alteram* [sc. *caueam*] *seruos inmisisti, ex altera liberos eiecisti.*

[76] Wiseman 1974.167–8 (rejected a priori by Goldberg 1998.9). Cf. Nicolaus of Damascus *FGrH* 90 F 127.9.19 on Caesar's games in 46 BC: δυοῖν ὀντοῖν θεάτροιν, Caesar was in charge of the 'Roman theatre', young Octavius of the 'Greek'.

[77] Cicero *De haruspicum responso* 22: *cum ille seruorum eludentium multitudini senatum populumque Romanum uincto ipso consessu et constrictum spectaculis atque impeditum turba et angustiis tradidisset.* Cf. Goldberg 1998.6–9, Marshall 2006.37.

[78] Suggested by Hanson 1959.14 n. 29, 25.

[79] Velleius Paterculus 1.15.3 (*Cassius censor a Lupercali in Palatium uersus theatrum facere instituit*); Livy *Epitome* 48, Valerius Maximus 2.4.2, Orosius 4.21.4, Augustine *City of God* 1.31.

[80] Appian *Civil Wars* 1.28.125, with North 1992. Fire: Obsequens 39, Valerius Maximus 1.8.11; Goldberg 1998.11.

[81] Cf. Dionysius of Halicarnassus 1.32.3–33.1 on the Lupercal and the Victoria temple; see Wiseman 1981 = 1987.187–204.

The *theatrum* mentioned in Cicero's letter of September 57 BC is best explained in the same way. At the *ludi Romani* (and at the *ludi plebeii* in November) there would be performances going on in front of Jupiter's own temple on the Capitol, and also simultaneously at a 'theatre' in the Forum. It has long been known that the speech of the troupe-manager (*choragus*) in Plautus' *Curculio*, detailing all the types of people to be found in different parts of the Forum,[82] must have been composed for performance in the Forum itself; now, however, the careful analysis of C. W. Marshall has made it likely that it presupposes a stage roughly on the site of the later *rostra* of Caesar, with the audience facing south-east into the main Forum piazza.[83] That is, the theatre was at the foot of the Capitol slope, notionally within sight of Jupiter Optimus Maximus, whose temple loomed on the summit to the west. Indeed, from 63 BC onwards it was literally within Jupiter's sight, for in that year, by order of the *haruspices*, a statue of the god was erected on the Capitol, facing east in order to see the Forum and the Senate-house.[84]

When Caesar planned a huge permanent theatre up against the Capitol slope, he probably had in mind Jupiter's games, the *ludi Romani* and the *ludi plebeii*.[85] His reconstruction of the Forum piazza destroyed the old *rostra* and the Comitium, which had been theatre-like in layout and probably used for theatre games;[86] it is possible that his siting of the new *rostra* was intended to reproduce the same combination of features.

The details escape us, but what is clear enough is the multiple use of the various platforms available in the Forum—as *rostra*, *tribunalia*, or stages, depending on what day it was—and the availability of temporary

---

[82] Plautus *Curculio* 462–84; cf. Marshall 2006.26–8 for the job of the *choragus*.

[83] Marshall 2006.40–3.

[84] Cicero *In Catilinam* 3.20 (*in excelso . . . [ut] solis ortum et forum curiamque conspiceret*), cf. 3.22 (*ad uos senatumque conuerso*).

[85] Suetonius *Diuus Iulius* 44.1 (*theatrum summae magnitudinis Tarpeio monti accubans*); not to be confused with his other projected theatre, which became the Theatre of Marcellus (Dio Cassius 43.49.2–3, 53.30.5, Augustus *Res gestae* 21.1 *ad aedem Apollinis*). Cf. nn. 79–80 above for the Lupercal theatre project and the *ludi Megalenses*.

[86] Livy 27.36.8 (n. 66 above); cf. Pliny *Nat. Hist.* 34.26 (*in cornibus comitii*), with 36.117 and Vitruvius 5.6.5 on the *cornua* of theatres. See Carafa 1998.132–55 for the shape of the republican Comitium; Bravo 2006 and Marshall 2006.44–5 for its probable use as a theatre, exploiting the *gradus curiae* (Livy 1.36.4, 1.48.3, Cicero *Ad Q. fratrem* 2.1.3).

or permanent viewing arrangements for the Roman People, whether as the audience at the games or as participants in the theatre of politics. It is against that background, ill-understood but essential for understanding the culture of the Roman republic, that we should try to imagine such apparently disparate phenomena as Varro's satires, the patriotic historical plays called *fabulae praetextae*, and the aristocratic funeral pageants described by Polybius.[87] They should not be separated off under the headings of social or literary history.

IV

If the permanent theatre at the Lupercal had been built, it would have provided seats for spectators not only at the *ludi Megalenses* in April but also at the Lupercalia festival itself on 15 February. The naked *Luperci* were performers (*ludii*); they made, quite literally, a spectacle of themselves.[88] Between the goat-sacrifice at dawn and the ritual meal at midday, the young men evidently spent their time at the Lupercal in athletic competitions;[89] after that, full of wine and equipped with thongs cut from the skin of the newly butchered goats, they set off around the city, running this way and that (*discurrere* is the term used) and whipping whomever they met, particularly women.[90]

That too was a spectacle. The young women were expected to bare their bodies for the lash,[91] and it is clear from the language of our sources that the Lupercalia presented a sexy show.[92] No doubt the *Luperci* went where the crowds were.[93] Varro refers to them going up

[87] Polybius 6.52.11–55.4, esp. 53.1–2 on the scene at the *rostra*.

[88] Varro *Antiquitates diuinae* fr. 80 Cardauns = Tertullian *De spectaculis* 5.3: *sicut et Lupercos ludios appellant, quod ludendo discurrant.* Valerius Maximus 2.2.9a: *equestris uero ordinis iuuentus omnibus annis bis urbem spectaculo sui... celebrabat* (i.e. the Lupercalia and the *transuectio equitum*).

[89] Ovid *Fasti* 2.267–8 (dawn), 364 (midday), 365–8, and *Origo gentis Romanae* 22.2–3 (competitions); evidence for the ritual discussed at Wiseman 1995.80–6.

[90] Valerius Maximus 2.2.9a on their preparation: *epularum hilaritate ac uino largiore prouecti.*

[91] Ovid *Fasti* 2.445–6: *iussae sua terga puellae | pellibus exsectis percutienda dabant.*

[92] See e.g. Livy 1.5.2 (*per lusum atque lasciuiam*), Valerius Maximus 2.2.9a (*iocantes*), Plutarch *Caesar* 61.2 (ἐπὶ παιδιᾷ καὶ γέλωτι), Dio Cassius 46.19.4 (ἐν τῷ παιγνιώδει τῶν γιγνομένων).

[93] Ovid *Fasti* 5.102: *cum lustrant celebres uellera secta uias.*

and down the Sacra Via, and we know that the climax of the day took place in the Forum, 'with the Roman People looking on'.[94] The *Luperci* were normally young equestrians, but men of senatorial rank might take part too.[95] There were two 'teams', the *Luperci Fabiani* and the *Luperci Quinctiales*, joined in 44 BC by a third, the *Luperci Iuliani*, newly created in honour of Caesar.[96] The first time the *Iuliani* took part they were led by the consul Antony, and it turned out to be a fateful occasion. The earliest narrative account, by Nicolaus of Damascus, is worth looking at closely.[97]

The historian begins by explaining the occasion for his non-Roman readers:[98]

μετὰ δὲ ταῦτα ἑορτὴ ἐν τῇ Ῥώμῃ ἐγένετο χειμῶνος (Λουπερκάλια καλεῖται), ἐν ᾗ γηραιοί τε ὁμοῦ πομπεύουσι καὶ νέοι γυμνοί, ἀληλιμμένοι τε καὶ διεζωσμένοι τούς τε ὑπαντῶντας κατακερτομοῦντες καὶ τύπτοντες αἰγείοις δοραῖς.

After that there took place at Rome a winter festival called Lupercalia, in which the parade consists of both old and young men, naked, oiled, and belted, who jeer at those they meet and strike them with goatskin thongs.

Nicolaus must be mistaken about the old men (γηραιοί), who are mentioned in no other source. That the *Luperci* were oiled is confirmed by Cicero, who adds that they were drunk.[99] By 'belted' (Ovid calls them *cinctuti*) he means wearing only goatskin loincloths, *diazomata*.[100]

---

[94] Varro *De gente populi Romani* fr. 21 Fraccaro = Augustine *City of God* 18.12 (*Lupercorum per sacram uiam adscensum atque descensum*); Cicero *Philippics* 2.85 (spectators *toto foro*), 3.12 (*populo Romano inspectante*, cf. n. 21 above).

[95] Valerius Maximus 2.2.9a (*equestris ordinis iuuentus*); Plutarch *Antony* 12.1 (τῶν εὐγενῶν νέοι πολλοὶ καὶ τῶν ἀρχόντων), *Caesar* 61.2 (τῶν εὐγενῶν νεανίσκων καὶ ἀρχόντων πολλοὶ); Cicero *Pro Caelio* 26 (M. Caelius), *Ad Atticum* 12.5.1 (Q. Cicero junior).

[96] *ILS* 1923, 4948, *CIL* 6.33421; Festus (Paulus) 78L, Festus 308L, Ovid *Fasti* 2.377–8. *Iuliani*: Dio Cassius 44.6.2, Cicero *Philippics* 13.31; implied by Aelius Tubero fr. 3P = Dionysius of Halicarnassus 1.80.1 (τριχῇ γὰρ ἐνενέμηντο).

[97] See Toher 2003 and 2006 for Nicolaus on Caesar, esp. 2003.141–3 on the Lupercalia.

[98] *FGrH* 90 F 130.21.71.

[99] Cicero *Philippics* 3.12 (Antony *nudus unctus ebrius*), 13.31 (Antony *obrutus uino, unguentis oblitus*); cf. Valerius Maximus 2.2.9a (n. 90 above).

[100] Ovid *Fasti* 5.101; Aelius Tubero fr. 3P = Dionysius of Halicarnassus 1.80.1 (γυμνοὺς ὑπεζωσμένους τὴν αἰδῶ ταῖς δοραῖς τῶν νεοθύτων), Plutarch *Romulus* 21.5 (ἐν περιζώμασι γυμνοί); see Wiseman 1995.82–3. Compare Thucydides 1.6.5 on the first Olympic athletes, διαζώματα ἔχοντες περὶ τὰ αἰδοῖα.

τότε δὲ ἐνστάσης, ἡγεμὼν ἡρέθη Μάρκος Ἀντώνιος· καὶ προῄει διὰ τῆς ἀγορᾶς, ὥσπερ ἔθος ἦν, συνείπετο δὲ αὐτῷ καὶ ἄλλος ὄχλος.

On that occasion Marcus Antonius had been appointed leader. He proceeded through the Forum, as the custom was, and the rest of the crowd followed him.

It is not clear whether Nicolaus is thinking here of the other *Luperci*, or (more likely) of the crowd of onlookers in the Forum. Antony was making for the new *rostra*:[101]

καθημένῳ δὲ Καίσαρι ἐπὶ τῶν ἐμβόλων λεγομένων ἐπὶ χρυσοῦ θρόνου, καὶ ἱμάτιον ἁλουργὲς ἀμπεχομένῳ πρῶτον Λικίνιος δάφνινον ἔχων στέφανον, ἐντὸς δὲ διάδημα περιφαινόμενον προσέρχεται <καὶ> (ἦν γὰρ ὑψηλὸς ὁ τόπος ἐφ᾽ οὗ Καῖσαρ ἐδημηγόρει) βασταχθεὶς ὑπὸ τῶν συναρχόντων κατέθηκεν αὐτοῦ πρὸ τῶν ποδῶν τὸ διάδημα.

Caesar was sitting on what they call the *rostra*, on a golden throne wearing a purple robe. First, Licinius came forward, holding a laurel wreath in which a diadem was visible all round. Since the place from which Caesar used to address the People was high above the ground, he was lifted up by his colleagues and placed the diadem before Caesar's feet.

Licinius is otherwise unidentified.[102] The platform of the Caesarian *rostra* was about 3.7 metres above the pavement,[103] so at first sight his exploit may have been taken as just more showing-off by the athletic *Luperci*. However, the diadem-wreath made it much more significant than that:[104]

βοῶντος δὲ τοῦ δήμου ἐπὶ τὴν κεφαλὴν τίθεσθαι καὶ ἐπὶ τοῦτο Λέπιδον καλοῦντος τὸν ἱππάρχον, ὁ μὲν ὤκνει·

The People shouted to put it on Caesar's head, and called on Lepidus, the *magister equitum*, to do it. But he hesitated.

According to Cicero's tendentious memory of the event, Lepidus groaned, wept, and turned away in anguish.[105] Nicolaus knows nothing of that.

---

[101] Dio Cassius 43.49.1; this must have been very soon after its inauguration.
[102] Toher 2003.142 suggests the name may be a textual corruption for Λ. Κίννας, but that seems unnecessary (and would Nicolaus have abbreviated the *praenomen*?).
[103] Verduchi 1999.215.
[104] *FGrH* 90 F 130.21.72; cf. Cicero *Philippics* 2.85 on the diadem as a *meditatum et cogitatum scelus*.
[105] Cicero *Philippics* 5.38, 13.17.

ἐν τούτῳ δὲ Κάσσιος Λογγῖνος, εἷς τῶν ἐπιβουλευόντων, ὡς δῆθεν εὔνους ὤν, ἵνα καὶ λανθάνειν μᾶλλον δύναιτο ὑποφθὰς ἀνείλετο τὸ διάδημα καὶ ἐπί τά γόνατα αὐτοῦ ἔθηκεν. συνῆν δὲ καὶ Πόπλιος Κάσκας.

Meanwhile Cassius Longinus, one of the conspirators, anticipated him and placed the diadem on Caesar's knees. His purpose was to avoid detection by appearing well-disposed to Caesar; Publius Casca was also involved.

Since Cassius was one of the praetors, and Casca may have been one of the tribunes,[106] it is likely that they were on the *rostra* with Caesar.

Καίσαρος δὲ διωθουμένου καὶ τοῦ δήμου βοῶντος, ταχὺ προσδραμὼν Ἀντώνιος, γυμνὸς ἀληλιμμένος ὥσπερ ἐπόμπευεν, ἐπὶ τὴν κεφαλὴν ἐπιτίθησιν.

As Caesar pushed it away and the People shouted, Antony quickly ran forward, naked and oiled as in the parade, and placed it on his head.

According to Cicero, the People were shouting that Caesar should reject the diadem,[107] but Nicolaus' narrative implies the opposite. As for Antony, he was certainly on the *rostra* by now; indeed, Cicero says that he addressed the People.[108] He had probably come up by the steps at the back.

Καῖσαρ δὲ ἀνελόμενος αὐτὸ εἰς τὸν ὄχλον ἔρριψε. καὶ οἱ μὲν τελευταῖοι ἐκρότησαν ἐπὶ τούτῳ, οἱ δὲ πλησίον ἐβόων δέχεσθαι καὶ μὴ διωθεῖσθαι τὴν τοῦ δήμου χάριν.

Caesar took it off and threw it into the crowd. At this those at the back applauded, but those close to him were shouting that he should accept it and not reject the People's gift.

We don't know who 'those at the back' were, but we may guess that their applause was prearranged.

---

[106] For Casca's tribunate (44 or 43 BC?) see Dio Cassius 44.52.2 and 46.49.1, with Broughton 1986.194–5. Toher 2003.141–2 says Cassius too was tribune in 44—but that was L. Cassius, the conspirator's brother.

[107] Cicero *Philippics* 2.85 (offered *cum plangore populi*, rejected *cum plausu*), 13.31 (*gementem populum Romanum*).

[108] Cicero *Philippics* 2.85 (*escendis, accedis ad sellam*), 3.12 (*est contionatus*), 13.31 (*populum Romanum ad seruitutem cohortari*).

Nicolaus now analyses the rival views.[109] Some people were angry at this manifestation of power inappropriate to a democracy; some went along with it in order to gain Caesar's favour; some put it about that Antony had done it with Caesar's approval; many wanted Caesar to be openly a king.

παντοδαπαὶ μὲν φῆμαι ἐν τῷ ὁμίλῳ ἦσαν. τὸ δ᾽ οὖν δεύτερον Ἀντωνίου ἐπιτεθέντος ὁ δῆμος ἐβόησε Χαῖρε βασιλεῦ τῆς ἑαυτοῦ γλώττης. ὁ δὲ οὐ δεχόμενος ἐκέλευσεν εἰς τὸ τοῦ Καπιτωλίου Διὸς ἱερὸν ἀποφέρειν αὐτό· ἐκείνῳ γὰρ μᾶλλον ἁρμόττειν. καὶ πάλιν ἐκρότησαν οἱ αὐτοὶ ὥσπερ καὶ πάλαι.

All sorts of things were being said in the crowd, but when Antony placed it on his head a second time, the People shouted 'Hail, king' in their own language. But Caesar did not accept it. He ordered it to be taken to the temple of Capitoline Jupiter, to whom, he said, it was more appropriate. And the same people as before applauded again.

At this point Nicolaus introduces an alternative version, in which Antony told one of the bystanders to put the diadem on Caesar's statue; that more than anything, he says, motivated the conspirators.[110] But his main narrative clearly implies that Caesar's order was obeyed, and the diadem taken to the Capitol.

Dio's version of the event has Antony saying 'Through me [as consul], the Roman People grant you this', and Caesar replying 'Jupiter alone is king of the Romans'. According to Plutarch, Caesar stood up and pulled the toga down from his throat, shouting out that that anyone who wanted to kill him could do so.[111] Cicero has Antony announce that henceforth the day of the Lupercalia would be marked in the *fasti* with this notice: 'The consul Marcus Antonius, by order of the People, offered the kingship to Gaius Caesar, dictator in perpetuity; and Caesar refused it.'[112] That was what the whole performance meant. Caesar would not be king.

He had no bodyguard. He could rely on the goodwill of the Roman People, who had voted him the same personal inviolability that

---

[109] *FGrH* 90 F 130.21.73: ἄλλοι γὰρ ἄλλην γνώμην περὶ τῶν δρωμένων εἶχον.

[110] *FGrH* 21.74–5: λέγεται δὲ καὶ ἕτερος λόγος. The change of source is not noted by Toher (2003.141).

[111] Dio Cassius 44.11.3, Plutarch *Antony* 12.4.

[112] Cicero *Philippics* 2.87: *ascribi iussit in fastis ad Lupercalia C. Caesari dictatori perpetuo M. Antonium consulem populi iussu regnum detulisse, Caesarem uti noluisse.*

protected their tribunes.[113] The Senate and equestrian order had sworn a formal oath to guard his safety.[114] Exactly a month later, for reasons that seemed good to them, twenty-three senators broke their oath and stabbed him to death.

[113] Appian *Civil Wars* 2.109.455, 118.498 (οὐ γὰρ δορυφόροις ἠρέσκετο); 2.106.442, Dio Cassius 44.5.3 (*sacrosanctitas*).

[114] Suetonius *Diuus Iulius* 84.2, 86.1; Appian *Civil Wars* 2.145.604; Dio Cassius 44.7.4 (including *equester ordo*). Cf. Cicero *Pro Marcello* 32: *omnesque tibi, ut pro aliis etiam loquar quod de me ipse sentio, ... non modo excubias et custodias sed etiam laterum nostrorum oppositus et corporum pollicemur.*

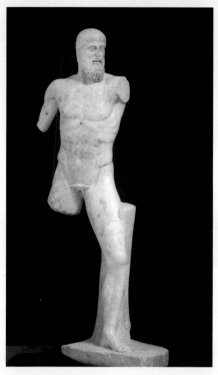

Fig. 6. Statue of Aristogeiton in the Capitoline collection (Centrale Montemartini), Rome. It was found in 1937 near S. Omobono, having evidently fallen from the Capitol above (along with the remains of the Fides temple).

9

The Ethics of Murder

I

The Roman republic began *post reges exactos*, after the expulsion of the kings. The Tarquins were driven out, not killed. Fifteen years later, in revolt against the arrogant patricians, the plebeians took up arms but did not use them; they withdrew to the Sacred Mount and a compromise was reached by negotiation.[1] Greek historians of Rome were particularly impressed.

Dionysius of Halicarnassus knew what would have happened in a Greek city: the democrats would have attacked the aristocrats, carried out a slaughter of the most prominent, and seized their property; or the privileged would have called in foreign allies and destroyed the entire democratic party in order to live in the city without fear. That neither of these things happened was, he thought, what made Rome worthy of imitation by all mankind, the most glorious of all her many wonderful achievements.[2] Less rhetorically, Appian began his great history of the civil wars with the same point:[3]

Ῥωμαίοις ὁ δῆμος καὶ ἡ βουλὴ πολλάκις ἐς ἀλλήλους περί τε νόμων θέσεως καὶ χρεῶν ἀποκοπῆς ἢ γῆς διαδατουμένης ἢ ἐν ἀρχαιρεσίαις ἐστασίασαν· οὐ μήν τι χειρῶν ἔργον ἔμφυλον ἦν, ἀλλὰ διαφοραὶ μόναι καὶ ἔριδες ἔννομοι, καὶ τάδε μετὰ πολλῆς αἰδοῦς εἴκοντες ἀλλήλοις διετίθεντο.

---

[1] *Armati*: Cicero *Pro Cornelio* fr. 22 Crawford = Asconius 76C; Sallust *Catiline* 33.3, *Jugurthine War* 31.6 and 17, *Histories* 1.11M, 1.55.23M, 3.48.1M; Appian *Civil Wars* 1.1.2 (ὁ δὲ δῆμος . . . οὐκ ἐχρήσατο τοῖς ὅπλοις παροῦσιν).
[2] Dionysius of Halicarnassus 7.66.4–5, contrasting Corcyra (Thucydides 3.70–85), Argos (Diodorus Siculus 15.57.3–58.4), Miletus (Athenaeus 12.523f–524b), and 'all of Sicily'.
[3] Appian *Civil Wars* 1.1.1; cf. Plutarch *Tiberius Gracchus* 20.1.

At Rome, the People and the Senate were often in conflict with each other, both about legislation and about debt-cancellation, land distribution, or elections. But there was no civil violence, only lawful differences and arguments, and even those they settled honourably by making mutual concessions.

Already in the second century BC Polybius had noted, with surprise and admiration, that the Romans kept their oaths.[4]

One oath that was kept for 360 years guaranteed the sacrosanct status of the tribunes and aediles of the *plebs*.[5] Without that sanction the rich and powerful would have had all the advantages, the strong (in Thucydides' phrase) doing what they were able to do and the weak suffering what they must.[6] The Romans had decided, as a citizen body, to prevent that from happening. Everything depended on good faith, honesty, responsibility—in Latin, *fides*. The Romans founded a temple to *Fides Publica* on the Capitol in 257 BC; how important the concept was can be seen from the contemporary Greek historian who attributed the temple to Roma herself, supposedly the daughter of Aeneas' son Ascanius.[7]

All of that came to an abrupt end in 133 BC. Here is Appian again:[8]

ξίφος δὲ οὐδέν πω παρενεχθὲν ἐς ἐκκλησίαν οὐδὲ φόνον ἔμφυλον, πρίν γε Τιβέριος Γράκχος δημαρχῶν καὶ νόμους ἐσφέρων πρῶτος ὅδε ἐν στάσει ἀπώλετο καὶ ἐπ᾽ αὐτῷ πολλοὶ κατὰ τὸ Καπιτώλιον εἰλούμενοι περὶ τὸν νεὼν ἀνηρέθησαν. καὶ οὐκ ἀνέσχον ἔτι αἱ στάσεις ἐπὶ τῷδε τῷ μύσει ...

No sword was ever brought into the assembly, and no civil bloodshed ever took place, until Tiberius Gracchus, a tribune of the *plebs* and engaged in legislation, was the first to be killed in political strife; and many others with him, crowded together on the Capitol, were killed around the temple. And the strife did not end with this abomination.

On the contrary, it led directly to civil war.[9]

---

[4] Polybius 6.56.14.
[5] Livy 3.55.10, cf. 2.33.1; Dionysius of Halicarnassus 6.89.3–4, Festus 422L.
[6] Thucydides 5.89 (the Athenians in the 'Melian dialogue').
[7] Temple: Cicero *De natura deorum* 2.61 (A. Calatinus triumphed in 257 BC). Historian: Agathocles of Cyzicus *FGrH* 472 F5 = Festus 328L (wrongly placing it on the Palatine).
[8] Appian *Civil Wars* 1.2.4–5; cf. 1.17.71 (τόδε μύσος).
[9] Appian *Civil Wars* 1.2.5–8; Velleius Paterculus 2.3.3–4.

II

What could justify such an act? It is easy to understand Gaius Gracchus' indignation ('My brother was the best of men, those who killed him are the worst'),[10] and the attitude of the few sources that reflect the People's view.[11] What needs explanation is the repeated assumption that Tiberius was 'lawfully killed',[12] and that Scipio Nasica, who was a private citizen when he led the senators to beat Tiberius and his supporters to death, deserved acclaim as a national hero.[13]

The two irreconcilable views are explained by Laelius in Cicero's *De republica*, written in the summer of 54 BC:[14]

nam, ut uidetis, mors Tiberii Gracchi et iam ante tota illius ratio tribunatus diuisit populum unum in duas partes.

'For, as you see, the death of Tiberius Gracchus, and even before that the whole policy of his tribunate, has divided one People into two parties.'

Was it the death, or was it the policy? The answer depended on which 'party' you belonged to.

Of course the rich objected to Gracchus' law for the distribution of *ager publicus*;[15] but that was precisely the sort of issue that the republic had been able to accommodate in the past by mutual

---

[10] C. Gracchus fr. 17 Malcovati = Charisius *Ars grammatica* 2.240 Keil (313 Barwick): *pessimi Tiberium fratrem meum optimum interfecerunt.*

[11] *Rhetorica ad Herennium* 4.31 (p. 10 above), 4.68; Sallust *Jugurthine War* 31.7, 42.1. Cicero is polite about the Gracchi when addressing the People (*De lege agraria* 2.10 and 31, *Pro Rabirio perduellionis reo* 14–15), and he does once admit that the result of Tiberius' death was an *atrox ac difficile rei publicae tempus* (*In Verrem* 2.4.108).

[12] *Iure caesus*: Cicero *De oratore* 2.106, *Pro Milone* 8, Velleius Paterculus 2.4.4 (Scipio Aemilianus' judgement); Cicero *Pro Plancio* 88, *De officiis* 2.43; cf. *Pro Milone* 14 (*e re publica*), *De officiis* 1.76 (*rei publicae profuit*).

[13] *Priuatus*: Cicero *In Catilinam* 1.3, *De domo* 91, *Pro Plancio* 88, *Brutus* 212, *Tusculan Disputations* 4.51, *De officiis* 1.76; Valerius Maximus 3.2.17. Hero: Cicero *De domo* 91 (*fortissimus uir*), *Pro Milone* 72 (*nominis sui gloria*), *De officiis* 1.109 (*magnus et clarus*), *Philippics* 8.13 (*uirtus, consilium, magnitudo animi*); Valerius Maximus 5.3.2e (*tantum laudis... meruisse*).

[14] Cicero *De republica* 1.31. The dramatic date is 129 BC; cf. *Ad Q. fratrem* 3.5.1 for the date of composition.

[15] See above, pp. 39–41.

concessions and compromise. They also objected to the way Tiberius defeated their attempts to prevent the passage of the law, as if it were self-evident that no reform should take place.[16] When the Senate met, in the temple of *Fides Publica* on the Capitol, there were calls for the presiding consul to take action, but he refused; an expert on the law, he evidently considered that Tiberius had done nothing illegal.[17]

'By following legal process,' Nasica is supposed to have said, 'the consul is effectively bringing about the collapse of Roman authority and all the laws with it.'[18] That is in a late and rhetorical source, but it is consistent with the Ciceronian evidence. Defending a *popularis* tribune in 65 BC, Cicero commented that Tiberius Gracchus was one of those whom the *optimates* considered 'seditious'.[19] That was also his own view two years later, when in a speech to the Senate he described Tiberius as 'undermining the republic'.[20] But what did the sedition consist of? In the speech for Milo it is specified as Tiberius' defeat of Octavius' veto by getting the People to vote him out of office.[21] That was certainly very contentious, but it was not illegal; Tiberius was after all acting with the People's authority.[22]

What Nasica had done was to take up arms as a private citizen.[23] According to Diodorus, he was enraged, and simply snatched up a piece of wood that lay to hand.[24] If that represents a plea of extenuating circumstances, Cicero will have none of it:[25]

---

[16] See above, pp. 7–8.

[17] P. Mucius Scaevola: Cicero *De domo* 91 (*qui in gerenda re publica putabatur fuisse segnior*), *Pro Plancio* 88 (*consul minus fortis*), *Tusculan Disputations* 4.51 (*consul languens*). Jurist: Cicero *De oratore* 1.212, *De legibus* 2.52, *De officiis* 2.47; Pomponius in *Digest* 1.2.2.39. Temple of *Fides*: Valerius Maximus 3.2.17, Appian *Civil Wars* 1.16.67.

[18] Valerius Maximus 3.2.17: *consul, dum iuris ordinem sequitur, id agit ut cum omnibus legibus Romanum imperium corruat.*

[19] Cicero *Pro Cornelio II* fr. 7 Crawford = Asconius 80C: *non Gai Gracchi, non Tiberi, neminem quem isti seditiosum existimant nominabo...*

[20] Cicero *In Catilinam* 1.3: *Ti. Gracchum mediocriter* [in comparison with Catiline] *labefactantem statum rei publicae.*

[21] Cicero *Pro Milone* 72: *Ti. Gracchum qui conlegae magistratum per seditionem abrogauit.*

[22] What Cicero calls *seditio* was the accepted principle that a tribune must devote himself to the will of the People: see Polybius 6.16.5 (with Badian 1972.708–9), Plutarch *Tiberius Gracchus* 11.3, 15.2, Appian *Civil Wars* 1.12.51.

[23] Cicero *Pro Plancio* 88: *arma quae priuatus P. Scipio ceperat. Pace* Lintott 1968.68, it is not 'difficult to ascertain who was responsible for beginning the violence'.

[24] Diodorus Siculus 34/35.7.2: καὶ ὁ Σκιπίων ξύλον ἁρπάσας ἐκ τῶν παρακειμένων, ὁ γὰρ θυμὸς παντὸς τοῦ δοκοῦντος εἶναι δυσκόλου περιεγένετο...

[25] Cicero *Tusculan Disputations* 4.51.

mihi ne Scipio quidem ille pontifex maximus, qui hoc Stoicorum uerum esse declarauit, numquam priuatum esse sapientem, iratus uidetur fuisse Ti. Graccho tum, cum consulem languentem reliquit atque ipse priuatus, ut si consul esset, qui rem publicam saluam esse uellent se sequi iussit.

I don't think even Scipio—I mean the *pontifex maximus*, who demonstrated the truth of this saying of the Stoics that the wise man is never a private citizen—was angry with Tiberius Gracchus at the time when he abandoned the feeble consul, and as if he, a private citizen, were consul himself, ordered those who wished the republic safe to follow him.

Nasica knew exactly what he was doing. He understood what was at stake, and he did what was necessary. In Cicero's great work of practical ethics, he has become an example of virtue in action.

By the time he wrote the *Tusculan Disputations*, Cicero's view had been focused by events—the killing of Clodius in 52 BC, and the outbreak three years later of a civil war which he believed would end in the death of the republic whichever side won.[26] In *De legibus*, probably written in the late fifties,[27] he gives prominence to Quintus' strongly expressed disapproval of the tribunate of the *plebs* as a pernicious institution, created at a time of sedition in order to promote sedition; Cicero himself defends it, but neither Quintus nor Atticus is convinced.[28] In the *Brutus*, composed in 46 BC, he writes of Tiberius Gracchus as executed by the republic itself, because of the extreme 'turbulence' of his tribunate; as for Nasica, he gave the republic liberty from Tiberius' 'domination'.[29]

The killing of Caesar confirmed the polarized positions of the two sides. In *De officiis* we read of Nasica punishing Tiberius' 'pernicious ventures'; in the *Philippics*, liberating the republic by his 'courage, wisdom, and greatness of mind'.[30] But only a few years later Sallust

[26] See above, p. 122.
[27] Dyck 2004.5–7; *De legibus* 2.42 refers to the death of Clodius.
[28] Cicero *De legibus* 3.19–26, esp. 19 (*nam mihi quidem pestifera uidetur, quippe quae in seditione et ad seditionem nata sit*) and 22 (*in ista quidem re uehementer Sullam probo*).
[29] Cicero *Brutus* 103 (*propter turbulentissimum tribunatum . . . ab ipsa re publica est interfectus*), 212 (*qui ex dominatu Ti. Gracchi priuatus in libertatem rem publicam uindicauit*). The latter passage may allude to Caesar's self-justification in *De bello ciuili* 1.22.5: *ut se et populum Romanum factione paucorum oppressum in libertatem uindicaret.*
[30] Cicero *De officiis* 1.109 (*qui Ti. Gracchi conatus perditos uindicauerit*); *Philippics* 8.13 (p. 208 below).

writes of Tiberius and Gaius Gracchus themselves liberating the republic from the criminal oligarchy of the aristocrats, and being killed for it.[31]

It was Cicero's version that prevailed. Two generations later, historians had to find vaguely portentous phrases for what Tiberius had done to account for the fate he must have deserved: he turned the state upside down, he led a criminal faction, he tried to overturn the constitution, he held the republic by the throat.[32] To be more specific, the Senate punished him with death for having dared to promulgate an agrarian law.[33] Just for that? No, of course not:[34]

> ... *cum Ti. Gracchus in tribunatu, profusissimis largitionibus fauore populi occupato, rem publicam oppressam teneret palamque dictitaret interempto senatu omnia per plebem agi debere.*

During his tribunate Tiberius Gracchus got control of the People's favour by lavish bribes. The republic was helpless under his power. Openly and repeatedly he urged that the Senate should be done away with, and all political business handled by the *plebs*.

And the men who killed him were 'the larger and better part of the Senate and the equestrian order, with those plebeians who were uninfected by pernicious policies'.[35]

III

That vagueness about what Tiberius was supposed to have done was there from the start. Publius Scaevola, the jurist consul who had

---

[31] Sallust *Jugurthine War* 42.1 (p. 37 above). He too may have had Caesar's formulation in mind (n. 29).

[32] Velleius Paterculus 2.2.3 (*summa imis miscuit*); Valerius Maximus 3.2.17 (*Gracchum cum scelerata factione*), 6.3.1d (he and his brother *statum ciuitatis conati erant conuellere*), 5.3.2e (*pestifera Ti. Gracchi manu faucibus apprensam rem publicam*). Cf. Velleius Paterculus 2.6.1 for his *furor*.

[33] Valerius Maximus 7.2.6b: *Ti. Gracchum tribunum plebis agrariam legem promulgare ausum morte multauit.*

[34] Valerius Maximus 3.2.17.

[35] Velleius Paterculus 2.3.2: *tum optimates, senatus atque equestris ordinis pars melior et maior, et intacta perniciosis consiliis plebs irruere in Gracchum*... Cf. Plutarch *Tiberius Gracchus* 18.1 (the armed friends and slaves of the rich).

refused to take action against him, nevertheless declared Nasica's action justified.[36] Scipio Aemilianus is said to have announced that Tiberius was justly killed 'if he had intended to take over the republic'.[37] What exactly did that mean?

When the Tarquins were expelled, the Romans swore an oath that they would never again let anyone reign in Rome.[38] The Roman historical tradition remembered three men who supposedly 'sought to reign' (the phrase is *regnum appetere* or *regnum occupare*), and were put to death for it: Spurius Cassius in 485 BC, Spurius Maelius in 439, and Marcus Manlius in 384.[39] The surviving narratives present all three as demagogues, and the anachronisms they contain clearly reveal the influence of contemporary politics on historians writing in the second and first centuries BC.[40] In particular, they were seen as precedents for the killing of Tiberius Gracchus.[41]

Greek historians of Rome translate *regnum* as *tyrannis*, and describe Cassius, Maelius, and Manlius as would-be *tyrannoi*.[42] In Plutarch's account of Tiberius Gracchus, Nasica at the Senate meeting urges the consul to suppress the *tyrannos*.[43] *Tyrannus* was also available as a loan-word in Latin, at least as early as Ennius and Plautus;[44] but no Latin author ever uses it of Cassius, Maelius, or

---

[36] Cicero *De domo* 91, *Pro Plancio* 88; on what grounds is not recorded.

[37] Velleius Paterculus 2.4.4: *respondit si is occupandae rei publicae animum habuisset, iure caesum* (cf. n. 12). See also Diodorus Siculus 34/35.7.3.

[38] Livy 2.1.9 (*neminem Romae passuros regnare*), Dionysius of Halicarnassus 5.1.3 (oath binding on posterity), Appian *Civil Wars* 2.119.499.

[39] Cassius: Cicero *De republica* 2.60, Livy 2.41, Dionysius of Halicarnassus 8.77–9. Maelius: Varro *De lingua Latina* 5.157, Cicero *De senectute* 56, Livy 4.13–15, Dionysius of Halicarnassus 12.1–4. Manlius: Varro *Annales* fr. 2P, Nepos *Chronica* fr. 5P = Aulus Gellius 17.12.24; Diodorus Siculus 15.35.3, Livy 6.11–20, Plutarch *Camillus* 36, Dio Cassius 7.26. All three as *exempla*: Cicero *De domo* 101, *Philippics* 2.114, Valerius Maximus 6.3.1, Ampelius 27.2–4. See Smith 2006a, esp. 49–52 (Cassius), 52–4 (Maelius), 54–5 (Manlius).

[40] See the analyses in Wiseman 1998a.99–101 (on Maelius) and Oakley 1997.476–93 (on Manlius).

[41] Cicero *De republica* 2.49, *De amicitia* 36 (dramatic date 129 BC in both cases); cf. *In Catilinam* 1.3, *Pro Milone* 72 (Manlius only).

[42] Dionysius of Halicarnassus 8.77.1, 8.79.4 (Cassius); 12.1.1, 12.4.4 (Maelius); Diodorus Siculus 15.35.3, Dio Cassius 7.26.2 (Manlius).

[43] Plutarch *Ti. Gracchus* 19.3: ὁ δὲ Νασικᾶς ἠξίου τὸν ὕπατον τῇ πόλει βοηθεῖν καὶ καταλύειν τὸν τύραννον.

[44] Ennius *Annales* fr. 104 Skutsch (of T. Tatius?), Plautus *Pseudolus* 703.

Manlius, much less of Tiberius Gracchus. Thanks to Herodotus and Plato, the word had very specific overtones: a *tyrannos* was not simply an autocrat, he was a rapist and a murderer, a man whose soul was driven by lust and passion.[45] Aristotle, more analytical, distinguished three types of *tyrannos*, but it was his third and worst type, 'to whose government no free man willingly submits',[46] that the word inevitably invoked when used without qualification.

The *tyrannos* was a figure specific to Greek politics, and in particular to that pathological alternation of mutual atrocity from which the Roman republic had kept itself so admirably free.[47] It is true that the Roman republic did soon go down that dreadful road: the respectively 'oligarchic' and 'democratic' proscriptions of 82 and 43 BC fit all too easily into the classic paradigm presented by Thucydides in his analysis of the Corcyra stasis.[48] It is also true, and for that very reason, that the *tyrannos* soon did come to be part of Roman political discourse, no longer an alien phenomenon, or one to be imagined only in the rhetorical schools,[49] but the description, accurate or otherwise, of contemporaries in the Roman Forum; the first politician to whom the term is attributed in Latin was Sulla.[50] That is a development to be considered in the next section. For the moment, we are concerned with what started the process in the first place.

No one could have been less like Plato's 'tyrannical man' than Tiberius Gracchus. Plutarch's repeated listing of his virtues is vindicated by the evidence of Cicero, who admits Tiberius' moral excellence when his case requires it.[51] Later historians dwelt on the great career he could have had,[52] if only he hadn't . . . done *what*, exactly?

---

[45] Herodotus 3.80.4–5, Plato *Republic* 8.565d–9.580c.

[46] Aristotle *Politics* 4.8.3 (1295a22). For the types of ruler who may be described as *tyrannoi*, see now Lewis 2006.

[47] See above, nn. 2–3.

[48] Thucydides 3.82–3.

[49] Already in *Rhetorica ad Herennium* 2.49 and Cicero *De inuentione* 1.102, 144. Cf. Seneca *Controuersiae* 3.6, 5.8, 7.6, 9.4; Petronius *Satyrica* 1.3.

[50] Sallust *Histories* 1.55.1 and 7M (speech of M. Lepidus). See in general Dunkle 1967.

[51] Cicero *De lege agraria* 2.31 (*aequitas, pudor*), *De haruspicum responso* 41 (*grauitas, eloquentia, dignitas*); Plutarch *Tiberius Gracchus* 2.4 (ἐπιείκεια, πραότης), 3.1 (ἀνδραγαθία, δικαιοσύνη, πρὸς τὰς ἀρχὰς ἐπιμέλεια, πρὸς τὰς ἡδονὰς ἐγκράτεια), 4.4 (εὐταξία, ἀνδρεία), 5.1 (τὸ συνετὸν καὶ ἀνδρεῖον).

[52] Velleius Paterculus 2.3.2, Valerius Maximus 6.3.1d.

It is agreed that the occupation of public land by the rich was illegal.[53] It is agreed that Tiberius was legally elected by the People to the sacrosanct office of tribune of the *plebs*, and that the agrarian law was legitimately passed; the issue was deeply controversial, but it was one of those political disagreements within the framework of the laws which the republic had traditionally been able to handle.[54] It is also agreed that Nasica acted as a private citizen on his own initiative.

The alleged precedents were of no help there. Sp. Cassius and M. Manlius were tried and condemned by due process of law;[55] Sp. Maelius was executed on the order of a properly appointed dictator.[56] Alternative versions had Cassius sentenced by his father in a domestic tribunal and Maelius by the Senate in a formal decision.[57] Even Cicero admits, when his case requires it, that no executive action could be legal without the authority of the People.[58] So why wasn't it murder?

It is sometimes suggested that Nasica acted in his capacity as *pontifex maximus*. A splendid recent article by Jerzy Linderski begins with the assumption that 'the constitution, civil and divine, was shattered when Tiberius had his fellow tribune Marcus Octavius deposed from office',[59] and concludes with this explanation of Nasica's act:[60]

Thus when Nasica displayed the purple border on his veiled head this was a striking arrangement: he was loudly proclaiming that he, the *pontifex maximus*, was proceeding to consecrate Tiberius and his followers to the wrath of the gods. The old religious and public regulations of the Republic, the *leges sacratae*, prescribed that the heads of those who attempted to establish

---

[53] See above, pp. 38–40.

[54] Appian *Civil Wars* 1.1.1 (pp. 177–8 above) on ἔριδες ἔννομοι.

[55] Cassius: Cicero *De republica* 2.60 (*populo cedente*), Livy 2.41.11 (*populi iudicio*), Dionysius of Halicarnassus 8.77.1 (ἐκκλησίαν συνάγειν ὄντες κύριοι); cf. Valerius Maximus 6.3.1b (*senatus populusque Romanus*). Manlius: Cicero *De domo* 101 (*iudicatus*), Livy 6.20.11–12 (*comitia centuriata*), Dio Cassius 7.26.1 (κατέγνω ὁ δῆμος).

[56] Cicero *De senectute* 56, Livy 4.14.3 and 15.1, Dionysius of Halicarnassus 12.2.4.

[57] Cassius: Livy 2.41.10, Dionysius of Halicarnassus 8.79. Maelius: Cincius Alimentus *FGrH* 810 F4 and Piso fr. 31 Forsythe = Dionysius of Halicarnassus 12.4.2–5.

[58] Cicero *De lege agraria* 2.27 (to the People, about Rullus): *hic autem tribunus plebis . . . uidebat potestatem neminem iniussu populi aut plebis posse habere.*

[59] Linderski 2002.339 = 2007.88 (no evidence offered).

[60] Linderski 2002.364–5 = 2007.113, cf. 350–1 = 99–100 (Nasica wearing the *toga praetexta*), 360–1 = 109–10 (Nasica wearing his toga reversed).

tyranny (*adfectatio regni*), and of those who injured the tribunes of the plebs, be forfeited to Jupiter, the guarantor of the constitution.

But there are serious problems with this interpretation.

In the first place, it seems clear that what infringed the constitutional conventions was Octavius' veto of a decision of the People in a legally constituted assembly;[61] the deposition of a tribune who had thwarted the People's will may have been presented by Nasica as a violation of *sacrosanctitas*, but that view is unlikely to have been generally accepted.[62]

Second, the *leges sacratae* to which Linderski refers are a law attributed to Publius Valerius in the first year of the republic,[63] and a law attributed to Lucius Valerius and Marcus Horatius after the overthrow of the Decemvirs in 449 BC.[64] Both those episodes were of course very thoroughly worked over in the Roman historiographical tradition; and since it is demonstrable that the later elaboration of that tradition included the creation of items that cast flattering light on the patrician Valerii,[65] it would be absurd to have any confidence in the authenticity of either of these two laws. They are just as likely to be evidence for the influence of Nasica's act on the historiography of the first century BC.

The third, and I think fatal, objection to the idea that Tiberius Gracchus was a *homo sacer* ritually put to death by the *pontifex maximus* is its total absence from the Ciceronian evidence.[66] One

---

[61] Detailed argument in Badian 1972.697–701, concluding that 'Octavius' veto was unexpected, his persistence in it a bombshell'; ibid. 706 ('a breach of all constitutional custom').

[62] See above, n. 22.

[63] Livy 2.8.2 (*sacrando cum bonis capite eius qui regni occupandi consilia inisset*), Plutarch *Publicola* 12.1 (νόμον ἄνευ κρίσεως κτεῖναι διδόντα τὸν βουλόμενον τυραννεῖν). The idea of mere intention being culpable seems to me to be prima facie evidence that this tradition is the work of a post-Gracchan historian. Contrast the rival tradition that Valerius' law prohibited the holding of any authority except by grant of the People (Dionysius of Halicarnassus 5.19.4, Plutarch *Publicola* 11.3).

[64] Livy 2.55.7: *ut qui tribunis plebis aedilibus iudicibus decemuiris nocuisset, eius caput Ioui sacrum esset.* Cf. Dionysius of Halicarnassus 6.89.3, attributing it to 'L. Brutus' as one of the founding college of tribunes after the first secession (see above, p. 62 n. 17—a late tradition).

[65] Documented in Münzer 1891 and Wiseman 1998a.75–89. The responsibility of Valerius Antias is not formally provable, but remains (in my view) overwhelmingly likely; Oakley 1997.91 and Rich 2005.147–8 are non-committal.

[66] See above, nn. 19–30.

could imagine a dramatist, or a declaimer in the rhetorical schools, presenting Nasica's act in the way Linderski describes, but Cicero has no notion of it. For him, Gracchus' crime was political, and Nasica punished him for it not as a *pontifex* but as a private citizen. I think it is reasonable to take Cicero as evidence for an optimate way of thinking that had hardly changed since the time of the event itself. So the question must still be asked: how could it not be murder to kill a citizen without trial?

The only possible explanation is that the rich unilaterally defined legislation against their financial interests as 'seeking to reign',[67] an act that must activate the oath sworn after the expulsion of Tarquin. It is easy to sympathize with the bitter irony of the tribune Memmius in Sallust:

sed sane fuerit regni paratio plebi sua restituere; quicquid sine sanguine ciuium ulcisci nequitur iure factum sit.

All right, let giving the *plebs* its own property back count as planning to reign; let anything that can't be avenged without shedding the blood of citizens count as a legal act.

Political assassination was unprecedented in republican Rome.[68] It was now being justified by an outrageously partisan reinterpretation of what the republic permitted and required.

So began 'the impunity of the sword',[69] the disastrous polarization of Roman politics into violent conflict and then civil war. The view that blamed it on what Gracchus did, rather than what was done to him, was an integral part of that 'arrogance of the aristocracy' which we explored in Chapter 2. It prevailed in the long run because an optimate politician who believed it was also a master of Latin prose, and later generations internalized Cicero's opinions along with his style.

---

[67] Cicero *De republica* 2.49, Sallust *Jugurthine War* 31.7.

[68] Sallust *Jugurthine War* 31.8; cf. Florus 2.1.2 (p. 8 above). It is not enough to argue that political violence was already 'a recognized political weapon' in 133 BC (Lintott 1968.175); murder of a tribune certainly wasn't.

[69] Velleius Paterculus 2.3.3: *hoc initium in urbe Roma ciuilis sanguinis gladiorumque impunitatis fuit.*

IV

We have seen in previous chapters how the Senate formalized its claim to decide what sort of political activity was acceptable and what was not. Gaius Gracchus tried to re-establish traditional norms with a law that no Roman citizen should be put to death without the authority of the People.[70] The Senate's answer was a decree requiring the consul to see to it that the republic should not be harmed—in effect, an invitation to take executive action without regard to the laws.[71]

Rightly contested though it was, since the laws were the foundation of republican liberty,[72] that expedient did at least offer a kind of quasi-constitutional authority for Opimius in 121 BC, Marius in 100, Catulus in 77, and Cicero in 63, all of whom executed Roman citizens without trial. But if murder was not quite the appropriate term to describe *those* deaths, it certainly was for a death on the Appian Way in 52 BC.

The facts are not in doubt.[73] On 18 January, Titus Milo was on his way to Lanuvium and Publius Clodius was returning from Aricia. When they passed each other near Bovillae, a minor affray broke out between their respective slave escorts. One of Milo's men, a gladiator called Birria, threw a javelin that hit Clodius in the shoulder. That was no doubt unpremeditated, but what happened next was done in cold blood. The wounded Clodius had been taken into a wayside tavern. Milo's men attacked the building, killed or drove off Clodius' slaves, dragged Clodius out, and finished him off. The body was left in the road.

When Milo was brought to trial, the jury was not persuaded by Cicero's plea that Milo's party had been ambushed and Clodius killed in self-defence.[74] More important for our purposes is the argument

---

[70] Cicero *Pro Rabirio perduellionis reo* 12 (to the People): *C. Gracchus legem tulit ne de capite ciuium Romanorum iniussu uestro iudicaretur.*

[71] Cicero *In Catilinam* 1.4, *Philippics* 8.14; see above, pp. 8 and 71.

[72] See e.g. Cicero *Pro Cluentio* 146 (*legum idcirco omnes serui sumus ut liberi esse possimus*), *De lege agraria* 2.102 (*libertas in legibus constitit*); Livy 2.1.1 (*liberi iam hinc populi Romani res...imperiaque legum potentiora quam hominum*). Still a powerful idea in AD 40: Josephus *Antiquities* 19.57, with Wiseman 1992.2–3.

[73] Asconius 31–2C; cf. 40C (evidence at Milo's trial), Dio Cassius 40.48.2.

[74] Asconius 41C; Cicero *Pro Milone* 6, 23–60. Cf. Macaulay's journal (12 Apr. 1850, Thomas 2008.2.233): 'The *Pro Milone* I think would have sufficed to make me find the defendant Guilty.'

Cicero did not make at the trial, but developed at length in the published version of his speech: if Milo had killed Clodius, he would have boasted of the fact.[75] Why? Because he would have freed the city from a tyrant:[76]

huius ergo interfector si esset, in confitendo ab eisne poenam timeret quos liberauisset? Graeci homines deorum honores tribuunt eis uiris qui tyrannos necauerunt—quae ego uidi Athenis, quae in aliis urbibus Graeciae! quas res diuinas talibus institutas uiris, quos cantus, quae carmina! prope ad immortalitatis et religionem et memoriam consecrantur—uos tanti conseruatorem populi, tanti sceleris ultorem non modo honoribus nullis adficietis sed etiam ad supplicium rapi patiemini? confiteretur, confiteretur, inquam, si fecisset, et magno animo et libenter, se fecisse libertatis omnium causa quod esset non confitendum modo sed etiam uere praedicandum.

If he were the killer of such a man, in admitting it would he have to fear punishment from those whom he had liberated? The Greeks bestow divine honours on those who have slain a tyrant. Why, in Athens and other cities of Greece I have seen religious ceremonies dedicated to such men with songs and hymns! They are consecrated with worship and commemoration little short of that of the immortals. And will you not only fail to grant such honours to the saviour of so great a people, the avenger of so great a crime, but even allow him to be dragged off to punishment? If Milo had done the deed he would admit it—yes, he would admit with pride and pleasure that for the sake of the liberty of all of us he had done what called not just for admission but in truth even for public declaration.

Given the hostility of the People,[77] Cicero could hardly have said such things at the trial itself.

The most famous of the Greek 'tyrant-slayers', and the reason why Cicero mentions Athens in particular, were the Athenians Harmodius and Aristogeiton. They killed Hipparchus (brother of the tyrant Hippias) in 514 BC, and were honoured by the Athenians as if they

---

[75] Cicero *Pro Milone* 72–91, esp. 72 (*impune Miloni palam clamare ac mentiri gloriose liceret, 'occidi, occidi'...*) and 77 (*clamaret T. Annius, 'adeste quaeso atque audite, ciues! P. Clodium interfeci'...*).

[76] Cicero *Pro Milone* 79–80.

[77] Asconius 37C (*maxima pars multitudinis* hostile to Milo and Cicero), 38C (*offensio inimicae multitudinis* against Cicero), 40C (Plancus urges the *populus* to make clear its *dolor* to the jury), 41C (*acclamatio Clodianorum* against Cicero at the trial); Balbus in Cicero *Ad Atticum* 9.7b.2 (Cicero asked Pompey for a bodyguard).

had killed the tyrant himself and liberated Athens.[78] Bronze statues of them were set up in a prominent position in the middle of the Agora, carried off by the Persians in 480 BC, and replaced by a new set in 477/6.[79] A marble copy of that famous statue-group was set up on the Capitol in Rome, at or near the temple of *Fides Publica* (see Fig. 6, p. 176).[80] When that happened is not known, but the choice of site (where Nasica had called on the senators to follow him) makes it more likely than not that it was an optimate gesture some time in the late republic.[81]

Cicero was not alone in believing that Milo's act was a benefaction to the republic. Cato, who was on the jury, let it be known that he took that view, and there were others who thought that that was the case Cicero should have made at the trial.[82] Marcus Brutus, whose coin issue two years earlier featured the goddess *Libertas* and the man who killed Spurius Maelius, wrote a defence of Milo on those lines and published it as if it were a court speech.[83]

Once again, as with Tiberius Gracchus, we may ask what Clodius had actually done to deserve summary execution outside the law. Cicero gives a long list of all his enormities, but they are no more than the usual material of Roman political invective between *inimici*;[84] the tyrant's characteristics of lust and violence are predictably emphasized,[85] but Cicero fails to make it clear why Clodius' election

---

[78] Herodotus 5.55, cf. 6.109.3 and 123.2 for their reputation; Thucydides 1.20.2, 6.53.3–59.1; [Aristotle] *Athenaion politeia* 18.2–6; cf. Aristophanes *Acharnians* 979, *Wasps* 1225–6 (the 'Harmodius song', *Poetae Melici Graeci* frr. 893–6). For the nature of the 'cult', see Parker 1996.136–7.

[79] Pausanias 1.8.5, Marmor Parium *FGrH* 239 F A54. The group is best known from a marble copy in Naples: Stewart 1990.135–6, plates 227–31.

[80] Stewart 1990, plate 228; Bertoletti et al. 1999.82–3 (II.58). For the site of discovery and the *Fides* temple, see Coarelli 1969.137–9, 156–9.

[81] See above, n. 17. Coarelli (1969.143–56) dates it to precisely 52 BC, but his inference from Cicero *Ad Atticum* 6.1.17 is very uncertain.

[82] Asconius 53–4C (Cato), 41C.

[83] Asconius 41C, Quintilian 3.6.93, 10.1.23; Crawford 1974.455–6 (no. 433). Cicero appeals to Ahala's killing of Maelius as a precedent (*Pro Milone* 72, 83).

[84] Cicero *Pro Milone* 73–5, 87; cf. 79 for his *inimicitia*.

[85] See Dunkle 1967, esp. 163, 167.

to the praetorship (for which he was a candidate) would have resulted in the rape of Roman citizens' wives and children.[86]

As always, later generations sided with Cicero.[87] Velleius Paterculus, however, does at least deserve credit for sensing the moral incoherence of the optimate position: the murder, he says, was salutary for the republic, but not a useful precedent.[88]

V

As we saw in Chapter 6, the rhetoric of *regnum* and tyranny was all-pervasive during Caesar's first consulship in 59 BC.[89] But Caesar was a legally elected consul,[90] and his legislation had the wholehearted support of the Roman People. His Gallic command was also by the vote of the Roman People (*lex Vatinia* in 59, *lex Trebonia* in 55), and his war commentaries show how conscious he was of the fact.[91] In 52 BC, the Roman People voted him the privilege of standing for his second consulship in absence; Pompey, the defender of the constitution, was in favour, and the proposal was made by all ten tribunes in a symbolic gesture of unanimity.[92] The *optimates* were determined to prevent that, even at the cost of civil war.[93]

For the citizens of Rome, civil war was the worst of evils. If Cicero, who had country houses to escape to, was afraid of the city being burned and plundered,[94] we may be sure that the fears of ordinary

---

[86] Cicero *Pro Milone* 76: *imperium ille si nactus esset . . . a liberis me dius fidius et coniugibus uestris numquam ille effrenatas suas libidines cohibuisset.* Cf. also 89: *oppressisset omnia, possideret, teneret.*

[87] See e.g. Plutarch *Caesar* 9.1 on Clodius: ὕβρει δὲ καὶ θρασύτητι τῶν ἐπὶ βδελυρίᾳ περιβοήτων οὐδενὸς δεύτερος.

[88] Velleius Paterculus 2.47.4: *exemplo inutili, facto salutari rei publicae.*

[89] See above, pp. 111–12.

[90] Despite bribery by the *optimates* at the election to try to keep him out: Suetonius *Diuus Iulius* 19.1 (*ne Catone quidem abnuente eam largitionem e re publica fieri*).

[91] See Wiseman 1998b.3–4.

[92] Cicero *Ad Atticum* 7.1.4, 7.3.4, 7.6.2, 8.3.3 (Pompey as *defensor rei publicae*), *Ad familiares* 6.6.5 (*populus iusserat*), *Philippics* 2.24; Caesar *De bello ciuili* 1.9.2 (*populi Romani beneficium*), 1.32.3.

[93] Civil war seen as inevitable: e.g. Caelius in Cicero *Ad familiares* 8.14.2 and 4 (Aug. 50), Cicero *Ad Atticum* 7.1.2 (Oct. 50).

[94] Cicero *Ad Atticum* 7.13.1, 8.2.3, *Ad familiares* 4.1.2, 14.14.1, 16.12.1.

192   *The Ethics of Murder*

people were even more acute. Older citizens remembered the horrors of 87 and 82 BC;[95] and everybody remembered the proscriptions.[96] At the eleventh hour, the danger seemed to have been avoided. Very late in his tribunate in 50 BC, Gaius Curio forced a division in the Senate on the motion that both Caesar and Pompey should resign their military commands and return to civilian life. Those in favour, 370; those against, 22. Curio hurried out of the meeting to report to the anxious citizens, who applauded and garlanded him with flowers.[97] But nothing came of it. The consul went to Pompey and asked him to defend the republic; Pompey agreed.[98]

Those voting figures, and their lack of effect, go some way towards justifying Caesar's explanation of the crossing of the Rubicon:[99]

se non malefici causa ex prouincia egressum sed uti a contumeliis inimicorum defenderet, ut tribunos plebis in ea re ex ciuitate expulsos in suam dignitatem restitueret, ut se et populum Romanum factione paucorum oppressum in libertatem uindicaret.

'I have not left my province in order to do harm, but to defend myself against the slanders of my enemies, to restore to their rightful position the tribunes of the *plebs*, who have been driven out of the city because of their concern with that matter, and to liberate myself and the Roman People from the factious dominance of a few men.'

Just twenty-two men, in fact, but they had achieved their aim in leaving Caesar no option. He had to put himself in the wrong by invading Italy.

If we turn, as we did in Chapter 6, to that wonderful sequence of letters to Atticus from December 50 to May 49 BC,[100] it becomes clear what Caesar meant by the slanders of his enemies. On a personal level Caesar and Cicero were friends, and throughout this time their

---

[95] 87 BC: Cicero *De oratore* 3.8–11, Diodorus Siculus 38/39.4.2–5, Livy *Epitome* 80, Appian *Civil Wars* 1.71.325–74.344. 82 BC: Livy *Epitome* 86, Appian *Civil Wars* 1.88.403–4. Relevance to 49 BC: Cicero *Ad Atticum* 7.7.7, 8.3.6, 9.10.3, 9.14.2, 10.8.7; Lucan 2.68–233, Dio Cassius 41.5.1, 41.8.5, 41.16.2–3. People were particularly afraid of Caesar's Gallic and German auxiliaries: Lucan 1.479–84, Dio Cassius 41.8.6.

[96] Prospect of new proscriptions: Cicero *Ad Atticum* 7.7.7, 8.11.4, 9.10.6, 9.11.3.

[97] Appian *Civil Wars* 2.30.118–19, Plutarch *Pompey* 58.5.

[98] See above, pp. 120, 122.

[99] Caesar *De bello ciuili* 1.22.5 (to Lentulus Spinther at Corfinium); cf. 1.5 for the expulsion of the tribunes M. Antonius and Q. Cassius.

[100] See above, pp. 122–3.

messages assure each other of their mutual *beneuolentia* and *amicitia*.[101] Cicero understood Caesar's political position perfectly well, and indeed claimed to share it:[102]

et illi semper et senatui cum primum potui pacis auctor fui nec sumptis armis belli ullam partem attigi iudicauique eo bello te uiolari, contra cuius honorem populi Romani beneficio concessum inimici atque inuidi niterentur.

I advocated peace to him [Pompey] always, and to the Senate as soon as I had opportunity. When arms were taken up, I had nothing to do with the war, and I judged you therein to be an injured party in that your enemies and those jealous of your success were striving to deprive you of a mark of honour accorded by the Roman People.

But in the private letters it is taken for granted that Caesar is a *tyrannus*; the only question was whether he would turn out to be a Phalaris or a Pisistratus.[103]

Caesar was evidently determined to counter this assumption. After the siege of Corfinium in February, he allowed Domitius Ahenobarbus and the other senatorial and equestrian officers to go free.[104] In order to make it clear to everyone what this signified, he wrote to his agents Oppius and Balbus, who could be relied on to circulate his letter as widely as possible:[105]

gaudeo mehercule uos significare litteris quam ualde probetis ea quae apud Corfinium sunt gesta. consilio uestro utar libenter et hoc libentius quod mea sponte facere constitueram ut quam lenissimum me praeberem et Pompeium darem operam ut reconciliarem. temptemus hoc modo si possimus omnium uoluntates recuperare et diuturna uictoria uti, quoniam reliqui crudelitate odium effugere non potuerunt neque uictoriam diutius tenere praeter unum

---

[101] Cicero *Ad Atticum* 8.2.1 (17 Feb.), 9.11a.2 (19/20 Mar.), 10.8b.1–2 (16 Apr.), 10.18.2 (19 May).

[102] Ibid. 9.11a.2 (to Caesar, 19/20 Mar.) (trans. D. R. Shackleton Bailey).

[103] Ibid. 7.5.4 (mid-Dec.), 7.11.1 (?21 Jan.), 7.12.2 (22 Jan., Φαλαρισμός), 7.20.2 (5 Feb., *Phalarimne an Pisistratum sit imitaturus*), 8.2.4 (17 Feb.), 8.16.2 (4 Mar., *hic Pisistratus*), 9.4.2 (12 Mar.), 9.13.4 (23 Mar.), 10.1.3 (3 Apr.), 10.4.2 (14 Apr.), 10.8.6 (2 May), 10.12a.1 (6 May). See Gildenhard 2006, esp. 200–2, and Lintott 2008.299–300.

[104] Caesar *De bello ciuili* 1.23.1–3. The date was 21 Feb. (Cicero *Ad Atticum* 8.14.1).

[105] *Ad Atticum* 9.7c.1 (*c.*5 Mar.) (trans. Shackleton Bailey). Cf. also 8.15a.3, 9.7b.1 (Balbus to Cicero on Caesar's avoidance of bloodshed, *c.*1 and 10 March).

L. Sullam, quem imitaturus non sum. haec noua sit ratio uincendi ut miser-icordia et liberalitate nos muniamus.

I am indeed glad that you express in your letter such hearty approval of the proceedings at Corfinium. I shall willingly follow your advice, all the more willingly because I had of my own accord decided to show all possible clemency and to do my best to reconcile Pompey. Let us try whether by this means we can win back the good will of all and enjoy a lasting victory, seeing that others have not managed by cruelty to escape hatred or to make their victories endure, except only L. Sulla, whom I do not propose to imitate. Let this be the new style of conquest, to make mercy and generosity our shield.

Cicero too had written congratulating Caesar on his clemency. Caesar replied:[106]

recte auguraris de me (bene enim tibi cognitus sum) nihil a me abesse longius crudelitate. atque ego cum ex ipsa re magnam capio uoluptatem tum meum factum probari abs te triumpho gaudio. neque illud me mouet quod ii qui a me dimissi sunt discessisse dicuntur ut mihi rursus bellum inferrent; nihil enim malo quam et me similem esse et illos sui.

You rightly surmise of me (you know me well) that of all things I abhor cruelty. The incident gives me great pleasure in itself, and your approval of my action elates me beyond words. I am not disturbed by the fact that those whom I have released are said to have left the country in order to make war against me once more. Nothing pleases me better than that I should be true to my nature and they to theirs.

Caesar might have been less elated if he had known Cicero's private thoughts.

Eleven days after Corfinium we find him grumbling to Atticus about the 'treacherous clemency' that was turning opinions in Caesar's favour.[107] When Atticus expressed the hope that Caesar would continue with his policy of moderation, Cicero's reply was forthright:[108]

qui hic potest se gerere non perdite? <uetat> uita, mores, ante facta, ratio suscepti negoti, socii, uires bonorum aut etiam constantia.

---

[106] Ibid. 9.16.2 (trans. Shackleton Bailey). See p. 104 above for Macaulay's admiration ('Noble fellow!' he wrote in the margin). On Caesar's *clementia* (the word was Cicero's, not Caesar's own), see Griffin 2003.159–65.

[107] Ibid. 8.16.2 (4 Mar.): *huius insidiosa clementia delectantur, illius iracundiam formidant.*

[108] Ibid. 9.2a.2 (8 Mar.) (trans. Shackleton Bailey). Cf. 9.10.9 (Atticus had written on 5 Mar.).

How can he behave otherwise than as a desperado? That is precluded by his life, his character, his past, the nature of the present enterprise, his associates, the strength of the honest men or just their persistence.

Since it was axiomatic for Cicero that Caesar was a *tyrannus*, despite all evidence to the contrary he must be cruel and violent, intent on massacring his opponents at the first opportunity:[109]

metuo ne omnis haec clementia ad unam illam crudelitatem colligatur. Balbus quidem maior ad me scribit nihil malle Caesarem quam principe Pompeio sine metu uiuere. tu, puto, hoc credis.

I am afraid that all this piling up of clemency may be simply a prelude to the cruelty we feared. Balbus senior for his part writes to me that Caesar would like nothing better than to live without fear under Pompey's primacy. You believe this of course!

Atticus might well believe it. But the key phrase was 'without fear'. If even moderate *optimates* like Cicero believed that Caesar was a Greek tyrant, there would always be someone wanting to act Harmodius or Aristogeiton.

In March of 49 BC Cicero was reading Plato's *Seventh Letter*, that classic narrative of tyranny and philosophy, and identifying his own position with that of Plato at the court of Dionysius.[110] He was, after all, the Roman Plato, author of the *Republic* and the *Laws*. He had given to Scipio in the first book of *De republica* a version of Plato's analysis of the tyrannical man which was very easily translatable into contemporary Roman terms. First, there is an 'excess of freedom', from which a tyrant emerges who gratifies the People with the property of private individuals (as it might be, Caesar's agrarian legislation in 59 BC). He is given powers which are then renewed (like Caesar in 59 and 55), and surrounds himself with armed men as Pisistratus did in Athens. The constitution can only be restored if he is 'suppressed' by the *optimates*.[111]

---

[109] *Ad Atticum* 8.9a.2 (25 Feb.) (trans. Shackleton Bailey). *Tyrannus*: n. 103 above. Massacre (*caedes*): *Ad Atticum* 10.8.2 (2 May), 10.10.5 (3 May).

[110] Ibid. 9.10.2 and 13.4 (18 and 23 Mar.), quoting Plato *Letters* 7.347e and 329d; Gildenhard 2006.203–5.

[111] Cicero *De republica* 1.68: *quos si boni oppresserunt, ut saepe fit, recreatur ciuitas.* See also 1.65: *quem si optimates oppresserunt...* At 1.66 Scipio quotes Plato *Republic* 8.562c–563e.

So was the Roman philosopher to guide the tyrant, as Plato had tried and failed to do in Syracuse, or just look forward to his 'suppression'? The Atticus correspondence reveals that the latter was certainly in Cicero's mind. He comforted himself with the knowledge that Caesar was mortal, and might be 'extinguished' in various ways.[112] And he took from 'Plato on tyrants' an augury that Caesar's period of power would be short-lived: 'he must fall, and I hope I live to see it'.[113]

However, Plato provided no indication of how the tyrant might be got rid of. By what means would the *optimates* 'suppress' him? The obvious precedent—and it was one Cicero himself had acted on—was summary execution authorized by the Senate. His own experience was certainly in his mind:[114]

non est committendum ut iis paream quos contra me senatus, ne quid res publica detrimenti caperet, armauit.

I must not stoop to yield obedience to men against whom the Senate placed arms in my hands 'lest harm come to the state'.

But less formal methods were also available. As well as reading Plato, Cicero was also exercising his mind on the rhetoricians' dilemmas about tyranny.[115] One of the themes he set himself was this: 'should one strive for the overthrow of a tyranny by *any* means?'[116]

Cicero knew very well that Caesar had the support of the Roman People,[117] just as he had had ten years before. But just as ten years before, Cicero did not care what the People thought. Their betters would decide.

VI

On 1 January 48 BC the constitutional question was definitively settled. The consuls of 49, who had left Rome after seventeen days

---

[112] *Ad Atticum* 9.10.3 (18 Mar.): *hunc primum mortalem esse, deinde etiam multis modis posse exstingui cogitabam.*
[113] Ibid. 10.8 (2 May): *auguria . . . illa Platonis de tyrannis* (§6); *corruat iste necesse est . . . id spero uiuis nobis fore* (§8). He gives Caesar's *regnum* just six months (§7).
[114] Ibid. 10.8.8 (2 May) (trans. Shackleton Bailey).
[115] Ibid. 9.4 (12 Mar.), 9.9.1 (17 Mar.).
[116] Ibid. 9.4.2: εἰ παντὶ τρόπῳ τυραννίδος κατάλυσιν πραγματευτέον.
[117] Ibid. 10.4.8 (14 April) on *populi studium.*

to follow Pompey to Greece, were out of office, and the Roman People had elected as their successors C. Iulius Caesar and P. Servilius Isauricus. Anyone who still thought that the republic resided in Pompey's camp would have to think again.[118] In the spring of 48 BC Cicero's son-in-law wrote to him across the battle-lines:[119]

satis factum est iam a te uel officio uel familiaritati, satis factum etiam partibus et ei rei publicae quam tu probabas. reliquum est, ubi nunc est res publica, ibi simus potius quam, dum illam ueterem sequamur, simus in nulla.

Enough has been done on your part for obligation and friendship; enough has been done for your party too, and the sort of republic of which you approved. It is time now to be where the republic actually is, rather than follow the old one and end up in none.

What separated the two conceptions of the republic was the sovereignty of the Roman People.

Cicero had thrown in his lot with the arrogant aristocracy (as Sallust would soon describe it), the 'factious few' who in the time of their dominance, on 7 January 49 BC, had driven two of the People's tribunes out of Rome with the threat of doing to them what their predecessors had done to the Gracchi and Saturninus.[120] That effectively deprived the People of its right of veto, and so decisions of the Senate after that date could be regarded as invalid—except in Pompey's camp.[121]

When the news of Pompey's defeat and death reached Rome in October 48 BC, Caesar was voted the consulship for five successive years, a dictatorship (his second) for a full year rather than the normal six months, and the tribunician power.[122] When the news of the defeat of the 'republicans' in Africa reached Rome in April 46

---

[118] [Caesar] *De bello Alexandrino* 68.1 (Caesar to Deiotarus): *quod homo tantae prudentiae ac diligentiae scire potuisset…ubi senatus populusque Romanus, ubi res publica esset, quis denique post L. Lentulum C. Marcellum consul esset.* See Sordi 2003.191.

[119] Dolabella in Cicero *Ad familiares* 9.9.2–3.

[120] Caesar *De bello ciuili* 1.5.3–5, 7.5–6; cf. Cicero *Ad familiares* 16.11.2, Livy *Epitome* 109, Dionysius of Halicarnassus 8.87.7–8, Plutarch *Antony* 5.4, Suetonius *Diuus Iulius* 31.1, Appian *Civil Wars* 2.33.131.

[121] Caesar *De bello ciuili* 1.5.1, 7.2–4; Cicero *Ad Atticum* 11.7.1 (*audio enim eum ea senatus consulta improbare quae post discessum tribunorum facta sunt*).

[122] Dio Cassius 42.20.3–4.

BC, Caesar was voted the position of *praefectus moribus* for three years, then successive annual dictatorships, and the right of granting magistracies and honours on behalf of the People.[123] When the news of young Pompey's defeat in Spain reached Rome in April 45 BC, Caesar was voted ten successive consulships, and authority over all military forces and public funds.[124] Early in 44 BC, Caesar was voted the censorship for life, without a colleague, and the *sacrosanctitas* of the tribunes; soon after that he was appointed dictator for life.[125]

I deliberately emphasize the verbs. These honours may have originated, as Dio implies, from senators eager to win Caesar's favour; but they were all voted on by the Roman People, and there is no reason to imagine that the People were bribed or coerced.[126] Caesar's power was not usurped, but granted constitutionally by the only authority competent to do so. Of course senior *optimates* thought the republic was dead,[127] because their own freedom of action was curtailed.[128] Curtailing their freedom of action was what the Roman People wanted. It did not follow that Caesar was a despot,[129] or that the rule of law had been abandoned.[130]

A glimpse of the republic at work is provided by the recently published inscription recording a treaty between Rome and the *koinon* of Lycia. On 24 July 46 BC the *praetor urbanus* L. Volcacius Tullus and the *praetor peregrinus* L. Roscius presided over the oath-taking in the Comitium, and the *fetiales* L. Billienus and L. Fabricius

---

[123] Dio Cassius 43.14.4–5; cf. Cicero *Ad familiares* 9.15.5 for the *praefectura moribus*.

[124] Dio Cassius 43.45.1–2.

[125] Dio Cassius 44.5.3, 8.4.

[126] Dio Cassius 46.13.1 (Calenus' speech): ἐψηφίσθη τε ὁμοίως ... καὶ ἤρεσε καὶ ἡμῖν [the Senate] καὶ τῷ δήμῳ. Cf. 42.19.1–2 (οἱ πρῶτοι and their motives); 42.21.1, 43.14.7 (ἐψηφίσθη); 43.45.1, 44.5.3 (ἐψηφίσαντο).

[127] See e.g. Cicero *Ad familiares* 9.16.3 (*in ciuitate libertas... nunc amissa*), 9.17.3 (*nos enim illi seruimus*), 9.26.1 (*seruitus nostra*); Ser. Sulpicius in *Ad familiares* 4.5.5 (Tullia died *cum res publica occideret*). When Cicero spoke in the Senate for M. Marcellus, it seemed to him that the republic was reviving a little (*Ad familiares* 4.4.3).

[128] See esp. *Ad familiares* 4.14.1, to Cn. Plancius in Jan. 45 BC: *sin autem in eo dignitas est si quod sentias aut re efficere possis aut denique libera oratione defendere, ne uestigium quidem ullum est reliquum nobis dignitatis.*

[129] Caesar as *rex*: Cicero *Ad Atticum* 13.37.2 (Aug. 45 BC); cf. *Ad familiares* 9.16.6 (analogy with Athenian and Syracusan *regna*).

[130] *Ad familiares* 9.16.3 (*cum a iure discessum est*), 9.26.4 (*si ulla nunc lex est*)— both to Papirius Paetus in 46 BC.

Licinus carried out the sacrifice and libation on behalf of the Roman People.[131] The arrangements that were sworn to had been decided by Gaius Caesar as *imperator*—during his brief visit to Asia in the autumn of 48 BC, after the battle of Pharsalus—and confirmed by a *senatus consultum*; they were guaranteed by what the Lycians' Greek text calls 'Caesar's law', evidently translating *lege Iulia*, which must be the legal authority the Senate and People had given him to decide on matters of peace and war.[132]

A day or two later Caesar himself reached Rome,[133] the first time in twelve years (apart from two brief and hurried visits in 49 BC) that the citizens had seen him in the capital. How would he use the power they had given him?

Not like Plato's tyrannical man. Cicero's public speeches, and more revealingly his letters, are full of grateful acknowledgements of the victor's moderation and generosity.[134] Caesar kept the promise he had made at the start of the war, not to imitate Sulla.[135] Cicero, who had feared proscriptions,[136] was well placed to appreciate that, remembering as he did what the *optimates* in Pompey's camp had planned.

In November 48 BC, while the memory was still fresh, he had written to Atticus:[137]

me discessisse ab armis numquam paenituit; tanta erat in illis crudelitas, tanta cum barbaris gentibus coniunctio, ut non nominatim sed generatim proscriptio

---

[131] Mitchell 2005.169–71 (lines 1–6, 74–6).

[132] Mitchell 2005.171, lines 62–4: καθὼς Γαίος Καῖσαρ ὁ αὐτοκράτωρ ἔκρεινεν ἥ τε σύγκλητος δογματίσασα συνεπεκύρωσεν· τῷ τε νόμωι τωι Καίσαρος πεφυλαγμένον καὶ κατηφαλισμένον ἐστιν. Dio Cassius 42.20.1 (autumn 48 BC): καὶ πολέμων καὶ εἰρήνης κύριον . . . πρὸς ἅπαντας ἀνθρώπους ἀπέδειξεν αὐτόν, κἂν μηδὲν μήτε τῷ δήμῳ καὶ τῇ βουλῇ περὶ αὐτὸν κοινώσηται. Discussion at Mitchell 2005.234–9.

[133] *De bello Africo* 98.2.

[134] 46 BC: *Pro Marcello* 12, 32 (*aequitas, misericordia*), *Pro Ligario* 15, 19 (*lenitas, clementia*); *Ad familiares* 4.4.2 (*nihil moderatius*), 4.9.4 (*liberalitas*), 4.13.2 (*summam erga nos humanitatem*), 6.6.8 (*mitis clemensque natura*), 6.6.10 (*admirari soleo grauitatem et iustitiam et sapientiam Caesaris*), 6.13.2 (*sua natura mitiorem facit*), 6.14.2 (*sane mollis et liberalis*). 45 BC: *Pro rege Deiotaro* 33–4 (*cuius in uictoria ceciderit nemo nisi armatus*), 40 (*eorum incolumitates quibus salutem dedisti*); *Ad familiares* 4.6.3 (*prudens et liberalis*).

[135] See above, n. 194. The contrast with Sulla is publicly acknowledged at *Pro Ligario* 12.

[136] See above, n. 96.

[137] Cicero *Ad Atticum* 11.6.2 (trans. Shackleton Bailey).

esset informata, ut iam omnium iudicio constitutum esset omnium uestrum bona praedam esse illius uictoriae.

I have never regretted quitting the war. There was so much cruelty on our side, such association with barbarian races; so that a proscription not by individuals but by whole classes had been sketched out, and it was already agreed by universal consent that the possessions of all of you should be the plunder of the victors.

Eighteen months later, probably before the outcome of the war in Africa was known, he made the same point to his friend Marcus Marius in Pompeii:[138]

extra ducem paucosque praeterea (de principibus loquor), reliquos primum in ipso bello rapacis, deinde in oratione ita crudelis ut ipsam uictoriam horrerem; maximum autem aes alienum amplissimorum uirorum.

Apart from the commander-in-chief and a few besides, all (I am referring to the principal figures) showed their greed for plunder in the war itself, and talked in so bloodthirsty a style that I shuddered at the prospect of victory. Moreover, those of the highest rank were up to their ears in debt.

Now, with Caesar's clemency before his eyes, he reminded his fellow ex-Pompeians what rapacious motives the leading *optimates* had had, and how cruel their victory would have been.[139] Late in 46 BC, when the war broke out in Spain, that prospect became real again: young Pompey was cruel and angry, and his victory would be murderous.[140] Cicero well understood what would happen if a civil war was won by 'angry, greedy, unbridled men'.[141]

Anger, cruelty, rapacity—the tyrant's characteristics were displayed not by Caesar but by the men who wished him dead. And anger, at least, was what motivated the conspirators.[142]

[138] Cicero *Ad familiares* 7.3.2 (Apr. 46 BC?) (trans. D. R. Shackleton Bailey). For the *optimates*' debts, see above, p. 124 n. 97.

[139] *Ad familiares* 6.6.6, to A. Caecina (*peropportunam et rebus domesticis et cupiditatibus suis illius belli uictoriam fore putabant*); 4.9.3, to M. Marcellus (*an tu non uidebas mecum simul quam illa crudelis esset futura uictoria?*); also in public at *Pro Marcello* 16–18. See p. 104 above for Macaulay's shrewd comment on Pompey.

[140] *Ad familiares* 15.19.4 (Cassius on young Pompey's *crudelitas*), 4.14.1 (*caedes* if he wins), 6.4.1 (*quam sit metuendus iratus uictor armatus*).

[141] *Ad familiares* 4.14.2, to Cn. Plancius in Jan. 45 BC (trans. Shackleton Bailey): *intellegebam et iratorum hominum et cupidorum et insolentium quam crudelis esset futura uictoria.*

[142] Nicolaus of Damascus *FGrH* 90 F 130.19.60; cf. Toher 2006.34–6, who rightly insists on the value of Nicolaus' work as the earliest extant narrative.

VII

Cicero was delighted by the killing of Caesar.[143] Immediately, his letters return to the prejudicial optimate terminology of 59 and 49 BC: the dead man is referred to constantly as *tyrannus*,[144] and the assassins, in a revealingly Greek expression, as *tyrannoctoni*.[145] The assassination itself was heroic or even godlike,[146] the most glorious of deeds,[147] the greatest in human history.[148] Of course Caesar was justly killed; that is not argued but taken for granted.[149] As Cassius put it, he was a wicked man.[150] It seems that nothing else needed to be said.

It is not easy to get inside this mindset. The author of *De republica* and *De legibus* knew perfectly well (and made the point at this very time) that acts of political violence could only be countered by more violence.[151] The figurehead of the conspiracy, Marcus Brutus, prided

[143] Cicero *Ad Atticum* 14.9.2 (*eius interfecti morte laetamur*), 12.1 (*laetitia*), 13.2 (*laetitiam autem apertissime tulimus omnes*), 14.4 (*laetitiam quam oculis cepi iusto interitu tyranni*), 22.2 (*nam aperte laetati sumus*): Apr.–May 44 BC.

[144] *Ad Atticum* 14.5.2, 6.2, 9.2, 14.2 and 4, 17.6 (Apr.–May 44 BC); 15.3.2, 20.2, *Ad familiares* 12.1.2 (May–June); *Ad Atticum* 16.14.1 (Nov.), *Ad M. Brutum* 11(12).3 (May 43 BC); *De officiis* 1.112, 2.23, 3.19, 3.84. For *rex* and *regnum*, see *Ad Atticum* 14.11.1, 21.3 (Apr.–May); *Ad familiares* 11.3.4, 8.1, 27.8 (Aug. 44 – Jan. 43 BC); *Ad M. Brutum* 5.1, 23.4 (Apr.–July 43 BC); *De officiis* 3.83. Contrast the public declaration in *Pro rege Deiotaro* 33–4: *quem nos liberi, in summa libertate nati, non modo non tyrannum sed clementissimum in uictoria ducem uidimus* (n. 134 above).

[145] *Ad Atticum* 14.6.2, 15.1, 21.3 (Apr.–May 44 BC); 16.15.3, *Ad familiares* 12.22.2 (Sept.–Nov.).

[146] ἥρωες, *heroicus* etc: *Ad Atticum* 14.4.2, 6.1, 11.1; 15.12.2. *Di, diuinus, caelestis*: *Ad Atticum* 14.11.1, 14.3; *Ad M. Brutum* 5.2, 23.4; *Philippics* 2.114.

[147] *Ad Atticum* 14.4.2 (*gloriosissime et magnificentissime confecerunt*); *Ad familiares* 12.3.1, to Cassius (*uestri…pucherrimi facti*); *De officiis* 3.19 (*ex omnibus praeclaris factis…pulcherrimum*); *Philippics* 2.25 (*gloriosissimi facti nomen*), 117 (*fama gloriosum*). Cf. Tacitus *Annals* 1.8.6: *aliis pessimum aliis pulcherrimum facinus*.

[148] *Ad familiares* 11.5.1, to D. Brutus: *in illa quidem re quae a te gesta est post hominum memoriam maxima*.

[149] *Ad Atticum* 14.14.4 (*iusto interitu tyranni*), 15.3.2 (*tyrannum iure optimo caesum*).

[150] *Ad familiares* 12.2.1, to Cassius: *ille ipse quem tu nequissimum caesum esse dixisti*. Cf. *Ad M. Brutum* 23.4: *magna pestis erat depulsa per uos, magna populi Romani macula deleta*.

[151] *Ad familiares* 12.3.1 (Oct. 44 BC): *quid enim est quod contra uim sine ui fieri possit?*

himself on being a stickler for constitutional propriety: 'what the
Senate has not yet decreed, nor the People ordered, I do not take it
upon myself to prejudge, I do not make myself the arbiter'.[152] And
yet Cicero assured Decimus Brutus that the very fact that he had
killed Caesar without public authority made his deed all the more
glorious.[153]

We may come some little way to understanding the paradox if we
look back at something Cicero had said twelve years before, in his
capacity as forensic orator. is His client had offended a patrician lady,
and he was afraid that her powerful family would suborn witnesses to
give false testimony against him:[154]

*neque ego id dico ut inuidiosum sit in eos quibus gloriosum etiam hoc esse
debet. funguntur officio, defendunt suos, faciunt quod uiri fortissimi solent;
laesi dolent, irati efferuntur, pugnant lacessiti. sed uestrae sapientiae tamen est,
iudices, non, si causa iusta est uiris fortibus oppugnandi M. Caelium, ideo
uobis quoque causam putare esse iustam alieno dolori potius quam uestrae fidei
consulendi ... hoc ex genere si qui se in hoc iudicium forte proiecerint, exclu-
ditote eorum cupiditatem, iudices, sapientia uestra, ut eodem tempore et huius
saluti et religioni uestrae et contra periculosas hominum potentias condicioni
omnium ciuium prouidisse uideamini.*

I say this with no intention of bringing ill will on those to whom this should
even be a matter of pride. *They* are performing their duty, defending their
own, doing what gallant gentlemen normally do: when injured they resent it,
when angered they strike out, when provoked they fight. But granted that
such gentlemen have good cause to attack Marcus Caelius, it is *your* responsibility, as wise jurymen, not to consider it reason enough to satisfy other
men's resentment instead of your own oath ... If it should happen that any
of that sort [bribed witnesses] push themselves forward into this trial, then
by your wisdom, gentlemen of the jury, you must shut your ears to their
avarice, and make it clear that you have given your attention equally to my
client's innocence, your own sworn responsibility, and the position of all
citizens against men whose power is dangerous.

[152] *Ad M. Brutum* 10(11).2 (May 43 BC) (trans. D. R. Shackleton Bailey): *quod
enim nondum senatus censuit nec populus Romanus iussit, id adroganter non praeiudico
neque reuoco ad arbitrium meum.*
[153] *Ad familiares* 11.7.2 (Dec. 44 BC): *nullo enim publico consilio rem publicam
liberauisti, quo etiam est res illa maior et clarior.*
[154] Cicero *Pro Caelio* 21–2 (Apr. 56 BC).

That is, the interests of the arrogant aristocracy do not coincide with those of the Roman citizen body as a whole. When injured they resent it, and their resentment (*dolor*) must be avenged.

Bearing that terminology in mind, let us look at the two places where Cicero comes closest to analysing the *optimates*' feelings about the assassination:[155]

o mi Attice, uereor ne nobis Idus Martiae nihil dederint praeter laetitiam et odi poenam ac doloris.

My dear Atticus, I'm afraid the Ides of March have given us nothing, except for joy and the satisfaction of our hatred and resentment.

ut tantum modo odium illud hominis impuri et seruitutis dolor depulsus esse uideatur.

so that what we have got rid of seems to be just hatred of a foul man and resentment of our slavery.

'Hatred' is a strong term, but it was clearly what Cicero meant.[156] And Caesar had been well aware of it, as a famous and well-attested story indicates. Seeing Cicero waiting to consult him on behalf of a friend, Caesar had commented,[157]

'ego dubitem quin summo in odio sim, cum M. Cicero sedeat nec suo commodo me conuenire possit? atqui si quisquam est facilis, hic est. tamen non dubito quin me male oderit.'

'How can I doubt that I am much hated, when Marcus Cicero is sitting there and can't see me at his own convenience? If anyone is easygoing, he is—but I don't doubt that he really hates me.'

It may seem frivolous to suggest that Caesar was killed because the *optimates* liked things to be at their own convenience, but something like that must be near the truth. When Suetonius, who was very well informed about the period, listed the reasons why 'it is thought that he was justly killed [*iure caesus*]',[158] all he could find were the powers

---

[155] *Ad Atticum* 14.12.1 (22 Apr. 44 BC), *Ad familiares* 12.1.1 (to Cassius, 3 May).
[156] As Macaulay recognized (p. 105 above). Cf. *Ad Atticum* 14.6.2 (*ea . . . propter quae illum oderamus*), *De officiis* 2.23 (*huius tyranni . . . interitus declarat quantum odium hominum ualeat ad pestem*).
[157] *Ad Atticum* 14.1.2, reported by C. Matius on 7 Apr. 44 BC.
[158] Suetonius *Diuus Iulius* 76.1 (for his knowledge of the Ciceronian and Augustan periods, see Wallace-Hadrill 1983.53–64). The suggestion that Suetonius' source for

and honours that were voted to Caesar by the Roman People, and then just a sequence of anecdotes alleging haughtiness or disrespect to the Senate.[159] A century earlier, Velleius Paterculus had a simpler explanation: the conspirators abused Caesar's clemency, and called him a tyrant to justify their act.[160]

Velleius' version is borne out by the evidence of Gaius Matius, writing to Cicero probably in October 44 BC. Matius had been criticized by the *optimates* for his grief at Caesar's death. 'They say that country should come before friendship—as though they have already proved that his death was to the public advantage.'[161] They didn't need to prove what to them was self-evident. Matius goes on:[162]

> *possum igitur, qui omnis uoluerim incolumis, eum a quo id impetratum est perisse non indignari, cum praesertim idem hominess illi et inuidiae et exitio fuerint? 'plecteris ergo' inquiunt 'quoniam factum nostrum improbare audes.' o superbiam inauditam! alios in facinore gloriari, aliis ne dolere quidem impunite licere!*

Well then, can I, who desired every man's preservation, help feeling indignant at the slaughter of the man who granted it—all the more when the very persons who brought him unpopularity were responsible for his destruction? 'Very well,' they say, 'you shall be punished for daring to disapprove of our action.' What unheard-of arrogance! Some may glory in the deed, while others may not even grieve with impunity!

However, the arrogance was not unheard-of. It had been manifest since the days of Scipio Nasica, the dogmatic insistence on an

---

the *iure caesus* judgement was Asinius Pollio (Canfora 1999.304–7 = 2007.274–6) seems to me to rely too heavily on Pollio's guarded words to Cicero in Mar. 43 BC (*Ad familiares* 10.31.3, *quam iucunda libertas et quam misera sub dominatione uita esset*); there is no sign that Pollio had any sympathy for the assassins (cf. *Ad familiares* 10.33.1), and in the late summer of 43 he joined forces with Antony.

[159] Suetonius *Diuus Iulius* 76 (powers and honours), 77–9 (anecdotes).

[160] Velleius Paterculus 2.56.3 (Brutus' and Cassius' disappointed ambitions), 57.1 (clemency and ingratitude), 58.2 (Brutus on 'the tyrant'—*ita enim appellari Caesarem facto eius expediebat*).

[161] Cicero *Ad familiares* 11.28.2, trans. Shackleton Bailey: *aiunt enim patriam amicitiae praeponendum esse, proinde ac si iam uicerint obitum eius rei publicae fuisse utilem.* Matius was replying to a letter in which Cicero had written *si Caesar rex fuerit, ut mihi quidem uidetur...* (ibid. 27.8).

[162] Ibid. 28.3 (trans. Shackleton Bailey); see Lintott 2008.359–62 for the Matius letters.

extreme partisan viewpoint, backed up where necessary by murderous violence ('you shall be punished').

In the speech for Caelius, Cicero's case had required him to champion the common interests of the citizen body against the dangerous power of the few. That was appropriate for the man who had prosecuted Verres. But Cicero's reaction to the deaths of Clodius and Caesar shows how far his political position had moved since 70 BC. In the great peroration to the second *Philippic*, he tells the senators how they should think of Caesar:[163]

muneribus monumentis congiariis epulis multitudinem imperitam delenierat; suos praemiis, aduersarios clementiae specie deuinxerat. quid multa? attulerat iam liberae ciuitati partim metu partim patientia consuetudinem seruiendi.

He had cajoled the ignorant populace with shows and buildings and largesses and feasts. He had bound his own followers with rewards, his adversaries by a show of clemency. In short, he had succeeded in habituating a free community to servitude, partly through its fears, partly through its long-suffering.

Those who had studied Greek philosophy could recognize 'tyranny'; to kill such a man was a beautiful act.[164] What did the ignorant Roman People know about it?

In fact, Cicero's position was not coherent. Very soon afterwards, writing *De officiis*, he claimed that Caesar had held the Roman People down by armed force,[165] and appealed to their own supposed approval of the assassination:[166]

quod potest maius esse scelus quam non modo hominem sed etiam familiarem occidere? num igitur se astrinxit scelere si qui tyrannum occidit quamuis familiarem? populo quidem Romano non uidetur, qui ex omnibus praeclaris factis illud pulcherrimum existimat.

What crime can be greater than murdering not just any individual but a close friend? But if a man murders a tyrant, even if he is a friend, has he thereby implicated himself in a criminal act? The Roman People in fact do not think so, for they regard this as the most noble of illustrious deeds.

---

[163] Cicero *Philippics* 2.116 (trans. D. R. Shackleton Bailey).
[164] Ibid. 117: *re pulchrum, beneficio gratum, fama gloriosum tyrannum occidere.*
[165] Cicero *De officiis* 3.84 (p. 207 below), with Dyck 1996.606, who can only assume an anachronistic reference to Caesar's veterans in Oct. 44 BC. For the date of composition see Dyck 1996.8–10.
[166] *De officiis* 3.19, trans. P. G. Walsh (World's Classics).

Really? We shall see in the next chapter how much truth there was in that.

Cicero's treatise on moral duty has been hugely influential, from the elder Pliny, who thought it should be read every day and learned by heart, to Voltaire, who declared that no truer or wiser book would ever be written.[167] But it was written very fast, at a time of acute political tension, and inevitably the topical references are tendentious and prejudicial. What are we to make, for instance, of the claim that Caesar's victory was 'fouler than Sulla's'?[168] Caesar had pardoned his enemies, and done his best in settling his veterans not to repeat the disastrous effects of Sulla's depredations.[169] But Cicero was not interested in dispassionate assessment. For him, Caesar in his pursuit of power had ignored everything that was right and honourable, overturned all the laws of gods and men, and destroyed liberty and the laws in a 'foul and accursed' oppression.[170]

The third book of *De officiis* does what Panaetius, Cicero's main source, had failed to do: discuss the compatibility of the honourable and the beneficial (*honestum* and *utile*). In the view of the common people, nothing could be more 'beneficial' than to be a king,[171] but Cicero disagrees. No doubt he has Plato in mind,[172] but he uses a Roman dramatist to make his point:[173]

[167] Pliny *Nat. Hist.* pref. 22: *uolumina ediscenda, non modo in manibus cotidie habenda*. Voltaire 1877–85.28.461 (*Lettres de Memmius à Cicéron*, 1771): 'on n'écrira jamais rien de plus sage, de plus vrai, de plus utile.' Again, Macaulay takes a different view (Journal, 1 Feb. 1856, Thomas 2008.4.243): 'The *Offices* I do not rate high, except for the style, which is, as usual, pellucid. As a system nothing could be more wretched. Particular remarks and illustrations are often excellent.' For the work's influence, see Dyck 1996.39–49.

[168] Cicero *De officiis* 2.27 (*uictoria etiam foediore*), on the expropriation of private property (cf. 1.43). For the vocabulary, cf. 3.83 on Caesar's *foedissimum et taeterrimum parricidium patriae*.

[169] Appian *Civil Wars* 2.94.395 (οὐ καθάπερ Σύλλας), Dio Cassius 42.54.1, Suetonius *Diuus Iulius* 38.1; see Keppie 1983.49–58 on Caesar's veteran settlements. For the anti-Sullan clemency, see p. 194 above.

[170] Cicero *De officiis* 3.82 (one of those who *omnia recta et honesta neglegunt*), 1.26 (*omnia iura et diuina et humana peruertit*), 3.83 (*legum et libertatis interitum earumque oppressionem taetram et detestabilem*).

[171] *De officiis* 3.84: *non habeo ad uolgi opinionem quae maior utilitas quam regnandi esse possit.*

[172] See e.g. Plato *Republic* 9.576a, 578b–c, 579b–580a.

[173] *De officiis* 3.84–5 (trans. P. G. Walsh); Accius fr. 691 Dangel (presumably from the *Atreus*).

possunt enim cuiquam esse utiles angores sollicitudines, diurni et nocturni metus, uita insidiarum periculorumque plenissima?

> *multi iniqui atque infideles regno, pauci beniuoli,*

inquit Accius. at cui regno? quod a Tantalo et Pelope proditum iure obtinebatur. nam quanto plures ei regi putas qui exercitu populi Romani populum ipsum Romanum oppressisset, ciuitatemque non modo liberam sed etiam gentibus imperantem seruire sibi coegisset? hunc tu quas conscientiae labes in animo censes habuisse, quae uulnera? cuius autem uita ipsi potest utilis esse cum eius uitae ea condicio sit ut qui illam eripuerit in maxima et gratia futurus sit et gloria?

For can worries, anxieties, fears by day and night, a life fraught with ambushes and hazards be useful to anyone? As Accius puts it,

> Kingship breeds many foes and faithless friends,
> Well-wishers all too few.

But to which kingship was he referring? Why, that bequeathed by Tantalus and Pelops, a kingdom held by right. How many more such foes and friends, then, do you imagine confronted the king who exploited the Roman People's army to subjugate the Roman People itself, and forced the state which was not only free but also the ruler of the world to become his slave? What blemish, what scars do you think he has on his conscience? Can anyone's life appear useful in his own eyes, when its status is such that the man who deprives him of it will be held in the greatest gratitude and esteem?

Cicero's eloquence is not easy to resist. But in justice one should remember that Caesar's power too was held by right, freely voted to him by the people Cicero pretends he had enslaved.[174]

Caesar was not a tyrant. The Senate had admitted as much when it voted on 17 March 44 BC to confirm his acts.[175] It also voted an amnesty for the assassins, but if Caesar was not a tyrant, what they had done was murder. In October, shortly before Cicero withdrew to Puteoli to write *De officiis*, Antony as consul addressed the Roman People about avenging Caesar's death, and told them that the deed had been carried out on Cicero's advice.[176] It wasn't true, but given Cicero's openly expressed opinions, it was all too easy to believe.

---

[174] See above, p. 198.

[175] Appian *Civil Wars* 2.128.535 and 135.563 (see pp. 224–6 below); Cicero *Ad Atticum* 14.6.2, 9.2, 10.1, 12.1 (Apr. 44 BC), *Ad familiares* 12.1.1–2 (May).

[176] Cicero *Ad familiares* 12.3.2 (to Cassius).

VIII

In February 43 BC, pursuing his determined policy to have war declared against Antony, Cicero attacked Q. Fufius Calenus in the Senate:[177]

atque ais eum te esse qui semper pacem optaris, semper omnis ciuis uolueris saluos. honesta oratio, sed ita si bonos et utilis et e re publica ciuis: sin eos qui natura ciues sunt, uoluntate hostes, saluos uelis, quid tandem intersit inter te et illos? pater tuus quidem, quo utebar sene auctore adulescens, homo seuerus et prudens, primas omnium ciuium P. Nasicae, qui Ti. Gracchum interfecit, dare solebat: eius uirtute, consilio, magnitudine animi liberatam rem publicam arbitrabatur. quid? nos a patribus num aliter accepimus? ergo is tibi ciuis, si temporibus illis fuisses, non probaretur, quia non omnis saluos esse uoluisset.

You describe yourself as one who has always prayed for peace, always wanted all citizens to survive. That is an honourable sentiment, but only if you mean good citizens, men of use and benefit to the commonwealth. But should you want the survival of people who are citizens by birth but public enemies by choice, where would be the difference between you and them? Your father was a strict man and a wise one. When I was young and he was old, I used to ask his advice. Among all Romans he used to give the place of honour to Publius Nasica, who killed Tiberius Gracchus, holding that Nasica's courage, judgement and unselfishness had brought freedom to the commonwealth. Have we not heard the same from *our* fathers? Well, if you had been alive in those days, you would not have approved of Nasica as a citizen because he had not wanted all citizens to survive.

Cicero went on to make the same point about Opimius and Gaius Gracchus, the consuls of 100 BC and Saturninus, himself and Catiline: 'in the body politic, let whatever is noxious be amputated so that the whole may be saved'.[178] Since Fufius had been a friend of Clodius, Cicero ironically defers to his supposed view that Clodius was a man of virtue and therefore 'a citizen to be preserved'.[179] No doubt that got a laugh, but one wonders how many senators shared the tacit

---

[177] Cicero *Philippics* 8.13–14, trans. Shackleton Bailey.

[178] Ibid. 14–15 (trans. Shackleton Bailey); cf. *Ad Atticum* 1.14.5–6, 16.2, Asconius 45C on Fufius and Clodius in 61 BC.

[179] *Philippics* 8.16: *sanctum, temperantem, innocentem, modestum, retinendum ciuem et optandum.*

premiss of his argument—that only those citizens he approved of deserved to be kept alive.

What others thought can be inferred only indirectly, from two posthumous attacks on Cicero which no doubt incorporate genuine contemporary arguments from texts now lost to us. 'Speakers hostile to the manner and memory of Cicero were active in the Augustan schools of rhetoric', and Pollio's classic history could provide them with authentic material from which to create plausible anti-Ciceronian orations.[180] One such may be the pseudo-Sallustian invective *In Ciceronem*, allegedly a speech in the Senate in 54 BC, which Quintilian thought was genuine; others must lie behind the speech Dio Cassius attributes to Fufius Calenus in the Senate in January 43 BC.[181]

Both authors attack Cicero's execution of the Catilinarians without trial, 'Sallust' with a damaging comparison to the methods of Sulla.[182] Dio's Calenus may be unfair in stating that Cicero 'killed Clodius by the hand of Milo, and Caesar by the hand of Brutus', but he is on much stronger ground in charging him with ingratitude to Caesar and encouragement of his assassins.[183] And each of the authors puts his finger unerringly on the arrogantly arbitrary nature of Cicero's political judgement.

Here is Dio's Calenus explaining Cicero to his peers:[184]

οὕτως οὔτε τὰ δίκαια πρὸς τοὺς νόμους οὔτε τὰ συμφέροντα πρὸς τὸ τῷ κοινῷ χρήσιμον ἐξετάζει, ἀλλὰ πάντα ἁπλῶς πρὸς τὴν ἑαυτοῦ βούλησιν διάγει . . .

So you see he doesn't estimate justice by the laws, or expediency by the public good, but manages everything simply according to his own wish.

And here is 'Sallust', ironically commenting on the most famous line in Cicero's epic poem:[185]

---

[180] Syme 1964.297, on Asconius 93–4C (speeches attributed to Catiline and C. Antonius in 64 BC) and Quintilian 10.5.20 (Cestius Pius' reply to the *Pro Milone*); Seneca *Suasoriae* 6.14 for Pollio as *infestissimus famae Ciceronis*.

[181] See Syme 1964.315–8 on ps.-Sallust ('swift and vivid, alert and scurrilous'); Millar 1964.52–5 on Dio Cassius 46.1–28.

[182] Dio Cassius 46.20.1–2; ps.Sallust *In Ciceronem* 5–6.

[183] Dio Cassius 46.2.3 (Milo and Brutus), 12.4 (ἀχάριστος), 22.3–5.

[184] Ibid. 46.22.7.

[185] ps.Sallust *In Ciceronem* 5, on Cicero *De consulatu suo* fr. 8 (Courtney 1993.159): *o fortunatam natam me consule Romam.*

te consule fortunatam, Cicero? immo uero infelicem et miseram, quae crude-
lissimam proscriptionem eam perpessa est, cum tu perturbata re publica metu
perculsos omnes bonos parere crudelitati tuae cogebas, cum omnia iudicia,
omnes leges in tua libidine erant, cum tu sublata lege Porcia, erepta libertate
omnium nostrum uitae necisque potestatem ad te unum reuocaueras.

[Rome] fortunate in your consulship, Cicero? Oh no—unfortunate and
wretched in suffering that most cruel proscription, when you took advantage of the political crisis to compel all the good men, panic-stricken as they
were, to obey your cruelty; when all the courts, all the laws, were dependent
on your whim; when by cancelling the *lex Porcia* and taking away our
freedom you had arrogated to yourself alone the power of life and death
over all of us.

In tua libidine is exactly right: that was the phrase the real Sallust used
of the abuse of power by the arrogant aristocracy in the time of the
Gracchi.[186]

Of course Cicero was not unique in being willing to bypass the rule
of law. What he did in 63 BC was backed by a resolution of the Senate.
What he applauded in 52 and 44 BC had not even that shred of
constitutional authority, but Cicero himself made no such distinction between the cases. By his standards, the deaths of the Catilinarians, of Clodius, and of Caesar were all equally and self-evidently
justified. What we must recognize is that his standards were those of
a factious minority. They did not coincide with those of the Roman
People, for whom the rule of law was the guarantee of their freedom
against exploitation and oppression.

---

[186] Sallust *Jugurthine War* 31.7 (speech of Memmius), 42.4: *non lex, uerum lubido*
eorum... ea uictoria nobilitas ex lubidine sua usa. Cf. 40.5 (*plebs*), 41.5 (*populus*) on
abuse of power by the other side.

10

After the Ides of March

I

The earliest surviving description of the murder of Caesar is the vivid and dramatic account in Nicolaus of Damascus, probably written about AD 15:[1]

εἰσιόντα δὲ αὐτὸν ὡς εἶδεν ἡ σύγκλητος, ὑπανέστη εἰς τιμῆς ἀξίωσιν. οἱ δὲ μέλλοντες ἐγχειρήσειν περὶ αὐτὸν ἦσαν. πρῶτος δὲ πάντων ἐπ᾽ αὐτὸν καθίει Τίλλιος Κίμβρος, ᾧ ἔφευγεν ἀδελφὸς ἐληλαμένος ὑπὸ Καίσαρος. ἐν προσχήματι δὴ τοῦ ἀντιβόλειν αὐτὸν λιπαρῶς ὑπὲρ τοῦ ἀδελφοῦ προσελθὼν ἥπτετο τῆς ἀναβολῆς, καί τι θρασύτερον εἴσω τὰς χεῖρας ἔχοντος ἐδόκει δρᾶν, ἐκώλυε τε, εἰ βούλοιτο ἀνίστασθαι καὶ ταῖς χερσὶ χρῆσθαι. ὀργιζομένου δ᾽ ἐπιστρεφῶς ἐκείνου...

When the Senate saw him coming in, they rose as a mark of honour. The intended assassins surrounded him. Tillius Cimber, whose brother was in exile, banished by Caesar, was the first of them all to approach him. In the assumed attitude of an earnest suppliant for his brother, he came forward and took hold of Caesar's robe. He certainly seemed to be acting more boldly than one who keeps his hands in his toga, and he was stopping him from standing up and using his hands if he wanted to. Caesar was seriously angry.

It was a mark of respect to keep one's hands out of sight inside the toga.[2] Suetonius adds that Caesar protested at Cimber's behaviour: 'That is violence!', he cried. Appian specifies that Cimber pulled the

---

[1] Nicolaus of Damascus *FGrH* 90 F 130.24.88. The date of Nicolaus' *Bios Kaisaros* is notoriously disputed, but I agree with Toher (2006.44 n. 38) that 'the conventions of the genre of ancient biography argue for a date of publication after the death of Augustus'.

[2] Cicero *Pro Caelio* 11, Seneca *Controuersiae* 5.6, Quintilian 12.10.21.

toga away from Caesar's neck, and shouted 'Friends, what are you waiting for?'[3] According to Plutarch and Dio, pulling the toga down was the signal for the attack.[4] Nicolaus continues with the assassins 'setting about their business':[5]

ταχὺ δὲ πάντες γυμνώσαντες τὰ ἐγχειρίδια ἐπ᾽ αὐτὸν ὥρμησαν. καὶ πρῶτος μὲν Σερουίλιος Κάσκας κατὰ τὸν ἀριστερὸν ὦμον ὀρθῷ τῷ ξίφει παίει μικρὸν ὑπὲρ τὴν κλεῖν, εὐθύνων ἐπ᾽ αὐτήν, ταραττόμενος δὲ οὐκ ἐδυνήθη.

They all drew their weapons and rushed at him. First, Servilius Casca, his sword vertical, struck him on his left shoulder a little below the collar-bone. He was aiming for it [?], but in the confusion he missed.

Either there is a textual corruption here or Nicolaus has misunderstood his source.[6] Plutarch and Appian both emphasize where Casca was standing: behind Caesar, and leaning over his head.[7] Appian says he struck at the throat, Plutarch that he wounded Caesar in the neck, near the shoulder.[8] Since he was on the left-hand side, it seems clear that he was holding his sword vertical for a two-handed thrust straight down into the heart; that was why Cimber had pulled the toga down. Caesar must have moved at the moment Casca struck.

Nicolaus goes on to say that Caesar stood up to defend himself. According to Plutarch, he turned round and grabbed Casca's sword-hand, with the cry 'Impious Casca, what are you doing?'; Suetonius adds that he stabbed Casca's arm with his pen.[9] Appian is more precise: 'Caesar wrenched his toga out of Cimber's grasp, gripped Casca's hand, and as he sprang off the seat whirled round and pulled Casca after him with enormous force. While he was in this position one of the others drove a dagger into his side, stretched as it was

---

[3] Suetonius *Diuus Iulius* 82.1 (*ista quidem uis est*), Appian *Civil Wars* 2.117.491.

[4] Plutarch *Caesar* 66.4, cf. *Brutus* 17.4 (Cimber used both hands); Dio Cassius 44.19.4.

[5] *FGrH* 90 F 130.24.88–9: ἔργου εἴχοντο οἱ ἄνδρες.

[6] Perhaps one should read εὐθύνων ἐπ᾽ αὐτὴν <τὴν καρδίαν>.

[7] Plutarch *Brutus* 17.4 (εἱστήκει γὰρ ὄπισθεν); Appian *Civil Wars* 2.117.492 (ἐφεστὼς ὑπὲρ κεφαλῆς).

[8] Appian *Civil Wars* 2.117.492; Plutarch *Caesar* 66.4, *Brutus* 17.4. Appian's 'wound to the *chest*' may be a conflation of Casca's blow with that of his brother (n. 11 below).

[9] *FGrH* 90 F 130.24.89; Plutarch *Caesar* 66.4 (μιαρώτατε Κάσκα), *Brutus* 17.5 (ἀνόσιε Κάσκα); Suetonius *Diuus Iulius* 82.2. Plutarch's adjectives presumably translate *impie* in a Latin source.

in the action of twisting.'[10] Who that was may be inferred from Nicolaus:[11]

καὶ ὃς τὸν ἀδελφὸν βοᾷ Ἑλλάδι γλώττῃ ὑπὸ θορύβου. ὁ δ' ὑπακούσας ἐρείδει τὸ
ξίφος κατὰ τῆς πλευρᾶς. μικρὸν δὲ Κάσσιος ὑποφθὰς εἰς τὸ πρόσωπον
ἐγκαρσίαν αὐτῷ πληγὴν δίδωσι, Δέκμος δὲ Βροῦτος ὑπὸ ταῖς λαγόσι
διαμπερὲς παίει, Κάσσιος δὲ Λογγῖνος ἑτέραν ἐπενδοῦναι πληγὴν σπεύδων
τοῦ μὲν ἁμαρτάνει, τυγχάνει δὲ τῆς Μάρκου Βρούτου χειρός, Μινούκιος δὲ καὶ
αὐτὸς τύπτων Καίσαρα παίει Ῥούβριον εἰς τὸν μηρόν.

In the confusion [Casca] shouted in Greek to his brother, who reacted by thrusting his sword down into Caesar's ribs. A moment before, Cassius gave Caesar a slanting blow in the face, Decimus Brutus struck him deep in the side, Cassius Longinus tried to land another blow but missed and hit the hand of Marcus Brutus, and Minucius, also trying to strike Caesar, struck Rubrius in the thigh.

Appian describes the same moment: 'Cassius also struck him in the face, Brutus in the thigh, and Bucilianus in the back, so that for a few moments Caesar kept turning from one to another of them with furious cries like a wild beast.'[12] Plutarch is more rhetorical: 'They hemmed Caesar in on every side. Whichever way he turned he met the blows of daggers and saw the cold steel aimed at his face and at his eyes. So he was driven this way and that, and like a wild beast in the toils, had to suffer from the hands of each one of them.'[13]

The repeated wild beast image confirms what is obvious anyway, that these narratives all derive, whether directly or indirectly, from the same original source, with each of our authors picking out particular details to emphasize. But it is clear that the later authors—Suetonius, Plutarch, Appian, Dio—also depend on a tradition unknown to Nicolaus, which contrasted Caesar's first furious resistance with his resignation when he saw Marcus Brutus attack

---

[10] Appian *Civil Wars* 2.117.492 (trans. John Carter, Penguin Classics).

[11] *FGrH* 90 F 130.24.89; cf. Plutarch *Caesar* 66.5, *Brutus* 17.5 for Casca shouting in Greek.

[12] Appian *Civil Wars* 2.117.493 (trans. John Carter, Penguin Classics); cf. Plutarch *Caesar* 66.6 for M. Brutus' blow εἰς τὸν βουβῶνα. See Pelling 2006.264 on the wild beast image: 'How much of all this is Appian himself, and how much is owed to Pollio? We cannot know.'

[13] Plutarch *Caesar* 66.6 (trans. Rex Warner, Penguin Classics); cf. also Dio Cassius 44.19.5.

him; at that point he allegedly covered his head with his toga and fell, decently covered, at the foot of Pompey's statue.[14] Nicolaus, by contrast, concludes immediately after the scene of the attackers wounding each other:[15]

πίπτει δὲ ὑπὸ πλήθους τραυμάτων πρὸ τοῦ Πομπηίου ἀνδριάντος. καὶ οὐδεὶς ἔτι λοιπὸν ἦν ὃς οὐχὶ νεκρὸν κείμενον ἔπαιεν ὅπως ἂν καὶ αὐτὸς δοκοίη τοῦ ἔργου συνῆφθαι, εἰς ὃ ἐ καὶ λ' λαβὼν τραύματα ἀπέπνευσε.

He fell under a hail of wounds in front of Pompey's statue. And there was not one of them who did not strike the body as it lay, to prove that he too was part of the deed. He finally breathed his last having received thirty-five wounds.

In the later authors it is only now, in their rush to strike the fallen Caesar, that the various attackers wounded each other.[16]

Nicolaus' detailed and circumstantial narrative has every chance of being authentic. Since there was a whole chamber full of eyewitnesses, watching in horror as the violence suddenly erupted, a contemporary historian would have had no difficulty finding informants with the scene still vivid in their memories. Asinius Pollio is the obvious possibility.[17] Such a well-informed early account would naturally have a deep influence on later historians;[18] but as we have seen, there was another source, not used by Nicolaus, which was also prestigious enough to influence the later tradition.

That source evidently pre-dates Valerius Maximus,[19] and I think the most likely candidate is Livy. By the time he got to book 116,

---

[14] Suetonius *Diuus Iulius* 82.2 (*tradiderunt quidam*); Plutarch *Caesar* 66.6–7 (λέγεται δὲ), *Brutus* 17.6; Appian *Civil Wars* 2.117.493; Dio Cassius 44.19.5 (ἤδη δέ τινες καὶ ἐκεῖνο εἶπον). Suetonius and Dio add his alleged words to Brutus (καὶ σύ, τέκνον;). See Toher 2006.34–5 for Nicolaus' lack of emphasis on Brutus.

[15] *FGrH* 90 F 130.24.90. The numeral may be corrupt; twenty-three is the canonical figure, as in the Triumvirs' edict (Appian *Civil Wars* 4.8.34); thus Livy *Epitome* 116, Valerius Maximus 4.5.6, Suetonius *Diuus Iulius* 82.2, Appian *Civil Wars* 2.147.612, Eutropius 6.25.

[16] Plutarch *Caesar* 66.7, *Brutus* 17.7; Appian *Civil Wars* 2.117.493.

[17] For Pollio as the historian who dared to tackle such dangerous contemporary themes, see Horace *Odes* 2.1.1–8 and 17–28, with Woodman 2003.196–213.

[18] See Wiseman 1998a.60–1 on Pollio as the likely source of the Rubicon scene in Plutarch, Appian, and Suetonius. For Pollio and Appian, see p. 113 n. 32 above.

[19] Valerius Maximus 4.5.6 (under the heading *de uerecundia*) for the 'decorous fall' story: *in hunc modum non homines exspirant sed di immortales sedes suas repetunt.*

perhaps about 5 BC,[20] Livy may have felt it necessary to provide Divus Iulius with an end more dignified than that of a trapped beast. Since Livy was a younger contemporary of Pollio,[21] whose account he cannot have ignored and may have followed in detail (with additions, subtractions, or adjustments as he saw fit), it is likely that our detailed information comes both from Pollio, via Nicolaus, and from Pollio-in-Livy, via Suetonius, Plutarch, Appian, and Dio.

II

There must have been a lot of blood. When Marcus Brutus stood up from Caesar's corpse and turned to speak to the Senate, the spell of horror was broken. Everyone rushed in panic to the doors.[22]

What the terrified senators had witnessed was not only murder but sacrilege. At the beginning of a new phase in the narrative, Appian sums up with a striking formulation:[23]

ἐκτελεσθέντος δὲ τοῖς φονεῦσι τοσοῦδε ἄγους ἐν ἱερῷ χωρίῳ καὶ ἐς ἄνδρα ἱερὸν καὶ ἄσυλον . . .

So great a pollution had the murderers committed, in a sacred place against a man whose person was sacred and inviolable.

Where the Senate met was a *templum*, either a temple in the normal sense or (as in this case) a meeting hall consecrated by the augurs as a sacred space.[24] Caesar himself had been granted the same *sacro-sanctitas* as the tribunes of the *plebs*;[25] any violence offered to him

---

[20] Cf. Syme 1959.71 = 1979.448.

[21] According to Jerome's *Chronica*, Pollio died in his eightieth year in Olympiad 195.4 (AD 5–6).

[22] Plutarch *Caesar* 67.1, *Brutus* 18.1; cf. Appian *Civil Wars* 2.118.494 (φυγή τε ἦν ἀνὰ τὸ βουλευτήριον αὐτίκα). Cicero, an eyewitness, gives a hint of the horror in *De diuinatione* 2.23: *trucidatus ita iaceret ut ad eius corpus non modo amicorum sed ne seruorum quidem quisquam accederet.*

[23] Appian *Civil Wars* 2.118.494.

[24] Aulus Gellius 15.7.7, from Varro's Εἰσαγωγικός of 71 BC.

[25] Appian *Civil Wars* 2.106.442, 144.601–2; Dio Cassius 44.5.3, 50.1.

was a pollution (ἄγος), an offence against the gods which would
have to be expiated one way or another. Already at the beginning
of his story Appian had described the murder of the tribune
Tiberius Gracchus in similar terms, and the way Suetonius and
Plutarch make Caesar react to Cimber's manhandling of him ('violence!') and Casca's first blow ('impious!'), makes it more likely
than not that this way of thinking went back to their common
source.[26]

The narrative of the next five days, thus derived indirectly from a
contemporary historian, gives us a rare glimpse of how matters may
have seemed to the Roman People. A recent and authoritative analysis of the events begins and ends as follows:[27]

The result, I shall argue, is a profoundly confused picture, whose lack of clear
resolution ultimately goes back to the fundamental indeterminacy of the
Popular Will in such circumstances—an indeterminacy that was exploited,
but also in the aggregate compounded, by the partisan interpretations of the
original actors...

Ultimately, then, precious little can be learned about the 'true' attitude of
the Roman People, or even of the urban *plebs*, from the confused
political theater of the days following Caesar's assassination and the fog of
controversy that quickly enshrouded the accounts. Perhaps the one incon-
trovertible fact is that there was no strong and unambiguous show
of popular anger toward the conspirators until Caesar's funeral (probably
on March 20).

With respect, I think our sources suggest quite a different conclusion.

What one needs to remember is how much the ordinary citizen
had to lose by civil war; people whose whole livelihoods could be
destroyed in the torching of a single workshop were naturally pre-
disposed in favour of peace and order.[28] Any motive that overcame
that predisposition must have been powerful indeed.

---

[26] Appian *Civil Wars* 1.2.5, 1.17.71 (τόδε μύσος); Suetonius *Diuus Iulius* 82.1;
Plutarch *Caesar* 66.4, *Brutus* 17.5 (n. 9 above).

[27] Morstein-Marx 2004.151, 157.

[28] A fact exploited by Cicero in his speeches to the People in 63 BC: *In Catilinam*
2.26, 3.22, 3.29 for the threat to *uestra tecta* (cf. 2.1, 2.10 on *flamma* and *incendia*).
The Senate voted a *supplicatio* in his honour *quod urbem incendiis, caede ciuis, Italiam
bello liberassem* (*In Catilinam* 3.15).

III

At the time of the murder several thousand of the Roman People were in the nearby theatre of Pompey watching a gladiatorial show.[29] That was one of the reasons why the assassins had picked that day for the deed; Decimus Brutus owned a troop of gladiators and had stationed them on a trumped-up excuse in the porticos between the theatre and the Senate-house.[30]

In the uproar that followed the senators' escape from the scene, as everyone scattered in panic, unaware of what was going on, the audience came streaming out of the theatre to add to the confusion. The gladiators ran to 'the railings of the Senate-house', no doubt to provide an escort for the assassins as they emerged waving their bloodstained weapons.[31] Marcus Brutus tried to reassure the crowd ('Nothing bad has happened, the tyrant is dead!'), but to no avail. The panic was total, with people shouting 'Run! Bolt doors! Bolt doors!'[32]

According to Appian, Lepidus was in the Forum when the first terrified citizens brought the news. He immediately hurried to the Tiber island, in order to deploy to the Campus Martius the force of soldiers that was encamped or billeted there; they were the advance guard for Caesar's imminent departure to the Parthian war.[33] If that is correct, he must narrowly have missed the assassins themselves, escorted by Decimus' gladiators and their own slaves and freedmen, as they hurried to the Forum to proclaim the news that tyranny was dead and freedom restored.[34]

[29] Nicolaus of Damascus *FGrH* 90 F 130.25.92; Appian *Civil Wars* 2.115.481, 118.495.

[30] Ibid. 23.81, 26.98; cf. Velleius Paterculus 2.58.2, Appian *Civil Wars* 2.122.513.

[31] Ibid. 25.91–2; Appian *Civil Wars* 2.118.494–5.

[32] Ibid. 25.92 (Brutus); Dio Cassius 44.20.1–2 (φεῦγε κλεῖε κλεῖε); cf. Appian *Civil Wars* 2.118.494–5 (some fatalities, including senators; markets plundered, doors bolted, houses defended from roofs), Plutarch *Caesar* 77.1 (doors bolted, stalls and shops abandoned).

[33] Appian 2.118.496, cf. 111.462, 114.476 for the Parthian war (Caesar intended to leave on 18 Mar.). Since we hear no more of looting or killing (n. 32 above), the soldiers must have restored order on the Campus soon after the assassins had left it.

[34] Nicolaus of Damascus *FGrH* 90 F 130.25.94, Appian *Civil Wars* 2.119.499, Dio Cassius 44.20.3; cf. Plutarch *Brutus* 18.7, *Caesar* 77.2 ('straight to Capitol').

They were evidently expecting to be hailed as heroes, and the popular reaction of fear and panic, as if in a captured city,[35] seems to have taken them by surprise. 'When the People did not run to join them, they were disconcerted and afraid.'[36] Anxious about 'Caesar's army'—the soldiers on the Tiber island—they went up from the Forum to the Capitol, where the gladiators established a defensive position.[37]

From there they will have seen what happened when three of Caesar's slaves appeared in the Forum carrying a litter. It was difficult for just three men, and they were unable to prevent the arms of the body within from trailing over the sides. The litter curtains were up, and Caesar's slashed face was all too visible as they carried their burden across the Forum towards their master's house:[38]

ἔνθα οὐδεὶς ἄδακρυς ἦν ὁρῶν τὸν πάλαι ἴσα καὶ θεὸν τιμώμενον· οἰμωγῇ τε πολλῇ καὶ στόνῳ συμπαρεπέμπετο ἔνθεν καὶ ἔνθεν ὀλοφυρομένων ἀπό τε τῶν τεγῶν καθ᾽ οὓς ἂν γένοιτο καὶ ἐν ταῖς ὁδοῖς καὶ προθύροις.

Everyone wept at the sight of the man who had once been honoured as equal to a god. Loud cries of grief and distress accompanied the litter on its way, as people lamented from the roofs of houses and in the streets and porches wherever it passed.

Calpurnia and her women received the body with bitter self-reproaches, and Caesar's friends began to prepare his burial.[39]

Did the assassins really expect the Roman People to share their own elation at the death of Caesar?[40] They must have believed that 'freedom from tyranny' would be not only welcome to the People, but also acceptable to the soldiers on the island and the large numbers of Caesar's veterans who were in the city, still under military discipline

---

[35] *FGrH* 90 F 130.25.94: διαδρομαὶ δὲ μυρίαι ἦσαν ἔν τε ταῖς ὁδοῖς καὶ κατ᾽ ἀγοράν . . . ἐῴκει τε ἡ πόλις ἁλισκομένη. Cf. Plutarch *Brutus* 18.8 for the διαδρομαί.

[36] Appian *Civil Wars* 2.119.501: τοῦ δήμου δὲ αὐτοῖς οὐ προσθέοντος ἠπόρουν καὶ ἐδεδοίκεσαν.

[37] Nicolaus of Damascus *FGrH* 90 F 130.25.94; Appian *Civil Wars* 2.119–20.502–3.

[38] *FGrH* 90 F 130.26.97; cf. Appian *Civil Wars* 2.118.498, Suetonius *Diuus Iulius* 82.3.

[39] *FGrH* 90 F 130.26.97–8.

[40] See above, p. 201.

and encamped in temples and sacred precincts.[41] (They were awaiting their land allocations and expecting to escort Caesar as he left for the war.) But was it a reasonable expectation? Three months later, at Brutus' country house at Antium, Cicero expressed the view that they should have summoned the Senate to the Capitol and done more to encourage the enthusiastic populace.[42] It is indeed possible to take that as genuine evidence for popular opinion, and by putting it against the narratives of Nicolaus and Appian to infer that the People's view of the assassins was 'relatively neutral, or ambiguous'.[43] But given the evidence amassed in Chapter 9, it may be better to see it as optimate wishful thinking (of course the true Roman People shares the opinion of the best citizens), an attitude which may also have deluded Brutus and Cassius themselves on the Ides of March.

Perhaps now, behind their defences on the Capitol, the assassins were having second thoughts. There was only one way to find out, and in due course, heavily guarded, they came down from the Capitol into the Forum. Brutus and Cassius were praetors; normally, their lictors would suffice to keep order at a *contio*. Casca was a tribune of the *plebs*; he should have needed no protection at all. But on this occasion the People's magistrates addressed them from the *rostra* surrounded by gladiators, with a force of their own slaves and dependents in support.[44]

They were heard in a strange silence, for which Nicolaus, our earliest and best authority, offers two very credible reasons. Yes, the People respected Brutus, for his virtues and his ancestry, but more important was anxiety: they didn't know what was going to happen, who was going to make the first violent move. It would have taken a brave citizen to voice dissent in the presence of armed men who were paid to kill; on the other hand, nothing prevented enthusiastic applause if that had seemed appropriate. In such circumstances,

---

[41] *FGrH* 90 F 130.25.94 ('Caesar's army'); Appian *Civil Wars* 2.119.501, 120.507 (cf. also 125.523, 135.565 for the veterans' leaders).

[42] Cicero *Ad Atticum* 15.11.2 (*c.*7 June): *senatum uocare, populum ardentem studio uehementius incitare.* Cf. *Ad Atticum* 14.10.1 (19 Apr.) for the Senate suggestion, made at the time.

[43] Morstein-Marx 2004.155–6, quotation from 157.

[44] Nicolaus of Damascus *FGrH* 90 F 130.26.99; cf. Appian *Civil Wars* 2.122.512–4.

silence could only be a negative judgement.[45] The assassins and their entourage returned to their place of safety on the Capitol.[46]

Some senior senators, including Cicero, joined them there for consultations, and that evening a deputation was sent to Antony and Lepidus inviting them to come and discuss the situation. The consul and the *magister equitum* said they would give their reply the following day.[47] As night fell on the anxious city, Antony ordered the magistrates to set guards and light fires to prevent disorder. Overnight, Lepidus brought his soldiers from the Campus Martius and deployed them in the Forum.[48]

Next morning, for the first time since the murder, the consul was present in authority in the Forum. Antony was armed, and soon other armed groups appeared among the crowd of citizens. Messengers were sent out to summon Caesar's friends and beneficiaries to join in the duty of avenging him. Antony sent representatives to the Capitol, but now that order was restored he probably wasn't interested in negotiating.[49] He announced a Senate meeting for the following day (17 March, the *Liberalia*), in the temple of Tellus close to his own house on the 'Carinae'.[50]

Meanwhile, he called his friends and advisers for a private discussion. Lepidus took the strong line: they should make war, attack the Capitol, and avenge Caesar. Hirtius was for diplomatic negotiations under a truce. Balbus (ἄλλος in the text must conceal his name) backed Lepidus, on the grounds that it would be impious, as well as

---

[45] *FGrH* 90 F 130.26.100 (καραδοκούντων πάντων ὅτι πρῶτον ὡς ἐν τοιῷδε τολμηθείη καὶ ἄρξειε τῆς νεωτεροποιίας), cf. Plutarch *Brutus* 18.12, *Caesar* 77.4 (noting the silence but ascribing it solely to respect for Brutus). Yavetz 1969.63–4, 65: 'The behaviour of the people bore the character of passive opposition...The people listened in silence but showed no sign of enthusiasm for the conspirators who promised them "freedom" with the help of armed gladiators.'

[46] *FGrH* 90 F 130.27.101. For the assassins' anxiety, cf. Appian *Civil Wars* 2.123.515 (οὐ γὰρ ἐθάρρουν πω τοῖς παροῦσι), Dio Cassius 44.21.2 (φοβούμενοι).

[47] *FGrH* 90 F 130.27.101; Cicero *Philippics* 2.89, *Ad Atticum* 14.10.1. Appian (*Civil Wars* 2.123–4.516–20) gives details of both speeches, no doubt taken from his source; see n. 60 below.

[48] *FGrH* 90 F 130.27.102–3; Appian *Civil Wars* 2.125.522 (cf. 126.525 on Lepidus, misdated), Dio Cassius 44.22.2.

[49] *FGrH* 90 F 130.27.103, 106.

[50] Cicero *Ad Atticum* 14.10.1, 14.14.2 for the date; 16 Mar. was a *dies ater*, ill-omened for public business (see above, p. 153 n. 3). Cf. Appian *Civil Wars* 2.126.525, Dio Cassius 44.22.3 for the Senate summons (misdated).

dangerous, to allow the murder of Caesar to go unpunished. Antony, however, agreed with Hirtius.[51] We may guess that as consul he did not want the responsibility of initiating open warfare in the city.

IV

At this point Nicolaus' narrative fails us. The account of the murder and its aftermath was a digression from his main subject, the young Octavius, to whose biography he now returns. Given our provisional analysis of the sources, that should mean that we lose our more direct access to the Pollio version and have to rely on Livy's elaboration of it, as transmitted at length by Appian and intermittently by Suetonius, Plutarch, and Dio. Two examples illustrate the way the story was developed.

According to Appian, as soon as the assassins had occupied the Capitol they decided to bribe the Roman People. So successful were they in this, thanks to the degeneration of the People by foreigners, ex-slaves, and idle beggars dependent on the corn-dole, that 'Cassius' people' were able to collect a crowd in the Forum shouting for peace, with the intention of rescuing the assassins.[52] Then the praetor Cornelius Cinna arrived, ostentatiously taking off his purple-bordered toga of office because it was the gift of a tyrant; he praised the assassins and ordered that they be invited down. The unbribed section of the crowd wouldn't have that, so the bribed ones contented themselves with shouting for peace. Then came Dolabella, as consul; he attacked Caesar and pretended to have been one of the conspirators himself. That encouraged the assassins' hirelings, who called for 'Cassius' people' to be brought down.[53] At that point, we have the *contio* of Brutus and Cassius in the Forum, as described by Nicolaus.[54]

[51] Nicolaus of Damascus *FGrH* 90 F 130.27.106.

[52] Appian *Civil Wars* 2.120–1.503–8; see Morstein-Marx 2004.152–5 on Appian's schematic distinction at this point between the 'hirelings' (μισθωτοί) and the 'honest part' of the People (τὸ καθαρὸν τοῦ πλήθους).

[53] Ibid. 2.121–2.509–11; for οἱ ἀμφὶ τὸν Κάσσιον see 121.508, 122.511. Cf. Plutarch *Brutus* 18.13 on the Cinna scene (placed *after* Brutus' speech in the Forum), Dio Cassius 44.22.1 on Dolabella's speech.

[54] Above, nn. 44–6.

This whole episode is patently unhistorical. When and how could the bribery-agents have been organized? In due course we discover that this is only the first of three linked scenes,[55] which may suggest that it was originally a scenario created for the stage;[56] an opening scene with Cassius' men distributing bribes becomes problematic only when transported from the theatre into a continuous historical narrative. I see no reason to doubt that Livy was capable of using such material,[57] but be that as it may, the episode is certainly an addition to the narrative known to Nicolaus.

The second Livian development is not an addition but a subtraction. Appian, Plutarch, and Dio all move straight from the night of the Ides to the morning of the Senate meeting at the Tellus temple, omitting a whole day.[58] That is inconsistent both with Nicolaus and with the contemporary evidence of Cicero,[59] but easily explained as Livy cutting out the inessentials in order to get his narrative more quickly from one dramatic scene to the next.

By this sleight of hand Livy omitted the discussion held by Antony with his advisers, and denied his readers Balbus' firm declaration that it would be impious (ἀνόσιον) not to avenge Caesar's death. But he had already made a major dramatic scene, with speeches, out of the embassy sent by the assassins to Antony on the night of the Ides, and put a forceful statement of Balbus' point into the mouth of Antony himself. Appian reproduces it as follows:[60]

κατὰ μὲν ἔχθραν ἰδίαν οὐδὲν ἐργασόμεθα· ἕνεκα δὲ τοῦ μύσους καὶ ὧν Καίσαρι πάντες ὠμόσαμεν, φύλακες αὐτῷ τοῦ σώματος ἢ τιμωροὶ παθόντι τι ἔσεσθαι,

---

[55] Second scene: the attack on Cinna before the Senate meeting (n. 66 below). Third scene: the hunt for Cinna and the killing of Cinna the poet by mistake (n. 122 below). Yavetz 1969.65–6 conflates the first two scenes, and assumes (wrongly, I think) that the episode is historical.

[56] See Wiseman 1998a.52–9 (pp. 54–5 above) for the possibility of such political dramas.

[57] *Pace* Keaveney 2006; see Wiseman 1998a.31–4, 43–8 (on Livy 1.46.2–9 and 39.8.1–14.2), 2008.24–38 (on triumph songs as part of historical dramas).

[58] Appian *Civil Wars* 2.126.524–5, Plutarch *Brutus* 19.1 (τῇ ὑστεραίᾳ), Dio Cassius 44.22.2–3.

[59] Above, nn. 49–50.

[60] Appian *Civil Wars* 2.124.520 (trans. John Carter, Penguin Classics); cf. 124.518 (εἴτε φιλίας ἕνεκα εἴτε τῶν ὁμωμοσμένων). 'The fact that Book 1 and most of Book 2 contain no speeches in direct discourse, in stark contrast to the last three, suggests that these speeches in large part derive from the source' (Gowing 1992.245).

εὔορκον ἦν τὸ ἄγος ἐξελαύνειν καὶ μετʼ ὀλιγωτέρων καθαρῶν βιοῦν μᾶλλον ἢ πάντας ἐνόχους ὄντας ταῖς ἀραῖς.

'We shall take no action that stems from private enmity; but in view of the defilement, and of the oath we all swore to Caesar to protect his person or exact vengeance if anything should happen to him, loyalty to our oath would entail driving out the pollution and sharing our lives with a smaller number of men who are undefiled, rather than all being liable to the curse.'

The word the translator renders as 'defilement' (μύσος) was used by Appian for the abomination of Tiberius Gracchus' murder;[61] now Antony invites Caesar's assassins to consider how the city may remain 'unpolluted'.[62]

The speeches that follow, in Appian's account of the Senate meeting and the popular assemblies associated with it, are full of allusions to the senators' broken oaths and the sacrilegious nature of the murder.[63] That may reflect the outlook of a historian writing in the middle years of Augustus,[64] but there is no reason to regard it as anachronistic. After all, Augustus was where he was because the citizens in 43 BC had given him authority to avenge the sacrilege.[65]

With these reservations in mind we can continue with Appian's narrative, glancing where necessary at Suetonius, Plutarch, and Dio, to see what can be inferred about the attitude of the Roman People.

V

Already before dawn on 17 March (to use the correct date) a crowd had gathered outside the temple of Tellus. Among the senators arriving for the meeting was Cornelius Cinna the praetor, wearing

---

[61] Appian *Civil Wars* 1.2.5, 1.17.71 (p. 178 above).

[62] Ibid. 2.124.520 (εὐαγές); cf. 118.494, 127.531 for the murder of Caesar as a pollution (ἄγος), 133.556 for the assassins as ἐναγεῖς.

[63] Ibid. 130.545 (Antony); 131.549–51, 132.553 (Lepidus); 134.560–2 (Antony); 137.571–8 (Brutus).

[64] Cf. Ovid *Fasti* 3.700 (*sacrilegae manus*), 705 (*nefas*), 706 (pollution); 5.569 (*pia arma*), 575 (*scelerato sanguine*).

[65] Appian *Civil Wars* 4.7.27 for the Triumvirate established on the proposal of the tribune P. Titius (cf. Dio Cassius 47.2.1, διὰ τῶν δημάρχων); 4.8.35 for the murder as μύσος in the Triumvirs' edict, 4.9.36 for their vengeance as θεοῦ συνεπιλαμβάνοντος.

the *toga praetexta* he had so histrionically cast off on the Ides. Those of the citizens who had not been bribed threw stones at him and chased him away, threatening to burn down the house in which he took refuge until Lepidus and his soldiers prevented them.[66] This episode is immediately suspect, as the second act of our putative drama. It may be relevant that a Lucius Cornelius Cinna, probably this man's son, plotted against Augustus about 16 BC and was pardoned by him;[67] that could have provided a context both for a 'historical' play and for Livy's exploitation of it.

When the meeting began, most of the senators were sympathetic to the assassins. An invitation was sent to them to come to the meeting under a safe conduct (it was declined), and then proposals were made that they should be publicly thanked, or even rewarded, for the killing of a tyrant.[68] An unusual procedure was demanded:[69]

ἤτουν σφίσι ψῆφον ἀναδοθῆναι περὶ τοῦ Καίσαρος ἐπὶ ὅρκῳ, καὶ εἰ καθαρῶς ἐθέλουσι κρῖναι, μηδέν᾽ αὐτοῖς ἐπιθεάσαι τὰ ἐξ ἀνάγκης ἐψηφισμένα ἄρχοντι ἤδη, ὧν οὐδὲν ἑκόντας οὐδὲ πρὶν ἢ δεῖσαι περὶ σφῶν αὐτῶν, ἀνῃρημένου τε Πομπηίου καὶ ἐπὶ Πομπηίῳ μυρίων ἄλλων, ψηφίσασθαι.

They asked to be allowed to vote on Caesar under oath, saying that if an unbiased judgement was wanted no-one was to call the gods to witness against them for decrees they had been forced to pass when Caesar was already in power, none of which they had passed voluntarily or before they had come to fear for their own lives after the death of Pompey and the subsequent death of thousands of others.

In fact, as Dio makes clear, the initiative for the decrees honouring Caesar had come from the senators themselves, for their own motives of flattery or malice.[70] As for the supposed reign of terror, the correspondence of Cicero is enough to disprove that, and to attest on the other hand the *optimates'* determination to believe that Caesar was

---

[66] Appian *Civil Wars* 2.126.526–7, cf. 528 for the μισθωτοί (n. 52 above).

[67] Seneca *De clementia* 1.9.2–12, with Griffin 1976.410–11; cf. Dio Cassius 55.14.1–22.1, who tells the story of Cn. Cinna *cos.* AD 5.

[68] Appian *Civil Wars* 2.127.529–30; cf. Suetonius *Tiberius* 4.1 on Ti. Claudius Nero (*de praemiis tyrannicidarum referendum censuit*).

[69] Ibid. 2.127.533 (trans. John Carter). For *sententiae* on oath, see Dionysius of Halicarnassus 7.39.2; Livy 26.33.14, 30.40.12, 42.21.5; Pliny *Nat. Hist.* 7.120; Tacitus *Annals* 1.14.4, 1.74.4, 2.31.3, 4.21.3.

[70] Dio Cassius 42.19.1–2 (48 BC), 43.44.1–3 (45 BC), 44.3.1–3 and 7.2–3 (44 BC).

necessarily a tyrant, however little he behaved like one.[71] That view was what they now wished to establish by their 'unbiased judgement'.

As the presiding consul, Antony pointed out that if such a vote resulted in a decision that Caesar was a usurper, then his body must be cast out unburied and all his acts must be annulled. 'But if you're willing to resign the offices and military commands you hold by his authority, I'll put the question.'[72]

While the senators argued among themselves, Antony and Lepidus left the temple to address the People. The usual custom of leaving the doors open for the citizens to hear the proceedings was clearly not followed on this occasion, when the temple was under armed guard.[73] But the crowd was restless, and had been shouting for Antony and Lepidus to come out. When they did so, someone shouted at Antony 'Be careful it doesn't happen to you too!' Antony pulled down the neck of his tunic to show the breastplate he was wearing. Not even a consul was safe without it.[74]

Some were shouting for vengeance, some for peace. 'Peace, yes,' said Antony, 'but with what security, when all those oaths couldn't keep Caesar safe?' As for vengeance, that was the proper option. 'But as consul I have to look out not for what's right but for what those in there say is expedient—a bit like Caesar, when he spared his captured enemies and was killed by them.'[75]

The other man on the temple steps was the *magister equitum*, in charge of Caesar's military forces and perhaps less constrained by constitutional propriety than the consul. The crowd turned to Lepidus and demanded that he avenge Caesar. At that point a roar went up from the much larger crowd down in the Forum. 'Come down to the *rostra*, where everyone can hear you!'[76] The Tellus temple was on the street that led from the Forum to the 'Carinae', probably about 400 or 500 metres from the Forum piazza itself.[77] We can be sure that

---

[71] See above, pp. 193–6.

[72] Appian *Civil Wars* 2.128.534–7.

[73] See above, p. 154 n. 5; Cicero *Ad Atticum* 14.14.2, *Philippics* 2.89 for the guards.

[74] Appian *Civil Wars* 2.130.542–3.

[75] Ibid. 2.130.544–6 (vengeance εὐορκότερα καὶ εὐσεβέστερα, 545).

[76] Ibid. 2.130.547.

[77] Dionysius of Halicarnassus 8.79.3 (κατὰ τὴν ἐπὶ Καρίνας φέρουσαν ὁδόν), cf. Suetonius *De grammaticis* 15.1 (*in Carinis ad Telluris*); Coarelli 1983.39–40, 1999.25 for the disputed topography.

the street was packed with people, and that what was said from the temple steps was repeated all the way down. But that was not enough: when such great issues were at stake, the Roman People demanded to be consulted in their own political space, the Roman Forum.

When Lepidus mounted the *rostra* and wept for Caesar, the cries were again for vengeance or for peace. Appian ascribes the latter to 'those who had taken the bribes', which looks like part of his source's elaboration;[78] and when the same group offer to make Lepidus *pontifex maximus*, and he reacts with ill-concealed delight, I think we may suspect the hand of a historian writing after 12 BC.[79]

Lepidus returned to the temple, and reported to Antony on the mood of the People.[80] Trusting that there would be no violent outbreak, the consul now put his compromise proposal to the Senate. First, Caesar's acts would be ratified, thus tacitly confirming that his rule had been lawful. Second, there would be no public praise of the assassins (that would be impious and wrong), but as an act of mercy for the sake of their families and friends, their deed would not be punished.[81] The *optimates* insisted that the ratification of Caesar's acts be accompanied by the explanation 'because it is in the public interest'.[82] Antony allowed them that scrap of self-justification, and the *senatus consultum* was passed.[83]

According to Appian, after the consul had closed the meeting but before the senators left the temple, a group of them surrounded Caesar's father-in-law Lucius Piso, urging him not to publish Caesar's will and to oppose a public funeral. When he refused, they threatened to prosecute him for withholding public money; the implication was that since Caesar was a tyrant, his property was automatically forfeit to the state. Piso demanded that the Senate be reconvened, and gave an indignant speech insisting that he would not betray his trust. The

[78] Appian *Civil Wars* 2.131.547–51; for the μισθωτοί see nn. 52 and 66 above.

[79] Ibid. 2.132.552; cf. Livy *Epitome* 117 (*in confusione rerum ac tumultu M. Lepidus pontificatum maximum intercepit*), Augustus *Res gestae* 10.2 (*eo mortuo qui ciuilis motus occasione occupauerat*).

[80] Ibid. 2.132.554: τὰ ἐν τῷ δήμῳ γιγνόμενα ... οὐδ' ἐν τῷ δήμῳ τι γεγενῆτο θερμότερον.

[81] Ibid. 2.132–4.554–62.

[82] Ibid.2.135.563–4: ἐπεὶ τῇ πόλει συμφέρει. The Latin phrase was probably *rei publicae causa* (cf. Velleius Paterculus 2.104.1, Suetonius *Tiberius* 21.3).

[83] On the motion of Cicero, whose speech invoked the Athenian amnesty of 403 BC (Cicero *Philippics* 1.1, Velleius Paterculus 2.58.4).

Senate passed a formal resolution that Caesar's will should be read in public, and that he should be given a public funeral.[84] Here too we may suspect a Livian elaboration. Piso's son, Lucius Piso 'the *pontifex*', was consul in 15 BC and one of the most prominent senators of his time.[85]

The next episode in Appian is an invitation from the assassins to 'the multitude' to come up to the Capitol. There Brutus gave a lengthy speech, defending himself and his comrades from the charge of oath-breaking, and reassuring Caesar's veterans that their land settlements were secure.[86] This too is suspect: it is linked causally with the supposed attack on Cornelius Cinna;[87] and Brutus' promise that he would pay out of public funds the price of the lands confiscated for the veterans is just what Augustus took pride in having done at the great demobilizations of 30 and 14 BC.[88] Brutus certainly did give a *contio* on the Capitol at some point, but it was probably on 16 March, the day the Livian tradition omits.[89]

These two episodes in Appian's narrative have displaced to the following morning the consuls' public announcement to the People of what the Senate had resolved.[90] It is, I think, close to inconceivable that they would have left the People in ignorance overnight, or that that would even have been possible. But there is no need for a priori argument, since Cicero makes it clear that the consuls' *contio* took place on the same day as the Senate meeting, as we should expect.[91] Whether the People were overjoyed, as Cicero alleges, may be doubted. The Senate had given them peace, but not vengeance; not

[84] Appian *Civil Wars* 2.135–6.566–9; cf. Cicero *Ad Atticum* 14.10.1, 14.14.3 for Atticus' optimate opinion that a public funeral would be disastrous.

[85] Tacitus *Annals* 6.10.3 for his father as censor (in 50 BC); Syme 1986.329–45.

[86] Appian *Civil Wars* 2.137–9.570–9 (oaths), 139–41.580–91 (land settlements); cf. 135.565 for the Senate's confirmation of the veterans' settlements. Dio Cassius (44.34.2–4) has a version of the same alleged speech, delivered to 'those in earshot' below the Capitol.

[87] Ibid. 2.137.570, referring back to 126.527 (n. 66 above).

[88] Ibid. 2.141.591. Cf. Augustus *Res gestae* 16.1: *id primus et solus omnium qui deduxerant colonias militum in Italia aut in prouincis ad memoriam aetatis meae feci.*

[89] Cicero *Ad Atticum* 15.1a.2, with Shackleton Bailey's note.

[90] Appian *Civil Wars* 2.142.593 (ἅμα δὲ ἡμέρᾳ).

[91] Cicero *Philippics* 1.32: *quo senatus die laetior, quo populus Romanus? qui quidem nulla in contione umquam frequentior fuit.* For post-Senate *contiones* see Morstein-Marx 2004.247–51.

everyone will have cheered when Brutus and Cassius came down from the Capitol and shook hands with the consuls.[92]

The gladiators must have come down too. I imagine they were redeployed as guards for the conspirators' houses.[93]

VI

Now that the Senate had confirmed the legitimacy of Caesar's rule, the will could be read and the preparations for a public funeral taken forward. It was probably on the morning of Day Four (18 March) that Lucius Piso came to Antony's house and the will was unsealed.[94] According to Plutarch, the Senate met that morning, with Brutus and Cassius present. They argued against a public reading of the will, and against a public funeral, but Antony insisted.[95] So the Roman People were summoned once again, and the will was read from the *rostra*.[96]

Each citizen was to receive a bequest of 300 sesterces, and Caesar's gardens beyond the Tiber were to belong to the Roman People in perpetuity.[97] That was welcome, but what disturbed the People most was the naming of Decimus Brutus, the owner of the gladiators, among the 'secondary heirs', to be adopted as Caesar's son if the young Octavius declined the honour.[98]

---

[92] Velleius Paterculus 2.58.3 (Antony *uelut pacis auctor*), Appian *Civil Wars* 2.142.594 (handshakes). The other consul was Dolabella, confirmed in office at the Senate meeting (Cicero *Philippics* 1.31).

[93] Appian *Civil Wars* 2.126.525 for the last mention of the gladiators; efficient guards are presupposed at 2.147.614, cf. Suetonius *Diuus Iulius* 85.1, Plutarch *Brutus* 20.7, *Caesar* 68.1, *Cicero* 42.3.

[94] Suetonius *Diuus Iulius* 83.1.

[95] Plutarch *Brutus* 19.4–20.1. This was evidently the meeting at which provincial commands were assigned to Brutus and Cassius (cf. Plutarch *Antony* 14.2).

[96] Appian *Civil Wars* 2.143.596; cf. Dio Cassius 44.35.2.

[97] Suetonius *Diuus Iulius* 83.2, Plutarch *Brutus* 20.3, Appian *Civil Wars* 2.143.596, Dio Cassius 44.35.3; cf. Cicero *Philippics* 2.109, Tacitus *Annals* 2.41.1 for the *horti*. 300 sesterces was the annual salary of a colonial *duumuir*'s secretary (*Lex coloniae Genetiuae* LXII.35–6, Crawford 1996.400).

[98] Appian *Civil Wars* 2.143.597, 146.611; Suetonius *Diuus Iulius* 83.2, cf. Dio Cassius 44.35.2.

The narratives of Appian, Plutarch, and Dio all move seamlessly from the reading of the will to the appearance in the Forum of Caesar's funeral procession, as if both took place on the same day.[99] But that seems very unlikely, since the funeral had only been authorized the day before, and the preparations for such a grand event could hardly have been completed overnight. It looks like another case of Livy streamlining his narrative by omitting the inessentials.[100]

But in that case, when did the funeral take place? On 19 March, the festival of *Quinquatrus*, the Salii danced in the Comitium in the presence of the *pontifices*.[101] It would be good to know (but we cannot) whether the ritual was performed that year, and if it was, whether the organizers of the funeral chose to avoid it or to exploit it. Were the Salii clashing the sacred shields when the *pontifex maximus* was brought through the Forum on his bier? Here is Appian's description of the scene on the morning of the funeral (whichever day that was):[102]

ἐπεὶ δὲ καὶ Πείσωνος τὸ σῶμα φέροντος ἐς τὴν ἀγορὰν πλῆθός τε ἄπειρον ἐς φρουρὰν συνέδραμον συν ὅπλοις, καὶ μετὰ βοῆς καὶ πομπῆς διψιλοῦς ἐπὶ τὰ ἔμβολα προυτέθη, οἰμωγή τε καὶ θρῆνος ἦν αὖθις ἐπὶ πλεῖστον, καὶ τὰ ὅπλα ἐπατάγουν οἱ ὡπλισμένοι.

When Piso then brought Caesar's body into the Forum a huge number of armed men gathered to guard it. It was laid with lavish pomp and cries of mourning on the *rostra*, whereupon wailing and lamentation arose again for a long time, and the armed men clashed their weapons.

The reference here is to Caesar's veterans,[103] but if it was 19 March they may have taken their cue from the Salii.

What we do know is that the bier was lavishly decorated, the musicians and actors were dressed in the robes they used for

---

[99] Ibid. 2.143.597–8, Plutarch *Brutus* 20.3–4, *Caesar* 68.1, Dio Cassius 44.35.3–4.

[100] See above, p. 222; this time we have no Nicolaus or Cicero as a corrective.

[101] *Fasti Praenestini* (Degrassi 1963.122–3); cf. Charisius in *Grammatici Latini* 1.81 Keil, Lydus *De mensibus* 4.55 on the *ancilia*. There is no evidence for Yavetz's assertion (1969.66) that 'the funeral should have been held on that day [19 Mar.] but was postponed to the morrow on account of the festival of the *Quinquatrus*'.

[102] Appian *Civil Wars* 2.143.598 (trans. John Carter).

[103] Suetonius *Diuus Iulius* 84.4 (*ueteranorum militum legionarii arma sua quibus exculti funeris celebrabant*); cf. Appian *Civil Wars* 2.133.557 (ἅμα τοῖς ὅπλοις ὡς ἐστρατεύοντο).

triumphal shows, and the *rostra* platform was set up as a stage,
complete with the crane that enabled actors to 'fly'.[104] The stage set
was a gilded replica of the temple of Venus Genetrix; the body lay on
an ivory couch with coverings of purple and gold; at the head of the
couch was a trophy of arms, with Caesar's gashed and bloodstained
robe hanging from a spear.[105] The Romans were used to 'funeral
games' at which the dead man himself was impersonated,[106] and the
choice of set suggests that the goddess too appeared, assuring her
descendant of a place in heaven when his body was taken to the
Campus to be burned on the pyre.[107] When Antony mounted the
rostra, he was not only a consul addressing the People; he was a
performer, literally on stage.

He began very calmly. 'I shall use your own words,' he told the
citizens, and ordered the herald to read the decrees, proposed in the
Senate and voted into law by the People, which honoured Caesar as
the father and benefactor of the *patria* and declared his person sacred
and inviolable.[108] After each item he added a few words of his own to
point up the contrast between these honours, which Caesar had
never asked for, and the fate that had befallen him.[109]

Then he had the oath read, 'by which they all undertook to protect
Caesar's person with all their might, and if anyone should conspire
against him, those who failed to defend him were to be accursed'. He
turned to his right, stretched out his hand towards the Capitol and
prayed in a loud voice to Jupiter, protesting his own willingness to
avenge Caesar according to his oath.[110] The senators didn't like that,

---

[104] Appian *Civil Wars* 2.146.607 (ὡς ἐπὶ σκηνῆς), 147.612 (μηχανή, cf. Phaedrus
5.7.6–9), 148.617 (τὴν πομπὴν δαψιλεστάτην οὖσαν); Suetonius *Diuus Iulius* 84.4
(*tibicines et scaenici artifices uestem quam ex triumphorum instrumento ad praesentem
usum induerant*).

[105] Suetonius *Diuus Iulius* 84.1.

[106] Diodorus Siculus 31.25.2, Suetonius *Diuus Vespasianus* 19.2 (*ut est mos*); see
Bettini 1991.39–43, Flower 1996.104–6.

[107] Ovid *Metamorphoses* 15.760–851 gives an idea of how it could be done.
Campus Martius pyre: Suetonius *Diuus Iulius* 84.1.

[108] Appian *Civil Wars* 2.144.600–01: ὅσα δὴ τῆς ἀρετῆς αὐτὸν ὑμεῖς ἀγάμενοι πάντες
ὁμαλῶς, ἥ τε βουλὴ καὶ μετὰ αὐτῆς ὁ δῆμος, ἔτι περιόντι ἐψηφίσασθε, ὑμετέραν καὶ οὐκ
Ἀντωνίου τάδε φωνὴν εἶναι τιθέμενος ἀναγνώσομαι. Suetonius *Diuus Iulius* 84.2: *per
praeconem pronuntiauit*.

[109] Ibid. 2.144.602–3: οὐ βιασάμενος οἷα τύραννος λαβεῖν τάσδε τὰς τιμάς, ἃς οὐδὲ
ᾔτησεν.

[110] Ibid. 2.145.604 (trans. John Carter). See p. 169 above for Jupiter overlooking
the Forum.

but he stopped short of direct accusation: it was not men, but some *daimon*, that had brought these events about.[111]

It was time for a change of tone:[112]

προπέμπωμεν οὖν τὸν ἱερὸν τόνδε ἐπὶ τοὺς εὐδαίμονας, τὸν νενομισμένον ὕμνον αὐτῷ καὶ θρῆνον ἐπᾴδοντες. τοιάδε εἰπὼν τὴν ἐσθῆτα οἷά τις ἔνθους ἀνεσύρατο, καὶ περιζωσάμενος ἐς τὸ τῶν χειρῶν εὔκολον, τὸ λέχος ὡς ἐπὶ σκηνῆς περιέστη κατακύπτων τε ἐς αὐτὸ καὶ ἀνίσχων, πρῶτα μὲν ὡς θεὸν οὐράνιον ὕμνει καὶ ἐς πίστιν θεοῦ γενέσεως τὰς χεῖρας ἀνέτεινεν

'Let us then conduct this sacred one to the abode of the blest, chanting over him our accustomed hymn and lamentation.' Having spoken thus, he gathered up his garments like one inspired, girded himself so that he might have the free use of his hands, took his position in front of the bier as in a play, bending down to it and rising again, raising his hands to heaven in order to testify to Caesar's divine birth.

In a clear, ringing voice he listed all Caesar's wars and victories; in a tone of grief and sorrow he mourned him as a friend unjustly slain.[113] Seizing the moment, he grasped the spear on the trophy and lifted it up to show the torn and bloodstained robe. The People joined in his lament like a chorus.[114]

After that the actors took over, singing arias from famous tragedies chosen for their aptness to the occasion.[115] The one that made the greatest impact was from Pacuvius' *Judgement of the Arms*, when the actor playing Caesar delivered Ajax's line: 'Did I save these men that they might destroy me?'[116] That angered the People, and there was worse to come. From ground level in the Forum, the citizens could not see Caesar's body on its bier on the high platform of the *rostra*, but now the crane lifted up into the view of all a wax image of the corpse, with all its wounds grievously visible.[117]

---

[111] Ibid. 2.145.605.

[112] Ibid. 2.145–6.606–7 (trans. Horace White, Loeb edn.).

[113] Ibid. 2.146.607–9.

[114] Ibid. 2.146.610 (ὁ δῆμος οἷα χορὸς); cf. Plutarch *Antony* 14.3, *Brutus* 20.4, *Cicero* 42.3.

[115] Ibid. 2.146.611 (θρῆνοι μετὰ ᾠδῆς κατὰ πάτριον ἔθος ὑπὸ χορῶν); Suetonius *Diuus Iulius* 84.2 (*cantata sunt quaedam ad miserationem et inuidiam caedis eius accommodata*).

[116] Suetonius *Diuus Iulius* 84.2, Appian *Civil Wars* 2.146.611.

[117] Appian *Civil Wars* 2.147.612 (ἐκ μηχανῆς).

According to Suetonius, the magistrates and senior senators now carried the bier down into the Forum, for the procession to proceed to the pyre in the Campus Martius. But the People angrily demanded that Caesar's body be burned in Pompey's Senate-house, where he had been killed, or else in Jupiter's Capitoline temple, where his murderers had taken refuge.[118] What they wanted was to burn the building along with the body, as they had done with the Senate-house at the funeral of Clodius in 52 BC.[119]

That precedent was evidently in people's minds:[120] if an ad hoc pyre could be built in the Forum for Clodius, so could it be for Caesar. What Suetonius reports next suggests that it may have been more than just a sudden improvisation by the crowd:[121]

repente duo quidam gladiis succincti ac bina iacula gestantes ardentibus cereis succenderunt confestimque circumstantium turba uirgulta arida et cum subselliis tribunalia, quicquid praeterea ad donum aderat, congessit.

Suddenly two men in sword-belts, each carrying two javelins, set light [to the bier] with burning tapers; immediately the throng of bystanders heaped dry branches on it, and tribunals with their benches, and whatever else was at hand as an offering.

The actors and musicians took off their triumphal robes, tore them up and added them to the blaze; the veterans threw in their weapons, and the women their jewellery.

In the midst of this orgy of grief, some of the crowd snatched firebrands from the pyre and ran to find the assassins and attack their houses. The houses were well defended (the gladiators no doubt doing their job), but we are told that the crowd then fell on Helvius Cinna, tribune, poet and friend of Caesar, and mistaking him for their bête noire Cornelius Cinna the praetor, tore him to pieces.[122]

---

[118] Suetonius *Diuus Iulius* 84.3, Dio Cassius 44.50.2; cf. Appian *Civil Wars* 2.147.613, 148.615, mistakenly reporting that the *curia Pompei* was indeed burned, and that the crowd took the corpse up to the Capitol to bury it ἐν ἱερῷ καὶ μετὰ θεῶν.

[119] See above, pp. 120–1. For the implied threat to the Jupiter temple, cf. Suetonius *Gaius* 5.1 on the news of the death of Germanicus: *lapidata sunt templa, subuersae deum arae.*

[120] Plutarch *Brutus* 20.5: ὥσπερ ἐπὶ Κλωδίου τοῦ δημαγωγοῦ πρότερον.

[121] Suetonius *Diuus Iulius* 84.3; cf. Appian *Civil Wars* 2.148.616, Plutarch *Brutus* 20.5, *Caesar* 68.1, *Antony* 14.4.

[122] Valerius Maximus 9.9.1 (*ex funere C. Caesaris domum suum petens*); Suetonius *Diuus Iulius* 85 (*statim a funere*); Plutarch *Brutus* 20.7–11, *Caesar* 68.1–3; Appian

That is probably unhistorical, another episode in the drama of Cornelius Cinna identified above. The People could hardly fail to recognize one of their own tribunes, the ominous dream he had had the night before looks very much like fiction, and it is suspicious that 'no part of him could be found for burial', since not even the most violent crowd can make a body disappear.[123] But the attacks on the houses certainly happened, and one house, that of Lucius Bellienus, was evidently destroyed.[124]

The main body of the Roman People remained in the Forum, keeping vigil at the pyre throughout the night. In due course, when it had burned itself out, Caesar's freedmen collected the bones for burial.[125]

VII

'Thus Gaius Caesar, to whom the Romans most owed their supremacy, was slain by his enemies and buried by the People.'[126] Appian's summary may be his own, or it may be taken from his source. But whether it is a judgement from forty years or two centuries after the event, it is in stark contrast with what one very well-informed senior senator had to say at the time.

Just seven months after Caesar's murder, writing his didactic treatise on moral obligations, Cicero stated that the Roman People regarded the killing of the tyrant as 'the most noble of illustrious

Civil Wars 2.147.613–4 (misplaced before the burning of the body); Dio Cassius 44.50.4.

[123] Previous episodes: nn. 52 and 66 above. Dream: Plutarch *Brutus* 20.9–10, *Caesar* 68.2. No part of him: Appian *Civil Wars* 2.147.614.

[124] Cicero *Philippics* 2.91, cf. *Ad Atticum* 14.10.1. Bellienus, probably the *fetialis* of the Lycia treaty (p. 198 above), is nowhere named among the assassins; but he may have been responsible for the murder of a friend of Caesar in Liguria (Caelius in Cicero *Ad familiares* 8.15.2).

[125] Appian *Civil Wars* 2.148.616 (τὴν νύκτα πανδημεὶ τῇ πυρᾷ παρέμενον); Dio Cassius 44.51.1.

[126] Appian *Civil Wars* 3.1.1: οὕτω μὲν δὴ Γαίος Καῖσαρ πλείστου Ῥωμαίοις ἄξιος ἐς τὴν ἡγεμονίαν γενόμενος ὑπὸ τῶν ἐχθρῶν ἀνήρητο καὶ ὑπὸ τοῦ δήμου τέθαπτο.

deeds'.[127] As Cicero saw it, those who were moved to vengeance at Caesar's funeral were just slaves and beggars.[128]

Normally, it would be methodologically unthinkable to contradict Cicero on the events of his own time by appeal to Appian, or even Livy. But when it is a matter of remembering the Roman People, the testimony of Cicero's late years is evidence only for the tendentious dogmas of the *optimates*. He speaks for the men Sallust would soon describe as *pauci potentes*.[129] And how few they were—like the twenty-two who voted against Curio's disarmament proposal in 50 BC,[130] or the twenty-three who five years later stabbed a defenceless man to death and were surprised not to be hailed as heroes for it.

As we have seen, there is much in Appian's narrative that almost certainly did not happen in March 44 BC, and some of that spurious material may well go back to Livy. But it is a reasonable surmise that the basic framework is authentic, probably established by Asinius Pollio at a time when the memory of the events was still fresh.[131] No doubt Pollio had his prejudices too, but as a self-styled lover of peace and liberty he was well placed to identify those who endangered both.[132] It is worth trying to catch even a distant echo of his version of events.

---

[127] Cicero *De officiis* 3.19 (p. 205 above).

[128] Cicero *Ad Atticum* 14.10.1 (*serui et egentes*), apparently accepted by Yavetz 1969.67; cf. *Philippics* 2.91 (*perditi*).

[129] Sallust *Catiline* 20.7 (Catiline's speech), *Jugurthine War* 31.19 (Memmius' speech), *Histories* 1.12M.

[130] See above, p. 192.

[131] See above, p. 214.

[132] Pollio in Cicero *Ad familiares* 10.31.2 (16 Mar. 43 BC): *natura autem mea et studia trahunt me ad pacis et libertatis cupiditatem.*

Epilogue

With the defeat of the *optimates* at Philippi, the deification of Caesar, and the establishment of a successor regime based on *tribunicia potestas*,[1] the People's cause eventually prevailed over that of the aristocracy. But the victory was short-lived.

In the new *saeculum* of Caesar Augustus the old issues no longer had the same urgency. The next generation grew up with their heads full of Virgil, whose sense of Roman politics is evident from the first simile of the *Aeneid*:[2]

> *ac ueluti magno in populo cum saepe coorta est*
> *seditio saeuitque animis ignobile uulgus*
> *iamque faces et saxa uolant, furor arma ministrant,*
> *tum, pietate grauem ac meritis si forte uirum quem*
> *conspexere, silent arrectisque auribus astant;*
> *ille regit dictis animos et pectora mulcet.*

Just as when often disorder has arisen among a great populace, the minds of the vulgar mob are savage, and already firebrands and stones are flying as fury supplies weapons—then, if they happen to have seen some man whose goodness and services give him authority, they fall silent and stand with attentive ears. He guides their minds with his words, and calms their hearts.

Virgil deplored 'the breath of popular favour', and made Cato the lawgiver of the virtuous dead.[3]

---

[1] Tacitus *Annals* 1.2.1 (*ad tuendam plebem tribunicio iure contentum*), 3.56.2 (*id summi fastigii uocabulum*).

[2] Virgil *Aeneid* 1.148–53 (Neptune calming the storm), quoted by Quintilian 12.1.27 on the *summus orator* who is also *uir bonus*; contrast *Aeneid* 11.336–41 on Drances, *seditione potens*.

[3] Virgil *Aeneid* 6.815–16 (*iactantior Ancus* | *nunc quoque iam nimium gaudens popularibus auris*), 8.670.

Cicero too was an all-pervasive influence. Since he was the classic paradigm in the rhetorical schools,[4] it was natural that educated Romans would understand the now distant history of republican politics in optimate terms. So, for instance, Valerius Maximus took it for granted that Tiberius Gracchus was an enemy of the republic, and Lucan's underworld had Sulla among the blessed and the Gracchi in Tartarus.[5] By the second century AD, the period from the Gracchi to Sulla was thought of as merely a numbered sequence of *seditiones*;[6] even Appian's detailed and intelligent account was influenced by that schematic framework.[7]

Though Sallust was still read,[8] his 'challenge to the arrogance of the aristocracy' was no longer necessary—or, perhaps, acceptable—for the understanding of the late republic. 'The situation had changed,'[9] and under the protection of the emperors the political significance of the Roman *plebs* was now just a memory:[10]

> *nam qui dabat olim*
> *imperium fasces legiones omnia, nunc se*
> *continet atque duas tantum res anxius optat,*
> *panem et circenses.*

For [the People] that once granted military command, the rods of office, legions, everything, now stays at home and longs anxiously for just two things, bread and chariot-races.

As Lily Ross Taylor put it sixty years ago, in the closing sentence of her Sather Lectures,[11] the Roman People 'had passed from the domination of an oligarchy to the domination of a monarch'.

Aristocrats, on the other hand, still prided themselves on family trees and famous names;[12] *their* contribution to the history of Rome

---

[4] Seneca *Controuersiae* 1.pref.11, cf. Velleius Paterculus 2.66.2–5, Valerius Maximus 5.3.4 (*caput Romanae eloquentiae*).

[5] Valerius Maximus 4.7.1, cf. 7.2.6b, 9.4.3, Velleius Paterculus 2.3.2, 2.6.2–3; Lucan 6.778–99, cf. 1.266–71.

[6] Ampelius *Liber memorialis* 26 (cf. 19.3–4); Florus 1.47.8, 2.1.1, 2.2–5.

[7] Appian *Civil Wars* 1.20.85 (ἐπὶ τῇ Γράκχου στάσει), 1.27.121 (ἡ στάσις ἡ τοῦ δευτέρου Γράκχου), 1.33.150 (τρίτον . . . τόδε ἔργον ἐμφύλιον ἦν τὸ Ἀπουληίου).

[8] See e.g. Martial 14.191: *primus Romana Crispus in historia*.

[9] Tacitus *Annals* 1.4.1 (*uerso ciuitatis statu*), 4.33.2 (*conuerso statu*).

[10] Juvenal 10.78–81 on the *turba Remi*; cf. ps.Seneca *Octauia* 288–99.

[11] Taylor 1949.182.

[12] The *locus classicus* is Juvenal 8.1–38, on which see Henderson 1997.1–72. Plutarch (*Solon-Publicola comparison* 1.2) notes the pride of the patrician Valerii of his own day in their descent from P. Valerius Publicola.

was in no danger of being forgotten. That is why the studies in this book have needed so much argument about obscure and controversial details, in an effort to counter the insidious influence of 'history as written by the victors'. The evidence does exist, but it has to be rescued and interpreted with a conscious effort to remember not just the great and powerful but the Roman People too. It turns out that their ancient ideology of a republic of equals (7 *iugera* per man) was still a living tradition in the first century BC; and Virgil's 'vulgar mob' that threw stones and wielded firebrands was the Roman People of 44 BC, reacting to murder and sacrilege.

Bibliography

Anderson 1982: William S. Anderson, *Essays on Roman Satire*. Princeton University Press.

Astbury 1967: Raymond Astbury, 'Varro and Pompey', *Classical Quarterly* 17: 403–7.

Astbury 1985: Raymond Astbury (ed.), *M. Terentii Varronis saturarum Menippearum fragmenta*. Leipzig: Teubner.

Badian 1958: E. Badian, *Foreign Clientelae (264–70 BC)*. Oxford: Clarendon Press.

Badian 1962a: E. Badian, 'Waiting for Sulla', *Journal of Roman Studies* 52: 47–61.

Badian 1962b: E. Badian, Review of Taylor 1960, *Journal of Roman Studies* 52: 200–10.

Badian 1964: E. Badian, *Studies in Greek and Roman History*. Oxford: Basil Blackwell.

Badian 1972: E. Badian, 'Tiberius Gracchus and the Beginning of the Roman Revolution', in Hildegard Temporini (ed.), *Aufstieg und Niedergang der römischen Welt* 1.1 (Berlin: De Gruyter): 668–731.

Baehr 1998: Peter Baehr, *Caesar and the Fading of the Roman World: A Study in Republicanism and Caesarism*. New Brunswick NJ: Transaction.

Balsdon 1971: J. P. V. D. Balsdon, 'Dionysius on Romulus: A Political Pamphlet?', *Journal of Roman Studies* 61: 18–27.

Batstone 2006: William W. Batstone, 'Literature', in Nathan Rosenstein and Robert Morstein-Marx (eds.), *A Companion to the Roman Republic* (Malden, Mass.: Blackwell): 543–63.

Beacham 1991: Richard C. Beacham, *The Roman Theatre and its Audience*. London: Routledge.

Beard 2007: Mary Beard, *The Roman Triumph*. Cambridge, Mass.: Harvard University Press.

Beesly 1866: E. S. Beesly, 'Cicero and Clodius', *Fortnightly Review* 5.4: 421–44.

Beesly 1878: E. S. Beesly, *Catiline, Clodius, and Tiberius*. London: Chapman and Hall.

Beness and Hillard 2001: J. L. Beness and T. W. Hillard, 'The Theatricality of the Deaths of C. Gracchus and Friends', *Classical Quarterly* 51: 135–40.

Bertoletti et al. 1999: Marina Bertoletti, Maddalena Cima, and Emilia Talamo, *Sculptures of Ancient Rome: The Collections of the Capitoline Museums at the Montemartini Power Plant.* Milan: Electa.

Bettini 1991: Maurizio Bettini, 'Sosia e il suo sosia: Pensare il "doppio" a Roma', in Renato Oniga (ed.), *Tito Maccio Plauto: Anfitrione* (Venice: Marsilio): 9–51.

Bravo 2006: José Román Bravo, '¿Terencio en el Comicio? Reflexiones sobre la primera y segunda representación de la *Hecyra*', in Andrés Pociña, Beatriz Rabaza, María de Fátima Silva (eds.), *Estudios sobre Terencio* (Granada: Editorial Universidad de Granada): 185–232.

Brennan 2004: T. Corey Brennan, 'Power and Process under the Republican "Constitution"', in Harriet I. Flower (ed.), *The Cambridge Companion to the Roman Republic* (Cambridge University Press): 31–65.

Briscoe 1971: J. Briscoe, 'The First Decade', in T. A. Dorey (ed.), *Livy* (London: Routledge and Keegan Paul): 1–20.

Broughton 1951: T. Robert S. Broughton, *The Magistrates of the Roman Republic*, vol. 1. New York: American Philological Association.

Broughton 1986: T. Robert S. Broughton, *The Magistrates of the Roman Republic*, vol. 3: suppl. Atlanta, Ga.: Scholars Press.

Brunt 1971: P. A. Brunt, *Social Conflicts in the Roman Republic.* London: Chatto and Windus.

Brunt 1988: P. A. Brunt, *The Fall of the Roman Republic and Related Essays.* Oxford: Clarendon Press.

Cameron 1995: Alan Cameron, *Callimachus and his Critics.* Princeton University Press.

Campbell 2000: Brian Campbell, *The Writings of the Roman Land Surveyors: Introduction, Text, Translation and Commentary* (*JRS* Monograph 9). London: Society for the Promotion of Roman Studies.

Canfora 1999: Luciano Canfora: *Giulio Cesare: Il dittatore democratico.* Bari: Laterza.

Canfora 2007: Luciano Canfora, *Julius Caesar: The People's Dictator* (trans. Marian Hill and Kevin Windle). Edinburgh University Press.

Carafa 1998: Paolo Carafa, *Il Comizio di Roma dalle origini all'età di Augusto* (*BCAR* suppl. 5). Rome: L'Erma di Bretschneider.

Cardauns 1976: Burkhart Cardauns, *M. Terentius Varro Antiquitates Rerum Divinarum.* Wiesbaden: Franz Steiner.

Cèbe 1972–99: Jean-Pierre Cèbe, *Varron, Satires Ménippées* (Collection de l'École française de Rome 9, 13 vols.). Rome: École française.

Chappuis 1868: C. Chappuis, *Fragments des ouvrages de M. Terentius Varron intitulés Logistorici, Hebdomades de imaginibus, De forma philosophiae.* Paris: Hachette.

Cichorius 1922: Conrad Cichorius, *Römische Studien*. Leipzig: Teubner.

Coarelli 1969: Filippo Coarelli, 'Le *Tyrannoctone* du Capitole et la mort de Tiberius Gracchus', *Mélanges d'archéologie et d'histoire de l'École française de Rome* 81: 137–60.

Coarelli 1983: Filippo Coarelli, *Il foro romano: Periodo arcaico*. Rome: Quasar.

Coarelli 1985: Filippo Coarelli, *Il foro romano: Periodo repubblicano e augusteo*. Rome: Quasar.

Coarelli 1987: Filippo Coarelli, *I santuari del Lazio in età repubblicana* (Studi NIS archeologia 7). Rome: Nuova Italia Scientifica.

Coarelli 1996a: F. Coarelli, 'Moneta in arce', *Lexicon topographicum urbis Romae* 3: 279–80.

Coarelli 1996b: Filippo Coarelli, *Revixit ars: Arte e ideologia a Roma: Dai modelli ellenestici alla tradizione repubblicana*. Rome: Quasar.

Coarelli 1999: F. Coarelli, 'Tellus, aedes', *Lexicon topographicum urbis Romae* 5: 24–5.

Coffey 1976: Michael Coffey, *Roman Satire*. London: Methuen.

Cook 1914: A. B. Cook, *Zeus*, vol. 1. Cambridge University Press.

Cornelius 1940: Friedrich Cornelius, *Untersuchungen zur frühen römischen Geschichte*. Munich: E. Reinhardt.

Cornell 1986: T. J. Cornell, 'The Foundation of the Historical Tradition of Early Rome', in I. S. Moxon, J. D. Smart and A. J. Woodman (eds.), *Past Perpectives: Studies in Greek and Roman Historical Writing* (Cambridge University Press): 67–86.

Cornell 1995: T. J. Cornell, *The Beginnings of Rome: Italy and Rome from the Bronze Age to the Punic Wars* (*c.1000–264 BC*). London: Routledge.

Cornell 1999: T. J. Cornell, review of Walt 1997, *Journal of Roman Studies* 89: 229–30.

Cornell 2005: 'The Value of the Literary Tradition', in Kurt A. Raaflaub (ed.), *Social Struggles in Archaic Rome: New Perspectives on the Conflict of the Orders*, ed. 2 (Oxford: Blackwell): 47–74.

Cotta Ramosino 2004: Laura Cotta Ramosino, *Plinio il Vecchio e la tradizione storica di Rome nella* Naturalis Historia (Studi di Storia greca e romana 9). Alessandria: Edizioni dell'Orso.

Courtney 1993: Edward Courtney (ed.), *The Fragmentary Latin Poets*. Oxford: Clarendon Press.

Cozza 1983: Lucos Cozza, 'Le tegole di marmo del Pantheon', in *Città e architettura nella Roma imperiale* (*Analecta Romana* suppl. 10, Odense University Press): 109–18.

Crawford 1974: Michael H. Crawford, *Roman Republican Coinage*. Cambridge University Press.

Crawford 1996: M. H. Crawford (ed.), *Roman Statutes* (*BICS* suppl. 64), 2 vols. London: Institute of Classical Studies.

Degrassi 1947: Atilius Degrassi (ed.), *Inscriptiones Italiae*, XIII *Fasti et elogia*, fasc. 1 *Fasti consulares et triumphales*. Rome: Libreria dello stato.

Degrassi 1963: Atilius Degrassi (ed.), *Inscriptiones Italiae*, XIII *Fasti et elogia*, fasc. 2 *Fasti anni Numani et Iuliani*. Rome: Istituto poligrafico dello stato.

Delbrueck 1907: Richard Delbrueck, *Hellenistische Bauten in Latium*, vol. 1. Strasbourg: K. J. Trübner.

Dench 2005: Emma Dench, *Romulus' Asylum: Roman Identities from the Age of Alexander to the Age of Hadrian*. Oxford University Press.

de Ste Croix 1981: G. E. M. de Ste Croix, *The Class Struggle in the Ancient Greek World from the Archaic Age to the Arab Conquests*. London: Duckworth.

Dunkle 1967: J. Roger Dunkle, 'The Greek Tyrant and Roman Political Invective of the Late Republic', *Transactions of the American Philological Association* 98: 151–71.

Dyck 1996: Andrew R. Dyck, *A Commentary on Cicero*, De Officiis. Ann Arbor: University of Michigan Press.

Dyck 2004: Andrew R. Dyck, *A Commentary on Cicero*, De Legibus. Ann Arbor: University of Michigan Press.

Fantham 2003: Elaine Fantham, 'Three Wise Men and the End of the Roman Republic', in Francis Cairns and Elaine Fantham (eds.), *Caesar against Liberty? Perspectives on his Autocracy* (ARCA 43, Cambridge: Francis Cairns): 96–117.

Feeney 2005: Denis Feeney, 'The Beginnings of a Literature in Latin', *Journal of Roman Studies* 95: 226–40.

Feig Vishnia 1996: Rachel Feig Vishnia, 'The Carvilii Maximi of the Republic', *Athenaeum* 84: 433–56.

Ferroni 1993: A. M. Ferroni, 'Concordia, aedes', *Lexicon topographicum urbis Romae* 1: 316–20.

Flacelière 1948: R. Flacelière, 'Sur quelques passages des *Vies* de Plutarque', *Revue des études grecques* 61: 67–103.

Flower 1996: Harriet I. Flower, *Ancestor Masks and Aristocratic Power in Roman Culture*. Oxford: Clarendon Press.

Flower 2006: Harriet I. Flower, *The Art of Forgetting: Disgrace and Oblivion in Roman Political Culture*. Chapel Hill: University of North Carolina Press.

Forsythe 1994: Gary Forsythe, *The Historian L. Calpurnius Piso Frugi and the Roman Annalistic Tradition*. Lanham, Md.: University Press of America.

Forsythe 2005: Gary Forsythe, *A Critical History of Early Rome: From Prehistory to the First Punic War.* Berkeley and Los Angeles: University of California Press.

Fraccaro 1907: Plinio Fraccaro, *Studi Varroniani: De gente populi Romani libri IV.* Padua: Draghi.

Frayn 1993: Joan M. Frayn, *Markets and Fairs in Roman Italy.* Oxford: Clarendon Press.

Freeman 1880: Edward A. Freeman, *Historical Essays, Second Series*, ed. 2. London: Macmillan.

Frier 1975: Bruce W. Frier, 'Licinius Macer and the *consules suffecti* of 444 BC', *Transactions of the American Philological Association* 105: 79–97.

Frier 1979/1999: Bruce W. Frier, *Libri annales pontificum maximorum: The Origins of the Annalistic Tradition* (Papers and Monographs 27). Rome: American Academy (ed. 2 1999, Ann Arbor: University of Michigan Press).

Frye 1957: Northrop Frye, *Anatomy of Criticism: Four Essays.* Princeton University Press.

Funaioli 1907: Hyginus Funaioli (ed.), *Grammaticae Romanae fragmenta.* Leipzig: Teubner.

Gabba 1956: Emilio Gabba, *Appiano e la storia delle guerre civili* (Biblioteca di cultura 59). Florence: La nuova Italia.

Gabba 1960: Emilio Gabba, 'Studi su Dionigi di Alicarnasso, 1: La Costituzione di Romolo', *Athenaeum* 38: 175–225.

Gabba 1991: Emilio Gabba, *Dionysius and the History of Archaic Rome* (Sather Classical Lectures 56). Berkeley and Los Angeles: University of California Press.

Gabba 2000: Emilio Gabba, *Roma arcaica: Storia e storiografia* (Raccolta di studi e testi 205). Rome: Storia e letteratura.

Gardner 1958: R. Gardner (trans.), *Cicero, The Speeches: Pro Sestio and In Vatinium* (Loeb Classical Library). Cambridge, Mass.: Harvard University Press.

Gelzer 1912: Matthias Gelzer, *Die Nobilität der römischen Republik.* Berlin: B. G. Teubner.

Gelzer 1962: Matthias Gelzer, *Kleine Schriften*, vol. 1. Wiesbaden: Steiner.

Gelzer 1969: Matthias Gelzer, *The Roman Nobility* (trans. Robin Seager). Oxford: Blackwell.

Gildenhard 2006: Ingo Gildenhard, 'Reckoning with Tyranny: Greek Thoughts on Caesar in Cicero's *Letters to Atticus* in Early 49', in Sian Lewis (ed.), *Ancient Tyranny* (Edinburgh University Press): 197–209.

Goldberg 1995: Sander M. Goldberg, *Epic in Republican Rome.* New York: Oxford University Press.

Goldberg 1998: Sander M. Goldberg, 'Plautus on the Palatine', *Journal of Roman Studies* 88: 1–20.

Goldberg 2006: Sander M. Goldberg, *Constructing Literature in the Roman Republic*. New York: Cambridge University Press.

Gowing 1992: Alain M. Gowing, *The Triumviral Narratives of Appian and Cassius Dio*. Ann Arbor: University of Michigan Press.

Gratwick 1982a: A. S. Gratwick, 'Drama', in E. J. Kenney and W. V. Clausen (eds.), *The Cambridge History of Classical Literature*: 2.1 *The Early Republic* (Cambridge University Press): 77–137.

Gratwick 1982b: A. S. Gratwick, 'The Satires of Ennius and Lucilius', ibid. 156–71.

Griffin 1976: Miriam T. Griffin, *Seneca: A Philosopher in Politics*. Oxford: Clarendon Press.

Griffin 1994: Miriam Griffin, 'The Intellectual Developments of the Ciceronian Age', in J. A. Crook, Andrew Lintott and Elizabeth Rawson (eds), *The Cambridge Ancient History*, ix (ed. 2) *The Last Age of the Roman Republic, 146–43 BC* (Cambridge University Press): 689–728.

Griffin 2003: Miriam Griffin, 'Clementia after Caesar: From Politics to Philosophy', in Francis Cairns and Elaine Fantham (eds.), *Caesar against Liberty? Perspectives on his Autocracy* (ARCA 43, Cambridge: Francis Cairns): 157–82.

Grueber 1910: H. A. Grueber, *Coins of the Roman Republic in the British Museum*, vol. 1. London: British Museum.

Gruen 1968: E. S. Gruen, *Roman Politics and the Criminal Courts, 149–78 BC*. Cambridge Mass.: Harvard University Press.

Gruen 1974: Erich S. Gruen, *The Last Generation of the Roman Republic*. Berkeley and Los Angeles: University of California Press.

Gruen 1992: Erich S. Gruen, *Culture and National Identity in Republican Rome* (Cornell Studies in Classical Philology 52). Ithaca, NY: Cornell University Press.

Gutberlet 1985: Dagmar Gutberlet, *Die erste Dekade des Livius als Quelle zur graccischen und sullanischen Zeit* (Beiträge zur Altertumswissenschaft 4). Hildesheim: Olms-Weidmann.

Hanson 1959: John A. Hanson, *Roman Theater-Temples* (Princeton Monographs in Art and Archaeology 33). Princeton University Press.

Hardie 1983: *Statius and the Silvae: Poets, Patrons and Epideixis in the Graeco-Roman World* (ARCA 9). Liverpool: Francis Cairns.

Harries 2006: Jill Harries, *Cicero and the Jurists: From Citizens' Law to the Lawful State*. London: Duckworth.

Hellegouarc'h 1963: J. Hellegouarc'h, *Le Vocabulaire latin des relations et des partis politiques sous la république*. Paris: Les Belles Lettres.

Henderson 1997: John Henderson, *Figuring Out Roman Nobility: Juvenal's Eighth Satire*. University of Exeter Press.

Henderson 2005: John Henderson, 'The Turnaround: A Volume Retrospect on Roman Satires', in Kirk Freudenburg (ed.), *The Cambridge Companion to Roman Satire* (Cambridge University Press): 309–18.

Hubaux 1958: Jean Hubaux, *Rome et Véies: Recherches sur la chronologie légendaire du Moyen Âge romain*. Paris: Les Belles Lettres.

Humphrey 1986: John H. Humphrey, *Roman Circuses: Arenas for Chariot Racing*. London: B. T. Batsford.

Hunt 1968: Christopher John Hunt, *Catalogue of the Library at Wallington Hall, Northumberland* (Library Publications, Extra Series 9). University of Newcastle upon Tyne.

Jehne 2006: Martin Jehne, 'Methods, Models, and Historiography', in Nathan Rosenstein and Robert Morstein-Marx (eds.), *A Companion to the Roman Republic* (Malden, Mass.: Blackwell): 3–28.

Jocelyn 1967: H. D. Jocelyn, *The Tragedies of Ennius* (Cambridge Classical Texts and Commentaries 10) Cambridge University Press.

Kaibel 1899: Georgius Kaibel, *Comicorum Graecorum fragmenta*: 1.1 *Doriensium comoedia, mimi, phlyaces*. Berlin: Weidmann.

Kaster 1998: Robert A. Kaster, *Guardians of Language: The Grammarian and Society in Late Antiquity*. Berkeley and Los Angeles: University of California Press.

Keaveney 2003: Arthur Keaveney, 'The Tragedy of Gaius Gracchus: Ancient Melodrama or Modern Farce?', *Klio* 85: 322–32.

Keaveney 2006: Arthur Keaveney, 'Livy and the Theatre: Reflections on the Theory of Peter Wiseman', *Klio* 88: 510–15.

Keppie 1983: Lawrence Keppie, *Colonisation and Veteran Settlement in Italy 47–14 BC*. London: British School at Rome.

Klotz 1937: Alfred Klotz, 'Diodors römische Annalen', *Rheinisches Museum* 86: 206–44.

Krenkel 2002: Werner A. Krenkel, *Marcus Terentius Varro Saturae Menippeae* (Subsidia Classica 6). St Katharinen: Scripta Mercaturae.

Latte 1960: Kurt Latte, *Römische Religionsgeschichte* (Handbuch der Altertumswissenschaft 5.4). Munich: C. H. Beck.

Lenaghan 1969: John O. Lenaghan, *A Commentary on Cicero's Oration De Haruspicum Responso* (Studies in Classical Literature 5). The Hague: Mouton.

Levick 1978: Barbara Levick, 'Concordia at Rome', in R. A. G. Carson and C. M. Kraay (eds.), *Scripta Nummaria: Essays Presented to Humphrey Sutherland* (London: Spink): 217–33.

Lewis 2006: Sian Lewis (ed.), *Ancient Tyranny*. Edinburgh University Press.

Linderski 1972: Jerzy Linderski, 'The Aedileship of Favonius, Curio the Younger and Cicero's Election to the Augurate', *Harvard Studies in Classical Philology* 76: 181–200.

Linderski 1995: Jerzy Linderski, *Roman Questions: Selected Papers* (HABES 20). Stuttgart: Franz Steiner.

Linderski 2002: J. Linderski, 'The Pontiff and the Tribune: The Death of Tiberius Gracchus', *Athenaeum* 90: 339–66.

Linderski 2007: Jerzy Linderski, *Roman Questions II: Selected Papers* (HABES 44). Stuttgart: Franz Steiner.

Lintott 1968: A. W. Lintott, *Violence in Republican Rome*. Oxford: Clarendon Press.

Lintott 1987: Andrew Lintott, 'Democracy in the Middle Republic', *Zeitschrift der Savigny-Stiftung* 104: 34–52.

Lintott 1992: Andrew Lintott, *Judicial Reform and Land Reform in the Roman Republic*. Cambridge University Press.

Lintott 1999: Andrew Lintott, *The Constitution of the Roman Republic*. Oxford: Clarendon Press.

Lintott 2008: Andrew Lintott, *Cicero as Evidence: A Historian's Companion*. Oxford University Press.

Luce 1968: T. J. Luce, 'Political Propaganda on Roman Republican Coins: Circa 92–82 BC', *American Journal of Archaeology* 72: 25–39.

Luce 1977: T. J. Luce, *Livy: The Composition of his History*. Princeton University Press.

Maas 1992: Michael Maas, *John Lydus and the Roman Past: Antiquarianism and Politics in the Age of Justinian*. London: Routledge.

Marshall 2006: C. W. Marshall, *The Stagecraft and Performance of Roman Comedy*. Cambridge University Press.

Marx and Engels 1979: Karl Marx and Frederick Engels, *Collected Works*, vol. 11. London: Lawrence and Wishart.

Mayer 2005: Roland Mayer, 'Sleeping with the Enemy: Satire and Philosophy', in Kirk Freudenburg (ed.), *The Cambridge Companion to Roman Satire* (Cambridge University Press): 146–59.

Mazzarino 1966: Santo Mazzarino, *Il pensiero storico classico*, II.1. Bari: Laterza.

Meadows and Williams 2001: Andrew Meadows and Jonathan Williams, 'Moneta and the Monuments: Coinage and Politics in Republican Rome', *Journal of Roman Studies* 91: 27–49.

Meier 1965: Christian Meier, 'Populares', *Paulys Realencyclopädie der classischen Altertumswissenschaft*, suppl. vol. 10: 549–615.

Meiser 1887: Karl Meiser, *Ueber historische Drama der Römer*. Munich: Königliche Akademie der Wissenschaften.

Merivale 1911: Charles Merivale, *History of Rome to the Reign of Trajan* (Everyman's Library). London: Dent.

Millar 1964: Fergus Millar, *A Study of Cassius Dio*. Oxford: Clarendon Press.

Millar 1984: Fergus Millar, 'The Political Character of the Classical Roman Republic, 200–151 BC', *Journal of Roman Studies* 74: 1–19.

Millar 1986: Fergus Millar, 'Politics, Persuasion, and the People before the Social War (150–90 BC)', *Journal of Roman Studies* 76: 1–11.

Millar 1989: Fergus Millar, 'Political Power in Mid-Republican Rome: Curia or Comitium?', *Journal of Roman Studies* 79: 138–50.

Millar 1995: Fergus Millar, 'Popular Politics in Rome in the Late Republic', in I. Malkin and Z. W. Rubisohn (eds.), *Leaders and Masses in the Roman World: Studies in Honor of Zvi Yavetz* (Leiden: Brill): 91–113.

Millar 1998: Fergus Millar, *The Crowd in Rome in the Late Republic* (Jerome Lectures 22). Ann Arbor: University of Michigan Press.

Millar 2000: Fergus Millar, 'The First Revolution: Imperator Caesar, 36–28 BC', in *La Révolution romaine après Ronald Syme: Bilans et perspectives* (Entretiens sur l'antiquité classique 46, Geneva: Fondation Hardt): 1–30.

Millar 2002a: Fergus Millar, *Rome, the Greek World, and the East*, vol. 1: *The Roman Republic and the Augustan Revolution* (ed. Hannah M. Cotton and Guy M. Rogers). Chapel Hill: University of North Carolina Press.

Millar 2002b: Fergus Millar, *The Roman Republic in Political Thought* (The Menahem Stern Jerusalem Lectures). Hanover, N. H.: University Press of New England.

Mirsch 1882: Paullus Mirsch, 'De M. Terenti Varronis Antiquitatum rerum humanarum libris XXV', *Leipziger Studien zur Classischen Philologie* 5: 1–144.

Mitchell 2005: Stephen Mitchell, 'The Treaty between Rome and Lycia of 46 BC', in M. Pintadui (ed.), *Papyri Graecae Schøyen* (Papyrologica Florentina 35, Florence): 161–258.

Mommsen 1886: Theodor Mommsen, 'Die Tatius-legende', *Hermes* 21: 570–87.

Mommsen 1887: Theodor Mommsen, *Römische Staatsrecht*, vol. 3.1. Leipzig: Hirzel.

Mommsen 1906: Theodor Mommsen, *Gesammelte Schriften*, vol. 4. Berlin: Weidmann.

Mommsen 1910: Theodor Mommsen, *History of Rome* (trans. W. P. Dickson, Everyman's Library). London: Dent.

Morstein-Marx 2004: Robert Morstein-Marx, *Mass Oratory and Political Power in the Late Roman Republic*. Cambridge University Press.

Mouritsen 2001: Henrik Mouritsen, *Plebs and Politics in the Late Roman Republic*. Cambridge University Press.

Münzer 1891: Fridericus Münzer, *De gente Valeria dissertatio inauguralis historica*. Oppeln: Erdmann Raabe.

Münzer 1920: Friedrich Münzer, *Römische Adelsparteien und Adelsfamilien*. Stuttgart: Metzler.

Münzer 1922: 'Licinius (61)', *Paulys Realencyclopädie der classischen Altertumswissenschaft* 13: 287–90.

Münzer 1999: Friedrich Münzer, *Roman Aristocratic Parties and Families* (trans. Thérèse Ridley). Baltimore, Md.: Johns Hopkins University Press.

Noè 2001: Eralda Noè, 'La memoria dell'antico in Columella: Continuità, distanza, conoscenza', *Athenaeum* 89: 319–43.

Norbrook 1999: David Norbrook, *Writing the English Revolution: Poetry, Rhetoric and Politics 1627–1660*. Cambridge University Press.

Norden 1892: Eduard Norden, 'In Varronis saturas Menippeas observationes selectae', *Jahrbücher für classische Philologie*, suppl. vol. 18: 265–352.

Norden 1966: Eduard Norden, *Kleine Schriften zum klassischen Altertum*. Berlin: De Gruyter.

North 1992: J. A. North, 'Deconstructing Stone Theatres', in *Apodosis: Essays presented to Dr. W. W. Cruickshank to mark his Eightieth Birthday* (London: St Paul's School): 75–83.

Oakley 1997: S. P. Oakley, *A Commentary on Livy Books VI–X*, vol. 1. Oxford: Clarendon Press.

Oakley 1998: S. P. Oakley, *A Commentary on Livy Books VI–X*, vol. 2. Oxford: Clarendon Press.

Ogilvie 1965: R. M. Ogilvie, *A Commentary on Livy Books 1–5*. Oxford: Clarendon Press.

Papi 1999: E. Papi, 'Tabernae Argentariae', *Lexicon topographicum urbis Romae* 5: 10–12.

Parker 1937: Harold T. Parker, *The Cult of Antiquity and the French Revolutionaries: A Study in the Development of the Revolutionary Spirit*. University of Chicago Press.

Parker 1996: Robert Parker, *Athenian Religion: A History*. Oxford: Clarendon Press.

Pelling 1985: C. B. R. Pelling, 'Plutarch and Catiline', *Hermes* 113: 311–29.

Pelling 1986: C. B. R. Pelling, 'Plutarch and Roman Politics', in I. S. Moxon, J. D. Smart, and A. J. Woodman (eds.), *Past Perpectives: Studies in Greek and Roman Historical Writing* (Cambridge University Press): 159–87.

Pelling 2002: Christopher Pelling, *Plutarch and History*. London: Classical Press of Wales.

Pelling 2006: Christopher Pelling, 'Breaking the Bounds: Writing about Julius Caesar', in Brian McGing and Judith Mossman (eds.), *The Limits of Ancient Biography* (Swansea: Classical Press of Wales): 255–80.

Peltonen 1995: Markku Peltonen, *Classical Humanism and Republicanism in English Political Thought 1570–1640*. Cambridge University Press.

Pinney 1974: Thomas Pinney (ed.), *The Letters of Thomas Babington Macaulay*, vol. 1. Cambridge University Press.

Pinney 1976: Thomas Pinney (ed.), *The Letters of Thomas Babington Macaulay*, vol. 3. Cambridge University Press.

Pohlenz 1924: M. Pohlenz, 'Eine politische Tendenzschrift aus Caesars Zeit', *Hermes* 59: 157–89.

Quinn 1982: Kenneth Quinn, 'The Poet and his Audience in the Augustan Age', in Hildegard Temporini and Wolfgang Haase (eds.), *Aufstieg und Niedergang der römischen Welt: Geschichte und Kultur Roms im Spiegel der neueren Forschung* 2.30.1: 75–180.

Raaflaub and Toher 1990: Kurt A. Raaflaub and Mark Toher (eds.), *Between Republic and Empire: Interpretations of Augustus and his Principate.* Berkeley and Los Angeles: University of California Press.

Ramsey 1999: John T. Ramsey, 'Mithridates, the Banner of Ch'ih-Yu, and the Comet Coin', *Harvard Studies in Classical Philology* 99: 197–253.

Rawson 1971: Elizabeth Rawson, 'Lucius Crassus and Cicero: The Formation of a Statesman', *Proceedings of the Cambridge Philological Society* 197 (NS 17): 75–88.

Rawson 1991: Elizabeth Rawson, *Roman Culture and Society: Collected Papers.* Oxford: Clarendon Press.

Relihan 2005: Joel Relihan, 'Late Arrivals: Julian and Boethius', in Kirk Freudenburg (ed.), *The Cambridge Companion to Roman Satire* (Cambridge University Press): 109–22.

Reynolds 1983: L. D. Reynolds (ed.), *Texts and Transmission: A Survey of the Latin Classics.* Oxford: Clarendon Press.

Rich 2005: John Rich, 'Valerius Antias and the Construction of the Roman Past', *Bulletin of the Institute of Classical Studies* 48: 137–61.

Rich and Williams 1999: J. W. Rich and J. H. C. Williams, '*Leges et Iura P. R. Restituit*: A New Aureus of Octavian and the Settlement of 28–27 BC', *Numismatic Chronicle* 159: 169–213.

Richard 1994: Carl J. Richard, *The Founders and the Classics: Greece, Rome, and the American Enlightenment.* Cambridge, Mass.: Harvard University Press.

Rickman 1980: Geoffrey Rickman, *The Corn Supply of Ancient Rome.* Oxford: Clarendon Press.

Riposati 1939: Benedetto Riposati, *M. Terenti Varronis De vita populi Romani: Fonti—Esegesi, Edizione critica dei frammenti* (Pubblicazioni dell'Università Cattolica del S. Cuore, serie quarta 33). Milan: Vita e Pensiero.

Ryan 1998: F. X. Ryan, 'A Lately Missing Aedile: M. Aufidius Lurco', *Athenaeum* 86: 517–21.

Salvadore 2004: Marcello Salvadore (ed.), *M. Terenti Varronis Fragmenta omnia quae extant*, II: *De vita populi Romani libri IV*. Hildesheim: Olms.

Schneidewin 1855: F. W. S[chneidewin], 'Ad. Emperius' marginalien zum Appianos', *Philologus* 10: 244.

Schofield 1995: Malcolm Schofield, 'Cicero's Definition of *Res Publica*', in J. G. F. Powell (ed.), *Cicero the Philosopher: Twelve Papers* (Oxford: Clarendon Press): 63–83.

Scullard 1970: H. H. Scullard, *From the Gracchi to Nero: A History of Rome from 133 BC to AD 68*, ed. 3. London: Methuen.

Seager 1977: Robin Seager, '"Populares" in Livy and the Livian Tradition', *Classical Quarterly* 27: 377–90.

Shackleton Bailey 1965: D. R. Shackleton Bailey, *Cicero's Letters to Atticus*, vol. 1 (Cambridge Classical Texts and Commentaries 3). Cambridge University Press.

Shackleton Bailey 1991: D. R. Shackleton Bailey, *Two Studies in Roman Nomenclature* (American Classical Studies 3). Atlanta, Ga.: Scholars Press.

Sherk 1969: Robert K. Sherk, *Roman Documents from the Greek East: Senatus consulta and epistulae to the Age of Augustus*. Baltimore: Johns Hopkins University Press.

Skutsch 1985: Otto Skutsch, *The Annals of Quintus Ennius*. Oxford: Clarendon Press.

Smith 2006a: Christopher Smith, '*Adfectatio regni* in the Roman Republic', in Sian Lewis (ed.), *Ancient Tyranny* (Edinburgh University Press): 49–64.

Smith 2006b: C. J. Smith, *The Roman Clan: The Gens from Ancient Ideology to Modern Anthropology*. Cambridge University Press.

Sordi 2003: Marta Sordi, 'Caesar's Powers in his Last Phase', in Francis Cairns and Elaine Fantham (eds.), *Caesar against Liberty? Perspectives on his Autocracy* (ARCA 43, Cambridge: Francis Cairns): 190–9.

Stewart 1990: Andrew Stewart, *Greek Sculpture: An Exploration*. New Haven: Yale University Press.

Strasburger 1939: H. Strasburger, 'Optimates', *Paulys Realencyclopädie der classischen Altertumswissenschaft* 18.1: 773–98.

Sumner 1973: G. V. Sumner, *The Orators in Cicero's* Brutus: *Prosopography and Chronology* (*Phoenix* suppl. vol. 11). University of Toronto Press.

Sutherland 1984: C. H. V. Sutherland, *The Roman Imperial Coinage*, rev. edn., vol. 1. London: Spink.

Sydenham 1952: Edward A. Sydenham, *The Coinage of the Roman Republic*. London: Spink.

Syme 1939: Ronald Syme, *The Roman Revolution*. Oxford: Clarendon Press.

Syme 1956: Ronald Syme, 'Seianus on the Aventine', *Hermes* 84: 257–66.

Syme 1959: Ronald Syme, 'Livy and Augustus', *Harvard Studies in Classical Philology* 64: 27–87.

Syme 1964: Ronald Syme, *Sallust* (Sather Classical Lectures 33). Berkeley and Los Angeles: University of California Press.

Syme 1979: Ronald Syme, *Roman Papers*, vol. 1 (ed. E. Badian). Oxford: Clarendon Press.

Syme 1986: Ronald Syme, *The Augustan Aristocracy*. Oxford: Clarendon Press.

Tatum 1999: W. Jeffrey Tatum, *The Patrician Tribune: Publius Clodius Pulcher*. Chapel Hill: University of North Carolina Press.

Taylor 1949: Lily Ross Taylor, *Party Politics in the Age of Caesar* (Sather Classical Lectures 22). Berkeley and Los Angeles: University of California Press.

Taylor 1960: Lily Ross Taylor, *The Voting Districts of the Roman Republic* (Papers and Monographs 20). American Academy in Rome.

Taylor 1966: Lily Ross Taylor, *Roman Voting Assemblies from the Hannibalic War to the Dictatorship of Caesar* (Jerome Lectures 8). Ann Arbor: University of Michigan Press.

Thomas 2008: William Thomas (ed.), *The Journals of Thomas Babington Macaulay*. London: Pickering and Chatto.

Toher 2003: Mark Toher, 'Julius Caesar and Octavian in Nicolaus', in Francis Cairns and Elaine Fantham (eds.), *Caesar Against Liberty? Perspectives on his Autocracy* (*PLLS* 11, Cambridge: Francis Cairns): 132–56.

Toher 2006: Mark Toher, 'The Earliest Depiction of Caesar and the Later Tradition', in Maria Wyke (ed.), *Julius Caesar in Western Culture* (Malden, Mass.: Blackwell): 29–44.

Trevelyan 1907: George Otto Trevelyan, *Marginal Notes of Lord Macaulay*. New York: Longman's, Green.

Trevelyan 1932: George Otto Trevelyan, *The Life and Letters of Lord Macaulay* (World's Classics edn., 2 vols.). London: Oxford University Press.

Trevor-Roper 1979: Hugh Trevor-Roper, 'Lord Macaulay: Introduction', in Lord Macaulay, *The History of England* (abridged edn., Harmondsworth: Penguin Books): 7–42.

Tucci 2005: Pier Luigi Tucci, ' "Where high Moneta leads her steps sublime": The "Tabularium" and the Temple of Juno Moneta', *Journal of Roman Archaeology* 18: 6–33.

Verduchi 1999: P. Verduchi, 'Rostra Augusti', *Lexicon topographicum urbis Romae* 4: 214–7.

Voltaire 1877–85: *Œuvres complètes de Voltaire*. Paris: Garnier Frères.

von Fritz 1932: F. von Fritz, 'Menedemos (11)', *Paulys Realencyclopädie der classischen Altertumswissenschaft* 15: 794–5.

von Premerstein 1937: A. von Premerstein, *Von Werden und Wesen des Prinzipats*. Munich: C. H. Beck.

von Ungern-Sternberg 2004: Jürgen von Ungern-Sternberg, 'The Crisis of the Republic', in Harriet I. Flower (ed.), *The Cambridge Companion to the Roman Republic* (Cambridge University Press): 89–109.

Wallace-Hadrill 1983: Andrew Wallace-Hadrill, *Suetonius: The Scholar and his Caesars*. London: Duckworth.

Wallace-Hadrill 2005: Andrew Wallace-Hadrill, '*Mutatas Formas*: The Augustan Transformation of Roman Knowledge', in Karl Galinsky (ed.), *The Cambridge Companion to the Age of Augustus* (Cambridge University Press): 55–84.

Walsh 1961: P. G. Walsh, *Livy: His Historical Aims and Methods*. Cambridge University Press.

Walt 1997: Siri Walt, *Der Historiker C. Licinius Macer: Einleitung, Fragmente, Kommentar* (Beiträge zur Altertumskunde 103). Stuttgart: Teubner.

Watson 1965: Alan Watson, 'The Divorce of Carvilius Ruga', *Tijdschrift voor Rechtsgeschiedenis* 33: 38–50.

Weinbrot 2005: Howard D. Weinbrot, *Menippean Satire Reconsidered: From Antiquity to the Eighteenth Century*. Baltimore, Md.: Johns Hopkins University Press.

Weinstock 1971: Stefan Weinstock, *Divus Julius*. Oxford: Clarendon Press.

Weiss 1925: E. Weiss, 'Lex Aebutia (1)', *Paulys Realencyclopädie der classischen Altertumswissenschaft* 12: 2320.

Welch 1991: Katherine Welch, 'Roman Amphitheatres Revived', *Journal of Roman Archaeology* 4: 272–81.

Welch 1994: Katherine Welch, 'The Roman Arena in Late-Republican Italy: A New Interpretation', *Journal of Roman Archaeology* 7: 59–80.

Welch 2007: Katherine E. Welch, *The Roman Amphitheatre: From its Origins to the Colosseum*. New York: Cambridge University Press.

Wiedemann 1996: Thomas Wiedemann, 'Mommsen, Rome and the German *Kaiserreich*', in Theodor Mommsen, *A History of Rome under the Emperors* (trans. Clara Krojzl, London: Routledge): 36–47.

Winterbottom 1970: Michael Winterbottom, *Problems in Quintilian* (*BICS* suppl. 25). London: Institute of Classical Studies.

Wirszubski 1950: C. Wirszubski, *Libertas as a Political Idea at Rome during the Late Republic and Early Principate*. Cambridge University Press.

Wiseman 1974: T. P. Wiseman, *Cinna the Poet and Other Roman Essays*. Leicester University Press.

Wiseman 1980: T. P. Wiseman, 'Looking for Camerius: The Topography of Catullus 55', *Papers of the British School at Rome* 48: 6–16.

Wiseman 1981: T. P. Wiseman, 'The Temple of Victory on the Palatine', *Antiquaries Journal* 61: 35–52.

Wiseman 1987: T. P. Wiseman, *Roman Studies Literary and Historical*. Liverpool: Francis Cairns.

Wiseman 1990: T. P. Wiseman, 'The Central Area of the Roman Forum', *Journal of Roman Archaeology* 3: 245–7.

Wiseman 1992: T. P. Wiseman, *Talking to Virgil: A Miscellany*. University of Exeter Press.

Wiseman 1994: T. P. Wiseman, 'The Senate and the *Populares*, 69–60 BC', in J. A. Crook, Andrew Lintott, and Elizabeth Rawson (eds.), *The Cambridge Ancient History*, ed. 2, vol. 9 (Cambridge University Press): 327–67.

Wiseman 1995: T. P. Wiseman, *Remus: A Roman Myth*. Cambridge University Press.

Wiseman 1998a: T. P. Wiseman, *Roman Drama and Roman History*. University of Exeter Press.

Wiseman 1998b: T. P. Wiseman, 'The Publication of *De Bello Gallico*', in Kathryn Welch and Anton Powell (eds.), *Julius Caesar as Artful Reporter: The War Commentaries as Political Instruments* (London: Duckworth): 1–9.

Wiseman 2000: T. P. Wiseman, 'Liber: Myth, Drama and Ideology in the Roman Republic', in Christer Bruun (ed.), *The Roman Middle Republic: Politics, Religion and Historiography c. 400–133 BC* (*AIRF* 23, Rome: Institutum Romanum Finlandiae): 265–99.

Wiseman 2002: T. P. Wiseman (ed.), *Classics in Progress: Essays on Ancient Greece and Rome*. Oxford University Press, for the British Academy.

Wiseman 2004: T. P. Wiseman, *The Myths of Rome*. University of Exeter Press.

Wiseman 2006: T. P. Wiseman, 'Fauns, Prophets, and Ennius' *Annales*', *Arethusa* 39: 513–29.

Wiseman 2008: T. P. Wiseman, *Unwritten Rome*. University of Exeter Press.

Woodman 2003: A. J. Woodman, 'Poems to Historians: Catullus 1 and Horace, *Odes* 2.1', in David Braund and Christopher Gill (eds.), *Myth, History and Culture in Republican Rome: Studies in Honour of T. P. Wiseman* (University of Exeter Press): 191–216.

Yavetz 1969: Z. Yavetz, *Plebs and Princeps*. Oxford: Clarendon Press.

Zucchelli 1976: Bruno Zucchelli, 'L'enigma del Τρικάρανος: Varrone di fronte ai triumviri', in Benedetto Riposati (ed.), *Atti del Congresso Internazionale di Studi Varroniani* (Rieti: Centro di Studi Varroniani): 609–25.

Chronological Index

Index Locorum

General Index